W9-CGK-920

CHEMISTRY 141

EXAMINATIONS

&

SOLUTIONS

FALL SEMESTER 2004
to
SPRING SEMESTER 2009

edited by

Wendy Whitford & Steve Poulios

Chemistry 141 Examinations and Solutions

(Volume 1 of a series of Examination books)

 Copyright © 2000-2009 CemVest
Printed in the United States of America

All rights reserved. No part of this publication may be reproduced or transmitted by any means, including electronic, mechanical, photocopying, recording, or otherwise, nor may any part of the publication be stored in any information retrieval system without the prior written permission of the publisher.

Published by the Okemos Press
Scientific and Technical Books
Okemos MI 48805-0085

Printed Summer 2009
Printed by
Sheridan Books, Inc., Ann Arbor, MI 48103

ISBN 0-9630471-6-7

CONTENTS

SOLUTIONS to EXAMS

EXAMINATION 1

CHEMISTRY 141 FALL 2004

Monday September 20th 2004

1. An atom has 13 neutrons and 10 electrons. If it is a cation with a charge of $+1$, what is the correct symbol for the element?

   a. F   c. Ne   e. Na   g. Mg
   b. Al   d. Si   f. Fe   h. Co

2. The oxoanions (polyatomic ions that contain oxygen) are named in a logical way. Based upon the formulas and names of the polyatomic ions that you have memorized, what would be the logical formula for the hyponitrite ion?

   a. NO_2^- c. NO^{2-} e. NO^- g. NO_3^-
   b. NO_2^{2-} d. NO_4^- f. N_2O^- h. NO_3^{2-}

3. What is the correct formula for the salt magnesium hydrogen sulfate?

   a. $MgHSO_4$ c. Mg_2HSO_4 e. $Mg(HSO_3)_2$ g. $Mg_2(HSO_3)_2$
   b. $MgHSO_3$ d. $Mg(HSO_4)_2$ f. Mg_2HSO_3 h. $MgSO_4$

4. Which statement is *correct*?

   a. All polyatomic ions have a negative charge (e.g. 1–, 2–, or 3–).
   b. All compounds are molecules.
   c. All molecules are compounds.
   d. All gases are diatomic.
   e. All binary compounds contain just two atoms.
   f. All elements have symbols consisting of two letters.
   g. All isotopes of an element have the same atomic number.

5. Which of the following compounds is an ionic compound?

   a. PF_3 c. CS_2 e. SO_2 g. CO_2
   b. CH_4 d. $MgCl_2$ f. CCl_4 h. H_2S

6. A new element X was discovered to have three isotopes. From the following information about the isotopes, calculate the atomic mass of this new element.

	mass	% abundance
^{118}X	117.88 amu	35.00%
^{119}X	118.80 amu	47.00%
^{120}X	119.75 amu	18.00%

   a. 117.92 amu   c. 118.13 amu   e. 118.65 amu   g. 119.21 amu
   b. 118.00 amu   d. 118.32 amu   f. 118.97 amu   h. 119.45 amu

7.   What is the mass, in grams, of 3.00 moles of dinitrogen tetroxide?

  a. 46 g c. 92 g e. 138 g g. 222 g i. 310 g
  b. 69 g d. 108 g f. 207 g h. 276 g j. 552 g

8.   What is the approximate % by mass of nitrogen in the agricultural fertilizer urea, NH_2CONH_2?

  a. 13% c. 33% e. 47% g. 61% i. 71%
  b. 27% d. 42% f. 53% h. 68% j. 79%

9.   Which one of the following changes is *not* an example of a chemical reaction?

  a. Sulfur burns in air to produce sulfur dioxide.
  b. Sulfur trioxide dissolves in water to produce sulfuric acid H_2SO_4.
  c. Methane gas CH_4 reacts with oxygen to produce carbon dioxide and water.
  d. Sugar (sucrose $C_{12}H_{22}O_{11}$) dissolves in water.
  e. Nitrogen and hydrogen react to form ammonia.
  f. Baking soda (sodium hydrogen carbonate) and vinegar (acetic acid) react to produce carbon dioxide.

10. Choose the one pair with *incorrectly* matching formula and name:

  a. MgO magnesium oxide   d. NO_2 nitrogen dioxide
  b. IF_3 iodine trifluoride   e. $NaHCO_3$ sodium hydrogen carbonate
  c. PCl_5 phosphorus pentachloride f. $Mg_2(PO_4)_3$ magnesium phosphate

11. How many moles of carbon atoms are there in 12 moles of dimethylaniline molecules $C_6H_5N(CH_3)_2$?

  a. 6 c. 12 e. 72 g. 108
  b. 8 d. 36 f. 96 h. 144

12. How many nitrogen atoms are there in 2.50 mg of nitrogen N_2?

  a. 2.15×10^{20} c. 4.30×10^{20} e. 1.08×10^{20} g. 2.15×10^{23}
  b. 1.08×10^{23} d. 1.51×10^{21} f. 3.00×10^{-22} h. 9.31×10^{-21}

13. Common table sugar has the formula $C_{12}H_{22}O_{11}$ (molar mass 342 g mol^{-1}). If a sugar cube has a volume of 4.29 cm^3 and a density of 1.58 g cm^{-3}, how many carbon atoms are in the sugar cube?

  a. 1.18×10^{20} c. 7.78×10^{21} e. 5.74×10^{22} g. 2.79×10^{23}
  b. 5.97×10^{20} d. 1.19×10^{22} f. 1.43×10^{23} h. 6.21×10^{23}

14. L-dopa, a drug for the treatment of Parkinson's disease, has the composition 54.8% carbon, 5.62% hydrogen, 7.10% nitrogen, and 32.6% oxygen. What is the empirical formula of L-dopa?

  a. $C_9H_{11}NO_4$ c. $C_4H_4NO_2$ e. $C_8H_{10}NO_3$ g. $C_8H_{11}NO_3$
  b. $C_7H_9NO_3$ d. $C_5H_6NO_2$ f. $C_3H_4NO_3$ h. $C_{10}H_{12}NO_4$

15. Methylhydrazine CH_3NHNH_2 burns in oxygen to produce nitrogen gas, carbon dioxide gas, and water. Write an equation for this reaction and balance the equation using whole number coefficients. The *sum of all* the coefficients for the reactants and products in the balanced equation is

  a. 8 c. 10 e. 12 g. 15 i. 17
  b. 9 d. 11 f. 13 h. 16 j. 19

16. A compound of boron and hydrogen is burned in oxygen and produces the boron oxide B_2O_3 and water. The number of moles of water produced was 2.5 times the number of moles of B_2O_3. What is the empirical formula of the boron hydrogen compound?

    a. BH c. BH_3 e. BH_4 g. B_2H_5 i. B_4H_5
    b. BH_2 d. B_2H_3 f. B_3H_4 h. B_3H_5 j. BH_{10}

17. According to the equation: $2\,NO \;+\; O_2 \;\rightarrow\; 2\,NO_2$

    If 8.0 grams of oxygen is consumed in this reaction, what mass of nitrogen dioxide will be produced?

    a. 8.0 g   c. 16 g   e. 32 g   g. 69 g
    b. 11.5 g   d. 23 g   f. 46 g   h. 92 g

18. Ethane gas C_2H_6 burns in oxygen gas to produce carbon dioxide and water. If 3.0 moles of ethane gas are ignited in 11.0 moles of oxygen gas, and the reaction goes as far as possible, how many moles of water are produced in the reaction? *(Hint: write the equation.)*

    a. 0.50 mol   c. 2.0 mol   e. 4.0 mol   g. 6.0 mol
    b. 1.0 mol   d. 3.0 mol   f. 4.5 mol   h. 9.0 mol

19. Nitrous oxide reacts with oxygen to produce nitrogen dioxide according to the equation:

    $$2\,N_2O \;+\; 3\,O_2 \;\rightarrow\; 4\,NO_2$$

    What mass of nitrogen dioxide can be made from 50 grams of nitrous oxide and 50 grams of oxygen?

    a. 31 g   c. 48 g   e. 76 g   g. 96 g
    b. 43 g   d. 55 g   f. 88 g   h. 105 g

20. Calcium carbonate reacts with hydrochloric acid HCl to form calcium chloride, water, and carbon dioxide. If 10.0 grams of calcium carbonate reacts with excess HCl to form 3.65 grams of carbon dioxide, what is the percent yield of the reaction?

    a. 36.5%   c. 80%   e. 87%   g. 95%
    b. 71%   d. 83%   f. 91%   h. 98%

EXAMINATION 1

CHEMISTRY 141 SPRING 2005

Monday January 31st 2005

1. Which of the following rows has the correct SI unit given for each unit of measure (choose the row where all of the SI units are correct).

	Mass	Length	Time	Amount
a.	gram	meter	second	mole
b.	gram	foot	second	dozen
c.	milligram	inch	minute	pair
d.	milligram	kilometer	second	mole
e.	kilogram	meter	hour	mole
f.	kilogram	meter	second	mole

2. A rocket is traveling at 12.0 km/s. What is this speed in miles/hour?

    a. 5.36×10^{-3}

    b. 2.07×10^{-3}

    c. 7.46

    d. 4.47×10^2

    e. 2.68×10^4

    f. 5.40×10^4

    g. 6.95×10^4

    h. 1.20×10^5

3. An iron cube measures 5.00 cm on each side. The density of iron is $7.86 \, \text{g cm}^{-3}$. How many iron atoms are in this cube?

    a. 7.87×10^{-24} atoms

    b. 2.92×10^{-23} atoms

    c. 1.76×10^3 atoms

    d. 1.71×10^{21} atoms

    e. 4.24×10^{23} atoms

    f. 2.86×10^{24} atoms

    g. 1.06×10^{25} atoms

    h. 5.92×10^{26} atoms

4. What is the correct name for $KClO_3$?

    a. potassium hypochlorite

    b. potassium chlorite

    c. potassium chlorate

    d. potassium perchlorate

    e. calcium chlorite

    f. calcium chloride

    g. phosphorus perchlorate

    h. potassium chloride

    i. calcium chlorate

    j. phosphorus hypochlorite

5. Butane (C_4H_{10}) burns in oxygen gas to produce carbon dioxide gas and water. Write an equation for this reaction and balance the reaction using whole number coefficients. What is the coefficient in front of oxygen gas in the equation?

    a. 6

    b. 7

    c. 9

    d. 11

    e. 13

    f. 15

    g. 17

    h. 19

6. Glucose, an important sugar in the human body, has a molecular formula of $C_6H_{12}O_6$. What is the % by mass of carbon in glucose?

    a. 6%

    b. 17%

    c. 25%

    d. 40%

    e. 50%

    f. 62%

    g. 80%

    h. 94%

7. The charges on monatomic ions of the representative elements depend upon the position of the element in the Periodic Table. In which row are all the charges assigned correctly?

	Mg	I	S	N	Na	Al
a.	+2	−1	−2	−3	+2	−5
b.	+2	−2	−3	−4	+1	+3
c.	+1	−1	−3	−2	+1	+3
d.	+3	−2	−2	−3	−1	−5
e.	+2	−1	−2	−3	+1	+3
f.	+2	−2	−2	−3	+2	+4

8. Which statement is *incorrect*?

a. Compounds may be ionic or molecular.
b. Hydrogen and oxygen exist naturally as diatomic molecules.
c. Sulfur trioxide SO_3 is a binary compound.
d. All molecules of methane CH_4 have exactly the same mass.
e. A neutron is slightly heavier than a proton.
f. Chromium and nickel are both transition elements.

9. Which of the following compounds is an ionic compound?

a. IF_7 c. $COCl_2$ e. CO g. SCl_4
b. CH_3CH_2OH d. RbF f. PF_5 h. ClO_2

10. A compound containing chromium (Cr) and silicon (Si) contains 73.52% chromium. What is the empirical formula of this compound?

a. $CrSi$ c. Cr_2Si_3 e. Cr_3Si g. Cr_2Si
b. Cr_3Si_2 d. $CrSi_3$ f. Cr_4Si_2 h. $CrSi_2$

11. How many moles of oxygen atoms are there in 192 g of ozone O_3?

a. 2.0 moles   c. 4.0 moles   e. 6.0 moles   g. 12 moles   i. 18 moles
b. 3.0 moles   d. 5.0 moles   f. 9.0 moles   h. 15 moles   j. 24 moles

12. How many grams of potassium are in 5.0 moles of potassium dichromate?

a. 0.064 g   c. 196 g   e. 520 g   g. 1471 g
b. 98 g   d. 391 g   f. 780 g   h. 3920 g

13. According to the following reaction, how many moles of Al_2O_3 can be formed when 0.36 moles of aluminum reacts with 0.36 moles of oxygen?

$$4\,Al \;+\; 3\,O_2 \;\rightarrow\; 2\,Al_2O_3$$

a. 0.09 mole   c. 0.18 mole   e. 0.27 mole   g. 0.72 mole
b. 0.12 mole   d. 0.24 mole   f. 0.32 mole   h. 2.0 moles

14. 5.00 grams of sulfur dioxide reacts with 5.00 grams of oxygen gas to produce sulfur trioxide. How many grams of the non-limiting reactant remain at the end of the reaction? (*Hint:* Write the equation.)

a. 0.390 g   c. 0.125 g   e. 1.25 g   g. 3.75 g
b. 0.075 g   d. 0.167 g   f. 2.50 g   h. 5.00 g

15. Which of the following statements is *not* an example of a physical change?

    a. Salt dissolves in water.
    b. A pot of water boils to form steam.
    c. Frost forms on a lawn.
    d. Leaves decay in the winter.
    e. Ice melts as the temperature rises in the Spring.
    f. Dry ice sublimes to form carbon dioxide vapor.

16. A compound with an empirical formula of CH_2O was found to have a molar mass of 150 g mol^{-1}. What is the molecular formula of this compound?

    a. CH_2O c. $C_3H_6O_3$ e. $C_5H_{10}O_5$ g. $C_7H_{14}O_7$
    b. $C_2H_4O_2$ d. $C_4H_8O_4$ f. $C_6H_{12}O_6$ h. $C_8H_{16}O_8$

17. The following diagrams represent a mixture of carbon atoms and sulfur atoms in the gas state before and after a reaction to form a carbon–sulfur compound. The carbon atoms are reperesented by the solid circles and the sulfur atoms are represented by the hollow circles. Write an equation for the reaction and then determine how many moles of the carbon–sulfur compound can be made from 9.0 moles of carbon atoms and 24 moles of sulfur atoms.

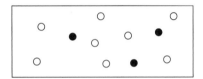 →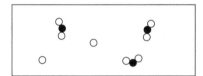

    a. 3.0 moles   c. 9.0 moles   e. 15 moles   g. 24 moles
    b. 6.0 moles   d. 12 moles   f. 18 moles   h. 31 moles

18. A compound of silicon and hydrogen ignites in air and produces silicon dioxide (SiO_2) and water. The number of moles of silicon dioxide produced was two-thirds the number of moles of water produced. What is the empirical formula of the silicon–hydrogen compound?

    a. SiH c. SiH_3 e. SiH_4 g. Si_2H_5 i. Si_3H_5
    b. SiH_2 d. Si_2H_3 f. Si_3H_2 h. Si_2H_6 j. Si_3H_6

19. Phosphorus pentachloride is formed by the following reaction:

$$PCl_3(g) \ + \ Cl_2(g) \ \rightarrow \ PCl_5(g)$$

A student performs this experiment in the laboratory and produces 119.3 g PCl_5 when she reacts 61.3 g Cl_2 with excess PCl_3. What is this student's percent yield?

    a. 5.5%   c. 39%   e. 57%   g. 82%
    b. 12%   d. 44%   f. 66%   h. 96%

20. 4.338 grams of an unknown compound of sulfur and chlorine was produced by reacting 0.800 g of sulfur with sufficient chlorine. All the sulfur was used in the reaction. What is the empirical formula of the unknown sulfur–chlorine compound?

    a. SCl c. SCl_2 e. SCl_3 g. S_3Cl i. SCl_5
    b. S_2Cl_2 d. S_2Cl f. S_2Cl_3 h. SCl_4 j. SCl_6

EXAMINATION 1

CHEMISTRY 141 FALL 2005

Monday September 19th 2005

1. In Major League Baseball, a typical pitch has a speed of about 95 mph (miles hour^{-1}). What is this speed in ms^{-1}?

    a. 95 ms^{-1} c. 560 ms^{-1} e. 5 ms^{-1}
    b. 220 ms^{-1} d. 90 ms^{-1} f. 42 ms^{-1}

2. An aquarium was filled with 5.00 gallons of water. How many moles of water are in the aquarium? (The density of water is 1.00 g mL^{-1})

    a. 1.00×10^{-3} mol   e. 341 mol
    b. 1.00 mol   f. 1050 mol
    c. 19.0 mol   g. 1.90×10^{4} mol
    d. 73.0 mol   h. 3.40×10^{5} mol

3. Which one of the following properties is extensive?

    a. volume   c. molecular mass   e. density
    b. color   d. boiling point   f. temperature

4. Copper has two isotopes, ^{63}Cu and ^{65}Cu; these two isotopes differ in that

    a. ^{65}Cu has more protons than ^{63}Cu.
    b. ^{65}Cu has more electrons than ^{63}Cu.
    c. ^{65}Cu has more neutrons than ^{63}Cu.
    d. the smallest unit of ^{65}Cu is an atom, whereas the smallest unit of ^{63}Cu is an ion.
    e. ^{65}Cu is an element, whereas ^{63}Cu is a compound.
    f. ^{65}Cu is a compound, whereas ^{63}Cu is an element.

5. Examples of a noble gas, a halogen, an alkali metal, and a transition metal, are, in that order:

	noble gas	*halogen*	*alkali metal*	*transition metal*
a.	helium He	chlorine Cl	sodium Na	tin Sn
b.	nobelium No	fluorine F	potassium K	copper Cu
c.	argon Ar	iodine I	lithium Li	iron Fe
d.	neon Ne	bromine Br	magnesium Mg	nickel Ni
e.	xenon Xe	hydrogen H	lithium Li	manganese Mn
f.	helium He	nitrogen N	lead Pb	titanium Ti

6. How many of the following compounds are ionic?

    $NaCH_3CO_2$ SCl_4 $Ca_3(PO_4)_2$ $NaCl$
    NO_2 $MgBr_2$ CO $Mg(NO_3)_2$

    a. none   c. 2   e. 4   g. 6   i. all are ionic
    b. 1   d. 3   f. 5   h. 7

7. Which of the following formulas is incorrect?

   a. KNO_3 c. $Al(NO_3)_3$ e. $LiNO_2$ g. $AlPO_4$ i. $Mg_3(PO_4)_2$
   b. $NaCl$ d. $Mg(CH_3CO_2)_2$ f. $Ca(HCO_3)_2$ h. $NaSO_4$ j. $LiClO_4$

8. How many moles of oxygen atoms are in 3.0 moles of copper(II) nitrate?

   a. 1   c. 3   e. 9   g. 15   i. 24
   b. 2   d. 6   f. 12   h. 18   j. 36

9. Which of the following questions is impossible to answer?

   a. What is the molar mass of benzene C_6H_6?
   b. What is the atomic mass of carbon?
   c. What is the molecular mass of nitrogen N_2?
   d. What is the formula mass of sodium chloride?
   e. What is the molar mass of sulfur?
   f. What is the atomic mass of phosphorus?

10. 3.00 moles of an unknown compound is known to have a mass of 67.0 grams. What is the molar mass of this compound?

   a. 0.045 g mol^{-1} c. 22.3 g mol^{-1} e. 67.0 g mol^{-1} g. 184 g mol^{-1}
   b. 3.17 g mol^{-1} d. 42.9 g mol^{-1} f. 129 g mol^{-1} h. 201 g mol^{-1}

11. The protein molecules in your body are made when chemical bonds are formed between small molecules called amino acids. One of these amino acids, glycine, has a molecular formula H_2NCH_2COOH. What is the molar mass of glycine?

   a. 92.00 g mol^{-1} c. 22.51 g mol^{-1} e. 25.23 g mol^{-1}
   b. 95.08 g mol^{-1} d. 43.07 g mol^{-1} f. 75.07 g mol^{-1}

12. How many chlorine atoms are in 10 grams of Cl_2?

   a. 4.2×10^{22} e. 3.4×10^{24}
   b. 8.5×10^{22} f. 1.7×10^{25}
   c. 1.7×10^{23} g. 4.5×10^{25}
   d. 6.0×10^{23} h. 8.5×10^{26}

13. An unknown element exists as three isotopes: ^{73}X (mass 72.975 u, 57.000% abundance), ^{75}X (mass 74.729 u, 40.000% abundance), and ^{77}X (mass 76.899 u, 3.000% abundance). What is the atomic mass of this element?

   a. 71.998   e. 75.234
   b. 72.347   f. 76.875
   c. 73.794   g. 77.631
   d. 74.955   h. 78.112

14. Ethanol C_2H_5OH is often added to gasoline used as a fuel in automobiles. What is the percentage % by mass of oxygen in ethanol?

   a. 17.3%   c. 29.1%   e. 39.2%   g. 49.7%
   b. 22.3%   d. 34.7%   f. 41.1%   h. 52.8%

15. Butane (C_4H_{10}) burns in oxygen gas to produce carbon dioxide gas and water. Balance the equation. How many moles of C_4H_{10} are required to react completely with 26 moles of O_2?

$$\_\_ C_4H_{10} \ + \ \_\_ O_2 \ \rightarrow \ \_\_ CO_2 \ + \ \_\_ H_2O$$

a. 1   c. 3   e. 5   g. 7
b. 2   d. 4   f. 6   h. 8

16. Nicotine, a compound found in cigarettes, is 74.04% carbon, 17.27% nitrogen, and 8.700% hydrogen by mass. What is the *empirical* formula of nicotine?

a. C_5NH_7 c. C_5NH_8 e. C_2NH_4 g. C_2NH_5
b. C_6NH_9 d. CNH_2 f. C_3NH_7 h. $C_3N_2H_8$

17. A compound of boron and hydrogen is burned in oxygen and produces the boron oxide B_2O_3 and water. The number of moles of water produced was three times the number of moles of B_2O_3. What is the empirical formula of the boron hydrogen compound?

a. BH c. BH_3 e. BH_4 g. B_2H_5 i. B_4H_5
b. BH_2 d. B_2H_3 f. B_3H_4 h. B_3H_5 j. BH_{10}

18. Hydrogen cyanide is produced industrially from the reaction of gaseous ammonia, oxygen, and methane. The *unbalanced* equation for this reaction is:

$$\_\_ NH_3(g) \ + \ \_\_ O_2(g) \ + \ \_\_ CH_4(g) \ \rightarrow \ \_\_ HCN(g) \ + \ \_\_ H_2O(g)$$

Balance the equation; what is the coefficient of water in the balanced equation?

a. 1   c. 3   e. 5   g. 7   i. 9
b. 2   d. 4   f. 6   h. 8   j. 10

19. If, in the reaction described in the previous question, 5.0 moles of ammonia, 8.0 moles of oxygen, and 4.0 moles of methane are used, which of the three reactants is the limiting reactant?

a. ammonia
b. oxygen
c. methane

20. Given the amounts of reactants described in the previous question, what is the maximum amount of hydrogen cyanide that can be formed?

a. 2.0 mol   c. 3.0 mol   e. 4.0 mol   g. 5.0 mol   i. 8.0 mol
b. 2.5 mol   d. 3.5 mol   f. 4.5 mol   h. 6.0 mol   j. 9.0 mol

EXAMINATION 1

CHEMISTRY 141 SPRING 2006

Monday January 30th 2006

1. A 5.0 gram cube of silver measures 0.78 cm on each side. What is the density of silver in $g \, mL^{-1}$? ($1 \, cm^3 = 1 mL$)

    a. $0.16 \, g \, mL^{-1}$ c. $6.4 \, g \, mL^{-1}$ e. $10.5 \, g \, mL^{-1}$ g. $390 \, g \, mL^{-1}$
    b. $2.4 \, g \, mL^{-1}$ d. $7.8 \, g \, mL^{-1}$ f. $227 \, g \, mL^{-1}$ h. $1137 \, g \, mL^{-1}$

2. In an Ironman distance triathlon, an athlete must swim 2.4 miles, bike 112 miles, and run 26.2 miles consecutively. What is the total distance an athlete will travel, in meters, by completing all three parts of this triathlon?

    a. $2.42 \times 10^2 \, m$ c. $4.22 \times 10^4 \, m$ e. $1.80 \times 10^5 \, m$ g. $3.96 \times 10^5 \, m$
    b. $3.86 \times 10^3 \, m$ d. $9.36 \times 10^4 \, m$ f. $2.26 \times 10^5 \, m$ h. $6.22 \times 10^5 \, m$

3. Which one of the following processes represents a chemical change?

    a. Salt dissolves in a pot of boiling water.
    b. Dynamite explodes to form a mixture of gasses.
    c. Dry ice (solid carbon dioxide) sublimes at room temperature to make carbon dioxide gas.
    d. Solid iodine vaporizes into a purple gas.
    e. Frost forms on a windshield.
    f. An ice cube melts.

4. John Dalton had several hypotheses about the nature of atoms that eventually became the foundation of modern atomic theory. Certain parts of Dalton's Theory have since been proven false. Which one of the following statements do we now understand to be false?

    a. All matter consists of atoms.
    b. Mass is conserved in a chemical reaction.
    c. Atoms combine in whole number ratios to form compounds.
    d. Chemical reactions are rearrangements of atoms.
    e. Atoms are indivisible.
    f. Atoms of the same element with different numbers of neutrons are called isotopes.

5. Consider two neutral atoms with the following symbols: $^{18}_{9}F$ and $^{18}_{8}O$. Which one of the following statements about these atoms is *incorrect*?

    a. The atoms are two different elements.
    b. The atoms have different atomic numbers.
    c. $^{18}_{8}O$ has more neutrons than $^{18}_{9}F$.
    d. The atoms have different mass numbers.
    e. $^{18}_{9}F$ has more protons than $^{18}_{8}O$.
    f. $^{18}_{9}F$ has more electrons than $^{18}_{8}O$.

6. Silver has 46 known isotopes, but only ^{107}Ag and ^{109}Ag occur naturally. The mass of ^{107}Ag is 106.90509 u and the mass of ^{109}Ag is 108.90476 u. What is the percent abundance of ^{107}Ag?

    a. 13.9%   c. 48.3%   e. 56.8%   g. 83.3%
    b. 24.6%   d. 51.7%   f. 71.6%   h. 94.2%

7. Classify the elements listed below based on their location on the Periodic Table. How many of the elements listed are alkali metals, alkaline earth metals, halogens and actinides? Choose the row where all responses are correct.

Pm	Mg	Cl	I	O
K	Ca	Li	Fe	Ar

	alkali metal	*alkaline earth metal*	*halogen*	*actinide*
a.	2	2	2	0
b.	1	3	2	1
c.	0	1	3	0
d.	4	2	3	1
e.	3	1	1	2
f.	2	0	3	3
g.	0	2	0	1
h.	4	0	1	1

8. How many of the following polyatomic ions have *incorrect* charges?

    NH_4^+ OH^{2-} ClO_4^- CrO_4^{4-} PO_4^{3-} SCN^- CO_3^- H_3O^+

    a. none (all are correct)   c. 2   e. 4   g. 6   i. all are incorrect
    b. 1   d. 3   f. 5   h. 7

9. What is the formula for calcium nitrite?

    a. CaN_2 c. $Ca(NO_3)_2$ e. $CaNO_2$ g. $CaNO_3$
    b. $Ca(NO_2)_2$ d. Ca_2NO_2 f. Ca_2NO_3 h. $Ca(NO_4)_2$

10. How many moles of phosphorus atoms are in 10.0 grams of P_4?

    a. 0.323   c. 1.23   e. 5.79   g. 10.0
    b. 0.646   d. 3.55   f. 8.76   h. 10.5

11. Insulin $C_{257}H_{383}N_{65}O_{77}S_6$ is a molecule produced by the pancreas to regulate carbohydrate metabolism. What is the molecular mass of insulin?

    a. 1203 g mol^{-1} c. 5808 g mol^{-1} e. 11343 g mol^{-1} g. 14232 g mol^{-1}
    b. 3522 g mol^{-1} d. 8656 g mol^{-1} f. 13221 g mol^{-1} h. 18085 g mol^{-1}

12. What is the percent by mass of oxygen in insulin $C_{257}H_{383}N_{65}O_{77}S_6$?

    a. 2.36%   c. 15.2%   e. 33.1%   g. 72.6%
    b. 9.55%   d. 21.2%   f. 53.1%   h. 86.8%

13. What is the mass, in grams, of 4.0 moles of copper(II) nitrate?

    a. 502.2 g   c. 731.8 g   e. 756.4 g   g. 878.3 g
    b. 622.3 g   d. 750.3 g   f. 799.2 g   h. 907.3 g

14.   What is the average mass of a molecule of phosphorus pentachloride?

a. 2.43×10^{-22} g   c. 6.02×10^{-23} g   e. 3.75×10^{-24} g   g. 6.37×10^{-26} g
b. 3.46×10^{-22} g   d. 4.93×10^{-24} g   f. 9.41×10^{-25} g   h. 7.98×10^{-27} g

15.   Creatine, a dietary supplement thought to improve athletic performance, is 36.6% carbon, 6.9% hydrogen, 32.0% nitrogen, and 24.4% oxygen by mass. What is the empirical formula of creatine?

a. $CHNO$ c. $C_2H_3NO_2$ e. $C_2H_5N_2O$ g. $C_4H_2N_3O_2$
b. CHN_3O_3 d. C_2H_4NO f. $C_2H_9N_2O$ h. $C_4H_9N_3O_2$

16.   A compound of carbon and hydrogen was completely burned in oxygen to produce six moles of carbon dioxide and seven moles of water. What is the *empirical* formula of this carbon–hydrogen compound? *(Hint: write the equation.)*

a. CH c. C_3H_7 e. C_4H_2 g. C_6H_{14}
b. CH_2 d. C_4H_{10} f. C_6H_7 h. C_7H_{12}

17.   Balance the following equation using whole number coefficients:

$$\underline{\hspace{1em}} C_3H_5N_3O_9 \ (l) \quad \rightarrow \quad \underline{\hspace{1em}} CO_2 \ (g) \ + \ \underline{\hspace{1em}} H_2O \ (g) \ + \ \underline{\hspace{1em}} N_2 \ (g) \ + \ \underline{\hspace{1em}} O_2 \ (g)$$

What is the coefficient of water in the balanced equation?

a.   1   c.   3   e.   5   g.   8   i.   12
b.   2   d.   4   f.   6   h.   10   j.   14

18.   Nitrous oxide reacts with oxygen to produce nitrogen dioxide according to the reaction:

$$2\,N_2O \quad + \quad 3\,O_2 \quad \rightarrow \quad 4\,NO_2$$

What mass of nitrogen dioxide is produced from 20 grams of nitrous oxide and 20 grams of oxygen?

a.   1.66 g   c.   18.34 g   e.   21.57 g   g.   38.34 g
b.   12.7 g   d.   20.24 g   f.   28.76 g   h.   41.78 g

19.   0.75 mole of chlorine gas reacts with 4.0 moles of fluorine gas to produce chlorine trifluoride. How many moles of the nonlimiting reactant remain at the end of the reaction? *(Hint: write the equation.)*

a.   0 mol   c.   1.5 mol   e.   2.25 mol   g.   3.5 mol
b.   0.75 mol   d.   1.75 mol   f.   3 mol   h.   4 mol

20.   Salicylic acid $C_7H_6O_3$ (molar mass 138.12 g mol^{-1}) reacts with acetic anhydride $(CH_3CO)_2O$ (molar mass 102.09 g mol^{-1}) to produce aspirin $C_9H_8O_4$ (molar mass 180.154 g mol^{-1}) and acetic acid CH_3CO_2H (molar mass 60.05 g mol^{-1}) according to the balanced equation:

$$C_7H_6O_3 \ (s) \ + \ (CH_3CO)_2O \ (l) \quad \rightarrow \quad C_9H_8O_4 \ (s) \ + \ CH_3CO_2H \ (l)$$

In one experiment, 3.03 grams salicylic acid and 6.48 grams acetic anhydride react to form 3.26 grams aspirin. What is the percent yield of this reaction?

a.   82.5%   c.   59.2%   e.   25.8%   g.   17.5%
b.   74.3%   d.   39.5%   f.   21.9%   h.   8.63%

EXAMINATION 1

CHEMISTRY 141 FALL 2006

Monday September 18th 2006

1.   An atom or ion has 11 protons, 12 neutrons, and 11 electrons. What is the symbol for the element and the charge, if any, for this atom or ion? (Choose the answer where *both* responses are correct.)

      symbol charge   *symbol charge*

    a. Mg   0   e. Na   0
    b. Mg   2+   f. Na   1+
    c. V   0   g. Ti   0
    d. V   1+   h. Ti   1+

2.   One of the following polyatomic ions has an incorrect charge. Which one?

    a. NO_2^- c. PO_4^{3-} e. SO_3^- g. $CH_3CO_2^-$ i. HPO_4^{2-}
    b. ClO^- d. CN^- f. MnO_4^- h. CO_3^{2-} j. ClO_3^-

3.   The following is a list of abbreviations for several base SI and common derived units:

    a. kg   b. s   c. K   d. mole   e. m   f. J

    Which is a derived unit (not a base unit)?

4.   Which of the following compounds has the greatest percent by mass of oxygen?

    a. HCl   c. $HClO_2$ e. $HClO_4$ g. $HBrO_3$
    b. HClO   d. $HClO_3$ f. $HBrO_2$ h. $HBrO_4$

5.   Which of the following is *not* an ionic compound?

    a. potassium chloride   c. magnesium nitride   e. calcium bromide
    b. manganese(II) oxide   d. sodium phosphate   f. phosphorus pentachloride

6.   What is the mass of one mole of cisplatin, $Cl_2H_6N_2Pt$?

    a. 195 g   c. 245 g   e. 300 g   g. 495 g
    b. 211 g   d. 276 g   f. 312 g   h. 526 g

7.   How many moles of nitrogen atoms are in 5 moles of urea molecules, $(NH_2)_2CO$?

    a. 1 mol   c. 4 mol   e. 6 mol   g. 8 mol   i. 12 mol
    b. 2 mol   d. 5 mol   f. 7 mol   h. 10 mol   j. 16 mol

8.   Which of the following compounds contains a transition metal?

    a. CO_2 d. PH_3 g. HCl
    b. $FeCl_2$ e. $MgSO_4$ h. $PbCl_2$
    c. $CaCl_2$ f. $CaCO_3$ i. $NaHCO_3$

9. Which of the following statements about formulas for compounds is *not* true?

    a. Molecular formulas indicate the number of atoms of each element in a molecule.
    b. Structural formulas show how the atoms are bonded together in a molecule.
    c. The empirical formula of a compound illustrates the simplest ratio of atoms of the elements present in a compound.
    d. The empirical and molecular formulas of a compound are *sometimes* the same.
    e. The empirical and molecular formulas of a compound are *always* the same.

10. How many of the elements listed below commonly exist as diatomic molecules?

oxygen	carbon	hydrogen	sulfur	helium
nitrogen	bromine	neon	phosphorus	iodine

    a. 1   c. 3   e. 5   g. 7   i. none of them
    b. 2   d. 4   f. 6   h. 8   j. all of them

11. How many moles of methane (CH_4) are there in 128 grams of methane?

    a. 2 mol   c. 4 mol   e. 6 mol   g. 8 mol   i. 10 mol
    b. 3 mol   d. 5 mol   f. 7 mol   h. 9 mol   j. 12 mol

12. Which one of the following formulas is incorrect?

    a. NaBr   d. $Ca(CH_3CO_2)_2$ g. $MgBr_2$
    b. $AlPO_4$ e. Li_2O h. KNO_3
    c. $CaCO_3$ f. NaClO   i. $MgHSO_4$

13. What is the mass, in grams, of 5.0 moles of carbon dioxide?

    a. 28 g   c. 56 g   e. 140 g   g. 220 g   i. 330 g
    b. 44 g   d. 88 g   f. 156 g   h. 280 g   j. 440 g

14. 100 mL of white vinegar contains 5.0 grams of acetic acid (CH_3CO_2H). How many moles of acetic acid are in a 1 pint (473 mL) bottle of vinegar?

    a. 8.3×10^{-4} mol   c. 0.82 mol   e. 40 mol   g. 95 mol
    b. 0.39 mol   d. 24 mol   f. 60 mol   h. 1.6×10^2 mol

15. A 100 mL graduated cylinder contains 54.0 mL water and weighs (cylinder and water) 123 g. A metal block is then immersed in the water in the cylinder. The level of the water in the cylinder is now 76.0 mL and the total mass (cylinder, water, and metal) is 194 g. What is the density of the metal?

    a. 2.28 g mL^{-1} d. 2.55 g mL^{-1} g. 3.23 g mL^{-1}
    b. 4.15 g mL^{-1} e. 0.11 g mL^{-1} h. 0.71 g mL^{-1}
    c. 3.73 g mL^{-1} f. 2.70 g mL^{-1} i. 0.34 g mL^{-1}

16. A compound containing carbon, hydrogen, and nitrogen is burned in air and produces carbon dioxide, water, and nitrogen dioxide. The mole ratio of the products of the reaction were 2.0 mol CO_2, 1.5 mol H_2O, and 1.0 mol NO_2. What is the empirical formula of the compound?

    a. CHN   c. CH_2N e. C_2H_2N g. $C_2H_3N_3$ i. $C_3H_2N_3$
    b. C_2HN d. C_2H_3N f. $C_2H_3N_2$ h. $C_3H_4N_2$ j. $C_4H_3N_2$

17. If 1.0 mol of the compound referred to in the previous question requires 15.0 mol of oxygen O_2 for complete combustion to CO_2, H_2O, and NO_2, what is the molecular formula of the compound?

a. $C_2H_2N_2$ c. $C_3H_4N_2$ e. $C_6H_{12}N_3$ g. $C_8H_{12}N_3$ i. $C_9H_{12}N_6$

b. $C_4H_6N_2$ d. $C_3H_4N_3$ f. $C_6H_9N_3$ h. $C_8H_{12}N_4$ j. $C_9H_{15}N_6$

18. Manganese dioxide (MnO_2) reacts with hydrochloric acid (HCl) to produce manganese(II) chloride, chlorine, and water according to the following equation:

$$\_MnO_2 \quad + \quad \_HCl \quad \rightarrow \quad \_MnCl_2 \quad + \quad \_Cl_2 \quad + \quad \_H_2O$$

Balance this equation using whole number coefficients. What is the coefficient of HCl in the balanced equation?

a. 1   c. 3   e. 5   g. 7   i. 9

b. 2   d. 4   f. 6   h. 8   j. 10

19. Chromium(III) oxide reacts with hydrogen sulfide (H_2S) to produce chromium(III) sulfide and water. If 2.0 moles chromium(III) oxide reacts with 2.0 moles hydrogen sulfide and the reaction goes to completion, how much of the non-limiting reactant remains? (*Hint:* Write the balanced equation.)

a. 0 mol   c. 2/3 mol   e. 4/3 mol   g. 2 mol

b. 1/2 mol   d. 1 mol   f. 5/3 mol   h. 3 mol

20. 61 g of an unknown element X reacts with excess chlorine to produce 114 g of a trichloride XCl_3. What is the element X?

a. zinc (Zn)   d. lead (Pb)   g. mercury (Hg)

b. tin (Sn)   e. antimony (Sb)   h. bromine (Br)

c. phosphorus (P)   f. aluminum (Al)   i. iodine (I)

EXAMINATION 1

CHEMISTRY 141 SPRING 2007

Monday January 29th 2007

1. *(5 points)* FM radio stations commonly express their frequency in units of megahertz (MHz). How many hertz (Hz) are equivalent to 93.7 MHz?

    a. 9.37×10^{-5} Hz   c. 9.37×10^{-1} Hz   e. 9.37×10^{2} Hz   g. 9.37×10^{6} Hz
    b. 9.37×10^{-2} Hz   d. 9.37×10^{1} Hz   f. 9.37×10^{5} Hz   h. 9.37×10^{7} Hz

2. *(5 points)* What is the formula for sodium bicarbonate?

    a. Na_2CO_3 c. $NaClO_4$ e. Na_2CrO_4 g. $NaCH_3CO_2$
    b. $Na(CO_3)_2$ d. $NaHCO_3$ f. $NaClO_2$ h. $NaCO_3$

3. A room has a length of 11 feet and a width of 13 feet. What is the area of the room in m^2?

    a. $43.6 \ m^2$ c. $0.319 \ m^2$ e. $2.06 \ m^2$ g. $1.33 \times 10^{9} \ m^2$
    b. $13.3 \ m^2$ d. $4.36 \times 10^{3} \ m^2$ f. $4.05 \ m^2$ h. $36.5 \ m^2$

4. A rectangular block of titanium is 9.5 cm long, 6.5 cm wide, 7.0 cm high, and has a mass of 1945 g. What is the density of titanium in $g \ cm^{-3}$?

    a. $3.5 \times 10^{-1} \ g \ cm^{-3}$ c. $4.5 \ g \ cm^{-3}$ e. $2.6 \ g \ cm^{-3}$ g. $9.8 \times 10^{1} \ g \ cm^{-3}$
    b. $4.3 \times 10^{2} \ g \ cm^{-3}$ d. $1.9 \times 10^{3} \ g \ cm^{-3}$ f. $9.8 \ g \ cm^{-3}$ h. $5.0 \times 10^{4} \ g \ cm^{-3}$

5. Which one of the following compounds contains a transition metal?

    a. CO_2 c. $LiCl$ e. $Mg(HSO_4)_2$ g. HCl i. NH_4NO_3
    b. $FeCl_2$ d. NH_3 f. $CaCO_3$ h. $NaHSO_4$ j. KOH

6. Which of the following cannot be physically separated into pure substances?

    a. salt dissolved into water   d. sand mixed with iron filings
    b. sugar mixed with flour   e. copper and chlorine in copper(I) chloride
    c. oil mixed with vinegar   f. carbon dioxide gas dissolved in soda

7. An atom or ion has 19 protons, 20 neutrons, and 19 electrons. What is the mass number, atomic number, and charge for this atom or ion? *(Choose the row where all responses are correct.)*

	mass number	atomic number	charge			mass number	atomic number	charge
a.	19	39	+1		f.	39	20	0
b.	20	39	0		g.	19	38	−1
c.	20	38	+2		h.	39	19	+1
d.	39	20	+1		i.	19	39	0
e.	39	19	0					

8. What is the mass of 3.0 moles of sulfur molecules (S_8)?

    a. 32 g   c. 256 g   e. 528 g   g. 770 g
    b. 128 g   d. 379 g   f. 672 g   h. 1080 g

9.   Which one of the following compounds is paired with an incorrect name?

   a. KNO_3 potassium nitrate   e. SF_6 sulfur pentafluoride
   b. XeF_4 xenon tetrafluoride   f. SO_3 sulfur trioxide
   c. $CuCl_2$ copper(II) chloride   g. BCl_3 boron trichloride
   d. Na_3PO_4 sodium phosphate   h. $NH_4CH_3CO_2$ ammonium acetate

10. How many hydrogen atoms are in 2 moles of phosphine PH_3?

   a. 6.022×10^{23} atoms   d. 2.409×10^{24} atoms   g. 4.215×10^{24} atoms
   b. 1.204×10^{24} atoms   e. 3.011×10^{24} atoms   h. 4.818×10^{24} atoms
   c. 1.807×10^{24} atoms   f. 3.613×10^{24} atoms

11. Which one of the following contains the greatest number of moles of sulfur atoms?

   a. 1.0 mol S_8 c. 3.0 mol SO_3 e. 6.0 mol H_2SO_4 g. 4.0 mol SO_4^{2-}
   b. 5.0 mol SO_2 d. 2.0 mol H_2S f. 7.0 mol SO_3^{2-} h. 3.0 mol HSO_4^-

12. Uracil ($C_4H_4O_2N_2$) is an organic base found in the nucleotides of ribonucleic acids (RNA). What is the molar mass of uracil?

   a. 28.02 g mol^{-1} c. 48.04 g mol^{-1} e. 80.04 g mol^{-1} g. 112.1 g mol^{-1}
   b. 32.00 g mol^{-1} d. 64.05 g mol^{-1} f. 84.07 g mol^{-1} h. 132.1 g mol^{-1}

13. 2 moles of an element have a mass of 130.8 grams. What is the element?

   a. He   c. Zn   e. Sr   g. Te   i. La
   b. Sc   d. Br   f. Ag   h. Xe   j. Pb

14. Sucralose is a non-nutrative sweetener with the molecular formula $C_{12}H_{19}Cl_3O_8$. The molar mass of sucralose is 397.6 g mol^{-1}. What is the percent by mass of chlorine in sucralose?

   a. 4.82 %   c. 32.2 %   e. 46.3 %   g. 81.7 %
   b. 26.7 %   d. 36.2 %   f. 65.1 %   h. 90.0 %

15. 1.302 grams of an organic compound containing carbon, hydrogen, and sulfur were burned in oxygen to produce 2.722 grams carbon dioxide, 0.558 grams water, and 0.992 grams sulfur dioxide. What is the empirical formula of the organic compound?

   a. CHS   c. C_2H_2S e. C_3H_6S g. C_4H_4S
   b. CHS_2 d. C_2HS f. $C_3H_3S_3$ h. $C_8H_8S_2$

16. Ethylenediamine is an organic compound found to contain 40.0 % carbon, 46.6 % nitrogen, and 13.4 % hydrogen by mass. If the molar mass of ethylenediamine is 60.1 g mol^{-1}, what is the molecular formula of ethylenediamine?

   a. CHN   c. $C_3H_3N_4$ e. $C_4H_3N_3$ g. $C_4H_4N_2$
   b. $C_2H_8N_2$ d. $C_3H_4N_3$ f. $C_8H_8N_4$ h. $C_4H_5N_4$

17. How many moles of O_2 are consumed in the complete combustion of 3 moles ethanol CH_3CH_2OH?

   a. 0.5 moles   c. 3 moles   e. 5 moles   g. 6.5 moles   i. 9 moles
   b. 2 moles   d. 3.5 moles   f. 6 moles   h. 8 moles   j. 10.5 moles

18. Balance the following equation using whole number coefficients.

$$\_\_ \ PbO \ + \ \_\_ \ NH_3 \ \rightarrow \ \_\_ \ Pb \ + \ \_\_ \ N_2 \ + \ \_\_ \ H_2O$$

What is the sum of all of the coefficients?

a. 9   c. 11   e. 13   g. 15   i. 17
b. 10   d. 12   f. 14   h. 16   j. 18

19. Phosphorus reacts with chlorine to produce phosphorus trichloride according to the reaction shown below. If 124 g P_4 react completely with 323 g Cl_2, how much PCl_3 will be produced?

$$P_4(s) \ + \ 6 \ Cl_2(g) \ \rightarrow \ 4 \ PCl_3(l)$$

a. 323 g   c. 549 g   e. 30 g   g. 714 g
b. 417 g   d. 626 g   f. 137 g   h. 94 g

20. 1.80 moles CCl_4 reacts with excess HF to produce CCl_2F_2 and HCl. When this reaction was done in the laboratory 1.55 moles CCl_2F_2 were produced. What is the percent yield of this reaction?

$$CCl_4 \ + \ 2 \ HF \ \rightarrow \ CCl_2F_2 \ + \ 2 \ HCl$$

a. 13%   c. 32%   e. 67%   g. 86%
b. 27%   d. 51%   f. 74%   h. 100%

21. 2.0 moles aluminum react with 2.0 moles chromium(III) oxide to produce aluminum oxide and chromium according to the following balanced equation.

$$2 \ Al(l) \ + \ Cr_2O_3(s) \ \rightarrow \ Al_2O_3(s) \ + \ 2 \ Cr(l)$$

Assuming the reaction goes as far as possible, which one of the following statements is false?

a. Aluminum is the limiting reactant.
b. It is possible to produce 4.0 moles of chromium.
c. In order to completely use both reactants, you would need twice as many moles of aluminum as chromium(III) oxide.
d. 1.0 mole of chromium(III) oxide remains at the end of the reaction.
e. There is no aluminum remaining at the end of the reaction.
f. The theoretical yield of chromium is 2.0 moles.
g. The maximum amount of aluminum oxide that can be produced is 1.0 mole.

22. A new element X was discovered to have five isotopes:

Based on this information, what is the atomic mass of element X?

isotope	mass	% abundance
^{86}X	85.925 amu	0.62%
^{87}X	86.787 amu	0.65%
^{88}X	87.976 amu	1.86%
^{89}X	88.989 amu	12.27%
^{90}X	89.855 amu	84.6%

a. less than 86 amu   f. greater than 90 amu
b. between 86 amu and 87 amu   g. exactly 86 amu
c. between 87 amu and 88 amu   h. exactly 88 amu
d. between 88 amu and 89 amu   i. exactly 90 amu
e. between 89 amu and 90 amu

EXAMINATION 1

CHEMISTRY 141 FALL 2007

Monday September 17th 2007

1. *(5 points)* What is the chemical symbol for the element potassium?

    a. P   c. Po   e. Ca   g. Pt

    b. Na   d. K   f. Pb   h. W

2. *(5 points)* Determine the number of significant figures in each of the numbers shown below. Then add these numbers of significant figures. What is the total?

    > 0.00176   14.05   106.90

    a. 8   c. 10   e. 12   g. 14

    b. 9   d. 11   f. 13   h. 15

3. All the following polyatomic ions have the correct charges but one has an incorrect formula. Which one?

    a. sulfite SO_3^{2-} d. sulfate SO_4^{2-} g. carbonate CO_3^{2-}

    b. cyanide CN^- e. permanganate MnO_4^- h. nitrate NO_2^-

    c. hypochlorite ClO^- f. hydrogen sulfate HSO_4^- i. acetate $CH_3CO_2^-$

4. A small rectangular metal block has the dimensions 1.2 inch × 1.8 inch × 1.0 inch. What is the volume of the metal block in cm^3?

    a. $2.2 \, cm^3$ c. $5.5 \, cm^3$ e. $14 \, cm^3$ g. $35 \, cm^3$

    b. $3.3 \, cm^3$ d. $7.7 \, cm^3$ f. $17 \, cm^3$ h. $46 \, cm^3$

5. Examples of an alkali metal, a halogen, a noble gas, and a transition metal, are, in that order: *Choose the row where all the descriptions fit.*

	alkali metal	halogen	noble gas	transition metal
a.	Na	Cl	Ar	Ni
b.	Mg	F	Ne	Pb
c.	Cs	I	H	Co
d.	K	N	Xe	Mn
e.	Li	I	He	Ca
f.	Sr	Br	H	Sn

6. How many of the following processes are physical changes?

    - a puddle of water evaporates in the sun
    - a silver fork tarnishes in air
    - sugar dissolves in hot water
    - an ice cube melts
    - gasoline burns to produce water and carbon dioxide
    - wax is molded into the shape of a candle

    a. none are physical changes   e. 4

    b. 1   f. 5

    c. 2   g. all are physical changes

    d. 3

7. Chlorine has an atomic mass of 35.453. It has two stable isotopes, one of which is ^{35}Cl which is 75.77% abundant. How many neutrons are in the nucleus of the other isotope?

    a. 17   c. 19   e. 21   g. 35
    b. 18   d. 20   f. 22   h. 37

8. John Dalton's hypotheses concerning the atomic nature of matter were based upon the observations and ideas of scientists of that time, including Dalton himself. Some of Dalton's hypotheses are listed below. One of these has since been found to be false. Which one?

    a. All matter consists of atoms.
    b. For all practical purposes, mass is conserved in chemical reactions.
    c. Elements combine in whole-number ratios to form compounds.
    d. Chemical reactions are rearrangements of atoms.
    e. Atoms are indivisible.

9. How many of the following substances are classified as binary molecular compounds?

    KBr $Mg(OH)_2$ H_2O K_3PO_4 CH_3OH
    CO PF_5 $NaCl$ O_3 HNO_3

    a. 0   c. 2   e. 4   g. 6   i. 8
    b. 1   d. 3   f. 5   h. 7   j. 9

10. 5 moles of an element have a mass of 260 grams. What is the element?

    a. No   c. Zn   e. Cr   g. Fe   i. Al
    b. Mo   d. Cl   f. Hg   h. Sb   j. Ca

11. How many moles of phosphorus atoms are there in 495.5 g of phosphorus P_4?

    a. 2.0 moles   c. 4.0 moles   e. 8.0 moles   g. 12 moles   i. 24 moles
    b. 3.0 moles   d. 6.0 moles   f. 9.0 moles   h. 16 moles   j. 32 moles

12. What is the mass of 5.00 moles of ammonia molecules (NH_3)?

    a. 17 g   c. 51 g   e. 85 g   g. 119 g
    b. 34 g   d. 68 g   f. 102 g   h. 136 g

13. What is the percent by mass of sodium in sodium carbonate?

    a. 16.1%   c. 27.7%   e. 43.4%   g. 55.6%
    b. 21.7%   d. 33.3%   f. 52.8%   h. 67.2%

14. What is the average mass of a single molecule of nitrogen dioxide?

    a. 2.43×10^{-24} g   c. 7.64×10^{-23} g   e. 2.12×10^{-22} g
    b. 5.87×10^{-23} g   d. 9.33×10^{-23} g   f. 3.97×10^{-23} g

15. A compound contains 59.96% C, 13.42% H, and 26.62% O by mass. 0.50 moles of the compound has a mass of 30.0 grams. What is the molecular formula of the compound?

    a. C_4H_7O c. $C_5H_{13}O$ e. $C_{15}H_{39}O_5$ g. C_3H_8O
    b. CHO d. $C_6H_{16}O_2$ f. $C_{10}H_{26}O_3$ h. C_2H_4O

16. Which sample contains the greatest mass of hydrogen?

    a. 3.0 moles of water H_2O
    b. 4.5 moles of methanol CH_3OH
    c. 5.0 moles of benzene C_6H_6
    d. 6.0 moles of sulfuric acid H_2SO_4

    e. 7.0 moles of ammonia NH_3
    f. 7.5 moles of hydrogen sulfide H_2S
    g. 9.0 moles of hydrogen fluoride HF

17. A compound of aluminum and selenium was burned in oxygen to produce alumina Al_2O_3 and selenium dioxide SeO_2. The number of moles of selenium dioxide produced was three times the number of moles of alumina produced. What is the formula of the compound of aluminum and selenium?

    a. AlSe
    b. $AlSe_2$
    c. Al_2Se
    d. $AlSe_3$
    e. Al_3Se
    f. Al_3Se_2
    g. Al_2Se_3
    h. Al_3Se_4

18. Balance the equation representing the reaction between methylhydrazine and dinitrogen tetroxide:

    $$\_\ CH_3NHNH_2 \ + \ \_\ N_2O_4 \ \rightarrow \ \_\ N_2 \ + \ \_\ H_2O \ + \ \_\ CO_2$$

    What is the sum of *all* the coefficients in the balanced equation?

    a. 12
    b. 15
    c. 18
    d. 20
    e. 22
    f. 27
    g. 30
    h. 32
    i. 34
    j. 36

19. 2.5 moles of methanol (CH_3OH) is burned in excess oxygen to produce carbon dioxide and water. How many moles of water are produced?

    a. 1
    b. 1.5
    c. 2
    d. 2.5
    e. 3
    f. 3.5
    g. 4
    h. 4.5
    i. 5
    j. 5.5

20. 7.36 g zinc reacts with 6.45 g sulfur to produce zinc sulfide according to the balanced reaction shown below. How much of each reactant remains after the maximum amount of zinc sulfide is produced?

    $$8\ Zn \ + \ S_8 \ \rightarrow \ 8\ ZnS$$

	zinc	sulfur		zinc	sulfur
a.	0 g	2.84 g	e.	1.17 g	0 g
b.	0 g	3.61 g	f.	2.52 g	0 g
c.	0 g	4.72 g	g.	5.49 g	0 g
d.	0 g	6.45 g	h.	7.36 g	0 g

21. 2.550 g of iron (Fe) reacts with excess sulfur to produce 5.475 g of an iron sulfide. What is the formula of the iron sulfide produced in this reaction?

    a. FeS
    b. FeS_2
    c. Fe_2S
    d. FeS_3
    e. Fe_3S
    f. Fe_3S_2
    g. Fe_2S_3
    h. Fe_3S_4

22. 3.000 grams of copper(II) sulfate $CuSO_4$ was dissolved in water and crystallized as 4.693 grams of a hydrate $CuSO_4.xH_2O$. All of the copper sulfate was recovered (100% yield). What is the value of x in the formula of the hydrate?

    a. 1
    b. 2
    c. 3
    d. 4
    e. 5
    f. 6
    g. 7
    h. 8
    i. 9
    j. 10

EXAMINATION 1

CHEMISTRY 141 SPRING 2008

Monday January 28th 2008

1. *(5 points)* Which one of the following units is NOT an SI base unit?

    a. kg   b. s   c. mole   d. m   e. K   f. g

2. *(5 points)* Normal human body temperature is 310.15K. What is normal human body temperature in degrees Celsius?

    a. 0 °C   c. 37 °C   e. 68 °C   g. 100 °C
    b. 25 °C   d. 54 °C   f. 98.6 °C   h. 212 °C

3. Which one of the following elements does *not* normally exist as a diatomic molecule?

    a. bromine   c. oxygen   e. iodine   g. fluorine
    b. hydrogen   d. carbon   f. nitrogen   h. chlorine

4. 4.63 kilometers is equivalent to _____ centimeters.

    a. 0.463 cm   c. 46.3 cm   e. 4.63×10^3 cm   g. 4.63×10^5 cm
    b. 4.63×10^{-5} cm   d. 4.63×10^2 cm   f. 4.63×10^4 cm   h. 4.63×10^6 cm

5. A one carat diamond has a mass of 200 mg. The density of diamond is 3.52 g cm^{-3}. What is the volume of this diamond?

    a. 5.68×10^{-2} cm^3 c. 1.63×10^{-2} cm^3 e. 0.284 cm^3 g. 56.8 cm^3
    b. 7.04×10^{-2} cm^3 d. 0.155 cm^3 f. 4.53 cm^3 h. 704 cm^3

6. How many of the following would be classified as an example of an intensive physical property?

    mass   color   molecular mass
    density   volume   temperature

    a. none   c. 2   e. 4   g. 6
    b. 1   d. 3   f. 5

7. Arrange the following isotopes in order of increasing number of protons (ie. fewest protons to most protons).

    ^{18}O ^{12}C ^{40}Ca ^{41}K ^{37}Cl

    a. ^{12}C ^{18}O ^{37}Cl ^{40}Ca ^{41}K
    b. ^{12}C ^{18}O ^{37}Cl ^{41}K ^{40}Ca
    c. ^{12}C ^{18}O ^{40}Ca ^{37}Cl ^{41}K
    d. ^{37}Cl ^{18}O ^{12}C ^{40}Ca ^{41}K
    e. ^{37}Cl ^{12}C ^{40}Ca ^{41}K ^{18}O
    f. ^{41}K ^{40}Ca ^{12}C ^{18}O ^{37}Cl
    g. ^{41}K ^{12}C ^{18}O ^{40}Ca ^{37}Cl

(8.) How many of the elements listed below are transition metals?

Ti	Ni	Ce	Pb	Ne
Ca	Na	Au	Cu	U

a. 1   c. 3   e. 5   g. 7   i. 9
b. 2   d. 4   f. 6   h. 8   j. 10

9.   Which one of the following statements is *false*?

a.   A molecule is composed of two or more different elements.
b.   A molecular formula gives the actual number of atoms in a molecule.
c.   Phosphorus pentafluoride is an example of a binary molecular compound.
d.   Metal atoms lose electrons to form cations.
e.   The molecules benzene (C_6H_6) and styrene (C_8H_8) have the same empirical formula.
f.   Calcium carbonate is an example of an ionic compound.

10.   Which one of the following formulas for polyatomic ions is *incorrect*?

a. SO_4^{2-} sulfate   e. PO_4^{3-} phosphate
b. ClO_3^- chlorate   f. CrO_4^{2-} chromate
c. NH_4^+ ammonium   g. ClO_4^- hypochlorite
d. NO_2^- nitrite   h. $CH_3CO_2^-$ acetate

11.   What is the molar mass of iron(III) chloride?

a.   91.3 g mol^{-1} c.   168 g mol^{-1} e.   306 g mol^{-1} g.   106 g mol^{-1}
b.   203 g mol^{-1} d.   162 g mol^{-1} f.   251 g mol^{-1} h.   313 g mol^{-1}

12.   You dissolve 0.0292 mole of sucrose $C_{12}H_{22}O_{11}$ in a glass of tea. How many grams of sucrose did you dissolve?

a.   0.0292 g   c.   10.0 g   e.   29.2 g   g.   171 g
b.   5.00 g   d.   12.0 g   f.   56.8 g   h.   342 g

13.   How many moles of hydrogen atoms are in 2.0 moles of ammonium carbonate?

a.   2   c.   6   e.   10   g.   14   i.   20
b.   4   d.   8   f.   12   h.   16   j.   24

14.   How many fluorine atoms are in 271 g boron trifluoride?

a. 6.02×10^{23} c. 7.22×10^{24} e. 4.27×10^{25} g. 3.99×10^{26}
b. 2.41×10^{24} d. 8.46×10^{24} f. 6.18×10^{25} h. 5.02×10^{26}

15.   4.263 grams of a compound was analyzed and found to contain 0.423 g of carbon, 2.50 g of chlorine, and 1.34 g of fluorine. What is the empirical formula of the compound?

a.   CClF   c.   CClF$_2$ e.   CCl$_6$F$_3$ g.   CCl$_2$F$_4$
b.   CCl$_2$F   d.   CCl$_2$F$_2$ f.   CCl$_3$F$_6$ h.   CCl$_3$F$_5$

16.   What is the percent by mass of oxygen in quinine $C_{20}H_{24}N_2O_2$?

a.   4.17%   c.   8.64%   e.   23.5%   g.   67.3%
b.   7.46%   d.   9.86%   f.   42.9%   h.   74.0%

17. A compound contains 71.56% chlorine, 24.27% carbon, and 4.07% hydrogen. The molar mass of the
     compound is approximately 100 g mol^{-1}. What is the molecular formula of the compound?

     a. $ClCH_2$ c. ClC_2H_2 e. $Cl_2C_2H_4$ g. ClC_5H_5
     b. Cl_2CH_2 d. $Cl_2C_2H_2$ f. $Cl_2C_4H_4$ h. $Cl_3C_3H_5$

18. A favorite lecture demonstration is the "volcano" produced when ammonium dichromate burns. An
     approximate equation for the reaction is:

     $$\underline{\quad} (NH_4)_2Cr_2O_7 \quad \rightarrow \quad \underline{\quad} Cr_2O_3 \quad + \quad \underline{\quad} N_2 \quad + \quad \underline{\quad} H_2O$$

     Balance the equation using whole number coefficients. What are the coefficients (in the order the
     reaction is written) for the balanced equation?

     a. 1, 1, 1, 1   c. 1, 1, 1, 2   e. 1, 1, 1, 4   g. 2, 2, 4, 5
     b. 4, 2, 1, 4   d. 1, 1, 2, 4   f. 4, 1, 1, 4   h. 2, 1, 1, 4

19. Potassium chlorate decomposes to make potassium chloride and oxygen gas. Write a balanced equation
     for this reaction. How many moles of oxygen gas are produced from the decomposition of 3.0 moles of
     potassium chlorate?

     a. 1.5 moles   c. 3.0 moles   e. 4.5 moles   g. 6.5 moles
     b. 2.0 moles   d. 4.0 moles   f. 5.0 moles   h. 9.0 moles

20. Nitrogen gas can be prepared by passing gaseous ammonia over solid copper(II) oxide at high tempera-
     tures. The other products of the reaction are copper metal and water vapor. If 18.1 g ammonia reacts
     with 90.4 g CuO and the reaction goes to completion, how many grams of N_2 gas will be formed?

     $$2\,NH_3(g) \quad + \quad 3\,CuO(s) \quad \rightarrow \quad N_2(g) \quad + \quad 3\,Cu(s) \quad + \quad 3\,H_2O(g)$$

     a. 1.60 g   c. 5.30 g   e. 12.9 g   g. 18.1 g
     b. 3.22 g   d. 10.6 g   f. 14.9 g   h. 72.3 g

21. Ammonia reacts with oxygen to produce nitrogen dioxide and water according to the following equa-
     tion:

     $$\underline{\quad} NH_3 \quad + \quad \underline{\quad} O_2 \quad \rightarrow \quad \underline{\quad} NO_2 \quad + \quad \underline{\quad} H_2O$$

     Balance this equation using whole number coefficients. If 4.0 moles of ammonia react with 7.0 moles of
     oxygen and the reaction goes to completion, how many moles of ammonia remain at the end of the
     reaction?

     a. 0   c. 2   e. 4   g. 6   i. 10
     b. 1   d. 3   f. 5   h. 7   j. 11

22. Methanol reacts with oxygen to produce carbon dioxide and water according to this balanced equation:

     $$2\,CH_3OH \quad + \quad 3\,O_2 \quad \rightarrow \quad 2\,CO_2 \quad + \quad 4\,H_2O$$

     6.21 g carbon dioxide was produced from the reaction of 6.40 g methanol in excess oxygen. What is the
     percent yield of carbon dioxide?

     a. 15.2%   c. 46.3%   e. 70.6%   g. 81.4%
     b. 36.4%   d. 57.4%   f. 78.2%   h. 100%

EXAMINATION 1

CHEMISTRY 141 FALL 2008

Monday September 15th 2008

The first four questions are worth 5 points each; the remaining 16 questions are worth 10 points each. The total number of points possible is 180.

1. Which one of the following units is the derived SI unit for density?

    a. $g \, mL^{-1}$ c. $kg \, m^{-3}$ e. $kg \, cm^{-3}$ g. $kg \, m$
    b. $g \, cm^2$ d. $m^3 \, kg^{-1}$ f. $g \, cm^{-3}$ h. $g \, L^{-1}$

2. Which of the following properties is extensive?

    a. mass   c. density   e. color
    b. temperature   d. molar mass   f. atomic number

3. How many significant figures should be shown in the correct answer to the following problem:

    $$(32.44 \; + \; 4.9 \; - \; 0.304) \, / \, 0.4461 \; = \; ???$$

    a. 1   c. 2   e. 4
    b. 2   d. 3   f. 5

4. Which one of the following elements would you classify as a transition element?

    a. sodium   c. sulfur   e. chlorine   g. magnesium
    b. iron   d. neon   f. lead   h. aluminum

5. Which one of the following names for polyatomic ions is *incorrect*?

    a. SO_4^{2-} sulfate   d. HCO_3^- hydrogen carbonate
    b. NO_2^- nitrite   e. MnO_4^- permanganate
    c. OH^- hydroxide   f. NH_4^+ ammonia

6. Which of the following statements is(are) *true*?

    I.   Atoms are indivisible.
    II. All molecules are compounds.
    III. Some elements exist as molecules.
    IV. All atoms of an element are identical.
    V.   All compounds are molecules.
    VI. Neutrons and protons are heavier than electrons.

    a. I only   c. III only   e. V only   g. II and III   i. II, IV, and VI
    b. II only   d. IV only   f. VI only   h. III and VI   j. III, V, and VI

7. A monatomic ion of an isotope of an unknown element contains 18 electrons, 15 protons, and 16 neutrons. What is the ion?

    a. $^{33}Mg^{2+}$ c. $^{31}P^{3+}$ e. ^{31}Ar g. $^{31}S^{2-}$ i. $^{16}S^{2-}$
    b. $^{16}P^{3-}$ d. $^{31}P^{3-}$ f. $^{31}Ga^{3+}$ h. $^{18}N^{3-}$ j. $^{31}Se^{3-}$

8. Boron exists as two naturally occurring isotopes, ^{10}B (10.012937 u) and ^{11}B (11.009305 u). What is the percent abundance of ^{11}B?

    a. 10.00%   c. 36.41%   e. 49.00%   g. 64.64%
    b. 20.00%   d. 42.07%   f. 50.00%   h. 80.00%

9. Which is a correct relationship between the mass of a substance and the number of moles of that substance?

    a. mass × molar mass = number of moles
    b. molar mass / mass = number of moles
    c. mass / molar mass = number of moles
    d. number of moles × mass = molar mass
    e. number of moles / mass = molar mass

10. Calculate the molar mass (formula mass) of aluminum sulfite.

    a. 59.1 g mol^{-1} c. 123 g mol^{-1} e. 241 g mol^{-1} g. 262 g mol^{-1} i. 294 g mol^{-1}
    b. 107 g mol^{-1} d. 150 g mol^{-1} f. 246 g mol^{-1} h. 273 g mol^{-1} j. 342 g mol^{-1}

11. What is the mass of 12 moles of carbon dioxide?

    a. 12 g   c. 88 g   e. 220 g   g. 336 g
    b. 44 g   d. 144 g   f. 288 g   h. 528 g

12. Which one of the following samples has the greatest mass?

    a. 0.5 mol magnesium chloride   e. 2.0 mol methane CH_4
    b. 5.0 mol hydrogen molecules   f. 1.0 mol argon
    c. 1.0 mol carbon dioxide   g. 0.25 mol sodium nitrate
    d. 0.5 mol potassium   h. 1.0 mol hydrogen chloride

13. Balance the following equation using whole number coefficients:

    $$\_\ N_2O_4 \quad + \quad \_\ NH_3 \quad \rightarrow \quad \_\ N_2 \quad + \quad \_\ H_2O$$

    What is the coefficient for N_2 in the balanced equation?

    a. 1   c. 3   e. 5   g. 7   i. 9
    b. 2   d. 4   f. 6   h. 8   j. 10

14. The compound 1,3,5-trinitrobenzene is a degradation product of the explosive TNT. What is the empirical formula for 1,3,5–trinitrobenzene (shown on the right)?

    a. CHNO   d. $C_6H_3N_3O_6$ g. $C_2H_2N_2O_2$
    b. $C_2H_2NO_2$ e. $C_6H_2N_2O_6$ h. C_2HNO_2
    c. C_3HNO_3 f. $C_6H_6N_3O_6$ i. $C_6H_6N_2O_6$

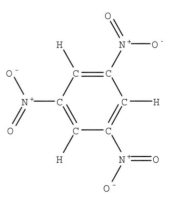

15. What is the percentage by mass of hydrogen in the compound $CH_3CH_2CH_2CH_2OH$?

    a. 9.3%   c. 17.2%   e. 23.8%   g. 34.8%
    b. 13.5%   d. 21.6%   f. 28.4%   h. 64.9%

16. The atomic mass of an unknown hypothetical element X is 33.42 g mol^{-1}. A 27.22 g sample of this unknown element combines with 84.10 g of another element Y to form a compound XY_2. What is the atomic mass (molar mass) of the element Y?

    a. 12.91 g mol^{-1} c. 25.81 g mol^{-1} e. 51.63 g mol^{-1} g. 103.2 g mol^{-1}
    b. 19.36 g mol^{-1} d. 38.72 g mol^{-1} f. 77.44 g mol^{-1} h. 154.9 g mol^{-1}

17. Ethyl mercaptan, a compound of carbon, hydrogen, and sulfur, is burned in air to produce carbon dioxide, sulfur dioxide, and water. It was determined that the number of moles of water produced was 1.5 times the number of moles of carbon dioxide produced in the combustion. The amount of sulfur dioxide produced was not measured. In a separate experiment, the molar mass of the compound was determined to be somewhere between 60 and 70 g mol^{-1}. What is the molecular formula of ethyl mercaptan?

    a. CH_2S c. CH_2S_2 e. C_2H_5S g. C_2H_7S i. C_2H_6
    b. CH_3S d. C_2H_4S f. C_2H_6S h. C_3H_8S j. C_5H_9

18. Aluminum sulfate crystallizes as a hydrate. In other words, the crystal contains water molecules and has the empirical formula $Al_2(SO_4)_3 \cdot xH_2O$ where x is unknown and represents the number of moles of water per mole of $Al_2(SO_4)_3$. A sample of the hydrate was analyzed and found to contain 8.10% aluminum. What is the value of x in this crystal?

Molar mass of Al   = 26.98 g mol^{-1}
Molar mass of $Al_2(SO_4)_3$ = 342.17 g mol^{-1}
Molar mass of H_2O = 18.016 g mol^{-1}

    a. 6   c. 10   e. 14   g. 16   i. 20
    b. 8   d. 12   f. 15   h. 18   j. 24

19. Nitroglcerin ($C_3H_5N_3O_9$) is a powerful and sensitive explosive. When it decomposes (explodes), it produces nitrogen, carbon dioxide, water, and oxygen according to the *unbalanced* equation shown below. Balance this equation using whole number coefficients. Assuming all the products are gases, how many moles of gas are produced in the decomposition of 1.00 mole of nitroglycerin?

$$\_\,C_3H_5N_3O_9 \;\rightarrow\; \_\,CO_2 \;+\; \_\,N_2 \;+\; \_\,H_2O \;+\; \_\,O_2$$

    a. 2.50 mol   c. 4.25 mol   e. 6.25 mol   g. 7.25 mol   i. 8.75 mol
    b. 3.75 mol   d. 5.50 mol   f. 6.75 mol   h. 8.25 mol   j. 9.50 mol

20. Ammonia reacts with oxygen according to the following balanced equation:

$$4\,NH_3(g) \;+\; 5\,O_2(g) \;\rightarrow\; 4\,NO(g) \;+\; 6\,H_2O(l)$$

If 3.0 mol ammonia reacts with 2.0 moles oxygen, and the reaction goes as far as possible, how many moles of which reactant are left unused at the end?

    a. 0.4 mol NH_3 c. 1.6 mol NH_3 e. 0.4 mol O_2 g. 1.6 mol O_2
    b. 1.4 mol NH_3 d. 2.4 mol NH_3 f. 1.4 mol O_2 h. 2.4 mol O_2

EXAMINATION 1

CHEMISTRY 141 SPRING 2009

Monday February 2nd 2009

The first four questions are worth 5 points each; the remaining 16 questions are worth 10 points each. The total number of points possible is 180.

1. How many significant figures should be shown in the correct answer to the following problem:

    $(23.56 - 1.4) / 1.345 = ???$

    a. 1   c. 3   e. 5
    b. 2   d. 4   f. 6

2. Use the following information to derive the SI unit for force: velocity = length / time
                                                                          acceleration = velocity / time
                                                                          force = mass × acceleration

    a. $kg\ m^{-1}\ s^{-2}$ c. $m\ s^2\ kg^{-1}$ e. $g\ m\ s^{-2}$ g. $g\ s^2\ m^{-1}$
    b. $kg\ m^2\ s^{-3}$ d. $m\ s^{-2}\ kg^{-1}$ f. $kg\ m\ s^{-2}$ h. $kg\ m^{-1}\ s^2$

3. Which one of the following elements does not exist as a molecule in nature?

    a. hydrogen   c. fluorine   e. bromine   g. oxygen   i. phosphorus
    b. nitrogen   d. chlorine   f. sulfur   h. tin   j. iodine

4. What is the correct formula for the ionic compound calcium hydrogen phosphate?

    a. $CaHPO_4$ c. $Ca(PO_2)_2$ e. $CaPO_4$ g. Ca_2HPO_4
    b. $Ca(H_2PO_4)_2$ d. $Ca_3(PO_4)_2$ f. $Ca_3(PO_3)_2$ h. Ca_3PO_3

5. A standard Army requirement is for a person to run 1.0 mile in 11.0 minutes. What is this speed in meters per second (ms^{-1})?

    a. $0.0024\ ms^{-1}$ c. $0.091\ ms^{-1}$ e. $2.4\ ms^{-1}$ g. $8.8\ ms^{-1}$ i. $91\ ms^{-1}$
    b. $0.0088\ ms^{-1}$ d. $0.45\ ms^{-1}$ f. $4.5\ ms^{-1}$ h. $9.1\ ms^{-1}$ j. $8776\ ms^{-1}$

6. Which of the following processes represent a chemical change?

    I.   Solid mercury melting at room temperature.
    II. Methane burns in air to produce carbon dioxide and water.
    III. Dissolving sugar in a cup of hot tea.
    IV. A silver fork tarnishing in air over time.
    V.   Boiling a pot of water.
    VI. Burning a piece of wood in a fireplace.

    a. I only   c. III only   e. VI only   g. II and IV   i. II, IV, and VI
    b. II only   d. IV only   f. I and III   h. I, III, and V j. all are chemical changes

7.   Gallium has two naturally occurring isotopes, ^{69}Ga (60.1% abundance) and ^{x}Ga. To the nearest whole number, how many neutrons are there in the nucleus of the ^{x}Ga isotope?

     a. 37   c. 39   e. 41   g. 43
     b. 38   d. 40   f. 42   h. 44

8.   The structural formula of vitamin C is shown to the right. What is the molecular formula of vitamin C?

     a. CHO   d. $C_3H_2O_3$ g. $C_6H_8O_6$
     b. CH_2O_3 e. $C_3H_4O_3$ h. $C_6H_4O_6$
     c. $C_2H_8O_6$ f. $C_4H_4O_6$ i. $C_6H_{10}O_3$

9.   How many moles of chlorine atoms are in 3.0 moles of carbon tetrachloride?

     a. 3   c. 5   e. 10   g. 14
     b. 4   d. 8   f. 12   h. 16

10. Calculate the molar mass (formula mass) of iron(II) acetate.

     a. 71.85 g mol^{-1} c. 115.9 g mol^{-1} e. 170.7 g mol^{-1} g. 173.9 g mol^{-1}
     b. 89.87 g mol^{-1} d. 169.8 g mol^{-1} f. 172.0 g mol^{-1} h. 177.9 g mol^{-1}

11. How many nitrogen atoms are in 1.0 mole of potassium nitrate?

     a. 6.022×10^{23} c. 1.801×10^{24} e. 3.011×10^{24} g. 4.215×10^{24}
     b. 1.204×10^{24} d. 2.401×10^{24} f. 3.613×10^{24} h. 4.818×10^{24}

12. What is the mass of 2.5 moles of phosphorus tribromide?

     a. 111 g   c. 271 g   e. 356 g   g. 677 g
     b. 184 g   d. 279 g   f. 591 g   h. 947 g

13. A compound found in antifreeze contains 38.7% carbon, 9.70% hydrogen, and 51.6% oxygen. If the molar mass of the compound is 62.0 g mol^{-1}, what is the molecular formula of the compound?

     a. $C_2H_6O_2$ c. CH_6O e. $C_3H_{10}O$ g. $C_3H_9O_3$
     b. CH_3O d. C_2H_6O f. CH_2O_3 h. $C_4H_7O_4$

14. Urea is a chemical used in plastics and adhesives. What is the percentage by mass of hydrogen in the compound urea $(NH_2)_2CO$?

     a. 6.71%   c. 23.3%   e. 31.8%   g. 50.0%
     b. 20.0%   d. 26.7%   f. 46.7%   h. 63.6%

15. Balance this equation using whole number coefficients.

     __ NaHCO$_3$ →   __ Na$_2$CO$_3$ +   __ H$_2$O   +   __ CO$_2$

     What is the coefficient of sodium bicarbonate in the balanced equation?

     a. 1   c. 3   e. 5   g. 7
     b. 2   d. 4   f. 6   h. 8

16. Silver(I) oxide decomposes to silver and oxygen gas according to the following unbalanced equation:

$$\_\_ Ag_2O(s) \quad \rightarrow \quad \_\_ Ag(s) \quad + \quad \_\_ O_2(g)$$

How many moles of silver are produced in the decomposition of 1.00 kg silver(I) oxide?

a. 2.16 mol   c. 4.00 mol   e. 6.98 mol   g. 16.2 mol
b. 3.73 mol   d. 4.32 mol   f. 8.63 mol   h. 17.3 mol

17. 47 g of an unknown element X reacts with excess chlorine to produce 232 g of a trichloride XCl_3. What is the element X?

a. Zn   c. P   e. Sb   g. Hg   i. I
b. Sn   d. Pb   f. Al   h. Br   j. N

18. 4.000 grams of a sample of a hydrate of nickel(II) nitrate $Ni(NO_3)_2 \cdot xH_2O$ was heated carefully to drive off the water. The mass was reduced to 2.513 grams. What is the value of x in the formula of the hydrate?

a. 1   c. 3   e. 5   g. 7   i. 9
b. 2   d. 4   f. 6   h. 8   j. 10

19. Ammonia reacts with oxygen to produce nitric oxide and water according to this balanced equation:

$$4\,NH_3(g) \quad + \quad 5\,O_2(g) \quad \rightarrow \quad 4\,NO(g) \quad + \quad 6\,H_2O(l)$$

How many moles of nitric oxide can be produced from the reaction of 4.0 moles ammonia with 3.0 moles oxygen?

a. 0.48   c. 2.4   e. 3.8   g. 5.5
b. 0.60   d. 3.6   f. 4.0   h. 7.0

20. Salicylic acid $C_7H_6O_3$ (molar mass 138.12 g mol^{-1}) reacts with acetic anhydride $(CH_3CO)_2O$ (molar mass 102.09 g mol^{-1}) to produce aspirin $C_9H_8O_4$ (molar mass 180.154 g mol^{-1}) and acetic acid CH_3CO_2H (molar mass 60.05 g mol^{-1}) according to the balanced equation:

$$C_7H_6O_3 \quad + \quad (CH_3CO)_2O \quad \rightarrow \quad C_9H_8O_4 \quad + \quad CH_3CO_2H$$

If the percent yield of this reaction is 82.5%, what mass of salicylic acid must be reacted with excess acetic anhydride to produce 5.0 grams aspirin?

a. 0.13 g   c. 3.9 g   e. 5.0 g   g. 6.1 g
b. 1.2 g   d. 4.6 g   f. 5.5 g   h. 7.9 g

EXAMINATION 2

CHEMISTRY 141 FALL 2004

Monday October 18th 2004

1. Classify the following solutes in aqueous solution as strong acid, weak acid, strong base, weak base, or salt. *Choose the row in which all the examples are correct.*

	strong acid	strong base	weak acid	weak base	salt
a.	H_2SO_4	NH_3	HF	NaOH	KCl
b.	H_3PO_4	KOH	CH_3CO_2H	NH_3	KNO_3
c.	HF	NaOH	HNO_2	NaCl	HNO_3
d.	HNO_2	$Mg(OH)_2$	HCO_2H	NH_3	KCN
e.	HCl	KOH	HF	NH_3	K_2SO_4
f.	HI	$NaClO_4$	H_2SO_3	$Ca(OH)_2$	KOH
g.	$HClO_3$	NaOH	HNO_2	NH_3	HCl

2. What is the molarity (*M*) of a 500 mL aqueous solution containing 10 g NaCl?

    a. $3.4 \times 10^{-4}\ M$ c. $0.34\ M$ e. $5.6\ M$ g. $13.8\ M$
    b. $0.020\ M$ d. $1.2\ M$ f. $12\ M$ h. $20\ M$

3. Identify all the spectator ions in the following reaction:

    $$LiOH(aq)\ +\ HBr(aq)\ \rightarrow\ LiBr(aq)\ +\ H_2O(l)$$

    a. Li^+ d. OH^- g. Li^+ and OH^-
    b. H^+ e. H^+ and OH^- h. Li^+ and H^+
    c. Br^- f. H^+ and Br^- i. Li^+ and Br^-

4. What are the oxidation numbers of

	Cl in $HClO_4$	S in H_2S	I in I_2?	*[Choose the row in which all the numbers are correct.]*
a.	+1	−1	−1	
b.	−1	−2	0	
c.	+5	+2	−1	
d.	+7	+2	−1	
e.	+1	−1	0	
f.	+7	−2	0	
g.	+7	−1	−1	

5. Which one of the following equations represents a redox reaction?

    a. $KOH(aq)\ +\ HI(aq)\ \rightarrow\ KI(aq)\ +\ H_2O(l)$
    b. $AgNO_3(aq)\ +\ NaCl(aq)\ \rightarrow\ AgCl(s)\ +\ NaNO_3(aq)$
    c. $Mg(s)\ +\ CO_2(s)\ \rightarrow\ MgO(s)\ +\ C(s)$
    d. $NH_3(aq)\ +\ H_2O(l)\ \rightarrow\ NH_4^+(aq)\ +\ OH^-(aq)$
    e. $HCl(aq)\ +\ H_2O(l)\ \rightarrow\ NH_4^+(aq)\ +\ OH^-(aq)$
    f. $CH_3CO_2H(aq)\ +\ MgCO_3(s)\ \rightarrow\ Mg^{2+}(aq)\ +\ CH_3CO_2^-(aq)\ +\ H_2O(l)\ +\ CO_2(g)$

6. Which one of the following physical properties is *not* a state function?

   a. enthalpy   c. temperature   e. pressure
   b. volume   d. heat   f. mass

7. A system consisting of a movable piston in a cylinder gains 30 kJ of heat. The piston moves up and does 25 kJ of work on the surroundings. What is the change in the internal energy ΔE of the system?

   a. −5 kJ   c. −25 kJ   e. −30 kJ   g. −55 kJ
   b. +5 kJ   d. +25 kJ   f. +30 kJ   h. +55 kJ

8. How much heat is required to raise the temperature of 20.0 g of water from 5.0°C to its boiling point and then completely vaporize it?

   Specific heat of water = 4.184 J K^{-1} g^{-1}
   Latent heat of vaporization of water = 2260 J g^{-1}

   a. 7.95 kJ   c. 31.2 kJ   e. 37.4 kJ   g. 45.2 kJ
   b. 53.1 kJ   d. 60.2 kJ   f. 67.4 kJ   h. 74.4 kJ

9. 10 g of steam at 100°C is bubbled into a mixture of 250 g of water and 100 g of ice at 0°C where all the steam condenses to water. How much of the ice melts?

   Specific heat of water = 4.184 J K^{-1} g^{-1}
   Latent heat of fusion of ice = 333 J g^{-1}
   Latent heat of vaporization of water = 2260 J g^{-1}

   a. 18 g   c. 36 g   e. 50 g   g. 80 g
   b. 20 g   d. 40 g   f. 68 g   h. 95 g

10. Acetylene gas burns in air with an extremely hot flame:

    $$2C_2H_2(g) \ + \ 5O_2(g) \ \rightarrow \ 4CO_2(g) \ + \ 2H_2O(g) \qquad \Delta H° = -2600 \text{ kJ}$$

    It requires 15 kJ of heat to melt one mole of iron metal at 1535°C. How much acetylene needs to be burned to melt 100 grams of iron?

    a. 0.26 g   c. 2.6 g   e. 26 g   g. 260 g
    b. 0.54 g   d. 5.4 g   f. 54 g   h. 540 g

11. Sulfuric acid is produced industrially in greater amounts than any other compound. The first stage in the production process is the oxidation of sulfur to sulfur dioxide. The second stage is the oxidation of sulfur dioxide to sulfur trioxide. Calculate the standard enthalpy change for the reaction:

    $$2 SO_2(g) \ + \ O_2(g) \ \rightarrow \ 2 SO_3(g) \qquad \Delta H° = ?$$

    given the following information:

    $$S(s) \ + \ O_2(g) \ \rightarrow \ SO_2(g) \qquad \Delta H° = -297 \text{ kJ}$$

    $$2 S(s) \ + \ 3 O_2(g) \ \rightarrow \ 2 SO_3(g) \qquad \Delta H° = -791 \text{ kJ}$$

    a. −179 kJ   c. −297 kJ   e. −791 kJ   g. −1088 kJ
    b. −197 kJ   d. −279 kJ   f. −971 kJ   h. −1385 kJ

12. For which substance does the standard enthalpy of formation ΔH_f° equal zero?

    a. $O_2(l)$ c. $C_6H_6(l)$ e. $NO(g)$ g. $Ag(s)$ i. $H(g)$

    b. $H_2O(l)$ d. $Ne(l)$ f. $K(g)$ h. $HCl(g)$ j. $Fe(l)$

13. Estimate the heat released in the reaction:

$$2\,H_2(g)\ +\ O_2(g)\ \rightarrow\ 2\,H_2O(g)$$

    provided the following bond energies:

        H–H bond in H_2:   436 kJ/mol

        O=O bond in O_2:   498 kJ/mol

        H–O bond in water: 467 kJ/mol

    a. −376 kJ/mol   d. −288 kJ/mol   g. −530 kJ/mol

    b. −218 kJ/mol   e. −336 kJ/mol   h. −662 kJ/mol

    c. −249 kJ/mol   f. −498 kJ/mol   i. −996 kJ/mol

14. Select the arrangement of electromagnetic radiation that starts with the lowest frequency and ends with the highest frequency:

a. radio	infrared	ultraviolet	gamma rays
b. microwave	radio	x-rays	visible
c. gamma rays	ultraviolet	infrared	radio
d. visible	x-rays	infrared	radio
e. ultraviolet	visible	infrared	microwave
f. gamma rays	microwave	x-rays	visible
g. radio	ultraviolet	infrared	gamma rays
h. radio	microwave	gamma rays	x-rays

15. What is the energy of one mole of photons with a wavelength of 1.0×10^{-6} m in the visible region?

    a. 2.0×10^{-19} J   c. 3.3×10^{25} J   e. 1.2×10^{5} J   g. 5.0×10^{18} J

    b. 4.0×10^{-16} J   d. 3.0×10^{42} J   f. 3.3×10^{-43} J   h. 3.6×10^{-7} J

16. Which one of the following sets of quantum numbers is correct for an electron in a 4d orbital?

	n	l	m_l
a.	4	0	0
b.	4	1	−1
c.	4	2	1
d.	4	2	−4
e.	3	0	0
f.	3	1	−1
g.	2	0	−2
h.	2	1	1

17. What is the correct ground state electron configuration for niobium (Nb)?

a. $1s^2\ 2s^2\ 2p^6\ 3s^2\ 3p^6\ 4s^2\ 3d^{10}\ 4p^6\ 5s^2\ 4d^5$

b. $1s^2\ 2s^2\ 2p^6\ 3s^2\ 3p^6\ 4s^2\ 3d^{10}\ 4p^6\ 5s^1\ 4d^3$

c. $1s^2\ 2s^2\ 2p^6\ 3s^2\ 3p^6\ 4s^2\ 3d^3$

d. $1s^2\ 2s^2\ 2p^6\ 3s^2\ 3p^6\ 4s^2\ 3d^{10}\ 4p^6\ 5s^5$

e. $1s^2\ 2s^2\ 2p^6\ 3s^2\ 3p^6\ 4s^2\ 3d^{10}\ 4p^6\ 5s^2\ 4d^3$

f. $1s^2\ 2s^2\ 2p^6\ 3s^2\ 3p^6\ 4s^2\ 3d^3\ 5s^2$

18. Start with the number of protons in the nucleus of a carbon atom

...subtract the number of 3p electrons in a sulfur atom

...multiply by the number of unpaired electrons in a nitrogen atom (in its ground state)

...subtract the number of orbitals in any set of f orbitals

...add the atomic number of oxygen

What's the result?

a. 1	c. 3	e. 5	g. 7	i. 9
b. 2	d. 4	f. 6	h. 8	j. 10

19. The Pauli Exclusion Principle states that

a. electrons remain unpaired as much as possible

b. the spin multiplicity is 2S + 1

c. no two electrons in a single atom can have the same set of values for the four quantum numbers

d. s orbitals in a principal quantum level n are always filled before p orbitals

e. electrons have two possible values for the electron spin quantum number m_s = +½ or −½

f. the number of orbitals within a sub-shell equals $2l + 1$

20. Of the elements

a. Na	c. Mg	e. Si	g. S	i. Cl
b. K	d. Ca	f. Ge	h. Se	j. Br

Which element is the smallest in atomic size and has the highest electronegativity?

EXAMINATION 2

CHEMISTRY 141 SPRING 2005

Monday February 28th 2005

1. Classify the following solutes in aqueous solution as strong acid, weak acid, strong base, weak base, or salt. *Choose the row in which all the examples are correct.*

	strong acid	strong base	weak acid	weak base	salt
a.	H_2SO_3	NH_3	HF	$NaOH$	$MgCl_2$
b.	$HClO_4$	KBr	HI	NH_3	$CaSO_4$
c.	H_3PO_4	KOH	HCN	NH_3	KBr
d.	HBr	$NaOH$	HNO_2	NH_3	KNO_3
e.	HNO_2	$Mg(OH)_2$	HCO_2H	NH_3	KCN
f.	HI	$NaClO_4$	H_2SO_4	$Ca(OH)_2$	$Mg(OH)_2$
g.	$HClO_3$	$NaOH$	HNO_3	NH_3	KH_2PO_4

2. If 10.0 mL of a 0.75 M solution of HCl is diluted to 250 mL, what is the molarity (M) of the resulting solution?

   a. 0.019 M c. 0.030 M e. 0.15 M g. 0.75 M
   b. 0.025 M d. 0.075 M f. 0.55 M h. 1.9 × 10³ M

3. Identify all the spectator ions in the following reaction.
   Note that the magnesium hydroxide is not soluble in aqueous solution.

   $$Mg(OH)_2(s) + 2\,HI(aq) \rightarrow MgI_2(aq) + 2\,H_2O(l)$$

   a. Mg^{2+} d. OH^- g. Mg^{2+} and I^-
   b. H^+ e. H^+ and OH^- h. Mg^{2+} and H^+
   c. I^- f. H^+ and I^- i. Mg^{2+} and OH^-

4. What are the oxidation numbers of

   Cr in $K_2Cr_2O_7$ P in P_4 O in O_2F_2?   *[Choose the row in which all the numbers are correct.]*

	Cr in $K_2Cr_2O_7$	P in P_4	O in O_2F_2
a.	+3	+5	+2
b.	+3	0	+1
c.	+6	0	−2
d.	+6	−3	−1
e.	+6	0	+1
f.	+7	+5	−2
g.	+12	−3	−2

5. Which one of the following substances will ionize completely in aqueous solution?

   a. CH_2CO_2H c. NH_3 e. HCN g. $HBrO_2$
   b. H_2SO_3 d. HNO_2 f. H_2SO_4 h. HF

6. Which one of the following equations does *not* represent a redox reaction?

   a. $Fe_2O_3(s) + 2\,Al(s) \rightarrow Al_2O_3(s) + 2\,Fe(l)$

   b. $Mg(s) + CO_2(s) \rightarrow MgO(s) + C(s)$

   c. $P_4(s) + 5\,O_2(g) \rightarrow P_4O_{10}(s)$

   d. $P_4O_{10}(s) + 6\,H_2O(l) \rightarrow 4\,H_3PO_4(aq)$

   e. $Na(s) + H_2O(l) \rightarrow Na^+(aq) + OH^-(aq)$

7. In a demonstration in class, a mixture of iron(III) oxide and aluminum powder was ignited. Which, if any, of the following statements is false?

   a. The reaction was endothermic.
   b. The reaction produced molten iron and aluminum oxide.
   c. The reaction was initiated using a magnesium fuse.
   d. The aluminum was oxidized and iron was reduced in the reaction.
   e. Aluminum–oxygen bonds are stronger than iron–oxygen bonds.
   f. All the above statements are true.

8. A system consisting of a movable piston in a cylinder gains 55 kJ of heat. The piston moves up and does 33 kJ of work on the surroundings. What is the change in the internal energy ΔE of the system?

   a. –22 kJ   c. –33 kJ   e. –55 kJ   g. –88 kJ
   b. +22 kJ   d. +33 kJ   f. +55 kJ   h. +88 kJ

9. How much heat is required to raise the temperature of 86.8 mL of benzene (1.0 mol) from 20.0°C to its boiling point and then completely vaporize it?

   Density of benzene = 0.90 g mL^{-1} Specific heat of benzene = 1.05 J K^{-1} g^{-1}
   Boiling point of benzene = 80.1°C   Latent heat of vaporization of benzene = 394 J g^{-1}

   a. 4.93 kJ   c. 30.8 kJ   e. 35.7 kJ   g. 42.9 kJ
   b. 25.8 kJ   d. 32.3 kJ   f. 37.1 kJ   h. 55.6 kJ

10. 30.0 g of liquid nitrogen at its boiling point (–196°C) was poured carefully into warm water at 30°C whereupon the nitrogen evaporated and 10.0 grams of ice was formed. What mass of liquid water is present at the end?

    Specific heat of water = 4.184 J K^{-1} g^{-1}
    Latent heat of fusion of ice = 333 J g^{-1}
    Latent heat of vaporization of liquid nitrogen = 200 J g^{-1}

    a. 5.21 g   c. 15.4 g   e. 21.3 g   g. 31.3 g
    b. 11.3 g   d. 18.7 g   f. 26.1 g   h. 205 g

11. Calculate the enthalpy change for the reaction $2\,NO_2(g) \rightarrow N_2O_4(g)$

    $\Delta H_f^\circ (N_2O_4(g)) = +9.16 \text{ kJ mol}^{-1}$
    $\Delta H_f^\circ (NO_2(g)) = +33.18 \text{ kJ mol}^{-1}$

    a. –14.86 kJ   c. –24.02 kJ   e. –48.04 kJ   g. –57.20 kJ   i. –68.33 kJ
    b. +14.86 kJ   d. +24.02 kJ   f. +48.04 kJ   h. +57.20 kJ   j. +68.33 kJ

12. Write a balanced equation for the reaction of ethane, C_2H_6, with oxygen, O_2, forming carbon dioxide, CO_2, and water. List the bonds broken and the bonds formed in the reaction. Then, based upon the bond energies listed below, calculate the energy released when 50.0 grams of ethane is burned in oxygen.

    C–C   346 kJ mol^{-1}
    C–H   413 kJ mol^{-1}
    O=O in O_2 498 kJ mol^{-1}
    C=O in CO_2 732 kJ mol^{-1}
    O–H   463 kJ mol^{-1}

    a. 228 kJ   c. 947 kJ   e. 1894 kJ   g. 2740 kJ
    b. 636 kJ   d. 1370 kJ   f. 2161 kJ   h. 3788 kJ

13. For which substance does the standard enthalpy of formation ΔH_f° equal zero?

    a. $O(g)$ c. $P_4(g)$ e. $SO_3(g)$ g. $Cu(l)$ i. $F(g)$
    b. $H_2O(l)$ d. $CH_4(g)$ f. $K(s)$ h. $H_2(s)$ j. $Mg(g)$

14. Calculate the enthalpy of reaction for the reaction of ethylene with fluorine gas

    $$C_2H_4(g) \;+\; 6\,F_2(g) \;\rightarrow\; 2\,CF_4(g) \;+\; 4\,HF(g) \qquad \Delta H^\circ = ?$$

    from the following information:

    $$H_2(g) \;+\; F_2(g) \;\rightarrow\; 2\,HF(g) \qquad \Delta H^\circ = -537 \text{ kJ}$$

    $$C(s) \;+\; 2\,F_2(g) \;\rightarrow\; CF_4(g) \qquad \Delta H^\circ = -680 \text{ kJ}$$

    $$2\,C(s) \;+\; 2\,H_2(g) \;\rightarrow\; C_2H_4(g) \qquad \Delta H^\circ = +52 \text{ kJ}$$

    a. −1165 kJ   c. −1269 kJ   e. −1949 kJ   g. −2486 kJ
    b. −1217 kJ   d. −1806 kJ   f. −2434 kJ   h. −2538 kJ

15. In which row are the values for typical wavelengths (in m) for regions of the electromagnetic spectrum correctly listed?

	radiowaves	x-rays	infrared	visible	ultraviolet	γ–rays
a.	10^{-2}	10^{-7}	10^{-7}	10^{-9}	10^{-5}	10^{-10}
b.	1	10^{-3}	10^{-5}	10^{-6}	10^{-7}	10^{-12}
c.	10^{-3}	10^{-9}	10^{-7}	10^{-3}	10^{-5}	10^{-11}
d.	1	10^{-9}	10^{-5}	10^{-6}	10^{-6}	10^{-9}
e.	10^{-3}	10^{-12}	10^{-7}	10^{-3}	10^{-5}	10^{-11}
f.	1	10^{-9}	10^{-5}	10^{-6}	10^{-7}	10^{-12}
g.	10^{-2}	10^{-12}	10^{-7}	10^{-9}	10^{-5}	10^{-10}

16. How many electrons are there in *all* the p orbitals of a bromine atom in its ground state?

    a. 2   c. 5   e. 8   g. 11   i. 17
    b. 3   d. 7   f. 10   h. 12   j. 35

17. When the ground state electron configuration of nitrogen is determined using the auf-bau principle, what are the values of the four quantum numbers for the *6th electron* placed in the electron orbitals available? Assume that the first electron to occupy an orbital has an $m_s = +\frac{1}{2}$ and the second electron added to the orbital has an $m_s = -\frac{1}{2}$.

	n	l	m_l	m_s
a.	1	0	0	$+\frac{1}{2}$
b.	1	1	-1	$-\frac{1}{2}$
c.	2	1	0	$+\frac{1}{2}$
d.	2	0	0	$+\frac{1}{2}$
e.	2	1	-1	$-\frac{1}{2}$
f.	0	0	0	$-\frac{1}{2}$
g.	3	2	-1	$+\frac{1}{2}$
h.	3	-2	1	$-\frac{1}{2}$

18. Start with the number of neutrons in the nucleus of a tritium atom
     ...subtract the number of 3s electrons in a sodium atom
     ...multiply by the number of unpaired electrons in a manganese (Mn) atom in its ground state
     ...add the atomic number of carbon
     ...subtract the number of orbitals in any set of f orbitals

     What's the result?

     a. 3   c. 5   e. 7   g. 9   i. 11
     b. 4   d. 6   f. 8   h. 10   j. 12

19. Which one of the following elements has the highest electronegativity?

     a. Na   c. Fe   e. Al   g. Cl
     b. K   d. Cs   f. Se   h. I

20. The bond energy of an H–Cl molecule is 431 kJ mol^{-1}. In other words, the enthalpy change for the following reaction is –431 kJ mol^{-1}:

$$H(g) \; + \; Cl(g) \quad \rightarrow \quad HCl(g) \qquad \Delta H° = -431 \text{ kJ}$$

     What frequency of light is required to provide sufficient energy to break H–Cl molecules?

     a. 1.08×10^{15} s^{-1} c. 2.11×10^{51} s^{-1} e. 4.74×10^{-52} s^{-1} g. 7.16×10^{-19} s^{-1}
     b. 3.17×10^{17} s^{-1} d. 4.18×10^{9} s^{-1} f. 1.08×10^{12} s^{-1} h. 1.40×10^{18} s^{-1}

EXAMINATION 2

CHEMISTRY 141 FALL 2005

Monday October 17th 2005

1. How many of the following electrolytes are classified as weak electrolytes?

    $HClO_4$ Na_2SO_4 HF $Ca(OH)_2$

    CH_3CO_2H HI $MgBr_2$ NH_3

    a. none   c. 2   e. 4   g. 6   i. 8 (all are weak)
    b. 1   d. 3   f. 5   h. 7

2. How many grams of sodium hydroxide are dissolved in water to make 2.00 L of a 3.30 M solution?

    a. 264 g   c. 174 g   e. 40.0 g   g. 6.60 g
    b. 226 g   d. 132 g   f. 24.2 g   h. 0.165 g

3. Write the net ionic equation for the following reaction and identify all the spectator ions. Note that the barium sulfate is *not* soluble in aqueous solution.

    $$Li_2SO_4(aq) \; + \; Ba(NO_3)_2(aq) \; \rightarrow \; BaSO_4(s) \; + \; 2\,LiNO_3(aq)$$

    a. Ba^{2+} d. SO_4^{2-} g. Li^+ and NO_3^-
    b. Li^+ e. Ba^{2+} and SO_4^{2-} h. Ba^{2+} and NO_3^-
    c. NO_3^- f. Li^+ and SO_4^{2-} i. Li^+ and Ba^{2+}

4. In the reaction below, identify the element reduced, the element oxidized, and the total (net) number of moles of electrons transferred in the reaction as it is written. *Choose the row in which all the answers are correct.*

    $$NaNO_3 \; + \; 4\,Zn \; + \; 7\,NaOH \; \rightarrow \; NH_3 \; + \; 4\,Na_2ZnO_2 \; + \; 2\,H_2O$$

	element reduced	element oxidized	net electrons transferred
a.	nitrogen	zinc	8
b.	sodium	zinc	1
c.	nitrogen	sodium	4
d.	zinc	nitrogen	4
e.	hydrogen	oxygen	1
f.	sodium	nitrogen	2
g.	oxygen	zinc	8
h.	oxygen	hydrogen	6
i.	nitrogen	zinc	4
j.	oxygen	zinc	4

5.   Consider the following statements concerning redox reactions:

     I   In a redox reaction, the number of electrons gained in reduction is equal to the number of electrons lost in oxidation.

     II   Hydrogen in a compound always has an oxidation state of +1.

     III   Whenever chlorine, bromine, and iodine are in compounds, their oxidation state is always −1.

     IV   The reducing agent is always oxidized, and the oxidizing agent is reduced, in a redox reaction.

     Which of the statements is(are) true?

     a.   I   c.   III   e.   I and II   g.   I and IV   i.   I, II and IV
     b.   II   d.   IV   f.   I and III   h.   II and III   j.   all of them

6.   166.5 J of heat are required to raise the temperature of a 15.0 gram block of iron from 25°C to 50°C. What is the specific heat of iron?

     a. $0.222 \, JK^{-1}g^{-1}$ c. $2.25 \, JK^{-1}g^{-1}$ e. $11.1 \, JK^{-1}g^{-1}$ g. $55.5 \, JK^{-1}g^{-1}$
     b. $0.444 \, JK^{-1}g^{-1}$ d. $6.66 \, JK^{-1}g^{-1}$ f. $37.3 \, JK^{-1}g^{-1}$ h. $99.9 \, JK^{-1}g^{-1}$

7.   20.0 g of water at 75°C is added to a mixture of 50.0 g ice and 50.0 g water at 0°C in an insulated container. How much ice *remains* after the system reaches a steady temperature?

     Specific heat of water = $4.184 \, JK^{-1}g^{-1}$
     Latent heat of fusion of ice = $333 \, Jg^{-1}$.

     a.   none (0 g)   c.   13.4 g   e.   31.2 g   g.   44.3 g
     b.   7.50 g   d.   18.8 g   f.   39.1 g   h.   50.0 g

8.   A system loses 40 kJ of heat and also does 25 kJ of work on its surroundings. What is the change in the internal energy ΔE of the system?

     a.   −15 kJ   c.   −25 kJ   e.   −40 kJ   g.   −65 kJ
     b.   +15 kJ   d.   +25 kJ   f.   +40 kJ   h.   +65 kJ

9.   Acetylene (C_2H_2) reacts with oxygen gas to form water and carbon dioxide. Write the balanced equation for this reaction. Given the following enthalpies of formation, how much energy is released when 3.00 mol of acetylene are burned?

     $\Delta H_f^{\circ}\,(C_2H_2(g)) = +227 \, kJ \, mol^{-1}$
     $\Delta H_f^{\circ}\,(CO_2(g)) = -394 \, kJ \, mol^{-1}$
     $\Delta H_f^{\circ}\,(H_2O(l)) = -286 \, kJ \, mol^{-1}$

     a.   847 kJ   c.   1301 kJ   e.   2721 kJ   g.   3903 kJ
     b.   907 kJ   d.   2541 kJ   f.   3222 kJ   h.   7806 kJ

10.   For which substance does the standard enthalpy of formation ΔH_f° equal zero?

     a. $Cl_2(l)$ c. $CH_4(g)$ e. $NO(g)$ g. $Fe(s)$ i. $H(g)$
     b. $H_2O(s)$ d. $He(l)$ f. $N_2(l)$ h. $CCl_4(l)$ j. $Ag(l)$

11. In 1923, Louis deBroglie suggested that all matter has wave-like characteristics. In particular, he developed an equation $\lambda = h/mv$ where λ is the wavelength associated with a moving particle of mass m and velocity v and h is Planck's constant. What is the deBroglie wavelength of a football (mass 500 g) moving at 30.0 ms^{-1}. [1 J = 1 kg m^{2}s^{-2}]

   a. 4.42×10^2 m   c. 9.86×10^{20} m   e. 4.42×10^{-35} m   g. 6.63×10^{-34} m
   b. 8.85×10^{10} m   d. 1.25×10^{-10} m   f. 7.77×10^{-25} m   h. 3.00×10^8 m

12. Which color in the visible part of the electromagnetic spectrum has the highest energy per photon?

   a. Red   c. Yellow   e. Blue   g. Violet
   b. Orange   d. Green   f. Indigo

13. What is the *total* number of orbitals in the first five principal quantum levels of an atom (n = 1, 2, 3, 4, and 5)?

   a. 9   c. 25   e. 36   g. 55   i. 75
   b. 16   d. 30   f. 40   h. 72   j. 80

14. The following diagrams represent electron orbitals of the hydrogen atom. Which labels correctly characterize each orbital?

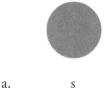

a.	s	p	d
b.	s	p	p
c.	p	d	p
d.	s	p	s
e.	p	d	d
f.	p	p	p
g.	s	d	p

15. What are possible values of the secondary quantum number, l, and the magnetic quantum number m_l when n = 2? *Choose the row in which all the answers are correct.*

	l			m_l				
a.	1				−1	0	1	
b.	0	1	2	−2	−1	0	1	2
c.	0	1		−2	−1	0	1	2
d.	0	1	2		−1	0	1	
e.	0			−2	−1	0	1	2
f.	0	1			−1	0	1	
g.			2	−2	−1	0	1	2
h.	0	1				0	1	

16. According to the *aufbau* principle, which orbital is filled after the 3d orbital?

   a. 4s   c. 4p   e. 4d   g. 3p
   b. 3f   d. 4f   f. 5s   h. 3s

17.   Start with the number of valence 3p electrons in a chlorine (Cl) atom
       ...subtract the number of orbitals in any one set of p orbitals,
       ...multiply by the positive charge on a magnesium (Mg) ion,
       ...add the value of n, the principal quantum number, for the valence s and p electrons of antimony (Sb)

       What's the result?

       a. 5   c. 7   e. 9   g. 11   i. 13
       b. 6   d. 8   f. 10   h. 12   j. 14

18.   Which of the following electron configurations represents the ground state electron configuration of
       technicium (Tc #43)?

       a. $1s^2\ 2s^2\ 2p^6\ 3s^2\ 3p^6\ 4s^2\ 3d^{10}\ 4p^6\ 5s^2\ 4d^3$
       b. $1s^2\ 2s^2\ 2p^6\ 3s^2\ 3p^6\ 4s^2\ 3d^{10}\ 4p^6\ 5s^2\ 5p^5$
       c. $1s^2\ 2s^2\ 2p^6\ 3s^2\ 3p^6\ 4s^2\ 3d^{10}\ 4p^6\ 5s^2\ 4d^5$
       d. $1s^2\ 2s^2\ 2p^6\ 3s^2\ 3p^6\ 4s^2\ 3d^{10}\ 4p^6\ 4d^7$
       e. $1s^2\ 2s^2\ 2p^6\ 3s^2\ 3p^6\ 4s^2\ 3d^{10}\ 4p^6\ 5s^2\ 4d^7$
       f. $1s^2\ 2s^2\ 2p^6\ 3s^2\ 3p^6\ 4s^2\ 3d^{10}\ 4p^6\ 5s^2\ 4d^{10}\ 5p^6\ 6s^2\ 5d^5$

19.   The longest wavelength of electromagnetic radiation that will cause the emission of a photoelectron
       from the surface of a metal is 250 nm. What is the energy per photon of this radiation?

       a. 5.52×10^{19} J   c. 7.95×10^{-19} J   e. 8.33×10^{-16} J
       b. 1.81×10^{-20} J   d. 1.81×10^{48} J   f. 7.95×10^{15} J

20.   Which statement is true?

       a. A fluorine atom is larger than a lithium atom
       b. Positive ions are always larger than their parent atoms
       c. The s electrons of a particular principal quantum level are better at shielding than the p electrons
       d. Elements in the Periodic Table are placed in order of increasing atomic mass
       e. The first ionization energy for the elements decreases from left to right across any period
       f. Cesium is the most electronegative element

EXAMINATION 2

CHEMISTRY 141 SPRING 2006

Monday February 27th 2006

1. Classify the following according to electrolyte strength. Choose the row where the correct number of molecules is represented in each category.

$HClO_4$ NH_3 $HClO_2$ $Mg(OH)_2$
$FeCl_3$ CH_3OH HF HBr

	strong electrolyte	weak electrolyte	non-electrolyte
a.	2	4	2
b.	2	5	1
c.	3	4	1
d.	3	3	2
e.	4	3	1
f.	4	4	0
g.	5	3	0

2. Which of the following molecular formulas is paired with an *incorrect* name?

   a. H_3PO_4 — phosphoric acid
   b. $NaOH$ — sodium hydroxide
   c. HNO_3 — nitric acid
   d. $HClO$ — hypochlorous acid
   e. CH_3CO_2H — acetic acid
   f. HNO_2 — nitrous acid
   g. H_2SO_3 — sulfuric acid
   h. $Ca(OH)_2$ — calcium hydroxide

3. What is the *net ionic equation* for the reaction of silver nitrate reacting with sodium chromate to produce solid silver chromate and sodium nitrate?

   a. $2\,AgNO_3(aq) + Na_2CrO_4(aq) \rightarrow Ag_2CrO_4(s) + 2\,NaNO_3(aq)$
   b. $2\,Ag^+(aq) + 2\,NO_3^-(aq) + 2\,Na^+(aq) + CrO_4^{2-}(aq)$
      $\rightarrow 2\,Ag^+(aq) + CrO_4^{2-}(aq) + 2\,Na^+(aq) + 2\,NO_3^-(aq)$
   c. $2\,Ag^+(aq) + 2\,NO_3^-(aq) + 2\,Na^+(aq) + CrO_4^{2-}(aq) \rightarrow Ag_2CrO_4(s) + 2\,Na^+(aq) + 2\,NO_3^-(aq)$
   d. $2\,Ag^+(aq) + CrO_4^{2-}(aq) \rightarrow Ag_2CrO_4(s)$
   e. $2\,AgNO_3(aq) + 2\,Na^+(aq) + CrO_4^{2-}(aq) \rightarrow 2\,Na^+(aq) + 2\,NO_3^-(aq) + Ag_2CrO_4(s)$
   f. $2\,Na^+(aq) + 2\,NO_3^-(aq) \rightarrow 2\,NaNO_3(aq)$

4. What is the oxidation number of oxygen in the following molecules and ions? Choose the row where all of the answers are correct.

	O_2F_2	O_2^{2-}	ClO_3^-
a.	+1	−1	−2
b.	−2	−2	−2
c.	+2	−2	−3
d.	−2	−1	−1
e.	+1	−4	−6
f.	−2	−4	−6

5.   Identify the element oxidized and the element reduced in the following reaction:

$$2\,Al(s) + 3\,Pb(NO_3)_2(aq) \rightarrow 2\,Al(NO_3)_3(aq) + 3\,Pb(s)$$

	element oxidized	*element reduced*		*element oxidized*	*element reduced*
a.	Al	N	f.	Pb	O
b.	Al	O	g.	N	Al
c.	Al	Pb	h.	N	O
d.	Pb	Al	i.	O	Pb
e.	Pb	N	j.	O	Al

6.   How many grams of sucrose $(C_{12}H_{22}O_{11})$ need to be added to 5.00 L of water to make a 0.25 M solution?

a.	3.65×10^{-3} g	c.	17.1 g	e.	342 g	g.	1.71×10^3 g
b.	1.25 g	d.	85.6 g	f.	428 g	h.	6.84×10^3 g

7.   100 mL of a 0.20 M sodium chloride solution was prepared by adding 10 mL of a concentrated sodium chloride solution to 90 mL of water. What is the molarity (M) of the concentrated sodium chloride solution?

a.	0.2 M	c.	1.7 M	e.	2.5 M	g.	4.8 M
b.	1.3 M	d.	2.0 M	f.	3.4 M	h.	5.5 M

8.   2 moles of cyclopropane (C_3H_6) burn in 9 moles oxygen gas (O_2) to produce 6 moles carbon dioxide and 6 moles water. Using the bond energies and the structural formulas of the molecules given below, calculate the change in enthalpy for this reaction. *(Hint: Write the balanced equation.)*

bond	*bond energy (kJ mol^{-1})*
C – C	346
C = O	803
C – H	413
O – H	463
O = O	498

a.	−9 kJ	d.	+1482 kJ	g.	−26706 kJ
b.	+9 kJ	e.	−3678 kJ	h.	+26706 kJ
c.	−1482 kJ	f.	+3678 kJ		

9.   In a class demonstration, you observed a reaction where iron oxide (Fe_2O_3) reacted with solid aluminum to produce aluminum oxide (Al_2O_3) and solid iron. This reaction is commonly known as the thermite reaction. Which of the following statements about the thermite reaction is *false*?

a.   The thermite reaction is exothermic.
b.   The bonds in Al_2O_3 are stronger than the bonds in Fe_2O_3.
c.   The thermite reaction is a redox reaction.
d.   The heat released in the thermite reaction was used to melt iron.
e.   The aluminum was reduced and the iron was oxidized.
f.   Oxygen did not gain or lose electrons in the thermite reaction.

10. How much energy is released when 10 grams argon gas at −186°C (the boiling point of argon) is completely condensed and cooled to −189°C?

    latent heat of vaporization of argon = 6.447 kJ mol⁻¹ → $6.447 \text{ kJ mol}^{-1}$
    specific heat of liquid argon = 1.05 J g⁻¹ K⁻¹ → $1.05 \text{ J g}^{-1} \text{ K}^{-1}$

    a. 31.5 J   c. 3714 J   e. 1614 J   g. 80 J
    b. 17.2 J   d. 1645 J   f. 5.2 J   h. 64501 J

11. How much ice melts when 15 grams water at 85°C is added to 100 grams ice and 50 grams water at 0°C?

    specific heat of liquid water = $4.184 \text{ J g}^{-1} \text{ K}^{-1}$ latent heat of fusion of water = 333 J g^{-1}
    latent heat of vaporization of water = 2260 J g^{-1}

    a. 0 g   c. 16 g   e. 54 g   g. 84 g
    b. 4 g   d. 27 g   f. 69 g   h. 100 g

12. What is the change in energy of the system when the surroundings do 30 kJ of work on the system and as a result the system loses 20 kJ of heat?

    a. +10 kJ   c. +20 kJ   e. +30 kJ   g. +50 kJ
    b. −10 kJ   d. −20 kJ   f. −30 kJ   h. −50 kJ

13. How many of the following substances have standard heats of formation equal to zero?

    C (s) O (g) NH_3 (g) H_2O (l)
    P_4 (s) Br_2 (l) Cl_2 (g) Hg (l)

    a. 0   c. 2   e. 4   g. 6   i. 8
    b. 1   d. 3   f. 5   h. 7

14. Methanol (CH_3OH) burns in oxygen to produce carbon dioxide and water:

    $$2 \, CH_3OH \, (g) + 3 \, O_2 \, (g) \;\rightarrow\; 2 \, CO_2 \, (g) + 4 \, H_2O \, (l)$$

    Given the heats of formation listed below, calculate the amount of heat released when 4 mol methanol is burned.

    $\Delta H_f^\circ \, (CH_3OH(g)) = -239 \text{ kJ mol}^{-1}$
    $\Delta H_f^\circ \, (CO_2(g)) \quad = -394 \text{ kJ mol}^{-1}$
    $\Delta H_f^\circ \, (H_2O(l)) \quad = -286 \text{ kJ mol}^{-1}$

    a. 1454 kJ   c. 397 kJ   e. 9640 kJ   g. 4820 kJ
    b. 5816 kJ   d. 2908 kJ   f. 793 kJ   h. 1589 kJ

15. An electron falls from level n = 3 to level n = 2 resulting in the release of 2.84×10^{-19} J of energy. What region of the electromagnetic spectrum corresponds to the energy released?

    a. radiowave   c. red light   e. ultraviolet light   g. gamma ray
    b. microwave   d. blue light   f. X-ray

16. The frequency of orange light is approximately 5×10^{14} s^{-1} and the frequency of violet light is approximately 7.5×10^{14} s^{-1}. How many photons of orange light have the same total energy as 2 photons of violet light?

a. 1   c. 2   e. 3   g. 4   i. 5
b. 1.5   d. 2.5   f. 3.5   h. 4.5   j. 5.5

17. When the ground state electron configuration of selenium (Se) is determined using the auf-bau principle, what are the values of the four quantum numbers for the *last electron* placed in the electron orbitals available? Assume the first electron added to an orbital has a spin of +½ and the second electron added to the orbital has a spin of –½.

	n	l	m_l	m_s			n	l	m_l	m_s
a.	4	0	0	+½		e.	3	0	0	+½
b.	4	1	–1	–½		f.	3	1	–1	–½
c.	4	1	–1	+½		g.	3	2	+1	+½
d.	4	2	+1	–½		h.	2	1	0	–½

18. The circles below represent the relative sizes of Na$^+$, Mg^{2+} and F$^-$. In which row are all of the atoms correctly identified?

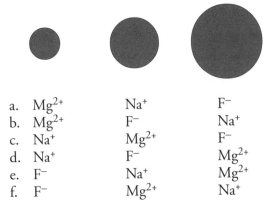

a.	Mg^{2+}	Na$^+$	F$^-$
b.	Mg^{2+}	F$^-$	Na$^+$
c.	Na$^+$	Mg^{2+}	F$^-$
d.	Na$^+$	F$^-$	Mg^{2+}
e.	F$^-$	Na$^+$	Mg^{2+}
f.	F$^-$	Mg^{2+}	Na$^+$

19. How many electrons are in *all* of the p orbitals of an atom of aluminum in the ground state?

a. 2   c. 4   e. 7   g. 9   i. 12
b. 3   d. 6   f. 8   h. 11   j. 13

20. What letters correspond to the following values of the secondary quantum number l? Choose the row where all of the choices are correct.

	$l = 2$	$l = 0$	$l = 3$	$l = 1$
a.	s	p	d	f
b.	s	f	d	p
c.	p	s	f	d
d.	p	s	d	f
e.	d	p	f	s
f.	d	s	f	p
g.	f	s	d	p
h.	f	d	p	s

EXAMINATION 2

CHEMISTRY 141 FALL 2006

Monday October 16th 2006

1. Which aqueous solution contains the greatest concentration of hydronium ions (H_3O^+) ions?

    a. $1.0\ M\ NH_3$ d. $1.0\ M\ NaOH$ g. $2.0\ M\ HF$
    b. $2.0\ M\ HNO_3$ e. $1.0\ M\ HClO_4$ h. $3.0\ M\ HCN$
    c. $2.0\ M\ HClO$ f. $2.0\ M\ CH_3CO_2H$ i. $3.0\ M\ H_2SO_3$

2. What mass of lithium nitrate is required to make 50 mL of a 0.10 M solution?

    a. $7.0 \times 10^{-2}\ g$ d. $5.7\ g$ g. $46\ g$
    b. $1.7 \times 10^2\ g$ e. $0.34\ g$ h. $9.2\ g$
    c. $70\ g$ f. $3.4 \times 10^2\ g$ i. $3.4\ g$

3. Which acid is named incorrectly?

    a. HNO_3 nitric acid   e. H_2SO_4 sulfuric acid
    b. $HClO_3$ chloric acid   f. HCl hydrochloric acid
    c. HNO_2 hydronitrous acid   g. $HBrO$ hypobromous acid
    d. HF hydrofluoric acid   h. H_3PO_4 phosphoric acid

4. Hydrocyanic acid HCN reacts with sodium hydroxide NaOH to produce sodium cyanide NaCN and water:

    $$HCN(aq)\ +\ NaOH(aq)\ \rightarrow\ NaCN(aq)\ +\ H_2O(l)$$

    Identify the spectator ion(s) in this reaction.

    a. Na^+ c. H^+ e. Na^+ and CN^- g. Na^+ and OH^-
    b. CN^- d. OH^- f. Na^+ and H^+ h. Na^+, CN^-, H^+ and OH^-

5. What is the oxidation number of the metal in each of the following compounds?

	VO	K_3PO_4	UO_2F_2	FeF_2	$(NH_4)_2Cr_2O_7$
a.	−2	−3	+4	+1	+2
b.	+2	+1	+6	+2	+3
c.	+1	+1	+2	+3	+6
d.	+1	+5	+6	+2	+2
e.	−2	+3	+4	−1	+3
f.	+3	−1	+2	+1	+6
g.	+2	+3	+6	+2	+2
h.	+3	+5	+1	−2	+3
i.	+2	+1	+6	+2	+6
j.	−2	+1	+2	+2	+3

6. An isolated system is heated and, as a result, does 40 kJ of work on its surroundings. The internal energy of the system increases by 25 kJ. How much heat was added to the system?

    a. 15 kJ   b. 20 kJ   c. 25 kJ   d. 40 kJ   e. 55 kJ   f. 65 kJ

7. The boiling point of acetone (C_3H_6O) is 56.2°C. How much energy is needed to heat to boiling and completely vaporize 3.9 g (5 mL) of acetone initially at room temperature (25°C)?

    The specific heat of liquid acetone = 2.16 J g^{-1} K^{-1}
    The latent heat of vaporization ΔH_{vap} of acetone = 525 J g^{-1}

a. 0.26 kJ	c. 2.1 kJ	e. 2.7 kJ	g. 4.0 kJ
b. 1.3 kJ	d. 2.3 kJ	f. 3.2 kJ	h. 4.6 kJ

8. A 55 g block of metal at 100°C is added to a mixture of 100 g of water and 20 g of ice in an insulated container. All the ice melted and the temperature in the container rose to 10°C. What is the specific heat of the metal?

    The specific heat of water = 4.184 J g^{-1} K^{-1}
    The latent heat of fusion ΔH_{fus} of water = 333 J g^{-1}

a. 1.23 J g^{-1} K^{-1}	d. 2.19 J g^{-1} K^{-1}	g. 2.87 J g^{-1} K^{-1}
b. 1.56 J g^{-1} K^{-1}	e. 2.36 J g^{-1} K^{-1}	h. 3.19 J g^{-1} K^{-1}
c. 1.95 J g^{-1} K^{-1}	f. 2.65 J g^{-1} K^{-1}	i. 3.37 J g^{-1} K^{-1}

9. What is the $\Delta H_{reaction}$ in kJ for the following reaction:

    $$Fe_3O_4(s) \ + \ CO(g) \ \rightarrow \ 3\,FeO(s) \ + \ CO_2(g)$$

    Standard enthalpies of formation:

    $Fe_3O_4(s)$ = –1117 kJ mol^{-1}
    $CO(g)$ = –110.5 kJ mol^{-1}
    $FeO(s)$ = –266.5 kJ mol^{-1}
    $CO_2(g)$ = –393.7 kJ mol^{-1}

a. +34.3 kJ	c. +3408 kJ	e. +1848 kJ	g. +607.5 kJ
b. –34.3 kJ	d. –3408 kJ	f. –1848 kJ	h. –607.5 kJ

10. Which equation represents the standard enthalpy of formation ΔH_f for ethene gas C_2H_4?

    a. $2C(s) \ + \ 4H(g) \ \rightarrow \ C_2H_4(g)$
    b. $2C(g) \ + \ 2H_2(g) \ \rightarrow \ C_2H_4(g)$
    c. $C_2(s) \ + \ H_4(g) \ \rightarrow \ C_2H_4(g)$
    d. $2C(s) \ + \ 2H_2(g) \ \rightarrow \ C_2H_4(g)$
    e. $2CO_2(s) \ + \ 2H_2O(l) \ \rightarrow \ C_2H_4(g) \ + \ 3O_2(g)$
    f. $C_2H_4(g) \ + \ 6F_2(g) \ \rightarrow \ 2CF_4(g) \ + \ 4HF(g)$

11. Solid carbon burns in oxygen to produce carbon dioxide with the liberation of 394 kJ per mole of carbon burned. The heat required to break up solid carbon into separate atoms is 710 kJ mol^{-1} and the O=O bond energy in oxygen O_2 is 498 kJ mol^{-1}. What is the C=O bond energy in carbon dioxide?

a. 197 kJ mol^{-1}	c. 407 kJ mol^{-1}	e. 604 kJ mol^{-1}
b. 312 kJ mol^{-1}	d. 557 kJ mol^{-1}	f. 801 kJ mol^{-1}

12. When electromagnetic radiation hits a metal surface, electrons can sometimes be ejected from the surface. Which type of electromagnetic radiation ejects the fastest moving or highest energy electrons?

    a. radiowave   d. visible light   f. x–rays
    b. microwave   e. ultraviolet light   g. γ–rays
    c. infrared light

13. Which one of the following statements is *true* regarding Planck's explanation of black body radiation?

    a. The vibrations of atoms in a solid are quantized.
    b. A black body is a device that can both reflect and emit light.
    c. As the temperature of a black body increases, the intensity of the emitted light decreases.
    d. As the temperature increases, a black body emits light with increasing wavelength.
    e. As the temperature increases, a black body emits light with decreasing frequency.

14. A local radio station broadcasts using electromagnetic waves with an energy of 5.89×10^{-26} J/photon. What is the frequency of this radio station in MHz?

    a. 101.7 MHz   c. 90.5 MHz   e. 100.7 MHz   g. 92.7 MHz
    b. 88.9 MHz   d. 99.1 MHz   f. 88.1 MHz   h. 94.9 MHz

15. What are *all* of the allowed values for the magnetic quantum number m_l when the principal quantum number is 3 and the secondary quantum number is 2?

    a. −3, 0, +3
    b. −2, 0, +2
    c. 0 only
    d. −1, 0, +1
    e. +2 only
    f. −2, −1, 0, +1, +2
    g. −3, −2, −1, 0, +1, +2, +3
    h. −2, −1, +1, +2

16. Which element has the ground state electron configuration $1s^2\ 2s^2\ 2p^6\ 3s^2\ 3p^6\ 4s^2\ 3d^{10}\ 4p^6\ 5s^2\ 4d^3$?

    a. Ta   c. Nb   e. As   g. Tc   i. Mn
    b. Zr   d. V   f. Mo   h. Sb   j. Cr

17. How many unpaired electrons are there in a sulfur atom in its ground state?

    a. 0   b. 1   c. 2   d. 3   e. 4   f. 5

18. Start with the number of orbitals in any set of p orbitals
    ...add the number of protons in the nucleus of a carbon atom
    ...add the number of d electrons in the valence shell of a manganese atom
    ...add the maximum value of the secondary quantum number l if the principal quantum number n equals 5.
    What's the result?

    a. 13   c. 15   e. 17   g. 19   i. 21
    b. 14   d. 16   f. 18   h. 20   j. 22

19. Ionization energy depends on:

      A. size
      B. nuclear charge
      C. electron configuration

  a. A only   c. C only   e. A and C   g. A, B, and C
  b. B only   d. A and B   f. B and C   h. none of the above

20. Which kind of bonding characterizes the following elements or compounds?
    Choose the row in which all of the answers are correct.

	Fe	N_2	CO
a.	ionic	metallic	polar covalent
b.	metallic	ionic	ionic
c.	metallic	covalent	polar covalent
d.	covalent	ionic	covalent
e.	covalent	covalent	covalent
f.	metallic	metallic	metallic
g.	covalent	polar covalent	covalent
h.	ionic	ionic	ionic

EXAMINATION 2

CHEMISTRY 141 SPRING 2007

Monday February 26th 2007

1. *(5 points)* A solution was prepared by dissolving 3.0 moles sodium hydroxide in 5.0 L water. What is the molarity (M) of this solution?

    a. 0.10 M c. 0.60 M e. 1.2 M g. 1.7 M
    b. 0.20 M d. 0.80 M f. 1.5 M h. 2.0 M

2. *(5 points)* Orange light has a wavelength of approximately 5.90×10^{-7} m. What is the frequency of this light?

    a. 1.97×10^{-15} s^{-1} c. 8.21×10^{3} s^{-1} e. 3.00×10^{8} s^{-1} g. 5.08×10^{14} s^{-1}
    b. 3.60×10^{-5} s^{-1} d. 5.90×10^{6} s^{-1} f. 6.68×10^{12} s^{-1} h. 1.22×10^{20} s^{-1}

3. Which one of the following statements is *false*?

    a. In a 1.0 M nitric acid solution, the concentration of hydronium ions is greater than the concentration of nitric acid molecules.
    b. Weak acids are weak electrolytes.
    c. In aqueous solution, glucose ($C_6H_{12}O_6$) will not ionize.
    d. A base will increase the concentration of hydroxide ions in solution.
    e. In aqueous solution, ammonia will completely ionize.
    f. Hydrochloric acid, sulfuric acid, and perchloric acid are all strong acids.

4. Aqueous magnesium nitrate reacts with aqueous sodium hydroxide to produce aqueous sodium nitrate and solid magnesium hydroxide. What is the net ionic equation for this reaction?

    a. $Mg(NO_3)_2(aq) + 2\,NaOH(aq) \rightarrow 2\,NaNO_3(aq) + Mg(OH)_2(s)$
    b. $Mg^{2+}(aq) + 2\,OH^-(aq) \rightarrow Mg(OH)_2(s)$
    c. $Mg^{2+}(aq) + 2\,Na^+(aq) + 2\,OH^-(aq) \rightarrow 2\,NO_3^-(aq) + Mg^{2+}(aq) + 2\,OH^-(aq)$
    d. $Mg^{2+}(aq) + 2\,Na^+(aq) + 2\,OH^-(aq) \rightarrow 2\,Na^+(aq) + Mg(OH)_2(s)$
    e. $Mg(NO_3)_2(aq) + 2\,OH^-(aq) \rightarrow 2\,Na^+(aq) + Mg(OH)_2(s)$
    f. $2\,Na^+(aq) + 2\,NO_3^-(aq) + 2\,OH^-(aq) \rightarrow 2\,Na^+(aq) + NO_3^-(aq)$
    g. $Mg^{2+}(aq) + 2\,NO_3^-(aq) + 2\,Na^+(aq) + 2\,OH^-(aq) \rightarrow 2\,Na^+(aq) + 2\,NO_3^-(aq) + Mg(OH)_2(s)$

5. Water is added to 75.0 mL of a 5.0 M H_2SO_4 solution until the volume is exactly 2.0 L. What is the concentration of the dilute solution?

    a. 0.030 M c. 0.187 M e. 0.750 M g. 5.0 M
    b. 0.150 M d. 0.375 M f. 2.75 M h. 187 M

6. A system does 75.4 J of work on its surroundings and at the same time 107.5 J of heat are transferred to the system. What are the signs associated with the heat and work for this process?

	q	w		q	w		q	w		q	w
a.	+	+	b.	−	−	c.	+	−	d.	−	+

7. What is the oxidation number of sulfur in each of these molecules / ions?
   Choose the row where all of the answers are correct.

	H_2S	SO_3^{2-}	SCl_2	S_8	K_2SO_4
a.	–1	–6	+2	–1	+6
b.	–1	+4	–2	0	+1
c.	–2	+6	+1	0	+6
d.	+2	+6	+1	0	0
e.	–2	+4	+1	–2	–2
f.	–2	–2	+2	–2	+1
g.	–2	+4	+2	0	+6
h.	+1	–6	–2	0	–2

8. In the following reaction, which element is reduced and what is the change in the oxidation number of the reduced element? *Choose the row where both answers are correct.*

   $$SiCl_4(l) \ + \ 2\,Mg(s) \ \rightarrow \ 2\,MgCl_2(s) \ + \ Si(s)$$

	element reduced	change in oxidation number
a.	Cl	–2
b.	Cl	+2
c.	Si	–2
d.	Si	+4
e.	Si	–4
f.	Mg	–2
g.	Mg	+4
h.	Mg	–4

9. How much heat is needed to heat to boiling and then completely vaporize 13.0 g of liquid neon initially at –270°C?

   Boiling point of Ne = –246°C
   Specific heat of liquid neon = 1.05 J g^{-1} K^{-1}
   Latent heat of vaporization of neon = 86.3 J g^{-1}

a.	330 J	c.	860 J	e.	1080 J	g.	1150 J
b.	500 J	d.	920 J	f.	1120 J	h.	1450 J

10. 10.0 g of liquid krypton at its boiling point (–153°C) was poured carefully into 5.00 g of warm water at 25°C whereupon all of the krypton evaporated and some ice was formed. How much ice formed?

    Specific heat of water = 4.184 J K^{-1} g^{-1}
    Latent heat of fusion of ice = 333 J g^{-1}
    Latent heat of vaporization of liquid krypton = 107.5 J g^{-1}

a.	0.230 g	c.	1.66 g	e.	2.77 g	g.	3.49 g	i.	5.00 g (all of the water freezes)
b.	0.760 g	d.	2.50 g	f.	3.26 g	h.	4.38 g		

11. Which of the following processes is/are exothermic?

   1. water evaporates
   2. the combustion of propane (C_3H_8)
   3. ice forms
   4. $2\,Na(s) + 2\,H_2O(l) \rightarrow 2\,NaOH(aq) + H_2(g) + 367.5\ kJ$

   a. 1 only   c. 3 only   e. 1 and 2   g. 2 and 3   i. 2, 3, and 4
   b. 2 only   d. 4 only   f. 3 and 4   h. 2 and 4   j. all are exothermic

12. What is the ΔH_{rxn} in kJ for the following reaction?

   $$5\,N_2O_4(l) + 4\,N_2H_3CH_3(l) \rightarrow 12\,H_2O(g) + 9\,N_2(g) + 4\,CO_2(g)$$

   $\Delta H_f^\circ\ N_2O_4(l) = -20\ kJ\ mol^{-1}$
   $\Delta H_f^\circ\ N_2H_3CH_3(l) = -54\ kJ\ mol^{-1}$
   $\Delta H_f^\circ\ H_2O(g) = -242\ kJ\ mol^{-1}$
   $\Delta H_f^\circ\ CO_2(g) = -394\ kJ\ mol^{-1}$

   a. +612 kJ   c. +710 kJ   e. +2082 kJ   g. +4164 kJ
   b. –612 kJ   d. –710 kJ   f. –2082 kJ   h. –4164 kJ

13. How many of the following substances have a ΔH_f° equal to zero?

   $O_3(g)$ $N_2(g)$ $Fe(l)$ $CO_2(g)$
   $He(l)$ $K(s)$ $Ar(g)$ $NH_3(l)$

   a. 0   c. 2   e. 4   g. 6   i. all of them
   b. 1   d. 3   f. 5   h. 7

14. Use the following information to calculate the molar enthalpy of formation (ΔH_f°) for $MnO_2(s)$:

   $4\,Al(s) + 3\,MnO_2(s) \rightarrow 3\,Mn(s) + 2\,Al_2O_3(s)$ $\Delta H^\circ = -1792\ kJ$
   $4\,Al(s) + 3\,O_2(g) \rightarrow 2\,Al_2O_3(s)$ $\Delta H^\circ = -3352\ kJ$

   a. –520 kJ   c. –1560 kJ   e. –2909 kJ   g. –5144 kJ
   b. +520 kJ   d. +1560 kJ   f. +2909 kJ   h. +5144 kJ

15. According to the following equation, how many moles of ethanol (C_2H_5OH) must burn to produce 4101 kJ heat?

   $$C_2H_5OH(l) + 3\,O_2(g) \rightarrow 2\,CO_2(g) + 3\,H_2O(l)\quad \Delta H^\circ = -1367\ kJ$$

   a. 1 mol   c. 3 mol   e. 5 mol   g. 7 mol
   b. 2 mol   d. 4 mol   f. 6 mol   h. 8 mol

16. Which one of the following was originally used to explain the line emission spectra of hydrogen?

   a. Rutherford's gold foil experiment
   b. Planck's black body radiation experiment
   c. the photoelectric effect
   d. Bohr's model of the atom
   e. Heisenberg's Uncertainty Principle
   f. Schrödinger's equation

17. A type of radiation has a frequency of 2.0 GHz (Gigahertz). What is the energy (in J) of one photon of this radiation?

    a. 1.33×10^{-24} J   c. 1.35×10^{-42} J   e. 3.26×10^{-12} J   g. 6.67 J
    b. 4.73×10^{-15} J   d. 0.15 J   f. 1.33×10^{-33} J   h. 9.03×10^{22} J

18. In which sequence are the regions of the electromagnetic spectrum arranged in decreasing energy per photon?

    a. infrared   yellow   blue   x-ray γ-ray
    b. ultraviolet   violet   infrared   red   microwave
    c. γ-ray x-ray   green   radiowave   microwave
    d. violet   ultraviolet   orange   red   radiowave
    e. microwave   blue   ultraviolet   infrared   orange
    f. γ-ray violet   yellow   radiowave   infrared
    g. x-ray   ultraviolet   red   microwave   radiowave

19. Which one of the following sets of quantum numbers is possible for an electron in a 5p orbital? *Choose the row where all answers are correct.*

	n	l	m_l			n	l	m_l
a.	5	1	−2		e.	5	1	+2
b.	5	2	0		f.	5	1	+1
c.	4	3	+3		g.	5	0	0
d.	3	3	−1		h.	4	3	−3

20. According to the Aufbau principle, the last electron for each of the following elements in the ground state will go into which orbital? *Choose the row where all answers are correct.*

	Na	Fe	Br	C			Na	Fe	Br	C
a.	2s	3p	3p	1s		e.	3d	3d	4s	3d
b.	2s	4d	4p	2p		f.	3s	3d	4p	2p
c.	3p	3d	3p	2s		g.	3p	5d	4s	2s
d.	3s	4d	4p	2p		h.	3s	3d	3p	2p

21. Which element has the ground state electron configuration: $1s^2 2s^2 2p^6 3s^2 3p^6 4s^2 3d^{10} 4p^6 5s^2 4d^1$?

    a. P   c. Te   e. La   g. Sc   i. Sr
    b. Ar   d. Ir   f. Y   h. Mo   j. Ca

22. Which ion in the following isoelectronic series is the largest?

    a. Y^{3+} b. Sr^{2+} c. Rb^+ d. Br^- e. Se^{2-}

EXAMINATION 2

CHEMISTRY 141 FALL 2007

Monday October 15th 2007

1. *(5 points)* Which one of the following solutes is classified as a weak acid in aqueous solution?

   a. HNO_3 c. KCN   e. H_2SO_4 g. NH_3 i. NH_4CN
   b. $Ca(OH)_2$ d. $HClO_3$ f. $NaClO_2$ h. H_3PO_4 j. HI

2. *(5 points)* Which statement is correct?

   a. molarity × moles = volume
   b. mass × number of moles = molar mass
   c. volume × molarity = mass
   d. mass × molar mass = number of moles
   e. molarity × volume = number of moles
   f. mass × volume = density

3. 170 g potassium hydroxide KOH is dissolved in water to make 1.0 L of a concentrated solution. How many mL of the concentrated solution need to be added to water to make 1.0 L of a 0.20 M KOH solution?

   a. 1.0 mL   c. 15 mL   e. 57 mL   g. 303 mL
   b. 3.0 mL   d. 20 mL   f. 66 mL   h. 600 mL

4. Which of the following choices represents the net ionic equation for the reaction between lithium hydroxide and hydrofluoric acid in aqueous solution?

   a. $OH^- + HF \rightleftharpoons F^- + H_2O$
   b. $LiOH + HF \rightleftharpoons LiF + H_2O$
   c. $Li^+ + OH^- + HF \rightleftharpoons Li^+ + F^- + H_2O$
   d. $LiOH + H^+ + F^- \rightleftharpoons Li^+ + F^- + H_2O$
   e. $Li^+ + OH^- + H^+ + F^- \rightleftharpoons Li^+ + F^- + H_2O$
   f. $LiOH + HF \rightleftharpoons Li^+ + F^- + H_2O$
   g. $OH^- + H^+ \rightleftharpoons H_2O$

5. What is the oxidation number of chromium in potassium dichromate $K_2Cr_2O_7$?

   a. +1   c. +4   e. +8   g. +12
   b. +2   d. +6   f. +10   h. +14

6. Consider the following redox reaction. What is the total number of electrons lost by the element being oxidized in this equation for the reaction?

   $$3\,PbO + 2\,NH_3 \rightarrow 3\,Pb + N_2 + 3\,H_2O$$

   a. 1   c. 3   e. 5   g. 7   i. 9
   b. 2   d. 4   f. 6   h. 8   j. 10

7. When a mixture of methane and oxygen burns, the internal energy of the system decreases by 180 J. The process causes the surroundings to be heated by 40 J. How much work was done by this system?

    a. w = –40 J   c. w = –140 J   e. w = –180 J   g. w = –220 J
    b. w = +40 J   d. w = +140 J   f. w = +180 J   h. w = +220 J

8. How much heat is required to heat to boiling and then completely vaporize 10.0 g of liquid neon initially at –300°C?

    Boiling point of Ne   = –246°C
    Specific heat of liquid neon   = 1.05 J g^{-1} K^{-1}
    Latent heat of vaporization of neon = 86.3 J g^{-1}

    a. 570 J   c. 870 J   e. 1090 J   g. 1310 J
    b. 710 J   d. 940 J   f. 1270 J   h. 1430 J

9. A 15.0 g block of aluminum is heated and dropped into a container of 10.0 g ice and 30.0 g water at 0°C. Assuming no heat is transferred to the surroundings, what must be the initial temperature of the aluminum block so that the final temperature of the system is 5.0°C?

    Specific heat of aluminum   = 0.902 J g^{-1} K^{-1}
    Specific heat of water   = 4.184 J g^{-1} K^{-1}
    Latent heat of fusion for water   = 333 J g^{-1}

    a. 67°C   c. 251°C   e. 313°C   g. 660°C
    b. 173°C   d. 298°C   f. 400°C   h. 1051°C

10. Calculate the change in enthalpy for this reaction:

    $$2\ Fe_3O_4\ (s)\ \rightarrow\ 6\ FeO\ (s)\ +\ O_2\ (g) \qquad \Delta H = ??$$

    Given:

    $$3\ Fe\ (s)\ +\ 2\ O_2\ (g)\ \rightarrow\ Fe_3O_4\ (s) \qquad \Delta H = -1118.4\ kJ$$
    $$Fe\ (s)\ +\ \tfrac{1}{2}\ O_2\ (g)\ \rightarrow\ FeO\ (s) \qquad \Delta H = -272.0\ kJ$$

    a. –604.8 kJ   c. –846.4 kJ   e. –1390.4 kJ   g. –1964.8 kJ
    b. +604.8 kJ   d. +846.4 kJ   f. +1390.4 kJ   h. +1964.8 kJ

11. Ethane C_2H_6 burns in oxygen to produce carbon dioxide and water according to the following balanced equation:

    $$2\ C_2H_6\ (g)\ +\ 7\ O_2\ (g)\ \rightarrow\ 4\ CO_2\ (g)\ +\ 6\ H_2O\ (g) \qquad \Delta H = -2856\ kJ$$

    How much ethane must burn to produce 5000 kJ of heat?

    a. 300 g   c. 163 g   e. 74.6 g   g. 37.4 g
    b. 220 g   d. 105 g   f. 52.6 g   h. 15.6 g

12. For which substance does the standard enthalpy of formation ΔH_f° equal zero?

    a. $Br_2(g)$ c. $CH_4(g)$ e. $NH_3(g)$ g. $Fe(l)$ i. $H_2(g)$
    b. $Na(l)$ d. $H_2O(l)$ f. $N_2O(g)$ h. $CO_2(s)$ j. $Ag(g)$

(13.) Hydrogen has been suggested as the fuel of the future. The following experiment was performed to compare the heat released by burning hydrogen with that released by burning methane (natural gas). In a constant volume (bomb) calorimeter having a heat capacity of 11.3 kJ K^{-1}, a 1.16 gram sample of hydrogen was burned in excess oxygen and the temperature increase was found to be 14.2°C. When a 1.50 gram sample of methane was burned in a similar experiment using the same calorimeter, the temperature increase was only 7.35°C. What is the ratio of heat released in burning 1.0 gram of hydrogen to that released in burning 1.0 g methane?

a. 0.20   c. 0.50   e. 1.5   g. 2.5   i. 3.0
b. 0.40   d. 1.0   f. 2.0   h. 2.75   j. 5.0

(14.) In a reaction in which an acid such as vinegar (acetic acid) reacts with baking soda (sodium hydrogen carbonate) to produce carbon dioxide gas, done in an ordinary kitchen, what can we say about the relative sizes of ΔH (the change in enthalpy) and ΔE (the change in internal energy)?

a. ΔH is larger than ΔE.
b. There is no difference between ΔH and ΔE.
c. Any difference between the two depends upon the path taken for the reaction.
d. ΔH is *always* larger than ΔE.
e. ΔH is smaller than ΔE.
f. In an exothermic reaction such as this ΔH must be larger than ΔE.

15. What is the energy of one photon of light that has a wavelength of 1.2×10^8 nm?

a. 1.7×10^{-24} J   c. 4.9×10^{-30} J   e. 6.6×10^{-34} J   g. 1.4×10^{-40} J
b. 3.4×10^{-26} J   d. 1.7×10^{-33} J   f. 3.1×10^{-37} J   h. 2.6×10^{-43} J

16. Which color in the visible part of the electromagnetic spectrum has the highest frequency?

a. Red   c. Green   e. Violet   g. Indigo
b. Orange   d. Blue   f. Yellow

17. Which statement is true?

a. If $m_l = 0$, the orbital must be a p orbital.
b. If n = 1, the orbital must be an s orbital.
c. If n = 3, the only allowed value of l is 2.
d. The d orbitals in a set have three different orientations.
e. The value of the quantum number n can never be larger than the value of the quantum number l.
f. The quantum number l indicates the orientation of the orbital.

18. How many of the following elements in their ground states have at least one unpaired electron in 4p orbitals?

        Ga   Sn   Kr   Ge
        Zn   As   K   Br

a. 0   c. 2   e. 4   g. 6   i. 8
b. 1   d. 3   f. 5   h. 7

19. According the *auf-bau* principle, which orbital, or set of orbitals, is filled after the 5d orbitals?

a. 6s   c. 5f   e. 4f   g. 6p
b. 6d   d. 6f   f. 7s   h. 7p

20. Titanium (Ti) exhibits an oxidation state IV rather than the usual II or III. What is the electron configuration for a Ti^{4+} ion?

   a. [Ar] $4s^2$ $3d^2$
   b. [Ar] $4s^2$
   c. [Ar] $4s^2$ $3d^6$
   d. [Ar]
   e. [Ar] $5s^2$ $4f^2$
   f. [Ar] $4s^2$ $4p^2$
   g. [Ar] $5s^2$ $4d^2$

21. Which element, among the choices below, has the highest first ionization energy?

   a. B   c. C   e. N   g. O   i. F
   b. Al   d. Si   f. P   h. S   j. Cl

22. Which kind of bonding characterizes the following elements or compounds?
     Choose the row in which all of the answers are correct.

	KCl	H_2O	Cu
a.	ionic	ionic	metallic
b.	ionic	covalent	metallic
c.	ionic	metallic	covalent
d.	covalent	ionic	covalent
e.	covalent	covalent	ionic
f.	covalent	metallic	metallic
g.	metallic	ionic	covalent
h.	metallic	covalent	ionic
i.	metallic	metallic	ionic

EXAMINATION 2

CHEMISTRY 141 SPRING 2008

Monday February 25th 2008

1. *(5 points)* Which one of the following is a strong electrolyte?

   a. HF
   b. CH_3CO_2H
   c. NH_3
   d. $HClO_2$
   e. NaF
   f. $C_{12}H_{22}O_{11}$ (sucrose)

2. *(5 points)* What is the maximum number of electrons that can fill all of the orbitals in the principal energy level of n=3?

   a. 2
   b. 3
   c. 4
   d. 8
   e. 9
   f. 16
   g. 18
   h. 25

3. Identify all of the spectator ion(s) in the reaction of lead(II) nitrate with sodium iodide in aqueous solution to produce sodium nitrate and solid lead(II) iodide.

   a. there are no spectator ions
   b. Pb^{2+} and I^-
   c. Pb^{2+} and Na^+
   d. NO_3^- and Na^+
   e. NO_3^- and $I^"$
   f. Pb^{2+}, NO_3^-, Na^+, and I^-

4. What is the oxidation number for phospohrus in each of these molecules?
   Choose the row where all of the answers are correct.

	H_3PO_2	$H_4P_2O_7$	PCl_5	P_4
a.	+1	+10	+5	0
b.	+1	+5	+5	0
c.	+1	+5	+1	−3
d.	−1	+10	+1	0
e.	+1	+5	−5	+4
f.	−1	+2	+1	−3
g.	−3	+10	+5	0
h.	−3	+5	+1	0

5. How many grams of sucrose $C_{12}H_{22}O_{11}$ must be added to sufficient water to make 5.00 L of a 0.25 M aqueous solution?

   a. 3.65×10^{-3} g
   b. 1.25 g
   c. 17.1 g
   d. 85.6 g
   e. 342 g
   f. 428 g
   g. 500 g
   h. 664 g

6. 50.0 mL of a 0.300 M HCl solution was added to 300 mL of a 0.120 M HCl solution. What is the molarity (M) of the resulting solution?

   a. 0.015 M
   b. 0.036 M
   c. 0.043 M
   d. 0.103 M
   e. 0.117 M
   f. 0.146 M
   g. 0.216 M
   h. 0.420 M

7.   Which one of the following processes is endothermic?

     a.   ammonia evaporates   d. $C(s)$ + $O_2(g)$ $\rightarrow$ $CO_2(g)$ ΔH = –394 kJ
     b.   water freezes   e.   the thermite reaction: Fe_2O_3 + 2 Al $\rightarrow$ Al_2O_3 + 2 Fe
     c.   propane (C_3H_8) burns

     Use the following information to answer questions 8 and 9:
          Specific heat of water   = 4.184 J K^{-1} g^{-1}
          Specific heat of copper   = 0.385 J K^{-1} g^{-1}
          Latent heat of fusion of ice = 333 J g^{-1}

8.   After absorbing 180 J of energy as heat, the temperature of a 35.0 g block of copper was 65°C. What was the initial temperature of the copper block?

     a.   15.2°C   c.   37.0°C   e.   63.4°C   g.   100.0°C
     b.   21.4°C   d.   51.6°C   f.   65.0°C   h.   116.6°C

9.   A 75.0 g block of copper at 100°C was added to an insulated vessel containing 50.0 g ice and 25.0 g water at 0°C. Assuming no heat escapes to the surroundings, what mass of liquid water is present in the vessel at the end?

     a.   8.7 g   c.   25.0 g   e.   39.2 g   g.   50.0 g
     b.   14.2 g   d.   33.7 g   f.   44.5 g   h.   75.0 g

10. Nitrogen monoxide gas reacts with oxygen gas to produce nitrogen dioxide gas according to this balanced equation:

          2 NO(g) + $O_2(g)$ $\rightarrow$ 2 NO$_2(g)$ ΔH = –114.1 kJ

     If 3.0 moles of nitrogen monoxide react with 2.0 moles of oxygen, what is the maximum amount of heat that will be released?

     a.   114.1 kJ   c.   228.2 kJ   e.   342.3 kJ   g.   456.4 kJ
     b.   171.2 kJ   d.   263.7 kJ   f.   392.2 kJ   h.   572.0 kJ

11. What are the reactants in the reaction that describes the standard enthalpy of formation (ΔH_f°) of sodium hydroxide?

     a.   Na(s) and $OH^-(aq)$ c.   Na(g), $O_2(g)$, and H(g) e.   Na(s), O(g), and H(g)
     b.   Na(s), $O_2(g)$, and $H_2(g)$ d. $Na_2(s)$, $O_2(g)$, and $H_2(g)$ f. $NaO_2(s)$ and $H_2(g)$

12. Calculate the enthalpy change (ΔH) in kJ for this reaction: 2 B(s) + 3/2 $O_2(g)$ $\rightarrow$ $B_2O_3(s)$ given the following information:

          $B_2O_3(s)$ + 3 $H_2O(g)$ $\rightarrow$ $B_2H_6(g)$ + 3 $O_2(g)$ ΔH = +2035 kJ
          2 $H_2O(l)$ $\rightarrow$ 2 $H_2O(g)$ ΔH = +88 kJ
          $H_2(g)$ + 1/2 $O_2(g)$ $\rightarrow$ $H_2O(l)$ ΔH = –286 kJ
          2 B(s) + 3 $H_2(g)$ $\rightarrow$ $B_2H_6(g)$ ΔH = +36 kJ

     a.   +1273 kJ   c.   +636 kJ   e.   +1873 kJ   g.   +1625 kJ
     b.   –1273kJ   d.   –636 kJ   f.   –1873 kJ   h.   –1625 kJ

13. Which of the following statement(s) is true according to Heisenberg's Uncertainty Principle?

    I. It is impossible to make precision measurements on both the position and momentum of microscopic particles in the same experiment.
    II. An experiment designed to detect waves will detect waves; if designed to detect particles, it will detect particles.
    III. Electrons, for example, have both wave and particle characteristics.
    IV. The microscopic quantum world does not behave the same as our normal world.
    V. Light with short enough wavelength to "see" inside an atom has enough energy to seriously disrupt the atom.

    a. I only   d. IV only   g. II and V
    b. II only   e. V only   h. III and IV
    c. III only   f. I and II   i. I, II, III, IV, and V

14. The transition of an electron from the first excited state to the ground state results in the release of a photon having a wavelength of approximately 93nm. What region of the electromagnetic spectrum corresponds to this wavelength?

    a. x-ray   c. visible light   e. radiowave   g. γ-ray
    b. infrared light d. microwave   f. ultraviolet light

15. Calculate the wavelength (in nm) of a photon emitted by a hydrogen atom when its electron drops from the n=5 state to the n=2 state. The change in energy for this transition is 4.85×10^{-19} J.

    a. 127 nm   c. 410 nm   e. 656 nm   g. 826 nm
    b. 225 nm   d. 486 nm   f. 732 nm   h. 854 nm

16. Louis deBroglie's equation ($\lambda = h / mv$) suggests that all matter has wave-like characteristics. What is the deBroglie wavelength (in m) of a 100 g ball traveling at 35 ms^{-1}? (1 J = 1 kg m^2 s^{-2})

    a. 6.6×10^{-34} m   c. 3.2×10^{-10} m   e. 6.3×10^{-43} m   g. 1.9×10^{-37} m
    b. 1.9×10^{-34} m   d. 7.0×10^{-7} m   f. 3.1×10^{-34} m   h. 1.6×10^{42} m

17. What information is provided by the magnetic quantum number m_l?

    a. energy   c. electron spin   e. number of valence electrons
    b. orientation   d. shape   f. electron configuration

18. According to the rules that govern the allowed values for the four quantum numbers for an electron in an atomic orbital, which set is not allowed?

	n	l	m_l	m_s			n	l	m_l	m_s
a.	0	0	0	$-\frac{1}{2}$		e.	3	2	0	$+\frac{1}{2}$
b.	1	0	0	$+\frac{1}{2}$		f.	3	1	-1	$-\frac{1}{2}$
c.	2	0	0	$+\frac{1}{2}$		g.	3	1	$+1$	$-\frac{1}{2}$
d.	2	1	-1	$-\frac{1}{2}$		h.	4	3	-3	$+\frac{1}{2}$

19. Uranium (U) is the heaviest element that occurs to any appreciable extent on Earth. In the ground state, uranium's <u>outermost</u> electrons are in which orbital?

    a. 4f   c. 5f   e. 6p   g. 7s
    b. 4g   d. 6s   f. 6d   h. 7p

20. What is the ground state electron configuration of Fe?

    a. $1s^2 2s^2 2p^6 3s^2 3p^6 3d^6$

    b. $1s^2 2s^2 2p^6 3s^2 3p^6 4s^2 3d^5 4p^1$

    c. $1s^2 2s^2 2p^6 3s^2 3p^6 4s^2 3d^8$

    d. $4s^2 3d^{10}$

    e. $1s^2 2s^2 2p^6 3s^2 3p^6$

    f. $1s^2 2s^2 2p^6 3s^2 3p^6 4s^2 3d^{10}$

    g. $1s^2 2s^2 2p^6 3s^2 3p^6 3d^8$

    h. $1s^2 2s^2 2p^6 3s^2 3p^6 4s^2 3d^6$

21. Which of the following elements has the smallest atomic radius?

    a. Eu   c. La   e. Sm   g. Ce

    b. Dy   d. Lu   f. Tb   h. Cs

22. How many of these elements or compounds exhibit covalent bonding?

Na	MgBr	Ti	NO
Cl_2	Al	CO_2	KF

    a. none   c. 2   e. 4   g. 6   i. 8

    b. 1   d. 3   f. 5   h. 7

EXAMINATION 2

CHEMISTRY 141 FALL 2008

Monday October 13th 2008

The first four questions are worth 5 points each; the remaining 16 questions are worth 10 points each. The total number of points possible is 180.

1. Molarity is a commonly used and useful unit of concentration. Which statement is correct?

   a. molarity × moles = volume
   b. mass × number of moles = molarity
   c. volume × molarity = mass
   d. mass × molarity = number of moles
   e. molarity × volume = number of moles
   f. mass × volume = molarity

2. What is the nitrate ion concentration in a 0.10 M strontium nitrate solution?

   | a. 0.05 M | c. 0.15 M | e. 0.25 M | g. 0.35 M | i. 0.45 M |
   | b. 0.10 M | d. 0.20 M | f. 0.30 M | h. 0.40 M | j. 0.50 M |

3. Which one of the following acids is paired with an *incorrect* name?

   a. H_3PO_4 phosphoric acid   e. CH_3CO_2H acetic acid
   b. H_2S hydrosulfuric acid   f. HCl hydrochloric acid
   c. HNO_3 nitric acid   g. $HClO_3$ chlorous acid
   d. H_2SO_3 sulfurous acid   h. $HClO$ hypochlorous acid

4. Which one of the following aqueous solutions will contain the highest concentration of hydronium ions?

   a. 3.0 M HCN   d. 2.0 M $HClO_4$ g. 3.0 M NH_3 i. 1.5 M $Ca(OH)_2$
   b. 2.5 M HF   e. 2.0 M HClO   h. 2.5 M NaOH   j. 2.0 M CH_3CO_2H
   c. 0.8 M HI   f. 1.5 M HCl

5. Which of the following choices represents the net ionic equation for the reaction between lithium hydroxide and hydrocyanic acid in aqueous solution?

   a. $OH^- + HCN \rightarrow CN^- + H_2O$
   b. $LiOH + HCN \rightarrow LiCN + H_2O$
   c. $Li^+ + OH^- + HCN \rightarrow Li^+ + CN^- + H_2O$
   d. $LiOH + H^+ + CN^- \rightarrow Li^+ + CN^- + H_2O$
   e. $Li^+ + OH^- + H^+ + CN^- \rightarrow Li^+ + CN^- + H_2O$
   f. $LiOH + HCN \rightarrow Li^+ + CN^- + H_2O$
   g. $OH^- + H^+ \rightarrow H_2O$

6.) What is the oxidation number of chromium in the following molecules and ions?
Choose the row where all the answers are correct.

	$K_2Cr_2O_7$	CrO	$Cr_2(SO_4)_3.6H_2O$
a.	+2	+1	+2
b.	+3	+2	+3
c.	+6	+1	+6
d.	+6	+2	+6
e.	+2	+2	+3
f.	+3	+1	+6
g.	+6	+2	+3
h.	+12	+2	+6

7.) In the reaction below, identify the element oxidized and the element reduced:

$$Cl_2 + H_2O \rightarrow H^+ + Cl^- + HOCl$$

	element oxidized	*element reduced*		*element oxidized*	*element reduced*
a.	chlorine	chlorine	f.	hydrogen	oxygen
b.	chlorine	hydrogen	g.	oxygen	oxygen
c.	chlorine	oxygen	h.	oxygen	hydrogen
d.	hydrogen	hydrogen	i.	oxygen	chlorine
e.	hydrogen	chlorine			

8. A 150 g block of copper (specific heat 0.385 $JK^{-1}g^{-1}$) at 86.5°C is dropped into an insulated vessel containing 50 g of ice and 50 g of liquid water. How much of the ice melts?

Latent heat of fusion of water = 333 Jg^{-1}

a. 5.0 g   c. 15.0 g   e. 25.0 g   g. 35.0 g   i. 45.0 g
b. 10.0 g   d. 20.0 g   f. 30.0 g   h. 40.0 g   j. all the ice melts

9. A system consisting of a cylinder with a movable piston absorbs 280 J of energy as heat. As a result, the piston moves up in the cylinder and does 130 J of work against an constant external pressure of 1.0 atmosphere (1.01×10^{-5} Pa). What is the change in the internal energy ΔE of the system?

a. +130 J   c. +150 J   e. +280 J   g. +410 J
b. –130 J   d. –150 J   f. –280 J   h. –410 J

10. How many kJ of energy is released in the combustion of 116.0 grams acetone C_3H_6O?

$$C_3H_6O + 4O_2 \rightarrow 3H_2O + 3CO_2 \quad \Delta H = -1790.4 \text{ kJ}$$

a. 15.4 kJ   c. 573 kJ   e. 1790 kJ   g. 2918 kJ
b. 30.9 kJ   d. 895.2 kJ   f. 1906 kJ   h. 3581 kJ

11. Calculate the change in enthalpy for this reaction:

$$4\,NH_3(g) \;+\; 3\,O_2(g) \;\rightarrow\; 2\,N_2(g) \;+\; 6\,H_2O(g) \qquad \Delta H = \text{???}$$

given the following information:

$$4\,NH_3(g) \;+\; 7\,O_2(g) \;\rightarrow\; 4\,NO_2(g) \;+\; 6\,H_2O(g) \qquad \Delta H = -1132\ kJ$$

$$6\,NO_2(g) \;+\; 8\,NH_3(g) \;\rightarrow\; 7\,N_2(g) \;+\; 12\,H_2O(g) \qquad \Delta H = -2740\ kJ$$

a. +1268 kJ   c. +2084 kJ   e. +3872 kJ   g. +5480 kJ   i. +8876 kJ
b. −1268 kJ   d. −2084 kJ   f. −3872 kJ   h. −5480 kJ   j. −8876 kJ

12. Determine the standard heat of formation of butane from the following data:

$$2\,C_4H_{10}(l) \;+\; 13\,O_2(g) \;\rightarrow\; 8\,CO_2(g) \;+\; 10\,H_2O(l) \qquad \Delta H^\circ = -5754\ kJ$$

ΔH°_f of $CO_2(g) = -393.5$ kJ mol^{-1}

ΔH°_f of $H_2O(l) = -285.8$ kJ mol^{-1}

a. +126.0 kJ mol^{-1} c. +252.0 kJ mol^{-1} e. +5880 kJ mol^{-1} g. +11760 kJ mol^{-1}
b. −126.0 kJ mol^{-1} d. −252.0 kJ mol^{-1} f. −5880 kJ mol^{-1} h. −11760 kJ mol^{-1}

13. The allowed energies for an electron in a hydrogen atom are usually given negative values, with zero energy indicating an electron completely free of the atom. As the electron moves closer to the nucleus, its energy decreases. The energy of an electron in the lowest energy level available to an electron in a hydrogen atom (the 1s orbital) is -2.18×10^{-18} J. What energy is required to completely ionize 1.0 mol of hydrogen atoms (to H^+ hydrogen ions) in the gas state?

a. 1.3×10^3 kJ   c. 3.6×10^6 kJ   e. 2.8×10^{12} kJ   g. 6.0×10^{22} kJ
b. 2.8×10^{-3} kJ   d. 1.3×10^6 kJ   f. 2.2×10^3 kJ   h. 2.3×10^4 kJ

14. In which sequence are the regions of the electromagnetic spectrum arranged in increasing energy per photon?

a. infrared   < yellow   < blue   < x-ray   < γ-ray
b. ultraviolet < violet   < infrared < red   < microwave
c. γ-ray   < x-ray   < green   < radiowave < microwave
d. violet   < ultraviolet < orange   < red   < radiowave
e. microwave < blue   < ultraviolet < infrared < γ-ray
f. γ-ray   < violet   < yellow   < radiowave < infrared
g. x-ray   < ultraviolet < red   < microwave < radiowave
h. radiowave < microwave < visible   < infrared < x-ray

15. Microwaves can be used in a microwave oven to cook food by heating water molecules. These waves have a wavelength of approximately 10^{-3} m. How many microwave photons need to be absorbed by 1.0 g water to raise the temperature by 1.0°C?

Specific heat of water = 4.184 J g^{-1}K^{-1}

a. 1.2×10^{22} c. 2.6×10^{22} e. 6.9×10^{22} g. 7.9×10^{22}
b. 2.1×10^{22} d. 4.3×10^{22} f. 7.1×10^{22} h. 8.3×10^{22}

16. The following statements concern the quantum numbers that characterize the allowed energy levels for an electron in an atom. Which statement is *not* true?

   a. If $m_l = +1$, the electron *must* be in a p orbital
   b. The value of n (principal quantum number) = the total number of nodes in the wavefunction + 1
   c. The number of orbitals in a set of p orbitals is *always* equal to 3
   d. The order of orbital energies within a principal quantum level is *always* s < p < d < f ...
   e. If n = 5, then the secondary quantum number *l* can be 0, 1, 2, 3, or 4
   f. Electrons in s and p orbitals shield the nuclear charge more effectively than electrons in d and f orbitals

17. Which one of the following sets of quantum numbers is not allowed?

	n	*l*	m_l
a.	1	0	0
b.	2	0	0
c.	2	1	0
d.	3	1	−1
e.	3	−3	+1
f.	4	2	−2
g.	4	3	0

18. What is the ground state electron configuration of the chloride ion?

   a. $1s^2\ 2s^2\ 2p^6\ 3s^2\ 3p^6$
   b. $1s^2\ 2s^2\ 2p^6\ 3s^2\ 3p^5$
   c. $1s^2\ 2s^2\ 2p^6$
   d. $1s^2\ 2s^2\ 2p^6\ 3s^2\ 3p^4$
   e. $1s^2\ 2s^2\ 2p^6\ 3s^2\ 3p^3$
   f. $1s^2\ 2s^2\ 2p^6\ 3s^2\ 3p^6\ 4s^1$

19. In which list are the following atoms and ions arranged in order of increasing size?

   a. P^{3-} < Cl^- < Ar < K^+ < Mg^{2+} < Ca^{2+} < Al^{3+}
   b. Mg^{2+} < Ca^{2+} < Al^{3+} < P^{3-} < Cl^- < Ar < K^+
   c. Al^{3+} < P^{3-} < Cl^- < Mg^{2+} < Ca^{2+} < Ar < K^+
   d. K^+ < Ca^{2+} < Mg^{2+} < Al^{3+} < Ar < Cl^- < P^{3-}
   e. Al^{3+} < Mg^{2+} < Ca^{2+} < Ar < Cl^- < K^+ < P^{3-}
   f. Al^{3+} < Mg^{2+} < Ca^{2+} < K^+ < Ar < Cl^- < P^{3-}

20. Electron affinities (energy released when an electron is added to an atom of an element in the gas state) depend upon several factors. Which of the following elements would be predicted to have the lowest electron affinity (i.e. the least desire to accept an electron)?

   a. aluminum   b. silicon   c. phosphorus   d. sulfur   e. chlorine   f. argon

EXAMINATION 2

CHEMISTRY 141 SPRING 2009

Monday March 2nd 2009

The first four questions are worth 5 points each; the remaining 16 questions are worth 10 points each. The total number of points possible is 180.

1. Which one of the solutes shown below will remain predominately in the molecular form in aqueous solution?

    a. HNO_3 c. HBr   e. H_2SO_3 g. $HClO_4$
    b. KOH   d. NH_4F f. KCl   h. Na_3PO_4

2. What is the oxidation number of carbon in the compound $(NH_4)_2C_2O_4$?

    a. +1   c. +2   e. +3   g. +4   i. +6
    b. −1   d. −2   f. −3   h. −4   j. −6

3. How many unpaired electrons are in one sulfide ion in the ground state?

    a. 0   c. 2   e. 4   g. 6   i. 8
    b. 1   d. 3   f. 5   h. 7

4. According to the *aufbau* principle, which orbital is filled after the 4s orbital?

    a. 4p   c. 5s   e. 4f   g. 3p
    b. 4d   d. 5p   f. 3d   h. 2p

5. How many grams of sodium chloride must be added to water to make 3.5L of a 0.45 M solution?

    a. 0.027 g   c. 27 g   e. 92 g   g. 291 g
    b. 7.5 g   d. 75 g   f. 147 g   h. 455 g

6. 150 mL of the solution described in question 5 are added to 300 mL of water. What is the molarity M of the new solution?

    a. 0.15 M   c. 0.23 M   e. 0.38 M   g. 0.90 M
    b. 0.20 M   d. 0.30 M   f. 0.45 M   h. 1.35 M

7. What is the change in oxidation number for the element being reduced in this redox reaction?

    $$3\,HNO_2 \rightarrow HNO_3 + H_2O + 2\,NO$$

    a. +1   c. +2   e. +3   g. +4   i. +5
    b. −1   d. −2   f. −3   h. −4   j. −5

8. When a system containing a mixture of methane and oxygen burns, the internal energy of the system decreases by 180 J. How much heat is absorbed or released by the system if the system expands by 1.38 L at a constant pressure of 1.0 atm? (1 L atm = 101.325 J)

    a. −40 J   c. −140 J   e. −220 J   g. −390 J
    b. +40 J   d. +140 J   f. +220 J   h. +390 J

9. A 5.0 g piece of solid carbon dioxide (dry ice) is placed in an insulated container with 100 g of water at 0°C. As a result, all of the CO_2 sublimes at –78.5°C (converted directly from solid to gas) and some ice is formed. All of the CO_2 gas at –78.5°C escapes from the liquid. How much ice formed?

    Latent heat of fusion of ice = 333 J g^{-1} Latent heat of sublimation of CO_2 = 199 J g^{-1}

    a. 1.0 g   c. 5.0 g   e. 9.0 g   g. 13 g
    b. 3.0 g   d. 7.0 g   f. 11 g   h. 15 g

10. Isooctane C_8H_{18} is a component in gasoline that burns in oxygen according to this balanced equation:

    $$2 C_8H_{18} + 25 O_2 \rightarrow 16 CO_2 + 18 H_2O \qquad \Delta H = -10992 \text{ kJ}$$

    How many grams of isooctane must burn to release 3500 kJ of energy?

    a. 36.4 g   c. 72.7 g   e. 114 g   g. 255 g
    b. 63.7 g   d. 91.5 g   f. 175 g   h. 312 g

11. Calculate the change in enthalpy for this reaction:

    $$2 C(s) + 3 H_2(g) \rightarrow C_2H_6(g) \qquad\qquad \Delta H = ???$$

    given: $2 C_2H_6(g) + 7 O_2(g) \rightarrow 4 CO_2(g) + 6 H_2O(l)$ $\Delta H = -3120$ kJ

    $\ C(s) + O_2(g) \rightarrow CO_2(g)$ $\Delta H = -394$ kJ

    $\ 2 H_2(g) + O_2(g) \rightarrow 2 H_2O(l)$ $\Delta H = -572$ kJ

    a. +86 kJ   c. +944 kJ   e. +1474 kJ   g. +4086 kJ
    b. –86 kJ   d. –944 kJ   f. –1474 kJ   h. –4086 kJ

12. The complete combustion of one mole of acetone C_3H_6O results in the release of 1790 kJ of heat. Calculate the enthalpy of formation ΔH_f° of acetone given the following information:

    $$C_3H_6O(l) + 4 O_2(g) \rightarrow 3 CO_2(g) + 3 H_2O(l) \qquad \Delta H = -1790 \text{ kJ}$$

    ΔH_f° of $CO_2(g)$ = –393.5 kJ mol^{-1} and ΔH_f° of $H_2O(l)$ = –285.8 kJ mol^{-1}

    a. +3828 kJ mol^{-1} c. +2469 kJ mol^{-1} e. +1111 kJ mol^{-1} g. +248 kJ mol^{-1}
    b. –3828 kJ mol^{-1} d. –2469 kJ mol^{-1} f. –1111 kJ mol^{-1} h. –248 kJ mol^{-1}

13. Which scientist was primarily responsible for each of the following discoveries/theories?

	Explanation of the Photoelectric Effect	*Wave-Particle Duality*	*Uncertainty Principle*	*Quantization of Electron energy levels*
a.	Planck	DeBroglie	Heisenberg	Bohr
b.	Einstein	Born	Schrodinger	Born
c.	Einstein	DeBroglie	Schrodinger	Rutherford
d.	Bunsen	Einstein	Pauli	Born
e.	Einstein	DeBroglie	Heisenberg	Bohr
f.	Planck	Bohr	Rutherford	Heisenberg

14. A photon of light has an energy of 3.0×10^{-19} J. What is the wavelength (in nm) of this photon?

    a. 1.5×10^{-6} nm   c. 2.1×10^{-15} m   e. 4.5×10^5 nm   g. 6.6×10^{-45} nm
    b. 6.6×10^{-16} nm   d. 6.6×10^{-7} nm   f. 6.6×10^2 nm   h. 3.7×10^{-36} nm

15. Louie deBroglie's equation ($\lambda = h / mv$) suggests that all matter has wave-like characteristics. What is the deBroglie wavelength (in m) of a 141.5 g baseball thrown at a speed of 89 miles / hour? ($1\ J = 1\ kg\ m^2\ s^{-2}$)

    a. 1.2×10^{-34} m   c. 5.3×10^{-38} m   e. 1.2×10^{-37} m   g. 5.3×10^{-35} m
    b. 9.1×10^{-45} m   d. 1.2×10^{-28} m   f. 9.1×10^{-36} m   h. 6.6×10^{-34} m

16. In which sequence are the regions of the electromagnetic spectrum arranged in decreasing frequency?

a.	x-ray	UV	orange light	infrared	microwave
b.	visible	infrared	radio	microwave	γ-ray
c.	γ-ray	UV	infrared	x-ray	microwave
d.	orange light	infrared	blue light	UV	radio
e.	radio	blue light	UV	x-ray	γ-ray
f.	radio	microwave	infrared	green light	UV
g.	infrared	visible	UV	microwave	x-ray

17. Which one of the following sets of quantum numbers is allowed?

	n	l	m_l	m_s			n	l	m_l	m_s
a.	3	1	0	$+\frac{1}{4}$		d.	1	2	0	$-\frac{1}{2}$
b.	6	3	4	$-\frac{1}{2}$		e.	3	-2	0	$+\frac{1}{2}$
c.	2	1	-1	$+\frac{1}{2}$		f.	0	0	0	$-\frac{1}{2}$

18. What is the maximum theoretical number of electrons within the n = 6 energy level?

    a. 6   c. 18   e. 36   g. 60   i. 72
    b. 12   d. 24   f. 48   h. 64   j. 128

19. Start with the number of valence electrons in one atom of oxygen
    ...add the number of orbitals in any one set of d orbitals
    ...add the number of electrons in the 3s orbital of a sodium atom in the ground state
    ...subtract the number of electrons in the 3d orbital of a titanium atom in the ground state.

    What is the result?

    a. 1   c. 4   e. 6   g. 9   i. 12
    b. 2   d. 5   f. 8   h. 10   j. 13

20. Which element, fluorine or nitrogen, is more electronegative, has a larger atomic radius, and has a larger first ionization energy? Choose the row in which all responses are correct.

	More Electronegative	Larger Atomic Radius	Larger First Ionization Energy
a.	fluorine	fluorine	fluorine
b.	fluorine	fluorine	nitrogen
c.	fluorine	nitrogen	fluorine
d.	fluorine	nitrogen	nitrogen
e.	nitrogen	fluorine	fluorine
f.	nitrogen	fluorine	nitrogen
g.	nitrogen	nitrogen	fluorine
h.	nitrogen	nitrogen	nitrogen

EXAMINATION 3

CHEMISTRY 141 FALL 2004

Monday November 22nd 2004

1. What is the electron pair arrangement around the central atom in the molecule IF_5?

   a. linear
   b. trigonal pyramidal
   c. T-shaped
   d. trigonal planar
   e. square planar
   f. see-saw
   g. tetrahedral
   h. octahedral
   i. square pyramidal

2. Which of the following molecules is/are polar?

   1. NH_3 2. CH_4 3. $BeCl_2$ 4. $CHCl_3$ 5. XeF_4

   a. 1 and 4
   b. 1 and 5
   c. 2, 3, and 4
   d. 1 only
   e. 2, 3, and 5
   f. 5 only
   g. 1 and 3
   h. 2 and 4
   i. 1, 3, 4, and 5

3. Consider the sulfur compounds shown. What is the hybridization of atomic orbitals on the sulfur atom in each molecule?

	$SOCl_2$	SO_3	SF_4
a.	sp^2	sp^2	sp^3
b.	sp^3	sp^3	sp^3d
c.	sp^2	sp^3	sp^3
d.	sp^3	sp^2	sp^3d
e.	sp	sp^3	sp^3d
f.	sp^3d	sp	sp^2
g.	sp^3d	sp^3	sp^3
h.	sp^3d	sp^3d	sp

4. What is the FNF bond angle in the molecule NF_3?

   a. 180°
   b. between 120° and 180°
   c. 120°
   d. between 109° and 120°
   e. 109°
   f. between 109° and 90°
   g. 90°
   h. less than 90°

5. How many lone pairs of electrons are there around the central atom in the molecule XeO_2F_2?

   a. 0   c. 2   e. 4   g. 6
   b. 1   d. 3   f. 5   h. 8

6. A balloon is filled with 0.75 L of helium gas at 1 atm pressure and 25°C. The balloon is released and floats upward in the atmosphere. The temperature drops to –25°C and the balloon expands to 1.50 L. What is the pressure at this altitude? Assume the gas behaves ideally.

   a. 0.21 atm   c. 0.42 atm   e. 0.60 atm   g. 1.20 atm
   b. 0.25 atm   d. 0.50 atm   f. 0.83 atm   h. 2.40 atm

7. How many σ bonds and π bonds are there in the hydrogen cyanide molecule HCN?

    a. two σ bonds
    b. three σ bonds
    c. four σ bonds
    d. one σ bond and one π bond
    e. two σ bonds and two π bonds
    f. three σ bonds and three π bonds
    g. one σ bond and three π bonds
    h. two π bonds
    i. three π bonds

8. A 6.0 L vessel contains nitrogen gas at 3.5 atm pressure and 25°C. Without changing the volume or the temperature, helium gas is introduced into the vessel until the total pressure equals 5.0 atm. Then, again without changing the volume or the temperature, oxygen gas is introduced into the vessel until the total pressure equals 7.5 atm. What is the partial pressure of oxygen gas in the vessel at the end?

a. 0.50 atm	c. 1.00 atm	e. 1.33 atm	g. 1.67 atm	i. 2.5 atm
b. 0.75 atm	d. 1.25 atm	f. 1.50 atm	h. 2.0 atm	j. 4.0 atm

9. An aqueous solution of hydrogen peroxide (H_2O_2) is 30.0% by mass and has a density of 1.11g mL^{-1}. What is the *molality* of this solution?

a. 0.185 m	c. 0.815 m	e. 9.79 m	g. 33.3 m
b. 0.333 m	d. 5.73 m	f. 12.6 m	h. 882 m

10. It takes 2.0 minutes for 0.10 mol of helium to effuse. How long will it take for 0.10 mol of ethane C_2H_6 to effuse?

a. 0.13 min	c. 0.37 min	e. 2.74 min	g. 5.5 min
b. 0.27 min	d. 0.73 min	f. 3.73 min	h. 15 min

11. Cinnamaldehyde (molar mass 132.15 g mol^{-1}) is a non-ionizing covalent compound that is used as a flavoring agent. What mass of cinnamaldehyde must be added to 175 g ethanol to produce a solution with a boiling point of 82.7°C?

    Boiling point of pure ethanol = 78.5°C.
    K_b for ethanol = 1.22.

a. 62.4 g	c. 76.2 g	e. 83.7 g	g. 138 g
b. 67.8 g	d. 79.6 g	f. 85.0 g	h. 175 g

12. For which of the following processes does the entropy (of the process) increase?

    1. Frost forms on a car windshield on a winter morning.
    2. Water boils.
    3. A pack of playing cards is shuffled.
    4. Iodine crystals sublime to iodine vapor.

a. only 1	c. only 3	e. 2 and 3	g. 2 and 4	i. none
b. only 2	d. only 4	f. 1 and 4	h. 2, 3, and 4	j. all

13. Two gases, nitric oxide (NO) and oxygen (O_2), are confined in two separate glass flasks, connected by a tap of negligible volume. Initially, there is 5.0 L of NO at a pressure of 3.0 atm and 3.0 L of O_2 at 2.0 atm. The tap is opened, allowing the gases to mix and react. Assume constant temperature and that the reaction goes to completion, producing as much nitrogen dioxide (NO_2) as possible according to the following equation. What is the total pressure, in atm, in the system after the reaction?

$$2\ NO\ (g)\ +\ O_2\ (g)\ \rightarrow\ 2\ NO_2\ (g)$$

a. 3/8 atm	c. 3/4 atm	e. 1.0 atm	g. 13/8 atm	i. 2.0 atm
b. 5/8 atm	d. 7/8 atm	f. 5/4 atm	h. 15/8 atm	j. 2.5 atm

14. The unit cell of a compound of titanium and oxygen contains one titanium atom and two oxygen atoms in the center of the cell, a titanium atom on each of the corners of the cell, and four oxygen atoms on the faces of the unit cell. What is the empirical formula of the compound?

a. TiO	c. Ti_2O	e. Ti_2O_3	g. Ti_3O	i. Ti_9O_2
b. TiO_2	d. Ti_3O_2	f. Ti_9O_6	h. TiO_3	j. Ti_4O_2

15. Which of the following properties of water is/are due to the intermolecular hydrogen bonding between the water molecules?

1. Water has a high heat of vaporization.
2. Ice floats on water.
3. The boiling point of water is much higher than the boiling points of molecules of comaparable size.
4. The specific heat of water ($4.184\ J\ K^{-1}\ g^{-1}$) is much higher than that of lead ($0.128\ J\ K^{-1}\ g^{-1}$).

a. 1 and 2	c. 1 and 4	e. 2 and 4	g. 1, 3, and 4	i. none of them
b. 1 and 3	d. 2 and 3	f. 1, 2, and 3	h. 2, 3, and 4	j. all of them

16. A reaction takes place within a system. As a result, the entropy of the system decreases—the system becomes more ordered. What *must* be true?

1. The entropy S of the universe increases.
2. The entropy S of the surroundings increases.
3. The reaction is exothermic.
4. The Gibb's free energy G of the system decreases.

a. 1 only	e. 1 and 2
b. 2 only	f. 2 and 4
c. 4 only	g. 3 and 4
d. 1 and 4	h. 1, 3, and 4

i. none of them
j. all of them

17. Which *one* of the following statements is true?

a. Increasing the pressure on an ideal gas at constant temperature slows the molecules down.
b. Gases behave more ideally at lower temperatures.
c. Above the critical point the pressure is sufficiently high to cause the molecules to stick together.
d. The smaller the gas molecule, the higher its kinetic energy at the same temperature.
e. All molecules in a sample of a gas travel at the same speed at a particular temperature.
f. The principal cause for the deviation of a gas from ideal behavior is the intermolecular attraction.

18. Which of the following aqueous solutions will have the lowest freezing point?

   a. 0.50 m $Ca(NO_3)_2$ d. 0.40 m Li_3PO_4
   b. 0.70 m $NaOH$ e. 0.60 m $NiSO_4$
   c. 1.20 m $C_{12}H_{22}O_{11}$ (sugar)   f. 0.65 m HCl

19. The phase diagram for a single substance is illustrated on the right. Which set of choices below represents the correct assignment of labels?

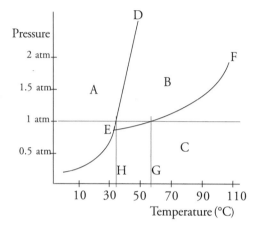

	Triple point	Gas state	Normal boiling pt	Solid state	Critical point
a.	D	B	H	A	E
b.	E	A	G	B	A
c.	E	C	H	C	F
d.	F	B	G	B	E
e.	F	A	H	C	F
f.	E	C	G	A	F
g.	E	C	G	A	D
h.	D	B	H	C	E
i.	F	A	G	C	E

20. Which process is exothermic?

   a. Evaporation of a liquid
   b. Dissolving a typical salt in water
   c. Breaking a hydrogen molecule into atoms
   d. Sublimation of solid carbon dioxide
   e. Freezing water
   f. Breaking up a crystalline lattice
   g. Any spontaneous process

EXAMINATION 3

CHEMISTRY 141 SPRING 2005

Monday April 11th 2005

1. What is the average bond order of the N–O bond in the nitrate ion NO_3^-?

    a. 0.5   d. 1.33   g. 2.5
    b. 1.0   e. 1.5   h. 3.0
    c. 1.25   f. 2.0   i. 4.0

2. Based upon the formal charges on the three atoms, which Lewis dot structure of the cyanate ion NCO^- is (are) the best?

    $$[\ddot{\ddot{N}}=C=\ddot{\ddot{O}}\,]^- \qquad [:N\equiv C-\ddot{\ddot{O}}:]^- \qquad [:\ddot{N}-C\equiv O:]^-$$
    I   II   III

    a. I   c. III   e. I and III   g. all are equally good
    b. II   d. I and II   f. II and III

3. What is the electron pair arrangement around the central atom in the molecule IF_3 and the shape of the molecule?

	electron pair arrangement	*molecular shape*
a.	T-shaped	trigonal bipyramid
b.	tetrahedral	tetrahedral
c.	tetrahedral	trigonal pyramid
d.	octahedral	square pyramid
e.	octahedral	trigonal pyramid
f.	trigonal bipyramid	trigonal pyramid
g.	trigonal planar	trigonal planar
h.	trigonal bipyramid	T-shaped
i.	trigonal bipyramid	trigonal planar
j.	tetrahedral	V-shaped

4. Which of the following molecules is/are polar?

    1. PCl_3 2. SF_6 3. H_2O 4. CCl_4 5. XeF_2

    a. 1 only   d. 4 only   g. 1 and 3   i. 1 and 5
    b. 2 only   e. 5 only   h. 1 and 4   j. 3 and 5
    c. 3 only   f. 1 and 2

5. What is the hybridization of atomic orbitals on the xenon atom in $XeOF_4$?

    a. sp   b. sp^2 c. sp^3 d. sp^3d e. sp^3d^2

6. How many lone pairs of electrons are there around the central atom in the polyatomic ion $PCl_2Br_2^+$?

    a. 0   c. 2   e. 4   g. 6
    b. 1   d. 3   f. 5   h. 8

7. How many σ bonds are there in a molecule of sulfuric acid H_2SO_4?

a. 2	c. 4	e. 6	g. 8	i. 10
b. 3	d. 5	f. 7	h. 9	j. 11

8. A 8.0 L vessel contains 5.0 moles of hydrogen gas, 3.0 moles of helium gas, and 2.0 moles of oxygen gas at a pressure of 25 atm. What is the temperature of the gas (assuming the mixture is ideal)?

a. −29°C	c. 0°C	e. 14°C	g. 47°C	i. 244°C
b. −2.4°C	d. 2.4°C	f. 25°C	h. 121°C	j. 313°C

9. What is the partial pressure of the oxygen gas in the mixture described in the previous question?

a. 0.50 atm	c. 1.5 atm	e. 3.0 atm	g. 5.0 atm	i. 15 atm
b. 1.0 atm	d. 2.0 atm	f. 4.0 atm	h. 10 atm	j. 25 atm

10. Suppose that an additional 7.0 moles of hydrogen is added to the mixture (described in question 8) without changing the temperature or the volume. What is the partial pressure of oxygen in the new mixture?

a. 0.33 atm	c. 1.0 atm	e. 3.0 atm	g. 4.0 atm	i. 10 atm
b. 0.67 atm	d. 2.67 atm	f. 3.33 atm	h. 5.0 atm	j. 16.7 atm

11. Suppose that an additional 4.0 moles of oxygen is now added to the mixture (described in question 10) without changing the temperature or the volume. What is the partial pressure of oxygen in the new mixture?

a. 0.50 atm	c. 1.5 atm	e. 3.0 atm	g. 5.0 atm	i. 15 atm
b. 1.0 atm	d. 2.0 atm	f. 4.0 atm	h. 10 atm	j. 25 atm

12. The mixture (after the addition of the 7.0 moles of hydrogen and 4.0 moles of oxygen) is now ignited (to form water). The mixture is cooled to the original temperature and the volume does not change. If the water completely condenses, what is the total pressure of gas in the vessel?

a. 0.50 atm	c. 2.0 atm	e. 5.0 atm	g. 10 atm	i. 15 atm
b. 1.0 atm	d. 2.5 atm	f. 7.5 atm	h. 12.5 atm	j. 25 atm

13. What is the density of argon gas at 1.00 atm pressure and 25.0°C?

a. 0.00103 g L^{-1}	c. 0.49 g L^{-1}	e. 1.63 g L^{-1}	g. 5.07 g L^{-1}
b. 0.041 g L^{-1}	d. 0.61 g L^{-1}	f. 3.26 g L^{-1}	h. 19.5 g L^{-1}

14. Which one of the following molecules cannot hydrogen bond with a water molecule?

a. NH_3	c. HF	e. NH_2NH_2	g. CH_4
b. CH_3OH	d. CH_3CO_2H	f. $CH_3CH_2NH_2$	h. OH^-

15. Niobium oxide crystallizes in the cubic system with the unit cell shown. The niobium atoms are on the faces of the cube and the oxygen atoms are on the edges. What is the empirical formula of niobium oxide?

    ○ niobium
    ● oxygen

a. NbO	c. Nb_2O	e. Nb_2O_3	g. Nb_3O
b. NbO_2	d. Nb_3O_2	f. NbO_3	

(16.) At its freezing point, solid water (ice) has a lower density than liquid water. The reason for this is

    a.   the low molar mass of water
    b.   the high specific heat of water
    c.   the polarity of the water molecule
    d.   the hydrogen bonding between water molecules
    e.   the high melting point of water

(17.) The substances hydrogen H_2, butane C_4H_{10}, sodium chloride NaCl, and diamond C have melting points that vary considerably. Order these substances in increasing melting point. [Butane is the fuel in disposable lighters.]

a.	hydrogen	<	butane	<	sodium chloride	<	diamond
b.	butane	<	hydrogen	<	sodium chloride	<	diamond
c.	butane	<	hydrogen	<	diamond	<	sodium chloride
d.	hydrogen	<	diamond	<	sodium chloride	<	butane
e.	diamond	<	sodium chloride	<	hydrogen	<	butane
f.	sodium chloride	<	butane	<	diamond	<	hydrogen
g.	hydrogen	<	sodium chloride	<	butane	<	diamond

18.   The phase diagram for a single substance is illustrated on the right. Which set of choices below represents the correct descriptions?

	The sign of ΔH for the transition	The sign of ΔS for the transition	The sign or value of ΔG at point
	A	**B**	**C**
a.	+	+	+
b.	+	+	−
c.	+	−	+
d.	+	−	−
e.	+	+	0
f.	−	−	0
g.	+	−	0
h.	−	+	0
i.	−	−	−
j.	−	+	+

19.   What is the molality of 1.00 L of a 50.0% by mass aqueous solution of acetic acid CH_3CO_2H?

    a. 0.017 *m*   c. 1.7 *m*   e. 8.3 *m*   g. 16.7 *m*
    b. 0.083 *m*   d. 6.4 *m*   f. 13.9 *m*   h. 50 *m*

20.   Which of the following aqueous solutions will have the *highest* melting point?

    a. 3.0 *m* glucose (sugar)   e. 1.6 *m* NaOH
    b. 2.0 *m* NaCl   f. 1.0 *m* CH_3CO_2H (acetic acid)
    c. 1.5 *m* KBr   g. 2.1 *m* KNO_3
    d. 0.70 *m* Na_2SO_4 h. 2.7 *m* NH_3

EXAMINATION 3
CHEMISTRY 141 FALL 2005
Monday November 21st 2005

To answer questions 1 through 3, use the following molecules or polyatomic ions:

CH_4	$CHCl_3$	N_2O	PF_5
HCN	NH_3	I_3^-	NO_2^-

1. How many of the molecules (or ions) have a trigonal bipyramidal electron pair arrangement?

    a. none c. 2 e. 4 g. 6 i. all
    b. 1 d. 3 f. 5 h. 7

2. How many of the molecules (or ions) have a linear shape?

    a. none c. 2 e. 4 g. 6 i. all
    b. 1 d. 3 f. 5 h. 7

3. How many of the molecules (or ions) are polar?

    a. none c. 2 e. 4 g. 6 i. all
    b. 1 d. 3 f. 5 h. 7

4. Consider the Lewis structure for acetic acid shown: What is the hybridization of the atomic orbitals of the carbon atom in the box?

    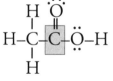

    a. sp c. sp^3 e. sp^3d^2
    b. sp^2 d. sp^3d

5. Which of the following statements about the nitrate ion is *not true?*

    a. The shape of the nitrate ion is trigonal planar.
    b. The sp^2 hybrid orbitals on the nitrogen atom form σ (sigma) bonds with the oxygen atoms.
    c. Nitrogen has an empty p orbital that is able to form π (pi) bonds with the oxygen atoms.
    d. Resonance is required to reconcile possible Lewis structures with the actual structure.
    e. The ONO bond angle is 120°.
    f. Electrons are delocalized over the entire ion in the π bond.

6. A triple bond consists of

    a. three π bonds e. one σ bond, one π bond, and one δ bond
    b. two π bonds and one σ bond f. two σ bonds and two π bonds
    c. one π bond and two σ bonds g. one σ bond and one π bond
    d. three σ bonds

7. A 4.0 L container is filled with 2.0 moles of oxygen gas at 25°C. How much more oxygen gas would you have to add to the container to increase the pressure to 50 atm, keeping the temperature and volume the same?

    a. 1.2 moles   c. 3.2 moles   e. 5.2 moles   g. 7.2 moles
    b. 2.2 moles   d. 4.2 moles   f. 6.2 moles   h. 8.2 moles

8. One of the possible Lewis structures for the covalent nitrosyl azide NNNNO is:

    $$:N\equiv N-\ddot{N}=\ddot{N}-\ddot{O}:$$

    From left to right, the formal charges on the atoms in this molecules are:

	N	N	N	N	O
a.	0	−1	0	0	+1
b.	0	−1	+1	+1	−1
c.	+1	0	0	0	−1
d.	−1	0	+1	+1	−1
e.	0	+1	0	0	−1
f.	+1	−1	0	−1	+1
g.	0	+1	0	+1	−2
h.	+1	0	+1	0	−2

9. A flask containing a gas is connected to an open-ended mercury manometer. The open end is exposed to the atmosphere (1 atm pressure). The mercury level in the open arm of the manometer is 50 cm below the mercury level in the arm connected to the flask containing the gas. What is the pressure of the gas in the vessel?

    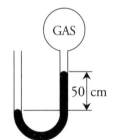

    a. 260 torr   c. 710 torr   e. 760 torr   g. 810 torr
    b. 500 torr   d. 755 torr   f. 765 torr   h. 1260 torr

10. A 6.0 L vessel contains 1.0 mole of neon gas, 2.0 moles of xenon gas, and 3.0 moles of helium gas at a pressure of 12.0 atm. What is the partial pressure of xenon gas in the vessel?

    a. 1.0 atm   c. 3.0 atm   e. 5.0 atm   g. 8.0 atm   i. 12.0 atm
    b. 2.0 atm   d. 4.0 atm   f. 6.0 atm   h. 10.0 atm   j. 36.0 atm

11. Maintaining a constant volume and temperature, an additional 3.0 moles of helium is added to the vessel described in the previous question. What are the partial pressures of helium and xenon in the vessel now?

	partial pressure of helium	*partial pressure of xenon*
a.	6.0 atm	2.0 atm
b.	9.0 atm	4.0 atm
c.	18.0 atm	6.0 atm
d.	4.0 atm	2.0 atm
e.	6.0 atm	4.0 atm
f.	12.0 atm	6.0 atm
g.	2.0 atm	2.0 atm
h.	12.0 atm	4.0 atm
i.	6.0 atm	6.0 atm

12. It takes 8.0 minutes for 1.00 mol of helium to effuse through a small hole. How long will it take for 1.00 mol of methane CH_4 to effuse through the same hole?

   a. 2.0 min   c. 6.0 min   e. 12 min   g. 32 min
   b. 4.0 min   d. 8.0 min   f. 16 min   h. 64 min

13. Consider the base adenine shown on the right. (This base forms a base-pair with thymine in DNA.) Which hydrogen atom(s) on the adenine molecule is(are) capable of forming hydrogen bonds?

   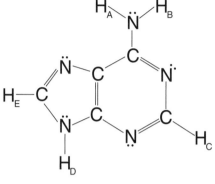

   a. A and B   f. A, B, and C
   b. C and E   g. A, B, and D
   c. C only   h. A, B, C, and D
   d. D only   i. C, D, and E
   e. E only   j. all of them

14. A substance with strong intermolecular forces of attraction would be expected to have

   A a high boiling point
   B a high vapor pressure
   C a high heat of vaporization
   D a high melting point

   a. A only   c. C only   e. A and B   g. C and D   i. B and C
   b. B only   d. D only   f. A and D   h. A, C, and D   j. A, B, C, and D

15. The unit cell of palladium sulfide is shown on the right. The small black spheres represent palladium ions, and the larger shaded spheres represent sulfide ions. How many sulfide ions belong to this unit cell?

   a. 1   c. 3   e. 5   g. 8   i. 12
   b. 2   d. 4   f. 6   h. 10   j. 15

16. For which of the following processes would you expect the change in entropy ΔS to be positive and the change in enthalpy ΔH to be negative (exothermic)?

   a. melting ice to form liquid water
   b. the sublimation of dry ice (solid CO_2)
   c. the burning of butane gas (C_4H_{10}) to form CO_2 gas and water vapor
   d. the condensation of water vapor to liquid water
   e. dissolving ammonium nitrate in water (the solution gets cold)
   f. the vaporization of ethanol C_2H_5OH

17. A phase diagram for a typical substance is illustrated on
    the right. What letters correctly identify the areas on the
    diagram?

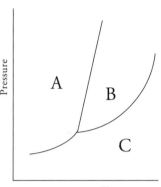

	solid	*liquid*	*vapor*
a.	A	B	C
b.	B	A	C
c.	A	C	B
d.	B	C	A
e.	C	A	B
f.	C	B	A

18. What is the molality of a 15.0% by mass solution of potassium hydroxide?

    a. 12.7 *m*   c. 8.53 *m*   e. 5.62 *m*   g. 1.72 *m*
    b. 9.42 *m*   d. 6.04 *m*   f. 3.15 *m*   h. 0.32 *m*

19. 30 grams of an unknown molecular solute is dissolved in 1 kg of water and the freezing point of the
    solution is –0.93°C. What is the molar mass of the solute?

    $K_f(H_2O) = -1.853$ K kg mol^{-1}.

    a. 0.02 g mol^{-1} c. 15 g mol^{-1} e. 60 g mol^{-1} g. 93 g mol^{-1}
    b. 0.50 g mol^{-1} d. 30 g mol^{-1} f. 77 g mol^{-1} h. 98 g mol^{-1}

20. A solution of two volatile liquids, A and B, behaves ideally according to Raoult's law. The vapor pressure
    of pure A at 25°C is 400 torr and the vapor pressure of pure B at the same temperature is 600 torr. If the
    vapor pressure above the solution is 550 torr, what is the mole fraction of A in the solution?

    a. 0.10   c. 0.20   e. 0.40   g. 0.75
    b. 0.15   d. 0.25   f. 0.50   h. 0.80

EXAMINATION 3

CHEMISTRY 141 SPRING 2006

Monday April 10th 2006

1. Which one of the following molecules / ions has a central atom that does not obey the octet rule?

    a. CH_2Cl_2 c. SO_3 e. CO_2 g. H_3O^+
    b. NO_3^- d. BF_3 f. NF_3 h. PO_4^{3-}

2. Arrange the molecules ethane (C_2H_6), ethene (C_2H_4), and ethyne (C_2H_2) in order of *increasing* carbon to carbon bond length.

    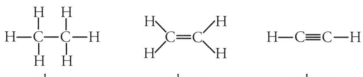

    ethane   ethene   ethyne

    a. ethane < ethene < ethyne   d. ethene < ethyne < ethane
    b. ethane < ethyne < ethene   e. ethyne < ethene < ethane
    c. ethene < ethane < ethyne   f. ethyne < ethane < ethene

3. What is the hybridization of the central atom in nitryl fluoride (FNO_2)?

    a. sp   c. sp^3 e. sp^3d^2
    b. sp^2 d. sp^3d

4. What is the electron arrangement and molecular shape of ClF_3?

electron arrangement	*molecular shape*
a. trigonal planar	trigonal planar
b. T-shaped	trigonal bipyramid
c. trigonal pryamid	bent
d. tetrahedral	trigonal pyramid
e. trigonal bipyramid	see-saw
f. octahedral	trigonal planar
g. trigonal bipyramid	T-shaped
h. octahedral	T-shaped

5. How many σ (sigma) bond(s) are in one molecule of aspirin?

    a. 1   c. 9   e. 16   g. 26
    b. 5   d. 14   f. 21   h. 30

6. Which one of the following molecules or ions is polar?

    a. O_2 c. CO_2 e. BF_3 g. CH_4
    b. I_3^- d. H_2S f. SF_6 h. NO_3^-

7. Consider a triple bond between two atoms. If the internuclear axis is the z-axis, which of the following orbitals could overlap to form a π (pi) bond?

    1. s and p_y 3. p_x and p_x 5. p_y and p_y
    2. p_z and p_z 4. p_x and d_{xz} 6. p_y and d_{xz}

    a. 2 only   c. 1 and 6   e. 2 and 3   g. 4 and 6   i. 3, 4 and 5
    b. 3 only   d. 3 and 6   f. 2 and 5   h. 2, 3 and 5 j. all of them

8. Based upon the formal charges on the three atoms, which Lewis dot structure(s) of carbonyl sulfide (COS) is (are) the best?

    $$[\ \ddot{O}=C=\ddot{S}\ ]^- \qquad\qquad [:\ddot{O}-C\equiv S:]^- \qquad\qquad [:O\equiv C-\ddot{S}:]^-$$

    $$\qquad\quad 1 \qquad\qquad\qquad\qquad\qquad 2 \qquad\qquad\qquad\qquad\qquad 3$$

    a. 1 only   c. 3 only   e. 1 and 3   g. all are equally good
    b. 2 only   d. 1 and 2   f. 2 and 3

9. A bubble at the bottom of a lake, where the temperature is 10°C and the pressure is 5.0 atm, has a volume of 5.0 mL. The bubble rises to the surface of the lake where the temperature is 25°C and the pressure is 1.0 atm. What is the volume of the bubble at the surface of the lake?

    a. 0.026 mL   c. 5 mL   e. 26 mL   g. 59 mL
    b. 2.2 mL   d. 19 mL   f. 38 mL   h. 63 mL

10. Suppose that there are two vessels connected by a tap that is closed. The first vessel is 2.0 liters in volume and contains methane (CH_4) gas at a pressure of 1.0 atm. The second vessel is 1.0 liter in volume and contains oxygen gas at 3.0 atm pressure. The tap is opened, the two gases mix, and react to form as much carbon dioxide and water vapor as possible. Assume the gases are ideal and the temperature is the same at the end of the experiment (100°C) as it was at the beginning. What is the partial pressure of carbon dioxide after the reaction has gone to completion?

    $$CH_4(g) + 2\,O_2(g) \quad\rightarrow\quad CO_2(g) + 2\,H_2O(g)$$

    a. 0 atm   c. 1/3 atm   e. 2/3 atm   g. 1 atm
    b. 1/6 atm   d. 1/2 atm   f. 3/4 atm   h. 5/3 atm

11. Two gases, krypton and argon, are contained within a glass bulb with a total pressure of 5.0 atm. There are 3.0 moles of argon in the bulb and the partial pressure of argon is 4.0 atm. How many moles of krypton are in the container?

    a. 0.25 mol   c. 0.75 mol   e. 1.25 mol   g. 1.75 mol
    b. 0.50 mol   d. 1.0 mol   f. 1.50 mol   h. 2.0 mol

12. Xenon effuses through a small hole at a rate of 1.6 mol min^{-1}. An unknown gas will effuse through the same hole at a rate of 2.0 mol min^{-1}. What is the molar mass of the unknown gas?

    a. 2 g mol^{-1} c. 32 g mol^{-1} e. 4 g mol^{-1} g. 40 g mol^{-1}
    b. 28 g mol^{-1} d. 70 g mol^{-1} f. 20 g mol^{-1} h. 84 g mol^{-1}

13. Compare methane (CH_4), chloromethane (CH_3Cl), and methanol (CH_3OH). Identify the molecule with the highest boiling point and the predominant intermolecular force in that molecule. *(Choose the row where both responses are correct.)*

	molecule with highest boiling point	*predominant intermolecular force*
a.	methane	london dispersion
b.	methane	dipole-dipole
c.	methane	H-bonds
d.	chloromethane	london dispersion
e.	chloromethane	dipole-dipole
f.	chloromethane	H-bonds
g.	methanol	london dispersion
h.	methanol	dipole-dipole
i.	methanol	H-bonds

14. A unit cell of a compound of strontium, titanium, and oxygen contains one strontium atom in the center of the cell, one titanium atom on each of the corners of the cell, and one oxygen atom on each face of the unit cell. What is the empirical formula of the compound?

a. $SrTiO$ c. $SrTiO_3$ e. $SrTi_2O_6$ g. $SrTi_4O_4$
b. $SrTiO_2$ d. $SrTi_2O_3$ f. $SrTi_3O_6$ h. $SrTi_8O_6$

15. For which of the following processes does the entropy (of the process) *increase?*

1. dry ice sublimes
2. salt crystallizing from solution
3. water vapor condenses
4. ammonia gas diffuses

a. 1 only c. 3 only e. 1 and 2 g. 1 and 4 i. 2 and 4
b. 2 only d. 4 only f. 1 and 3 h. 2 and 3 j. 1, 2, and 3

16. What is the *molality* (m) of a 5.0% by mass aqueous solution of acetic acid (CH_3CO_2H)? The molar mass of acetic acid is 60 g mol^{-1}.

a. 1.1 *m* c. 0.080 *m* e. 3.2 *m* g. 2.7 *m*
b. 0.88 *m* d. 0.65 *m* f. 0.50 *m* h. 5.6 *m*

17. The boiling point of benzene (C_6H_6) is 80°C. What are the signs for ΔH, ΔS, and ΔG for the vaporization of benzene at 100 °C? *(Choose the row in which all answers are correct.)*

	ΔH	ΔS	ΔG
a.	+	+	+
b.	+	+	−
c.	+	−	+
d.	+	−	−
e.	−	−	−
f.	−	−	+
g.	−	+	−
h.	−	+	+

18. An ideal solution of two liquids A and B contains 1 mole of A and 2 moles of B. At a particular temperature, the total vapor pressure above the solution is 760 torr and the vapor pressure of pure A is 300 torr. What is the vapor pressure of pure B at this temperature?

a. 300 torr   c. 380 torr   e. 600 torr   g. 990 torr
b. 330 torr   d. 460 torr   f. 760 torr   h. 1290 torr

19. The phase diagram for carbon is illustrated below. Which point(s) represent the triple point(s) in the phase diagram?

a. A   f. A and B
b. B   g. B and C
c. C   h. C and E
d. D   i. A and E
e. E   j. B, C and E

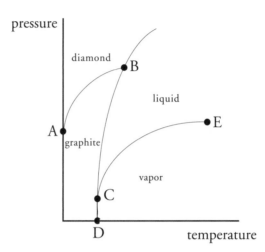

20. A 0.50 *m* solution of magnesium nitrate elevates the boiling point of water by 0.75 degrees. What molality of a sodium chloride solution is needed to raise the boiling point of water by the same amount?

a. 2.0 *m*   c. 1.5 *m*   e. 1.0 *m*   g. 0.50 *m*
b. 1.75 *m*   d. 1.25 *m*   f. 0.75 *m*   h. 0.25 *m*

EXAMINATION 3

CHEMISTRY 141 FALL 2006

Monday November 20th 2006

1. The central atom in a molecule has two nonbonding pairs of electrons and three bonding pairs of electrons in its valence shell. What is the arrangement of these pairs of electrons around the central atom?

    a. linear
    b. trigonal planar
    c. tetrahedral
    d. square planar
    e. trigonal pyramidal
    f. trigonal bipyramidal
    g. square pyramidal
    h. octahedral

2. Three possible Lewis structures for the fulminate ion CNO^- are illustrated below. What are the formal charges on the indicated elements in each structure?

    $$[\ddot{C} = N = \ddot{O}]^- \qquad [:C = \ddot{N} - \ddot{O}:]^- \qquad [:C \equiv N - \ddot{O}:]^-$$

    I II III

	C in structure I	N in structure II	N in structure III
a.	0	0	0
b.	−1	0	0
c.	−2	−1	0
d.	0	0	−1
e.	−1	−1	−1
f.	−2	0	+1
g.	0	+1	+1
h.	−1	0	+1
i.	−2	+1	0
j.	0	0	+1

3. How many lone pairs of electrons are there in the valence shell of the central atom in the molecule $SeOF_2$?

    a. 0   b. 1   c. 2   d. 3   e. 4   f. 5

4. For which one of the following molecules is the concept of resonance necessary to reconcile possible Lewis structures with the actual electronic structure of the molecule?

    a. H_2O
    b. CO_2
    c. BrF_3
    d. SO_2
    e. H_2CO
    f. H_2
    g. CCl_4
    h. XeO_3
    i. O_2
    j. BF_3

5. What is the shape of the polyatomic ion IF_4^-?

    a. tetrahedral
    b. square planar
    c. trigonal pyramidal
    d. trigonal bipyramidal
    e. square pyramidal
    f. octahedral

6.   How many of the following molecules are polar?

CH_3Cl NO_2 BrF_3 PH_3 $XeOF_4$
HCN H_2CO H_2O CH_2Br_2 SO_2

a. 1   c. 4   e. 6   g. 8   i.   none of them
b. 3   d. 5   f. 7   h. 9   j.   all of them

7.   Imagine a diatomic molecule in which the axis connecting the two nuclei is the z axis. Various combina-
tions of atomic orbitals on the two atoms lead to orbitals for the molecule. Which row correctly lists the
molecular orbitals formed by the two orbitals (one on one atom and the second on the other atom)?

	p_x and p_x	p_z and p_z	s and p_x	p_z and s
a.	σ	σ	σ	σ
b.	π	σ	π	σ
c.	p	σ	σ	no interaction
d.	σ	π	no interaction	π
e.	σ	π	π	σ
f.	π	σ	σ	σ
g.	π	σ	no interaction	σ
h.	σ	σ	no interaction	σ

8.   What is the hybridization of the atomic orbitals on the xenon atom in the molecule XeF_4?

a. sp   b. sp^2 c. sp^3 d. sp^2d e. sp^3d f. sp^3d^2

9.   A 5.0 L vessel contains 1.0 mole He, 4.0 moles N_2, and 5.0 moles Ar at a pressure of 40 atm. What is the
partial pressure of nitrogen in the vessel? An additional 2.0 moles of nitrogen is added to the vessel with
no change in the volume or the temperature. What is the partial pressure of nitrogen now?

	Initial partial pressure of N_2	*Partial pressure after adding 2.0 moles nitrogen*
a.	2.0 atm	2.0 atm
b.	2.0 atm	3.0 atm
c.	4.0 atm	6.0 atm
d.	4.0 atm	12.0 atm
e.	8.0 atm	8.0 atm
f.	8.0 atm	12.0 atm
g.	8.0 atm	24.0 atm
h.	16.0 atm	16.0 atm
i.	16.0 atm	24.0 atm
j.	16.0 atm	32.0 atm

10.   Suppose that a 2.0 liter vessel contains N_2O gas at 2.0 atm pressure. Suppose that a second vessel, 3.0
liter in volume, contains oxygen at 3.0 atm pressure. Now suppose that the two vessels are connected by
a pipe of negligible volume and the two gases mix and react to produce as much nitrogen dioxide as
possible. Assume that the temperature remains constant. What is the pressure in the apparatus at the end
of the reaction?

$$2\,N_2O(g)\ +\ 3\,O_2(g)\ \rightarrow\ 4\,NO_2(g)$$

a. 3/5 atm   c. 1 atm   e. 7/5 atm   g. 9/5 atm   i.   11/5 atm
b. 4/5 atm   d. 6/5 atm   f.   8/5 atm   h. 2 atm   j.   12/5 atm

11. The Rankine temperature scale is an absolute Fahrenheit temperature scale—just as the Kelvin scale is an absolute Celsius temperature scale. In other words, the Rankine scale has a value of 0°R at absolute zero and a degree size equal to one Fahrenheit degree. What is the boiling point of water on the Rankine scale?

a. 491.7°R   c. 523.7°R   e. 591.7°R
b. 639.7°R   d. 671.7°R   f. 703.7°R

12. In an effusion experiment, it takes a sample of helium gas 240 seconds to effuse through a small hole. Under the same conditions, how long would it take the same number of moles of methane gas (CH_4) to effuse through the same hole?

a. 15 s   c. 90 s   e. 180 s   g. 480 s   i. 1920 s
b. 60 s   d. 120 s   f. 360 s   h. 960 s   j. 3840 s

13. The cubic unit cell of a metal alloy is illustrated on the right. The two metals are copper (black circles on the top and bottom faces and on the edges) and silver (shaded circles). How is the lattice of silver atoms described and what is the stoichiometry of the alloy?

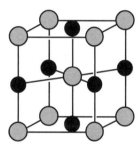

	Silver atom lattice	Stoichiometry
a.	simple cubic	Cu_2Ag
b.	simple cubic	$CuAg$
c.	simple cubic	$CuAg_2$
d.	body-centered cubic	Cu_2Ag
e.	body-centered cubic	$CuAg$
f.	body-centered cubic	$CuAg_2$
g.	face-centered cubic	Cu_2Ag
h.	face-centered cubic	$CuAg$
i.	face-centered cubic	$CuAg_2$

14. The vapor pressure curve on a phase diagram...

a. indicates that the vapor pressure of a liquid is zero at the triple point
b. starts at the triple point and ends at the critical point
c. shows that the vapor pressure decreases as the temperature increases
d. indicates that liquid water cannot exist at a temperature lower than the triple point
e. crosses the 1 atm pressure line at the freezing point

15. Identify the strongest intermolecular force of attraction in ammonia, hydrogen iodide, methane (CH_4), and nitrogen trichloride. Choose the row where all responses are correct.

	NH_3	HI	CH_4	NCl_3
a.	hydrogen bond	hydrogen bond	London dispersion	dipole-dipole
b.	dipole-dipole	hydrogen bond	hydrogen bond	London dispersion
c.	dipole-dipole	dipole-dipole	London dispersion	London dispersion
d.	hydrogen bond	dipole-dipole	London dispersion	dipole-dipole
e.	hydrogen bond	dipole-dipole	hydrogen bond	dipole-dipole
f.	dipole-dipole	hydrogen bond	dipole-dipole	London dispersion
g.	hydrogen bond	London dispersion	London dispersion	dipole-dipole

16. The sublimation of iodine is a spontaneous process at 298K. What are the signs for ΔG, ΔH, and ΔS for this reaction at 298K?

	ΔG	ΔH	ΔS
a.	+	−	−
b.	+	−	+
c.	−	−	−
d.	−	−	+
e.	+	+	−
f.	+	+	+
g.	−	+	−
h.	−	+	+

17. Which one of the following statements is false?

   a. The entropy of the universe must increase for any spontaneous process.
   b. Gibbs free energy must increase for any spontaneous process.
   c. At equilibrium, the change in enthalpy is equal to the temperature times the change in entropy.
   d. The change in entropy is negative for a condensation process.
   e. An enthalpy–driven process is one in which the change in enthalpy and the change in entropy are both negative.
   f. A positive change in entropy represents an increase in disorder.

18. A solution is made by dissolving 0.30 mol isopropanol (C_3H_7OH) in 0.80 mol water. What is the *molality* of the solution?

   The density of water is 1.00 g mL^{-1}
   The density of isopropanol is 0.785 g mL^{-1}.

a. 0.375 *m*	c. 15.6 *m*	e. 0.273 *m*	g. 2.67 *m*
b. 8.02 *m*	d. 0.727 *m*	f. 20.8 *m*	h. 13.1 *m*

19. Which one of the following aqueous solutions has the *highest* freezing point?

   a. 0.4 *m* NaCl
   b. 3.0 *m* NH$_3$
   c. 0.3 *m* Na$_3$PO$_4$
   d. 1.2 *m* HF
   e. 0.6 *m* KCl
   f. 0.5 *m* Na$_2$CO$_3$
   g. 2.0 *m* NH$_4$CH$_3$CO$_2$
   h. 0.8 *m* MgBr$_2$

20. An ideal solution is prepared by mixing 2.0 moles of ethanol with 6.0 moles of methanol. At the temperature of the liquid, the vapor pressure of pure ethanol is 60.5 torr and the vapor pressure of pure methanol is 126.0 torr. What is the total vapor pressure above the solution at this temperature?

a. 109.6 torr	d. 187.0 torr	g. 66.0 torr
b. 94.5 torr	e. 6.25 torr	h. 76.9 torr
c. 27.2 torr	f. 34.3 torr	

EXAMINATION 3

CHEMISTRY 141 SPRING 2007

Monday April 9th 2007

1. *(5 points)* What is the name of the electron arrangement from which the molecular shape shown below was derived?

    a. linear   c. tetrahedral   e. trigonal bipyramidal
    b. trigonal planar   d. trigonal pyramidal f. octahedral

2. *(5 points)* Which one of the following is <u>not</u> a concentration unit?

    a. parts per million   c. molality   e. mole fraction
    b. molarity   d. mass percent   f. pascal

3. Which one of the following molecules / ions has a central atom that does not obey the octet rule?

    a. H_3O^+ c. NO_3^- e. CO_2 g. CH_3Cl
    b. SBr_2 d. BO_3^{3-} f. FNO_2 h. H_2S

4. What is the electron arrangement and molecular shape for the ion SF_3^+?
    (Choose the row where both answers are correct.)

	electron arrangement	molecular shape
a.	trigonal bipyramidal	trigonal pyramidal
b.	tetrahedral	trigonal planar
c.	trigonal planar	trigonal planar
d.	trigonal planar	tetrahedral
e.	tetrahedral	bent
f.	tetrahedral	trigonal pyramidal
g.	trigonal bipyramidal	see-saw
h.	octahedral	square planar

5. What is the average bond order for each of the following ions?
    (Choose the row in which all answers are correct.)

	NO_2^-	IO_4^-	NO_3^-
a.	2.0	1.0	1.0
b.	1.0	1.0	1.0
c.	1.5	1.0	1.33
d.	1.0	1.5	1.33
e.	1.5	1.0	1.5
f.	2.0	2.0	2.0
g.	1.5	1.33	1.5
h.	1.33	1.33	1.33

6. For which of the following molecules / ions is resonance <u>not</u> needed to reconcile the Lewis structure with the actual structure?

a. O_3 c. CO_3^{2-} e. COS   g. $BeCl_2$

b. SO_3 d. SCN^- f. N_2O h. C_6H_6 (benzene)

7. What is the hybridization of the valence orbitals on the indicated oxygen, carbon, and nitrogen atoms in the following molecule? *(Choose the row in which all responses are correct.)*

	oxygen	carbon	nitrogen
a.	sp	sp	sp^2
b.	sp	sp^2	sp^3
c.	sp	sp^3	sp
d.	sp^2	sp	sp^2
e.	sp^2	sp^2	sp^3
f.	sp^2	sp^3	sp
g.	sp^3	sp	sp^2
h.	sp^3	sp^2	sp^3
i.	sp^3	sp^3	sp

8. How many π bonds are in one molecule of HCN?

a. zero   c. 2   e. 4   g. 6

b. 1   d. 3   f. 5   h. 7

9. Consider a double bond between two atoms. If the internuclear axis is the y–axis, which of the following orbitals could overlap to form the σ (sigma) bond?

1. s and p_y 3. p_x and p_x 5. s and p_z

2. p_x and p_y 4. p_y and p_y 6. d_{xy} and p_x

a. 1 and 2   d. 1 and 4   g. 2, 4, and 6

b. 2 and 3   e. 3 and 6   h. 1 only

c. 1 and 6   f. 1, 4, and 5   i. 1, 3, 4, and 5

10. Suppose there are two vessels connected by a tap that is closed. The first vessel is 3.0 liters in volume and contains nitrogen gas at a pressure of 5.0 atm. The second vessel is empty (contains no gas). When the tap is opened the pressure of the nitrogen gas drops to 1.5 atm. What is the volume of the second vessel?

a. 4.0 L   c. 6.0 L   e. 8.0 L   g. 10.0 L

b. 5.5 L   d. 7.0 L   f. 9.25 L   h. 13.0 L

11. A 4.0 liter vessel contains 1.0 moles of helium gas, 2.0 moles of hydrogen gas, and 5.0 moles of nitrogen gas at a temperature of 25°C. What is the partial pressure of the nitrogen gas?

a. 2.56 atm   c. 12.2 atm   e. 30.6 atm   g. 48.9 atm

b. 6.11 atm   d. 24.7 atm   f. 37.4 atm   h. 52.9 atm

12. Suppose that there are two vessels that are connected by a tap that is closed. The first vessel is 4.0 liters in volume and contains water vapor at a pressure of 3.0 atm. The second vessel is 2.0 liters in volume and contains oxygen dichloride at a pressure of 1.0 atm. The tap is opened, the two gases mix and react to form as much hydrogen hypochlorite (HClO) as possible. Assume that the gases are ideal and the temperature is constant. What is the partial pressure of hydrogen hypochlorite after the reaction has gone to completion?

$$H_2O(g) + OCl_2(g) \rightarrow 2\,HClO(g)$$

a. 0 atm	c. 2/3 atm	e. 5/3 atm	g. 7/3 atm	i. 3 atm
b. 1/3 atm	d. 1 atm	f. 2 atm	h. 8/3 atm	j. 4 atm

13. Gas A effuses through a small hole at a rate of $1.05\ ms^{-1}$ and Gas B effuses through the same small hole at a rate of $0.25\ ms^{-1}$. If there are 4 grams of gas A in one mole of A, what is gas B?

a. H_2	c. O_2	e. CH_4	g. F_2
b. Xe	d. CO	f. Cl_2	h. CO_2

14. A unit cell of an unknown compound contains element X in a face centered cubic arrangement. How many atoms of element X are in one unit cell of this compound?

a. 1	c. 3	e. 5	g. 7	i. 10
b. 2	d. 4	f. 6	h. 8	j. 12

15. Arrange these four substances in order of increasing melting or boiling point: propane (C_3H_8), water, hydrogen, sodium.

a.	hydrogen	propane	water	sodium
b.	hydrogen	water	propane	sodium
c.	propane	water	hydrogen	sodium
d.	water	sodium	propane	hydrogen
e.	sodium	propane	hydrogen	water
f.	hydrogen	propane	sodium	water
g.	propane	hydrogen	sodium	water

16. Which one of the following statements best explains why the boiling point of water is much higher than the boiling point of H_2S?

a. There are no intermolecular forces between water molecules, so they move faster than H_2S molecules.
b. Water molecules have a lower molar mass than H_2S molecules.
c. The strongest intermolecular force in water are dispersion forces.
d. Solid water is less dense than solid H_2S.
e. The strongest intermolecular force in water are hydrogen bonds which are much stronger than the intermolecular forces in H_2S.

(17.) For which of the following processes is ΔS positive?

    1. a solute dissolves in a solvent to make a solution
    2. carbon dioxide sublimes
    3. water freezes
    4. a container of gas is heated

    a. 3 only   c. 1 and 4   e. 2 and 4   g. 2 only   i. 1, 2 and 3
    b. 1 and 2   d. 2 and 3   f. 2, 3 and 4   h. 1, 2 and 4   j. all of them

(18.) At 298K, nitrogen gas reacts with hydrogen gas to produce ammonia gas. Is this spontaneous reaction enthalpy driven or entropy driven?

    a. enthalpy driven   b. entropy driven

19. Use the phase diagram below to identify the triple point, the normal boiling point, and the liquid phase.

	triple point	*normal boiling point*	*liquid phase*
a.	J	D	B
b.	D	G	C
c.	E	G	C
d.	D	F	B
e.	D	F	C
f.	E	G	A
g.	H	D	B
h.	H	F	C

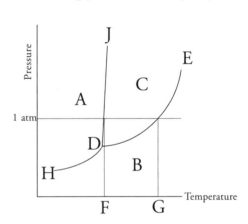

20. A solution made from two volatile liquids, benzene and toluene, has a normal boiling point of 98.6°C. The mole fraction of benzene in this solution is 0.30. Assuming ideal behavior, what must the vapor pressure of pure benzene be at 98.6°C if the vapor pressure of pure toluene is 0.70 atm at 98.6°C?

    a. 0.30 atm   c. 1.3 atm   e. 0.20 atm   g. 0.75 atm
    b. 1.0 atm   d. 0.50 atm   f. 1.5 atm   h. 1.7 atm

21. What is the *molality* (m) of a 15% by mass aqueous solution of ethylene glycol ($C_2H_6O_2$)? The molar mass of ethylene glycol is 62 g mol^{-1}.

    a. 2.85 m c. 3.65 m e. 4.47 m g. 0.71 m
    b. 2.14 m d. 4.02 m f. 0.61 m h. 1.82 m

22. Which one of the following aqueous solutions has the <u>lowest</u> freezing point?

    a. 0.25 m sodium sulfate
    b. 0.30 m ammonium nitrate
    c. 0.45 m potassium hydroxide
    d. 0.40 m acetic acid
    e. 0.35 m potassium chromate
    f. 0.50 m ammonia

EXAMINATION 3

CHEMISTRY 141 FALL 2007

Monday November 19th 2007

1. How many lone pair(s) of electrons are around the central atom in the following molecules or ions?

	SF_4	$HOCl$	PO_4^{3-}
a.	0	1	2
b.	0	2	1
c.	2	0	1
d.	2	1	0
e.	1	2	0
f.	1	0	2

2. What is the shape of the polyatomic ion ClF_4^+?

a.	tetrahedral	d.	bent	g.	trigonal bipyramidal
b.	square planar	e.	see-saw	h.	square pyramidal
c.	octahedral	f.	T-shaped	i.	trigonal pyramidal

3. What is the average bond order in the linear N_3^- ion?

a.	0.67	c.	1.33	e.	1.67	g.	3.0
b.	1.0	d.	1.5	f.	2.0	h.	4.0

4. What hybridization of atomic orbitals on the central atom of iodine trifluoride IF_3 is necessary to accommodate the arrangement of electron pairs on the iodine atom?

    a. sp b. sp^2 c. sp^3 d. sp^3d e. sp^3d^2

5. Resonance is...

    a. the fundamental frequency with which a molecule vibrates
    b. the rapid movement of electrons from one bond in a molecule to another
    c. the change in the character of a bond from single to double
    d. a way to reconcile Lewis structures with the real electronic structure of a molecule
    e. an alternating sequence of single and double bonds along a chain of carbon atoms

6. If a molecule was described as having a square-planar shape, how many lone pairs of electrons would you expect on the central atom of the molecule?

    a. 0   b. 1   c. 2   d. 3   e. 4   f. 5   g. 6

7. Which of the following molecules is/are polar?

    1. PH_3 2. SF_6 3. OF_2 4. $CHCl_3$

a.	1 only	e.	1 and 3	i.	1, 2 and 4
b.	2 only	f.	1 and 4	j.	1, 3 and 4
c.	3 only	g.	3 and 4		
d.	1 and 2	h.	1, 2 and 3		

8. What are the formal charges on the individual atoms in the structure for the thiocyanate ion shown below:

	C	N	S
a.	+1	+1	0
b.	+1	−1	−1
c.	+1	+1	−1
d.	0	−1	0
e.	0	+1	−2
f.	−1	+1	0
g.	−1	+1	−1

$$[:C\equiv N-\overset{..}{\underset{..}{S}}:]^-$$

9. How many of the hydrogen atoms in one molecule of cysteine (shown on the right) are capable of participating in a hydrogen bond?

a. 0   c. 2   e. 4   g. 6
b. 1   d. 3   f. 5   h. 7

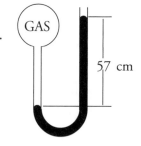

10. How many σ bonds are in one molecule of cysteine (shown above)?

a. zero   c. 5   e. 12   g. 14   i. 16
b. 1   d. 7   f. 13   h. 15   j. 18

11. A U-tube mercury manometer is open to the atmosphere (1 atm) on the right arm and is connected to a glass vessel containing a gas on the left arm as shown. The level of the mercury in the tube is 57 cm higher in the right arm. What is the pressure of the gas in the glass vessel?

a. 0.25 atm   c. 0.75 atm   e. 1.25 atm   g. 1.75 atm
b. 0.50 atm   d. 1.00 atm   f. 1.50 atm   h. 2.00 atm

12. A 5.0L vessel contains 3.0 moles helium, 4.0 moles nitrogen, and 3.0 moles oxygen. If the temperature is 25 °C, what is the partial pressure of each gas in the vessel?

	P_{He}	$P_{nitrogen}$	P_{oxygen}
a.	10.2 atm	14.7 atm	12.4 atm
b.	14.7 atm	19.6 atm	14.7 atm
c.	16.3 atm	16.3 atm	16.3 atm
d.	1.23 atm	1.64 atm	1.23 atm
e.	19.6 atm	14.4 atm	17.2 atm
f.	36.6 atm	48.9 atm	36.6 atm

13. A 6.0 liter vessel contains 2.0 moles of helium gas, 3.0 moles of argon gas, and 5.0 moles of neon gas at a total pressure of 20.0 atm. An additional 6.0 moles of argon gas is added to the mixture without changing the temperature or the volume (for a total of 9.0 moles of argon). What is the partial pressure of argon in the new mixture?

a. 3.0 atm   c. 9.0 atm   e. 12.0 atm   g. 18.0 atm   i. 24.0 atm
b. 6.0 atm   d. 10.0 atm   f. 15.0 atm   h. 20.0 atm   j. 26.0 atm

14. Nitric oxide (NO) and oxygen (O_2), are confined in two separate glass flasks connected by a tap. Initially, there is 4.0 L of NO at a pressure of 3.0 atm and 3.0 L of O_2 at 2.0 atm. The tap is opened, allowing the gases to mix and react. The reaction goes to completion producing as much nitrogen dioxide (NO_2) as possible according to the following equation. Assume that the temperature remains constant. What is the total pressure, in atm, in the system after the reaction?

$$2\,NO(g) \quad + \quad O_2(g) \quad \rightarrow \quad 2\,NO_2(g)$$

   a. 4/7 atm   c. 3/4 atm   e. 6/7 atm   g. 12/7 atm   i. 18/7 atm
   b. 5/7 atm   d. 7/8 atm   f. 1.0 atm   h. 2.0 atm   j. 24/7 atm

15. Water has several unusual or anomalous properties including a high boiling point, a high heat of vaporization, a high value for van der Waals constant $\underline{a}$, a high value for Trouton's constant ΔS_{vap}, etc. The predominant reason for these properties is...

   a. the small molar mass of H_2O
   b. the high abundance of water on the surface of this planet
   c. the strength of the bonds in the water molecule
   d. hydrogen bonding
   e. the high speed at which water molecules travel in the vapor state
   f. the high surface tension of liquid water

16. A cubic unit cell of a compound X and Y has four X atoms completely inside the unit cell. There is one Y atom on each corner, four Y atoms on the edges, two Y atoms on the faces, and one Y atom completely inside the unit cell. What is the stoichiometry of the compound?

   a. XY   c. XY_2 e. X_3Y g. X_3Y_2 i. X_5Y_4
   b. X_2Y d. XY_3 f. X_2Y_3 h. X_4Y_5 j. X_4Y_{15}

17. The Second Law of Thermodynamics can be expressed in many ways—including some of the statements below. Which statement is not an expression of the Second Law?

   a. All systems spontaneously approach equilibrium.
   b. For a spontaneous change, the entropy of the universe must increase.
   c. The change in the free energy of a system, ΔG, equals $\Delta H - T\Delta S$.
   d. For any spontaneous process, if the entropy of the system decreases then the entropy of the surroundings must increase.
   e. For any spontaneous process, ΔG must be negative.

18. Which one of the following aqueous salt solutions has the *highest* boiling point?

   a. 0.60 *m* magnesium nitrate $Mg(NO_3)_2$
   b. 0.70 *m* potassium nitrate KNO_3
   c. 0.50 *m* sodium sulfate Na_2SO_4
   d. 0.80 *m* sodium perchlorate $NaClO_4$
   e. 0.40 *m* sodium phosphate Na_3PO_4
   f. 0.80 *m* potassium permanganate $KMnO_4$

19. 368 grams of sulfuric acid H_2SO_4 is dissolved in enough water to make one liter of solution. The density of the solution is 1.230 g ml^{-1}. What is the *molality* of the solution?

   a. 0.75 *m*   c. 2.14 *m*   e. 3.05 *m*   g. 4.35 *m*
   b. 1.04 *m*   d. 2.82 *m*   f. 3.26 *m*   h. 4.60 *m*

(20.) Which of the following is caused by an increase in the entropy of a solution?

      I.   elevation of the boiling point
      II.   reduction of the freezing point
      III. lowering the vapor pressure

    a. I only   c. III only   e. I and III   g. I, II, and III
    b. II only   d. I and II   f. II and III

The last two questions (21 and 22) are written in pairs (a and b) and are worth five points each. Answer only one of each pair—you may choose which of each pair you answer—do not answer both! Make only one mark per line on your answer sheet! The first question of each pair is written specifically for students attending the 6:00 pm lectures by Prof. McHarris but you may answer either one of each pair regardless of which lecture you attend. The first question of each pair is based on the movie An Inconvenient Truth.

Answer either 21a or 21b:

21a.   If the Greenland icecap were to melt because of global warming, one of the first effects would be:

    a. Greenland would receive much greater rainfall.
    b. The Sahara would become less desolate.
    c. Polar bears would thrive on the newly uncovered ground in Greenland.
    d. Europe would turn into an icebox.
    e. Antarctica would absorb the released water, and its ice sheet would thicken.

21b.   The predominant reason why gases deviate from ideal behavior is because...

    f. molecules have a finite size
    g. molecules move fast in the gas state
    h. gases condense at low temperatures
    i. molecules attract one another
    j. kinetic energies depend only upon temperature

Answer either 22a or 22b:

22a.   Measuring the isotope ratios of oxygen in the bubbles captured in Antarctic ice cores allows scientists to determine:

    a. the increase of carbon dioxide in the atmosphere
    b. the extent of the rainfall in each year represented in the layers of the core
    c. the ratio of fresh water to salt water in the ice cores
    d. the temperature variation from year to year in the layers of ice
    e. whether or not Antarctica was ever forested

22b.   Which concentration unit is expressed in units of moles of solute per kilogram of solvent?

    f. mass fraction   h. mass percent   j. mole fraction
    g. molarity   i. molality

EXAMINATION 3

CHEMISTRY 141 SPRING 2008

Monday April 7th 2008

1. How many bonding pair(s) of electrons are around the central atom in ozone O_3?

    a. 1   c. 3   e. 5   g. 7
    b. 2   d. 4   f. 6   h. 8

2. Which of the following molecules / ions require resonance to reconcile the Lewis structure with the actual structure?

    I: CCl_4 II: CO_3^{2-} III: SO_3 IV: PO_4^{3-} V: BCl_3

    a. II and III   d. I, II, and III   g. III, IV, and V
    b. I and IV   e. II, III, and IV   h. II, III, IV, and V
    c. II and V   f. II, III, and V   i. I, II, III, IV, and V

3. What is the average bond order in the nitrite ion?

    a. 1.0   c. 1.5   e. 2.0   g. 2.5
    b. 1.33   d. 1.67   f. 2.33   h. 3.0

4. What is the shape of the molecule ClF_5?

    a. octahedral   d. square planar   g. square pyramidal
    b. T-shaped   e. see-saw   h. trigonal pyramidal
    c. tetrahedral   f. bent   i. trigonal bipyramidal

5. What is the change in hybridization (if any) of atomic orbitals on the boron atom according to the following reaction?

    $$BF_3 \; + \; NH_3 \; \rightarrow \; F_3B\text{--}NH_3$$

    a. sp to sp^3 d. sp to sp^2 g. sp to sp^3d
    b. sp^2 to sp^3 e. sp^3 to sp^3d h. sp^2 to sp^3d^2
    c. sp^2 to sp^3d f. sp^3 to sp^3d^2 i. there is no change in hybridization

6. Which one of the following statements is *false*?

    a. All linear molecules are nonpolar.
    b. A non polar molecule can have polar bonds.
    c. Water is a polar molecule.
    d. Propane (C_3H_8) is a nonpolar molecule.
    e. Sulfur trioxide is a nonpolar molecule.
    f. A carbon-fluorine bond is more polar than a carbon-bromine bond.

7. How many σ bonds and π bonds are there in the nitrogen molecule?

    a. two σ bonds   d. one σ and one π bond   g. one σ bond and two π bonds
    b. three σ bonds   e. two σ bonds and one π bond   h. two π bonds
    c. four σ bonds   f. three σ bonds and three π bonds i. three π bonds

8. A 3.0 L glass vessel contains helium gas at a pressure of 0.5 atm and a temperature of 25°C. Keeping the temperature constant, oxygen gas is added to the vessel until the total pressure is 2.5 atm. What is the partial pressure of oxygen gas in the vessel?

   a. 0.5 atm   c. 1.5 atm   e. 2.5 atm   g. 5.5 atm
   b. 1.0 atm   d. 2.0 atm   f. 3.0 atm   h. 6.0 atm

9. Suppose that there are two vessels connected by a tap that is closed. The first vessel is 3.0 L in volume and contains hydrogen gas as 1.0 atm pressure. The second vessel is 2.0 L in volume and contains nitrogen gas at 2.0 atm pressure. The tap is opened, the gases mix, and react to form as much ammonia as possible. Assume the gases are ideal and the temperature is constant. What is the total pressure in the apparatus at the end of the reaction?

$$3 H_2(g) + N_2(g) \rightarrow 2 NH_3(g)$$

   a. 1/5 atm   c. 3/5 atm   e. 1.0 atm   g. 2.0 atm
   b. 2/5 atm   d. 4/5 atm   f. 7/5 atm   h. 3.0 atm

10. In an effusion experiment, it takes 1.0 mole of chlorine gas 4.0 minutes to effuse through a small hole. Under the same conditions, how long would it take for 1.0 mole of neon gas to effuse through the same hole?

    a. 0.13 min   c. 2.1 min   e. 4.4 min   g. 7.5 min
    b. 0.47 min   d. 3.6 min   f. 6.2 min   h. 9.1 min

11. Which one of the following molecules would you expect to have the lowest boiling point?

    a. H_2O b. H_2S c. H_2Se d. H_2Te e. H_2Po

12. In how many of these substances would you expect hydrogen bonding to play a significant role?

    H_2CO HF OF_2 PH_3 CH_3Cl H_2O NH_2NH_2 C_2H_6

    a. none   c. 2   e. 4   g. 6   i. 8
    b. 1   d. 3   f. 5   h. 7

13. In the cubic crystal system, a structural unit on the corner of a unit cell is shared among how many unit cells?

    a. none   c. 2   e. 4   g. 6   i. 8
    b. 1   d. 3   f. 5   h. 7

14. Determine the sign for the change in entropy (ΔS) for each of these processes.
    Choose the row in which all responses are correct.

	Liquid bromine vaporizes	A block of lead melts	Sugar dissolves in water
a.	+	+	+
b.	+	+	−
c.	+	−	+
d.	+	−	−
e.	−	+	+
f.	−	+	−
g.	−	−	+
h.	−	−	−

15. The sublimation of carbon dioxide is a spontaneous process at 298K. What are the signs for ΔH, ΔS, and ΔG for this reaction at 298K?

	ΔH	ΔS	ΔG
a.	−	+	+
b.	−	+	−
c.	−	−	+
d.	−	−	−
e.	+	+	+
f.	+	+	−
g.	+	−	+
h.	+	−	−

16. Which one of the following statements about the phase diagram of carbon (shown on the right) is correct?

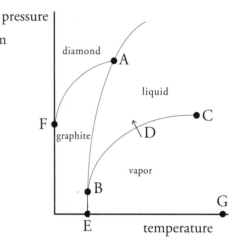

  a. The solid state of carbon exists in two phases.
  b. There is only one triple point in this phase diagram.
  c. Point A is the critical point.
  d. Letter D (arrow) represents a phase change where both ΔH and ΔS are positive.
  e. At constant temperature (point G), increasing the pressure will cause carbon to undergo a phase change.
  f. ΔG is negative at point B.

17. A solution is 30% by mass solute and 70% by mass solvent. The density of the solution is 1.19 g mL^{-1}, and the molar mass of the solute is 90 g mol^{-1}. What is the molarity (M) of this solution?

  a. 5.5 M   c. 4.0 M   e. 2.5 M   g. 1.5 M
  b. 4.5 M   d. 3.0 M   f. 2.0 M   h. 1.0 M

18. What is the *molality* (*m*) of the solution described in question 17?

  a. 0.013 *m*   c. 1.09 *m*   e. 3.52 *m*   g. 8.43 *m*
  b. 0.210 *m*   d. 3.17 *m*   f. 4.76 *m*   h. 11.1 *m*

19. Which one of the following statements is true when you heat water to 100°C at a pressure of 1 atm?

  a. $\Delta G = 0$
  b. $\Delta S = 0$
  c. $\Delta H = 0$
  d. The change of state is an endothermic process
  e. The system becomes more ordered
  f. You cause an enthalpy-driven reaction

20. Which one of the following aqueous solutions would you expect to have the *lowest* freezing point?

  a. 1.5 *m* HCl   d. 3.0 *m* NH$_3$ g. 2.0 *m* HF
  b. 0.5 *m* NaCl   e. 0.65 *m* MgBr$_2$ h. 1.5 *m* NaOH
  c. 0.4 *m* sugar   f. 1.2 *m* KCl   i. 1.0 *m* Na$_3$PO$_4$

The last two questions (21 and 22) *are written in pairs* (a and b) *and are worth five points each. Answer only one of each pair - you may choose which of each pair you answer - do not answer both! Make only one mark per line on your answer sheet! The first question of each pair is written specifically for students attending the 4:00 pm lecture by Prof. McHarris but you may answer either one of each pair regardless of which lecture you attend. The first question in each pair is based on the movie* An Incovenient Truth.

Answer either 21a or 21b:

21a.   If the Greenland icecap were to melt because of global warming, one of the first effects would be:

   a.   Greenland would receive much greater rainfall.
   b.   The Sahara would become less desolate.
   c.   Polar bears would thrive on the newly uncovered ground in Greenland.
   d.   Europe would turn into an icebox.
   e.   Antarctica would absorb the released water, and its ice sheet would thicken.

21b.   How many electrons (dots) would be included in the Lewis dot symbol for the sulfide ion?

   f.   2   g.   6   h.   8   i.   14   j.   18

Answer either 22a or 22b:

22a.   The narrator of *An Inconvenient Truth* is

   a.   Barack Obama   c.   John McCain   e.   Hillary Clinton
   b.   Al Gore   d.   George W. Bush

22b.   A 4.5 L vessel contains 2.0 moles of oxygen gas at a temperature of 25°C. What is the pressure, in atm, of the oxygen gas?

   f.   0.9 atm   h.   8.4 atm   j.   55.0 atm
   g.   1.7 atm   i.   10.9 atm

EXAMINATION 3
CHEMISTRY 141 FALL 2008
Monday November 24th 2008

The first four questions are worth 5 points each; the remaining 16 questions are worth 10 points each. The total number of points possible is 180.

1. How many valence shell electron pairs are there around the phosphorus atom in the molecule $POCl_3$?

    a. 1   b. 2   c. 3   d. 4   e. 5   f. 6

2. What is the arrangement of bonding and non-bonding electron pairs around the central atom in the molecule SF_4?

    a. linear   c. trigonal planar   e. tetrahedral
    b. trigonal bipyramidal   d. octahedral

3. According to the ideal gas equation, the volume of an ideal gas is directly proportional to

    I.   the density of the gas
    II. the pressure of the gas
    III. the temperature of the gas
    IV. the number of moles of the gas

    a. I   c. III   e. I and II   g. I and III   i. II and III
    b. II   d. IV   f. II and IV   h. III and IV   j. I, III and IV

4. Of all the van der Waals forces of intermolecular attraction, which one is the strongest and most significant from a biological point of view?

    a. London dispersion forces
    b. Dipole-dipole attraction
    c. Hydrogen bonding

5. In the following pairs of molecules, one molecule is polar and the other molecule is nonpolar. Determine which one of each pair is the polar molecule. *Choose the line where all responses are correct.*

	BeF_2 and SF_2	BF_3 and BrF_3	CCl_4 and SCl_4
a.	BeF_2	BF_3	CCl_4
b.	BeF_2	BF_3	SCl_4
c.	BeF_2	BrF_3	CCl_4
d.	BeF_2	BrF_3	SCl_4
e.	SF_2	BF_3	CCl_4
f.	SF_2	BF_3	SCl_4
g.	SF_2	BrF_3	CCl_4
h.	SF_2	BrF_3	SCl_4

6. How many π bonding *pairs* of electrons are there in a benzene (C_6H_6) molecule?

    a. none   c. 2   e. 4   g 6
    b. 1   d. 3   f. 5

7. Based upon the formal charges on the three atoms, rank the following Lewis dot structures of the cyanate ion (OCN^-) in the order: best > not so bad > worst.

$$[\ddot{O}=C=\ddot{N}]^- \qquad [:\ddot{O}-C\equiv N:]^- \qquad [:O\equiv C-\ddot{N}:]^-$$

   1   2   3

	best	not so bad	worst
a.	1	2	3
b.	1	3	2
c.	2	1	3
d.	2	3	1
e.	3	1	2
f.	3	2	1

8. Consider the xenon compounds shown. What is the hybridization of atomic orbitals on the xenon atom in each molecule?

	XeF_2	XeF_4	XeO_4
a.	sp	sp^3	sp^3
b.	sp	sp^3	sp^3d^2
c.	sp^2	sp^3	sp^3
d.	sp^3	sp^3	sp^3d^2
e.	sp^3	sp^3d	sp^3
f.	sp^3d	sp^3d	sp^3d^2
g.	sp^3d	sp^3d^2	sp^3
h.	sp^3d	sp^3d^2	sp^3d
i.	sp^3d^2	sp^3d^2	sp^3d^2

9. A U-tube mercury manometer connects two vessels. One vessel contains Gas A at a pressure of 5 atm. The difference in the heights of the mercury in the two sides of the manometer is 38 cm. What is the pressure of Gas B in the second vessel?

   a. 342 torr   c. 418 torr   e. 3762 torr   g. 3838 torr
   b. 380 torr   d. 3420 torr   f. 3800 torr   h. 4180 torr

10. 5 moles of hydrogen gas effuses through a small hole in 60 seconds. How long does it take for 5 moles of oxygen gas to effuse through the same hole under the same conditions?

   a. 3.8 s   c. 30 s   e. 90 s   g. 4 min
   b. 15 s   d. 45 s   f. 2.0 min   h. 16 min

11. A molecular compound with strong intermolecular forces of attraction would be expected to have

   a. a low boiling point   d. a high melting point
   b. a high vapor pressure   e. a low value for van der Waals constant $\underline{a}$
   c. a low heat of vaporization

12. A 20 liter vessel contains 2.0 moles of helium gas, 3.0 moles of argon gas, and 5.0 moles of neon gas at a total pressure of 15.0 atm.

   A. What is the partial pressure of helium?

   An additional 5.0 moles of argon gas is added to the mixture without changing the temperature or the volume.

   B. What is the partial pressure of helium in the new mixture?

   Now an additional 4.0 moles of helium is added to the mixture without changing the temperature or the volume.

   C. What is the partial pressure of helium now?

P_{He}:	A	B	C
a.	2.0 atm	2.0 atm	6.0 atm
b.	3.0 atm	2.0 atm	4.0 atm
c.	3.0 atm	2.0 atm	6.0 atm
d.	3.0 atm	3.0 atm	6.0 atm
e.	3.0 atm	3.0 atm	9.0 atm
f.	4.0 atm	4.0 atm	8.0 atm
g.	4.0 atm	4.0 atm	12 atm

13. In the unit cell of an unknown compound of two elements A and B shown on the right, the black spheres on the top and bottom faces and the edges represent A atoms, and the shaded spheres represent B atoms. What is the stoichiometry of the compound?

   a. AB   c. A_3B e. A_2B g. A_2B_3
   b. AB_2 d. A_3B_2 f. AB_3 h. A_7B_8

14. What must be true for a system undergoing an endothermic spontaneous change?

	ΔG_{sys}	ΔH_{sys}	ΔS_{sys}			ΔG_{sys}	ΔH_{sys}	ΔS_{sys}
a.	+	+	+		e.	−	+	+
b.	+	+	−		f.	−	+	−
c.	+	−	+		g.	−	−	+
d.	+	−	−		h.	−	−	−

15. A vapor pressure curve...

   a. indicates that the vapor pressure of a liquid is zero at the triple point
   b. starts at the triple point and ends at the critical point
   c. shows that the vapor pressure decreases as the temperature increases
   d. separates those conditions on a phase diagram where the liquid state and the solid state are stable
   e. crosses the 1 atm pressure line at the freezing point
   f. is almost vertical on a PV phase diagram illustrating that liquids are incompressible

16. Calculate the molarity (M) and molality (m) of a 20% by mass aqueous sodium chloride solution. The density of this solution is 1.148 g mL^{-1} at 25°C. *Choose the row in which both responses are correct.*

	molarity (M)	molality (m)		molarity (M)	molality (m)
a.	0.250	0.300	e.	4.28	3.93
b.	0.300	0.250	f.	3.93	4.28
c.	0.254	0.234	g.	3.42	6.15
d.	0.234	0.254	h.	6.15	3.42

17. A solution is made by dissolving 50.0 g sucrose (molecular formula $C_{12}H_{22}O_{11}$, a nonvolatile solute, molar mass 342.3 g mol^{-1}) in 100 g water. What is the vapor pressure of water over this solution if the vapor pressure of pure water at the same temperature is 71.9 torr?

a.	1.84 torr	c.	54.3 torr	e.	71.9 torr	g.	86.2 torr
b.	24.0 torr	d.	70.1 torr	f.	73.8 torr	h.	97.4 torr

18. Arrange these aqueous solutions in order of *decreasing* freezing point (highest freezing point to lowest freezing point):

   0.15 m Na_2SO_4

   0.10 m NaBr

   0.10 m $Mg(NO_3)_2$

   0.30 m HCl

   a. Na_2SO_4 > HCl > $Mg(NO_3)_2$ > NaBr
   b. NaBr > $Mg(NO_3)_2$ > Na_2SO_4 > HCl
   c. HCl > Na_2SO_4 > NaBr > $Mg(NO_3)_2$
   d. NaBr > $Mg(NO_3)_2$ > HCl > Na_2SO_4
   e. NaBr > Na_2SO_4 > $Mg(NO_3)_2$ > HCl
   f. Na_2SO_4 > NaBr > HCl > $Mg(NO_3)_2$

19. A catalyst...

   a. increases the amount of product at equilibrium
   b. is not involved chemically in the reaction
   c. changes the route the reaction takes between reactants and products
   d. increases the activation energy required in the reaction
   e. increases the kinetic energy of the reactant molecules
   f. shifts the equilibrium state toward the product side
   g. must be continually replenished as it is used up in the reaction

20. An ideal solution consists of 4 moles of butanol (vapor pressure at room temperature = 12.5 torr) and 5 moles of ethanol (vapor pressure at room temperature = 59 torr). What is the mole fraction of ethanol *in the vapor* above the liquid at room temperature? Consider the butanol and ethanol *vapor* only—i.e. we're not concerned about any air originally present.

a.	0.10	c.	0.25	e.	0.45	g.	0.60	i.	0.80
b.	0.15	d.	0.30	f.	0.55	h.	0.70	j.	0.85

EXAMINATION 3

CHEMISTRY 141 SPRING 2009

Monday April 20th 2009

The first four questions are worth 5 points each; the remaining 16 questions are worth 10 points each. The total number of points possible is 180.

1. How many lone pair(s) of electrons are around the central atom in xenon difluoride XeF_2?

    a. 0   c. 2   e. 4   g. 6
    b. 1   d. 3   f. 5   h. 7

2. How many π (pi) bonds are in one molecule of tetracyanoethylene?

    a. 2   c. 4   e. 6   g. 8   i. 14
    b. 3   d. 5   f. 7   h. 9   j. 18

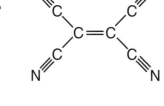

3. The phase diagram for a single substance is illustrated on the right. Which set of choices below represents the correct assignment of labels?

	critical point	*liquid state*	*normal melting point*
a.	F	C	I
b.	D	C	H
c.	F	A	I
d.	E	B	H
e.	E	A	I
f.	D	B	H
g.	F	B	I
h.	D	A	H

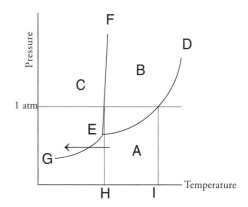

4. In the phase diagram shown in question 3, what are the signs for ΔH and ΔS moving from area A to area C (as indicated by the arrow)?

	ΔH	ΔS			ΔH	ΔS
a.	+	+		c.	−	−
b.	+	−		d.	−	+

Use the following choices to answer questions 5 and 6:

    a. NO_2^+ c. SO_3 e. CH_4 g. BCl_3
    b. SO_3^{2-} d. H_2S f. I_3^- h. XeF_4

5. Which one of the molecules / ions has a tetrahedral electron pair arrangement and a trigonal pyramidal shape?

6. In which of the molecules / ions are the valence atomic orbitals on the central atom sp^3d hybridized?

7. What is the average bond order in the ozone molecule O_3?

    a. 1.0   c. 1.5   e. 2.0   g. 3.0
    b. 1.33   d. 1.67   f. 2.5   h. 4.0

8. How many of the molecules shown below are polar?

    BF_3 CCl_4 CO_2 NH_3 SF_6 BrF_5

    a. 0   c. 2   e. 4   g. 6
    b. 1   d. 3   f. 5

9. Use the bond energies given below to calculate the change in enthalpy (ΔH) for this reaction:

    $CO(g)$ + $Cl_2(g)$ $\rightarrow$ $COCl_2(g)$ C–O   358 kJ mol^{-1}
                                                             C=O   732 kJ mol^{-1}
                                                             C O   1072 kJ mol^{-1}
                                                             Cl–Cl 242 kJ mol^{-1}
                                                             C–Cl   339 kJ mol^{-1}

    a. –96 kJ   c. –278 kJ   e. –436 kJ   g. –810 kJ
    b. +96 kJ   d. +278 kJ   f. +436 kJ   h. +810 kJ

10. Consider a triple bond between two atoms. If the internuclear axis is the y-axis, which of the following orbitals could overlap to form a p (pi) bond?

    a. p_y and p_y c. p_y and d_{xy} e. s and p_x g. p_y and p_z
    b. s and p_y d. p_x and p_x f. p_z and d_{xz} h. p_y and p_x

11. A greenish-yellow gaseous compound of chlorine and oxygen has a density of 7.71 g L^{-1} at 36°C and a pressure of 2.88 atm. What is the molecular formula of this compound?

    a. ClO c. ClO_2 e. ClO_3 g. ClO_4
    b. Cl_2O d. Cl_3O f. Cl_4O h. Cl_2O_3

12. Suppose that there are two vessels connected by a tap that is closed. The first vessel is 1.0 L in volume and contains acetylene C_2H_2 gas at 2.0 atm pressure. The second vessel is 3.0 L in volume and contains oxygen gas at 1.0 atm pressure. The tap is opened, the gases mix, and react to form as much carbon dioxide gas and water vapor as possible. Assume the gases are ideal and the temperature is constant. What is the total pressure in the apparatus at the end of the reaction?

    $2 C_2H_2(g)$ + $5 O_2(g)$ $\rightarrow$ $4 CO_2(g)$ + $2 H_2O(g)$

    a. 1.1 atm   c. 2.75 atm   e. 0.9 atm   g. 1.25 atm
    b. 1.2 atm   d. 1.75 atm   f. 0.6 atm   h. 1.0 atm

13. Suppose a new temperature scale (°A) was invented for which 20°A is the freezing point of water and 170°A is the boiling point of water. What is the normal human body temperature (98.6°F) on the new scale?

    a. 19°A   c. 45°A   e. 76°A   g. 111°A
    b. 25°A   d. 56°A   f. 90°A   h. 141°A

14. It takes 2.0 minutes for 0.1 mol of helium gas to effuse through a small hole. At the same temperature, how long would it take for 0.1 mol of the toxic gas phosphine PH_3 to effuse through the same hole?

    a. 0.24 minutes   c. 0.69 minutes   e. 5.8 minutes   g. 15 minutes
    b. 0.58 minutes   d. 1.5 minutes   f. 6.9 minutes   h. 17 minutes

15. Consider the five substances ethane C_2H_6, methanol CH_3OH, hydrogen H_2, water, and sodium chloride at the same temperature. Arrange these substances in order of increasing melting or boiling point.

a.	C_2H_6	CH_3OH	H_2	H_2O	NaCl
b.	H_2	C_2H_6	CH_3OH	H_2O	NaCl
c.	NaCl	H_2O	CH_3OH	C_2H_6	H_2
d.	H_2	H_2O	CH_3OH	C_2H_6	NaCl
e.	H_2	H_2O	C_2H_6	CH_3OH	NaCl
f.	CH_3OH	H_2O	H_2	C_2H_6	NaCl

16. Amino acids are molecules capable of forming hydrogen bonds. Which hydrogen atom(s) in histidine (shown to the right) is / are capable of forming hydrogen bonds?

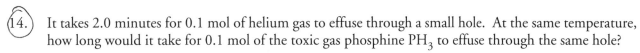

    a. A, B, C   f. B, C, D
    b. F, B   g. A, D, F
    c. G, E   h. C, D, F
    d. E, F, G   i. B, E, G
    e. B, G   j. all of them

17. Gold crystallizes in a face-centered cubic unit cell. How many gold atoms are in one unit cell?

    a. 1   c. 3   e. 5   g. 7   i. 10
    b. 2   d. 4   f. 6   h. 8   j. 12

18. Carbonated water is made by dissolving carbon dioxide gas in water. What are the signs for ΔG, ΔH, and ΔS for this process?

	ΔG	ΔH	ΔS			ΔG	ΔH	ΔS
a.	+	+	+		e.	−	+	+
b.	+	+	−		f.	−	+	−
c.	+	−	+		g.	−	−	+
d.	+	−	−		h.	−	−	−

19. How many grams of sodium chloride must be dissolved in 250 mL water to make a 0.35 m solution? The density of water is 1.0 g mL^{-1}.

    a. 3.61 g   c. 9.50 g   e. 26.3 g   g. 71.4 g
    b. 5.11 g   d. 14.7 g   f. 41.7 g   h. 87.5 g

20. Which one of the following aqueous solutions has the highest boiling point?

    a. 0.60 m Na_3PO_4 c. 0.80 m $KMnO_4$ e. 1.35 m CH_3CO_2H g. 2.0 m NH_3
    b. 0.50 m NaCl   d. 0.75 m $NaClO_4$ f. 0.40 m H_2SO_4 h. 1.1 m HF

FINAL EXAMINATION

CHEMISTRY 141 FALL 2004

Thursday December 16th 2004

1.   An atom has 42 neutrons and 36 electrons and has a charge of -3. What is the correct symbol for the element?

    a. Co   c. Mo   e. Y   g. As
    b. Kr   d. Rh   f. Zn   h. C

2.   What is the correct formula for the salt calcium hydrogen carbonate?

    a. $CaHCO_2$ c. Ca_2HCO_3 e. $Ca_3(HCO_3)_2$ g. $Ca(CO_3)_2$
    b. $CaHCO_3$ d. $Ca(HCO_3)_2$ f. $Ca_2(HCO_3)_3$ h. $CaCO_3$

3.   Which statement is *incorrect*?

    a. All compounds are made of elements
    b. A solution is a homogeneous mixture
    c. All binary compounds contain just two atoms
    d. Isotopes of an element have different mass numbers
    e. The halogens exist naturally as diatomic molecules
    f. Mass is conserved in a chemical reaction
    g. Mass is an extensive property

4.   Which of the following compounds is an ionic compound?

    a. NH_3 c. CO   e. LiCl   g. C_2H_6
    b. CH_4 d. O_3 f. N_2O_4 h. F_2

5.   What is the mass, in grams, of 3.00 moles of magnesium phosphate?

    a. 87.6 g   c. 333.5 g   e. 503.7 g   g. 692.6 g   i. 978.3 g
    b. 262.9 g   d. 357.8 g   f. 642.8 g   h. 788.6 g   j. 1000 g

6.   A can of soda contains 39 grams of sugar ($C_{12}H_{22}O_{11}$, molar mass = 342 g mol^{-1}). How many hydrogen atoms are there in all the sugar molecules in one can of soda?

    a. 6.9×10^{22} c. 1.5×10^{24} e. 5.2×10^{26} g. 4.2×10^{-24}
    b. 1.4×10^{23} d. 3.7×10^{26} f. 1.9×10^{-25} h. 1.0×10^{-21}

7.   An oxide of gadolinium (atomic number 64) contains 86.76% Gd by mass. What is the empirical formula of the compound?

    a. GdO   c. GdO_2 e. Gd_2O_2 g. Gd_2O_3 i. Gd_4O_3
    b. $GdO_{1.5}$ d. GdO_3 f. Gd_3O_2 h. Gd_3O_4 j. Gd_4O_6

8. Ammonia reacts with fluorine gas to produce dinitrogen tetrafluoride and hydrogen fluoride. Write the balanced equation. How many moles of ammonia are needed to react completely with 2.0 moles of fluorine?

    a. 0.20 mol   c. 0.70 mol   e. 2.0 mol   g. 4.0 mol
    b. 0.40 mol   d. 0.80 mol   f. 2.4 mol   h. 5.0 mol

9. Benzene C_6H_6 burns in oxygen to produce carbon dioxide and water. Write an equation for this reaction and balance the equation using whole number coefficients. What is the coefficient for water in the equation?

    a. 1   c. 3   e. 5   g. 7   i. 9
    b. 2   d. 4   f. 6   h. 8   j. 12

10. Nitrous oxide reacts with oxygen to produce nitrogen dioxide according to the equation:

    $$2\,N_2O \;+\; 3\,O_2 \;\rightarrow\; 4\,NO_2$$

    If 5.0 moles of nitrous oxide reacts with 8.0 moles of oxygen, how many moles of what reactant are left at the end of the reaction unused?

    a. 0.5 mol N_2O f. 0.5 mol O_2
    b. 1.0 mol N_2O g. 1.0 mol O_2
    c. 1.5 mol N_2O h. 1.5 mol O_2
    d. 2.0 mol N_2O i. 2.0 mol O_2
    e. 2.5 mol N_2O j. 2.5 mol O_2

11. What is the molarity (M) of a 1.25 L aqueous solution containing 238.7 g cobalt(II) chloride?

    a. 0.44 M c. 0.68 M e. 1.47 M g. 2.00 M
    b. 0.55 M d. 1.30 M f. 1.84 M h. 2.30 M

12. What description is correct for the reaction: $2\,Mg \;+\; CO_2 \;\rightarrow\; 2\,MgO \;+\; C$

	oxidation no. of C in CO_2	element that is oxidized	reducing agent
a.	+4	Mg	CO_2
b.	+4	C	CO_2
c.	+4	Mg	Mg
d.	+2	Mg	Mg
e.	+2	C	CO_2
f.	−4	Mg	Mg
g.	−4	C	CO_2
h.	−4	Mg	CO_2

13. Identify all the spectator ions in the following reaction:

    $$HCN(aq) \;+\; KOH(aq) \;\rightarrow\; KCN(aq) \;+\; H_2O(l)$$

    a. H^+ d. CN^- g. K^+ and OH^-
    b. OH^- e. H^+ and OH^- h. H^+ and CN^-
    c. K^+ f. K^+ and CN^- i. K^+, CN^- and OH^-

14.   What are the oxidation numbers for sodium, phosphorus, and oxygen in the compound $Na_5P_3O_{10}$?

Choose the row in which all the numbers are correct.

	Na	P	O
a.	+1	+5	−2
b.	+5	+15	−20
c.	+1	−1	+2
d.	+5	+3	+10
e.	+1	−3	−2
f.	+1	+3	−2
g.	−1	+5	+2
h.	−1	+15	−1

15.   A system consisting of a movable piston in a cylinder gains 800 J of heat. The piston moves up and does 450 J of work on the surroundings. What is the change in the internal energy ΔE of the system?

a. −350 J   c. −450 J   e. −800 J   g. −1250 J
b. +350 J   d. +450 J   f. +800 J   h. +1250 J

16.   20 g of steam at 100°C is bubbled into a mixture of 50 g of water and 200 g of ice at 0°C where all the steam condenses to water. What is the composition of the system at the end?

Specific heat of water = 4.184 J K^{-1} g^{-1}
Latent heat of fusion of ice = 333 J g^{-1}
Latent heat of vaporization of water = 2260 J g^{-1}

	water	ice
a.	75 g	175 g
b.	89 g	161 g
c.	95 g	175 g
d.	109 g	161 g
e.	156 g	114 g
f.	186 g	64 g
g.	206 g	64 g
h.	211 g	39 g
i.	231 g	39 g
j.	248 g	22 g

17.   Calculate the enthalpy change for the reaction:

$$NO(g) + O(g) \rightarrow NO_2(g) \qquad\qquad \Delta H° = ?$$

from the following information:

$$NO(g) + O_3(g) \rightarrow NO_2(g) + O_2(g) \qquad \Delta H° = -199 \text{ kJ}$$

$$O_3(g) \rightarrow 1.5\, O_2(g) \qquad\qquad \Delta H° = -142 \text{ kJ}$$

$$O_2(g) \rightarrow 2\, O(g) \qquad\qquad \Delta H° = +494 \text{ kJ}$$

a. −588 kJ   c. −304 kJ   e. +150 kJ   g. +353 kJ   i. +190 kJ
b. −552 kJ   d. −57 kJ   f. +153 kJ   h. +437 kJ   j. +94 kJ

18. For which substance does the standard enthalpy of formation ΔH_f° equal zero?

    a. $O_2(l)$ c. $CH_4(g)$ e. $NO(g)$ g. $Cl_2(g)$ i. $H(g)$
    b. $H_2O(l)$ d. $Ne(l)$ f. $K(g)$ h. $NH_3(g)$ j. $Fe(l)$

19. Which one of the following sets of quantum numbers is invalid for an electron of a calcium atom in its ground state?

	n	l	m_l
a.	1	0	0
b.	2	0	0
c.	2	1	−1
d.	2	1	0
e.	3	2	0
f.	3	1	+1
g.	3	1	−1
h.	4	0	0

20. Which element has the ground state electron configuration $1s^2\, 2s^2\, 2p^6\, 3s^2\, 3p^6\, 4s^2\, 3d^{10}\, 4p^4$?

    a. Se   c. S   e. Sb   g. Br
    b. Cr   d. Te   f. As   h. Ar

21. Start with the number of protons in the nucleus of a lithium atom
    ...multiply by the number of 3s electrons in a magnesium atom
    ...add the number of unpaired electrons in an oxygen atom in its ground state
    ...subtract the number of π orbitals in a triple bond
    ...add the number of neutrons in the nucleus of the isotope ^{14}C ...What's the result?

    a. 6   c. 10   e. 12   g. 14   i. 18
    b. 8   d. 11   f. 13   h. 15   j. 20

22. Of the elements

    a. Li   c. Be   e. C   g. O   i. F
    b. K   d. Ca   f. Ge   h. Se   j. Br

    which element is the most metallic in character and has the largest atomic radius?

23. Draw the *best* Lewis structure for the dicyanamide ion NCN^{2-}. What is the average bond order of the CN bonds in the dicyanamide ion?

    a. 1   c. 1.5   e. 2.0   g. 3.0
    b. 1.33   d. 1.67   f. 2.5

24. What is the shape of the ion ClF_4^-?

    a. linear   d. trigonal planar   g. tetrahedral
    b. trigonal pyramidal e. square planar   h. octahedral
    c. T-shaped   f. see-saw   i. square pyramidal

25. What is the hybridization of atomic orbitals on the beryllium atom in the molecule $BeCl_2$?

    a. sp
    b. sp^2

    c. sp^3
    d. sp^3d

    e. sp^3d^2

26. What is the ONO bond angle in the nitrite ion NO_2^-?

    a. 180°
    b. slightly less than 180°
    c. slightly more than 120°
    d. 120°

    e. slightly less than 120°
    f. slightly more than 109°
    g. 109°
    h. slightly less than 109°

27. A 10.0 L vessel contains nitrogen gas at 5.0 atm pressure and 25°C. Without changing the volume or the temperature, oxygen gas is introduced into the vessel until the total pressure equals 7.5 atm. Then, again without changing the volume or the temperature, more nitrogen gas is introduced into the vessel until the total pressure equals 15.0 atm. What is the partial pressure of nitrogen gas in the vessel at the end?

    a. 2.50 atm
    b. 5.00 atm

    c. 7.50 atm
    d. 10.0 atm

    e. 12.5 atm
    f. 15.0 atm

    g. 17.5 atm
    h. 20.0 atm

    i. 25.0 atm
    j. 30.0 atm

28. For which of the following processes does the entropy (of the process) increase?

    1. Water freezes to form ice.
    2. Ethanol and water are mixed to make a solution.
    3. A gas is cooled down.
    4. Gasoline (C_8H_{18}) is burned to produce carbon dioxide and water.

    a. only 1
    b. only 2

    c. only 3
    d. only 4

    e. 2 and 3
    f. 1 and 4

    g. 2 and 4
    h. 2, 3, and 4

    i. none
    j. all

29. Two gases, nitrous oxide (N_2O) and oxygen (O_2), are confined in two separate glass flasks, connected by a tap of negligible volume. Initially, there is 4.0 L of N_2O at a pressure of 2.0 atm and 6.0 L of O_2 at 3.0 atm. The tap is opened, allowing the gases to mix and react. Assume constant temperature and that the reaction goes to completion, producing as much nitrogen dioxide (NO_2) as possible according to the following equation. What is the total pressure, in atm, in the system after the reaction?

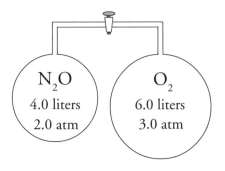

$$2\,N_2O\,(g) + 3\,O_2\,(g) \rightarrow 4\,NO_2\,(g)$$

    a. 1/5 atm
    b. 2/5 atm

    c. 3/5 atm
    d. 4/5 atm

    e. 1.0 atm
    f. 7/5 atm

    g. 9/5 atm
    h. 2.0 atm

    i. 11/5 atm
    j. 14/5 atm

30. Lead oxide crystallizes in the tetragonal system and has the unit cell illustrated. The oxygen atoms are the larger spheres and are on the faces of the unit cell. The lead ions are the smaller circles and have the positions illustrated. What is the stoichiometry of the oxide?

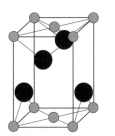

lead
oxygen

    a. PbO
    b. PbO_2

    c. Pb_2O
    d. Pb_3O_2

    e. PbO_3
    f. Pb_2O_3

    g. Pb_5O_2
    h. Pb_5O_4

31. A spontaneous endothermic reaction occurs within a system. What are the signs of ΔG, ΔH, and ΔS?

	ΔG_{sys}	ΔH_{sys}	ΔS_{sys}
a.	+	+	+
b.	+	+	−
c.	+	−	+
d.	+	−	−
e.	−	+	+
f.	−	+	−
g.	−	−	+
h.	−	−	−

32. When an aqueous solution contains a nonvolatile solute such as sodium chloride, the boiling point of the solution is raised above 100°C. If the solution of sodium chloride is heated to its boiling point under standard conditions, what is the vapor pressure of the solution at its boiling point?

a. 0.90 atm
b. 0.95 atm
c. 1.00 atm
d. 1.05 atm
e. 1.10 atm
f. it depends upon the concentration of the sodium chloride

33. What is the freezing point of a solution made by dissolving 3.50 g of potassium chloride in 100 g of water? K_f for water = 1.86 K m^{-1}.

a. −0.50°C
b. −0.87°C
c. −0.94°C
d. −1.30°C
e. −1.75°C
f. −2.62°C
g. −3.49°C
h. −5.10°C

34. The equilibrium constant K for the following reaction is 16.00.

$$H_2(g) \; + \; CO_2(g) \; \rightleftharpoons \; H_2O(g) \; + \; CO(g)$$

Initially, 0.25 moles each of H_2 and CO_2 are injected into an 1.0 liter flask. Calculate the concentration of the $CO_2(g)$ at equilibrium.

a. 0.02 *M*   c. 0.08 *M*   e. 0.12 *M*   g. 0.20 *M*   i. 0.30 *M*
b. 0.05 *M*   d. 0.10 *M*   f. 0.15 *M*   h. 0.25 *M*   j. 0.33 *M*

35. Which statement is *false*?

a. An acid is called *strong* if it is stronger than the hydronium ion H_3O^+.
b. Potassium cyanide is a strong electrolyte.
c. HNO_2 is a weak acid.
d. At 25°C, the lower the pH, the more acidic the solution.
e. A neutral solution is one in which $[H_3O^+] = [OH^-]$.
f. The pH of pure water decreases if the temperature is raised.
g. Salts of weak acids or bases hydrolyze in aqueous solution.
h. The conjugate partner of a strong acid is a strong base.

36. Consider the following disturbances on the equilibrium system shown. In which, if any, direction will the system shift to restore equilibrium in each case? The reaction is exothermic in the forward direction.

$$4NH_3(g) \; + \; 3O_2(g) \; \rightleftharpoons \; 2N_2(g) \; + \; 6H_2O(g)$$

	increase pressure	decrease temperature	add more $O_2(g)$	remove $N_2(g)$
a.	left	right	right	right
b.	left	right	left	left
c.	left	left	right	left
d.	left	left	left	right
e.	right	right	right	left
f.	right	right	left	right
g.	right	left	right	right
h.	right	left	left	right

37. In the following aqueous equilibrium, label the components according to the Brønsted-Lowry theory of acids and bases:

$$H_2PO_4^- \; + \; H_2O \; \rightleftharpoons \; HPO_4^{2-} \; + \; H_3O^+$$

	$H_2PO_4^-$	H_2O	HPO_4^{2-}	H_3O^+
a.	base	acid	acid	base
b.	base	acid	base	acid
c.	base	base	acid	acid
d.	acid	acid	base	base
e.	acid	base	base	acid
f.	acid	base	acid	base

38. The first half of a Brønsted-Lowry equilibrium in aqueous solution is illustrated:

$$F^- \; + \; H_2O \; \rightleftharpoons$$

Complete the equilibrium:

a. $H_3O^+ \; + \; HF$ e. $H_2F^+ \; + \; OH^-$
b. $HF \; + \; OH^-$ f. $F_2 \; + \; H_2O_2$
c. $HF \; + \; H_2O$ g. $H_3O^+ \; + \; OH^-$
d. $OF_2 \; + \; H_2$ h. $OF_2 \; + \; HF$

39. Which solute will produce an acidic solution when dissolved in water?

a. K_2CO_3 e. $NaHCO_3$
b. KNO_3 f. $NaCN$
c. NH_4ClO_3 g. $NaCl$
d. LiF h. $Mg(OH)_2$

40. The pH of a 0.250 *M* solution of an unknown weak acid is 4.20. Calculate the hydrogen ion concentration in this solution at 25°C.

a. $3.22 \times 10^{-3} \, M$ c. $6.31 \times 10^{-5} \, M$ e. $6.31 \times 10^{-7} \, M$ g. $1.58 \times 10^{-10} \, M$
b. $4.91 \times 10^{-4} \, M$ d. $5.35 \times 10^{-6} \, M$ f. $7.16 \times 10^{-9} \, M$ h. $2.23 \times 10^{-11} \, M$

FINAL EXAMINATION

CHEMISTRY 141 SPRING 2005

Tuesday May 3rd 2005

1. Which of the following rows has the correct derived SI unit given for each unit of measure (choose the row where all of the SI units are correct).

	Volume	Pressure	Density	Area
a.	m^3	newton	$g\ cm^{-3}$	m^2
b.	L	atm	$g\ L^{-1}$	sq in
c.	m^3	pascal	$kg\ m^{-3}$	m^2
d.	mL	newton	$g\ cm^{-3}$	cm^2
e.	m^3	torr	$kg\ L^{-1}$	m^2
f.	cm^3	pascal	$g\ cm^{-3}$	sq ft

2. An iron cube measures 50.0 mm on each side. The density of iron is $7.86\ g\ cm^{-3}$. What is the mass of the metal?

    a. 3.18 g
    b. 9.36 g
    c. 15.9 g
    d. 197 g
    e. 318 g
    f. 393 g
    g. 983 g
    h. 983 kg

3. What is the correct name for NH_4ClO_4?

    a. ammonium hypochlorite
    b. ammonia chlorite
    c. ammonium chlorate
    d. ammonia perchlorate
    e. ammonia chloride
    f. ammonium perchlorate
    g. ammonia hypochlorite
    h. monoammonium chloride
    i. ammonium monoperchlorate
    j. perchloric acid

4. Toluene ($CH_3C_6H_5$) burns in oxygen gas to produce carbon dioxide gas and water. Write an equation for this reaction and balance the reaction using whole number coefficients. What is the sum of *all* the coefficients in the properly balanced equation?

    a. 7
    b. 9
    c. 12
    d. 13
    e. 16
    f. 19
    g. 21
    h. 23

5. Sucrose is a disaccharide, a combination of glucose and fructose with the molecular formula $C_{12}H_{22}O_{11}$. What is the % by mass of oxygen in sucrose?

    a. 23%
    b. 31%
    c. 42%
    d. 47%
    e. 51%
    f. 63%
    g. 78%
    h. 84%

6. The mineral chromite contains iron (Fe), chromium (Cr) and oxygen (O). The percent by mass of iron is 25.0% and the percent by mass of chromium is 46.5%. What is the empirical formula of chromite?

    a. $FeCrO$
    b. $FeCrO_2$
    c. $FeCrO_4$
    d. $FeCr_2O_2$
    e. $FeCr_3O_6$
    f. $FeCr_2O_4$
    g. $Fe_2Cr_2O_3$
    h. Fe_2CrO_4

7. The charges on monatomic ions of the representative elements depend upon the position of the element in the Periodic Table. In which row are all the charges assigned correctly?

	K	Ca	Ga	O	P	Br
a.	+1	+1	+2	−3	−4	−1
b.	+1	+2	+3	−2	−3	−1
c.	+2	+3	+3	−1	−2	−1
d.	+2	+1	+2	−3	−1	−2
e.	+3	+2	+2	−2	−2	−2
f.	+3	+3	+3	−1	−3	−2

8. How many moles of phosphorus atoms are there in 248 g of phosphorus P_4?

    a. 1.0 mole   c. 3.0 moles   e. 6.0 moles   g. 9.0 moles   i. 18 moles
    b. 2.0 moles   d. 4.0 moles   f. 8.0 moles   h. 12 moles   j. 24 moles

9. According to the following reaction, how many moles of Al_2Cl_6 can be formed when 0.60 moles of aluminum reacts with 0.60 moles of chlorine?

    $$2\,Al \;+\; 3\,Cl_2 \;\rightarrow\; Al_2Cl_6$$

    a. 0.10 mole   c. 0.30 mole   e. 0.50 mole   g. 0.80 mole
    b. 0.20 mole   d. 0.40 mole   f. 0.60 mole   h. 1.20 moles

10. 52 grams of acetylene gas C_2H_2 reacts with 10 grams of hydrogen gas to produce ethane gas C_2H_6. How many grams of the non-limiting reactant remain at the end of the reaction? (*Hint:* Write the equation.)

    a. 0.5 g   c. 1.5 g   e. 4.0 g   g. 42 g
    b. 1.0 g   d. 2.0 g   f. 8.0 g   h. 47 g

11. A compound with an empirical formula of C_4H_3N was found to have a molar mass of 130 g mol^{-1}. What is the molecular formula of this compound?

    a. C_4H_3N c. $C_{12}H_9N_3$ e. $C_6H_8N_2$ g. $C_6H_{12}N_6$
    b. $C_8H_6N_2$ d. C_3H_4N f. $C_9H_{12}N_3$ h. $C_4H_6N_2$

12. A compound of magnesium and carbon reacts with excess water and produces magnesium hydroxide and a gas called propyne C_3H_4. The number of moles of magnesium hydroxide produced was twice the number of moles of propyne produced. What is the empirical formula of the magnesium–carbon compound?

    a. MgC   c. MgC_3 e. MgC_4 g. Mg_3C_2 i. Mg_3C_5
    b. MgC_2 d. Mg_2C f. Mg_2C_3 h. Mg_3C_4 j. Mg_4C_3

13. 25.0 mL of a 3.0 *M* solution of acetic acid is diluted to 150 mL. What is the molarity (*M*) of the resulting solution?

    a. 0.20 *M*   c. 0.33 *M*   e. 0.67 *M*   g. 1.0 *M*
    b. 0.25 *M*   d. 0.50 *M*   f. 0.75 *M*   h. 1.5 *M*

14. Classify the following solutes in aqueous solution as strong acid, base, weak acid, or salt.
    Choose the row in which all the examples are correct.

	strong acid	base	weak acid	salt
a.	H_2SO_4	NH_3	HCl	$MgCl_2$
b.	$HClO_3$	NH_3	HF	$CaSO_4$
c.	H_3PO_3	KOH	HCN	KBr
d.	HF	NaOH	HNO_2	KNO_3
e.	HNO_3	$Mg(CN)_2$	HCO_2H	KCN
f.	HI	NH_3	H_2SO_4	$CaCl_2$
g.	HNO_3	NaOH	HNO_2	NH_3

15. What are the oxidation numbers of sulfur in the substances

	$Na_2S_2O_3$	S_8	$H_4S_4O_6$	SO_2	*[Choose the row in which all the numbers are correct.]*
a.	+3	0	+2	+4	
b.	+3	0	+1	+2	
c.	+2	+8	0	+2	
d.	+2	+6	−3	−4	
e.	+2	0	+2	+4	
f.	+1	+6	+5	+2	
g.	+1	+2	−2	+4	

16. In a demonstration in class, phosphorus was ignited under water and the solution changed color. What gas was bubbled into and through the solution?

a. methane CH_4 c. hydrogen H_2 e. carbon dioxide CO_2
b. nitrogen N_2 d. hydrogen chloride HCl   f. oxygen O_2

17. A system consisting of a movable piston in a cylinder is heated and gains 75 kJ of heat. At the same time the piston is pushed into the cylinder and does 25 kJ of work. What is the change in the internal energy ΔE of the system?

a. −25 kJ   c. −50 kJ   e. −75 kJ   g. −100 kJ
b. +25 kJ   d. +50 kJ   f. +75 kJ   h. +100 kJ

18. 35 g of liquid water near its boiling point at 91°C was poured carefully into a mixture of 50 g of ice and 35 g of water at 0°C whereupon ice melted. What mass of liquid water is present at the end?

Specific heat of water = 4.184 J K^{-1} g^{-1}
Latent heat of fusion of ice = 333 J g^{-1}

a. 25 g   c. 40 g   e. 75 g   g. 110 g
b. 35 g   d. 65 g   f. 80 g   h. 120 g

19. For which substance does the standard enthalpy of formation ΔH_f° equal zero?

a. $O(g)$ c. $P_4(s)$ e. $SO_3(g)$ g. $Cu(l)$ i. $F(g)$
b. $H_2O(l)$ d. $CH_4(g)$ f. $NH_3(l)$ h. $H_2(s)$ j. $HCl(g)$

20. Calculate the standard enthalpy of formation of hydrogen fluoride (HF) given the following information:

$$2\,HF(g) \quad \rightarrow \quad H_2(g) \; + \; F_2(g) \qquad \Delta H° = +538\,kJ$$

   a. $-269\,kJ\,mol^{-1}$ c. $+269\,kJ\,mol^{-1}$ e. $+538\,kJ\,mol^{-1}$
   b. $-538\,kJ\,mol^{-1}$ d. $-1076\,kJ\,mol^{-1}$ f. $+1076\,kJ\,mol^{-1}$

21. Vinyl chloride CH_2CHCl can be made by the reaction of ethylene C_2H_4, hydrogen chloride HCl, and oxygen O_2:

List the bonds broken and the bonds formed in the reaction. Then, based upon the bond energies listed below, calculate the energy required or released in this reaction as written.

C–H	$415\,kJ\,mol^{-1}$	C–Cl	$330\,kJ\,mol^{-1}$
H–Cl	$430\,kJ\,mol^{-1}$	O–H	$460\,kJ\,mol^{-1}$
O=O in O_2	$495\,kJ\,mol^{-1}$		

   a. $-185\,kJ$ c. $-215\,kJ$ e. $-275\,kJ$ g. $-315\,kJ$ i. $-375\,kJ$
   b. $+215\,kJ$ d. $+245\,kJ$ f. $+275\,kJ$ h. $+315\,kJ$ j. $+425\,kJ$

22. Which statement concerning the electromagnetic spectrum is *correct*?

   a. Blue light travels faster than red light.
   b. The frequency of radio waves exceeds that of visible light.
   c. Photons of ultraviolet radiation have a higher energy than photons of infrared radiation.
   d. The wavelength of x-rays is longer than the wavelength of UV radiation.
   e. Microwave photons are considerably more dangerous than γ-ray photons.
   f. Visible radiation has a wavelength in the region of 4 to 7 nm.

23. Start with the number of protons in the nucleus of a beryllium atom,
   ...subtract the number of unpaired 2p electrons in a fluorine atom,
   ...multiply by the number of 3d electrons in a titanium (Ti) atom,
   ...add the atomic number of lithium,
   ...subtract the number of empty 3p orbitals in a silicon atom in its ground state. What's the result?

   a. 3   c. 5   e. 7   g. 9   i. 11
   b. 4   d. 6   f. 8   h. 10   j. 12

24. Which one of the following elements is the largest in size?

   a. Li   c. Be   e. N   g. F
   b. K   d. Ga   f. P   h. Br

25. How many lone pairs of electrons are there around the central atom in the ion IF_2^-?

   a. 0   c. 2   e. 4   g. 6
   b. 1   d. 3   f. 5   h. 8

26. What is the electron pair arrangement around the central atom in the molecule SF_4 and the shape of the molecule?

electron pair arrangement	*molecular shape*
a. T-shaped	trigonal bipyramid
b. trigonal	V–shaped
c. tetrahedral	trigonal pyramid
d. tetrahedral	square pyramid
e. tetrahedral	tetrahedral
f. tetrahedral	V–shaped
g. trigonal bipyramid	linear
h. trigonal bipyramid	see-saw
i. trigonal bipyramid	tetrahedral
j. octahedral	square planar

27. What is the hybridization of atomic orbitals on the xenon atom in XeF_4?

    a. sp   b. sp^2 c. sp^3 d. dsp^2 e. sp^3d f. sp^3d^2

28. A 8.0 L vessel contains 5.0 atm of hydrogen gas, 3.0 atm of helium gas, and 2.0 atm of oxygen gas at a total pressure of 10 atm. What is the mole fraction of oxygen in the mixture (assuming the mixture is ideal)?

a. 0.10	c. 0.30	e. 0.50	g. 0.70	i. 0.90
b. 0.20	d. 0.40	f. 0.60	h. 0.80	j. 1.0

29. Suppose that additional hydrogen is added to the mixture (described in question 28) without changing the temperature or the volume until the partial pressure of hydrogen reaches 10.0 atm. What is the partial pressure of helium in the new mixture?

a. 1.0 atm	c. 3.0 atm	e. 5.0 atm	g. 7.0 atm	i. 9.0 atm
b. 2.0 atm	d. 4.0 atm	f. 6.0 atm	h. 8.0 atm	j. 10 atm

30. Suppose that all the oxygen is removed from the mixture described in question 29 without changing the temperature or the volume. What is the new total pressure?

a. 2.0 atm	c. 4.0 atm	e. 7.5 atm	g. 10 atm	i. 13 atm
b. 3.0 atm	d. 5.0 atm	f. 8.0 atm	h. 12 atm	j. 15 atm

31. What is the mole fraction of acetic acid CH_3CO_2H in 1.00 L of a 60.0% by mass aqueous solution?

a. 0.12	c. 0.27	e. 0.36	g. 0.51
b. 0.21	d. 0.31	f. 0.42	h. 0.60

32. Vanadium carbide has the unit cell illustrated on the right.

    The large spheres represent the vanadium ions and the small spheres represent carbon.

    What is the empirical formula of vanadium carbide?

a. VC	c. V_2C	e. V_2C_3	g. V_3C
b. VC_2	d. V_3C_2	f. VC_3	h. $V_{14}C_{13}$

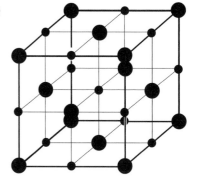

33. Which of the following aqueous solutions will have the *highest* boiling point?

    a. 3.0 *m* glucose (sugar)   e. 1.5 *m* NaOH

    b. 2.0 *m* NaCl   f. 3.0 *m* CH_3CO_2H (acetic acid)

    c. 1.5 *m* KBr   g. 2.2 *m* KNO_3

    d. 0.70 *m* Na_2SO_4 h. 2.7 *m* NH_3

34. The phase diagram for a single substance is illustrated on the right. Which set of choices below represents the correct descriptions?

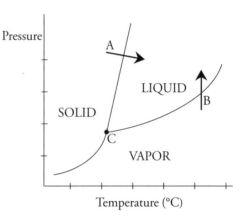

	A	B	C
a.	melting	condensation	critical point
b.	freezing	condensation	triple point
c.	melting	vaporization	critical point
d.	melting	sublimation	triple point
e.	vaporization	melting	triple point
f.	condensation	freezing	critical point
g.	freezing	vaporization	triple point
h.	melting	condensation	triple point
i.	sublimation	condensation	triple point

35. Which of the following statements about catalysts is true?

    a. A catalyst lowers the activation energy for a reaction.

    b. A catalyst is consumed (used up) in a reaction.

    c. A catalyst increases the energy of the products.

    d. A catalyst does not change the rate of a reaction.

    e. A catalyst lowers the energy of the reactants.

    f. A catalyst does not change the mechanism of a reaction.

36. The equilibrium constant K at a particular temperature for the following reaction is 9.00.

$$NO_2(g) \ + \ CO(g) \ \rightleftharpoons \ NO(g) \ + \ CO_2(g)$$

Initially, 2.0 moles each of NO_2 and CO are injected into an 1.0 liter flask. Calculate the concentration of the $CO_2(g)$ at equilibrium at this temperature.

    a. 0.25 *M*   c. 0.50 *M*   e. 0.75 *M*   g. 1.25 *M*   i. 1.50 *M*

    b. 0.33 *M*   d. 0.67 *M*   f. 1.00 *M*   h. 1.33 *M*   j. 1.67 *M*

37. In the following aqueous equilibrium, label the components according to the Brønsted-Lowry theory of acids and bases:

$$HCO_3^- \ + \ H_2O \ \rightleftharpoons \ H_2CO_3 \ + \ OH^-$$

a.	base	acid	acid	base
b.	base	acid	base	acid
c.	base	base	acid	acid
d.	acid	acid	base	base
e.	acid	base	base	acid
f.	acid	base	acid	base

38. Consider the following disturbances on the equilibrium system shown. In which, if any, direction will the system shift to restore equilibrium in each case? The reaction is exothermic in the forward direction.

$$Ti(s) \ + \ 2\,Cl_2(g) \ \rightleftharpoons \ TiCl_4(g)$$

	increase pressure	decrease temperature	add more $Ti(s)$	remove $Cl_2(g)$
a.	left	right	right	right
b.	left	right	no change	left
c.	left	left	right	left
d.	left	left	no change	right
e.	right	right	right	left
f.	right	right	no change	left
g.	right	left	right	right
h.	right	left	no change	right

39. The first half of a Brønsted-Lowry equilibrium in aqueous solution is illustrated:

$$PO_4^{3-} \ + \ H_2O \ \rightleftharpoons$$

Complete the equilibrium:

a. $H_3O^+ \ + \ OH^-$ e. $HPO_4^{2-} \ + \ OH^-$

b. $HPO_4^{2-} \ + \ H_3O^+$ f. $PH_3 \ + \ H_2O_2$

c. $H_3PO_4 \ + \ OH^-$ g. $H_3O^+ \ + \ H_2PO_4^-$

d. $P_4O_{10} \ + \ H_2$ h. H_3PO_4

40. What is the pH of a 0.0050 M NaOH solution?

a. 1.3   c. 5.3   e. 8.7   g. 11.7

b. 2.3   d. 7.0   f. 9.3   h. 12.7

FINAL EXAMINATION

CHEMISTRY 141 FALL 2005

Wednesday December 14th 2005

1. What is the speed in ms^{-1} of a tennis ball traveling with a speed of 120 mph (miles per hour)?

    a. $3.2\ ms^{-1}$ c. $42\ ms^{-1}$ e. $120\ ms^{-1}$ g. $361\ ms^{-1}$
    b. $11.6\ ms^{-1}$ d. $53.6\ ms^{-1}$ f. $193\ ms^{-1}$ h. $695\ ms^{-1}$

2. Examples of a noble gas, a halogen, an alkaline earth metal, and a transition metal, are, in that order:

	noble gas	*halogen*	*alkaline earth metal*	*transition metal*
a.	neon Ne	chlorine Cl	potassium K	tin Sn
b.	nobelium No	sodium Na	strontium Sr	copper Cu
c.	iodine I	argon Ar	calcium Ca	iron Fe
d.	krypton Kr	bromine Br	magnesium Mg	nickel Ni
e.	xenon Xe	hydrogen H	tin Sn	manganese Mn
f.	helium He	oxygen O	lead Pb	titanium Ti

3. How many of the following compounds are ionic?

    KCN NI_3 $AlPO_4$ NaBr
    SO_2 CaI_2 Li_2CO_3 $CsNO_3$

    a. none   c. 2   e. 4   g. 6   i. all are ionic
    b. 1   d. 3   f. 5   h. 7

4. There are three isotopes of hydrogen: protium ^1H, deuterium ^2H, and tritium ^3H. What are the correct numbers of neutrons in the nuclei of these three isotopes?

	protium	deuterium	tritium
a.	1	2	3
b.	3	2	1
c.	0	1	2
d.	0	2	3
e.	2	1	0
f.	1	2	0

5. Which of the following formulas is incorrect?

    a. Li_2HPO_4 c. $Al(NO_3)_3$ e. $LiNO_2$ g. $Al_2(SO_4)_3$ i. $Mg_3(PO_4)_2$
    b. RbCl   d. $Mg(CH_3CO_2)_2$ f. $CaCO_3$ h. $NaSO_4$ j. $KClO_3$

6. How many moles of oxygen atoms are in 2.0 moles of sodium phosphate?

    a. 2   c. 6   e. 10   g. 14
    b. 4   d. 8   f. 12   h. 16

7. What is the % by mass of carbon in aspirin, $C_9H_8O_4$?

   a. 5%   c. 35%   e. 60%   g. 82%
   b. 20%   d. 43%   f. 74%   h. 90%

8. 5.50 moles of an unknown compound is known to have a mass of 440 grams. What is the molar mass of this compound?

   a. 10.0 g mol^{-1} c. 25.0 g mol^{-1} e. 45.0 g mol^{-1} g. 75.0 g mol^{-1}
   b. 20.0 g mol^{-1} d. 30.0 g mol^{-1} f. 60.0 g mol^{-1} h. 80.0 g mol^{-1}

9. Balance the following equation:

   $$\_\_ C_8H_{18}O_3(l) \;+\; \_\_ O_2(g) \;\longrightarrow\; \_\_ H_2O(g) \;+\; \_\_ CO_2(g)$$

   What is the coefficient for oxygen in the balanced equation?

   a. 1   c. 5   e. 9   g. 11   i. 13
   b. 3   d. 8   f. 10   h. 12   j. 15

10. Assume you have 3.0 moles $C_8H_{18}O_3$ and 4.0 moles O_2 in the reaction described in the previous question. What is the maximum amount of carbon dioxide that can be produced?

    a. 2.9 moles   c. 5.5 moles   e. 11 moles   g. 24 moles
    b. 3.3 moles   d. 8 moles   f. 19 moles   h. 27 moles

11. The following spheres represent the sizes of Ca, Ca^{2+} and Mg^{2+}. Pick the row where all the species are correctly identified.

a.	Ca	Ca^{2+}	Mg^{2+}
b.	Mg^{2+}	Ca^{2+}	Ca
c.	Ca	Mg^{2+}	Ca^{2+}
d.	Ca^{2+}	Ca	Mg^{2+}
e.	Ca^{2+}	Mg^{2+}	Ca
f.	Mg^{2+}	Ca	Ca^{2+}

12. Which of the following electrolytes is classified as a weak electrolyte?

    a. $HClO_4$ c. H_2SO_4 e. HF   g. $Ca(OH)_2$ i. KOH
    b. NH_4NO_3 d. NaOH   f. NaCN   h. HI   j. $Mg(NO_3)_2$

13. What is the *molality* of a 22.0% by mass aqueous solution of sodium bicarbonate?

    a. 0.13 m c. 2.64 m e. 4.78 m g. 6.22 m
    b. 1.72 m d. 3.36 m f. 5.07 m h. 7.32 m

14. The internal energy of a system increases by 40 J. If 25 J of work was done by the system, what heat was transferred to or from the system to cause this increase?

    a. +15 J   c. +20 J   e. +25 J   g. +35 J   i. +65 J
    b. −15 J   d. −20 J   f. −25 J   h. −35 J   j. −65 J

15. Write the net ionic equation for the following reaction and identify all the spectator ions.

$$KOH(aq) + HCN(aq) \rightarrow KCN(aq) + H_2O(l)$$

    a. K^+ d. H_3O^+ g. CN^- and OH^-
    b. OH^- e. K^+ and CN^- h. K^+ and H_3O^+
    c. CN^- f. H_3O^+ and OH^-

16. How much heat is required to completely melt a 15 gram block of ice initially at –20°C?

Specific heat of ice = 2.1 $Jg^{-1}K^{-1}$
Specific heat of water = 4.184 $Jg^{-1}K^{-1}$
Latent heat of fusion of ice = 333 Jg^{-1}

    a. 0.630 kJ   c. 1.885 kJ   e. 5.625 kJ   g. 6.880 kJ
    b. 1.255 kJ   d. 4.995 kJ   f. 6.250 kJ   h. 7.565 kJ

17. Calculate the enthalpy change for the reaction:

$$NO(g) + O_3(g) \rightarrow NO_2(g) + O_2(g) \quad \Delta H° = ? \text{ kJ}$$

from the following information:

$$NO(g) + O(g) \rightarrow NO_2(g) \quad\quad \Delta H° = -304 \text{ kJ}$$
$$O_3(g) \rightarrow 1.5 \, O_2(g) \quad\quad \Delta H° = -142 \text{ kJ}$$
$$O_2(g) \rightarrow 2 \, O(g) \quad\quad \Delta H° = +494 \text{ kJ}$$

    a. –693 kJ   c. –656 kJ   e. –199 kJ   g. –446 kJ   i. +470 kJ
    b. –940 kJ   d. –343 kJ   f. +223 kJ   h. +940 kJ   j. +312 kJ

18. In the reaction below, identify the element reduced, the element oxidized, and the total (net) number of moles of electrons transferred in the reaction as it is written. Choose the row in which all the answers are correct.

$$Sn(s) + 2 H_2O(l) \rightarrow Sn^{2+}(aq) + 2 OH^-(aq) + H_2(g)$$

	element reduced	element oxidized	net electrons transferred
a.	tin	hydrogen	1
b.	hydrogen	tin	2
c.	oxygen	hydrogen	1
d.	oxygen	tin	4
e.	tin	hydrogen	2
f.	hydrogen	oxygen	1
g.	hydrogen	oxygen	2
h.	oxygen	tin	6

19. A radio station broadcasts at a frequency of 97.5 MHz. What is the energy of one photon of this radiation?

    a. 1.47×10^{41} J   c. 3.08 J   e. 3.9×10^{-2} J   g. 6.46×10^{-26} J
    b. 1.47×10^{35} J   d. 3.08×10^6 J   f. 3.9×10^{15} J   h. 6.46×10^{-32} J

20. Blue light has a wavelength of 400 nm and red light has a wavelength of 600 nm. How many photons of red light have the same total energy as 100 photons of blue light?

a. 25   c. 50   e. 100   g. 150   i. 300
b. 33   d. 67   f. 133   h. 200   j. 400

21. Which one of the following sets of quantum numbers is invalid?

	n	l	m_l
a.	1	0	0
b.	2	1	0
c.	2	1	−1
d.	2	0	0
e.	2	2	−1
f.	3	1	+1
g.	3	2	−1
h.	4	3	+2

22. How many electrons does a sulfur atom have in p orbitals (consider *all* the p orbitals that are occupied)?

a. 2   c. 5   e. 8   g. 12
b. 4   d. 6   f. 10   h. 16

23. $1s^2 2s^2 2p^6 3s^2 3p^6 4s^2 3d^{10} 4p^6 5s^2 4d^2$ is the ground state electron configuration for which element?

a. Ti   c. Sr   e. Sn   g. Nb
b. Zr   d. Y   f. Ge   h. V

24. How many of the following molecules contain hydrogen atoms(s) that is(are) capable of forming a hydrogen bond?

CH_3OH HBr   HF H_2O
C_4H_{10} N_2H_4 CH_3OCH_3 CH_3CO_2H

a. none   c. 2   e. 4   g. 6   i. all
b. 1   d. 3   f. 5   h. 7

25. What is the electron arrangement and molecular shape of the molecule TeF_4?

	electron arrangement	*molecular shape*
a.	trigonal planar	bent
b.	tetrahedral	tetrahedral
c.	tetrahedral	T-shaped
d.	trigonal bipyramid	see-saw
e.	trigonal bipyramid	trigonal bipyramid
f.	square pyramid	see-saw
g.	octahedral	trigonal bipyramid
h.	octahedral	tetrahedral
i.	octahedral	square planar

26. What is the hybridization of the atomic orbitals of the central atom in sulfur dioxide?

a. sp   c. sp^3 e. sp^3d^2
b. sp^2 d. sp^3d

27. What is the sum of all the formal charges on the atoms in the thiocyanate ion SCN^-?

a. +1   c. +3   e. −1   g. −3
b. +2   d. zero   f. −2   h. −4

28. According VSEPR theory, which molecule has the greatest number of lone (nonbonding) pairs of electrons around the central atom?

a. CH_4 c. N_2O e. H_2O g. NO_2^-
b. PF_5 d. I_3^- f. XeF_4 h. NH_3

29. A flask containing a gas is connected to an open-ended mercury manometer. The open end is exposed to the atmosphere (1 atm pressure). The mercury level in the open arm of the manometer is 38 cm below the mercury level in the arm connected to the flask containing the gas. What is the pressure of the gas in the vessel?

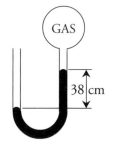

a. 0.50 atm   e. 2.5 atm
b. 1.0 atm   f. 3.0 atm
c. 1.5 atm   g. 3.5 atm
d. 2.0 atm   h. 4.0 atm

30. A 10.0 L vessel contains 2.0 mole of nitrogen gas, 3.0 moles of helium gas, and 5.0 moles of hydrogen gas at a pressure of 15.0 atm. What is the partial pressure of helium gas in the vessel?

a. 2.0 atm   c. 3.0 atm   e. 4.0 atm   g. 5.0 atm   i. 10.0 atm
b. 2.5 atm   d. 3.5 atm   f. 4.5 atm   h. 7.5 atm   j. 15.0 atm

31. Maintaining a constant volume and temperature, an additional 5.0 moles of hydrogen is added to the vessel described in the previous question. What are the partial pressures of all gases in the vessel now?

	partial pressure of nitrogen	*partial pressure of helium*	*partial pressure of hydrogen*
a.	3.0 atm	3.0 atm	7.5 atm
b.	3.0 atm	4.5 atm	7.5 atm
c.	3.0 atm	6.75 atm	15.0 atm
d.	3.0 atm	4.5 atm	15.0 atm
e.	4.0 atm	4.5 atm	15.0 atm
f.	4.5 atm	3.0 atm	7.5 atm
g.	4.5 atm	4.5 atm	7.5 atm
h.	4.5 atm	6.75 atm	7.5 atm
i.	4.5 atm	4.5 atm	15.0 atm

32. It takes 5.0 minutes for 1.0 mole of Ar gas to effuse through a small hole. How many moles of H_2 gas can effuse through the same hole in 5.0 minutes?

a. 1.5 moles   c. 3.5 moles   e. 5.5 moles   g. 7.5 moles
b. 2.5 moles   d. 4.5 moles   f. 6.5 moles   h. 8.5 moles

33. A unit cell of Na_2O is illustrated on the right.
The larger circles represent the oxygen atoms.
The small circles represent the sodium atoms.
How would you describe the lattice of oxygen atoms?

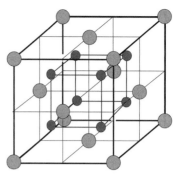

    a. simple cubic
    b. body-centered cubic
    c. face-centered cubic

34. Which of the following aqueous solutions will have the *lowest* freezing point? Assume salts dissociate completely.

    a. 3.5 *m* sugar
    b. 2.0 *m* NaCl
    c. 1.7 *m* LiBr
    d. 1.0 *m* K_2SO_4
    e. 1.6 *m* NaOH
    f. 3.0 *m* CH_3CO_2H (acetic acid)
    g. 2.2 *m* KNO_3
    h. 2.7 *m* NH_3

35. Which of the following would be expected to increase the rate of a reaction?

    A increase the concentration of the reactants
    B lower the activation energy
    C lower the reaction temperature
    D add a catalyst

    a. A only   c. C only   e. A and B   g. B and D   i. B and C
    b. B only   d. D only   f. A and D   h. A, B and D   j. A, B, C and D

36. Consider the following disturbances on the equilibrium system shown. In which, if any, direction will the system shift to restore equilibrium in each case? The reaction is exothermic in the forward direction.

$$C(s) + H_2O(g) \rightleftharpoons CO(g) + H_2(g)$$

	increase pressure	decrease temperature	add more $H_2O(g)$	remove $H_2(g)$
a.	left	right	right	right
b.	left	left	right	right
c.	left	right	left	right
d.	left	left	left	right
e.	right	right	right	left
f.	right	left	right	left
g.	right	right	left	left
h.	right	left	left	left

37. The first half of a Brønsted-Lowry equilibrium in aqueous solution is illustrated:

$$CO_3^{2-} + H_2O \rightleftharpoons$$

Complete the equilibrium:

    a. $H_3O^+ + OH^-$
    b. $HCO_3^- + H_3O^+$
    c. $H_2CO_3 + 2OH^-$
    d. $CO_2 + H_2O$
    e. $HCO_3^- + OH^-$
    f. $CO_2 + OH^-$
    g. $2H_3O^+ + CO_3^{2-}$
    h. $H_2CO_3 + H_3O^+$

38. Consider the following equilibrium:

$$2\ SO_2\ +\ O_2\ \rightleftharpoons\ 2\ SO_3$$

At equilibrium, the concentration of SO_2 is 1M, the concentration of O_2 is 5M and the concentration of SO_3 is 5M. What is the relationship between the equilibrium constant (K) and the reaction quotient (Q) if the concentration of SO_2 is increased to 3M but the concentrations of O_2 and SO_3 both remain at 5M?

a. Q < K   b. Q = K   c. Q > K

39. In the following aqueous equilibrium, label the components according to the Brønsted-Lowry theory of acids and bases:

$$HSO_3^-\ +\ H_2O\ \rightleftharpoons\ H_2SO_3\ +\ OH^-$$

	HSO_3^-	H_2O	H_2SO_3	OH^-
a.	base	acid	acid	base
b.	base	acid	base	acid
c.	base	base	acid	acid
d.	acid	acid	base	base
e.	acid	base	base	acid
f.	acid	base	acid	base

40. What is the pH of an 0.04 M $HClO_4$ solution?

a. 0.04   c. 3.4   e. 7.0   g. 10.6
b. 1.4   d. 5.6   f. 8.4   h. 12.6

FINAL EXAMINATION
CHEMISTRY 141 Spring 2006
Tuesday May 2nd 2006

1. A rectangular block of silver has a mass of 50 g and a volume of 4.76 mL. What is the mass of a cube of silver that measures 2.2 cm on each side? $(1 \text{ cm}^3 = 1 \text{ mL})$

    a. 327 g   c. 10.5 g   e. 232 g   g. 186 g
    b. 58.2 g   d. 112 g   f. 145 g   h. 270 g

2. Three isotopes of nickel are ^{58}Ni, ^{62}Ni and ^{64}Ni. How many neutrons are in each of these isotopes? *Choose the row in which all of the answers are correct.*

	^{58}Ni	^{62}Ni	^{64}Ni
a.	30	28	26
b.	30	30	30
c.	28	28	28
d.	36	34	30
e.	58	58	62
f.	58	62	64
g.	34	34	34
h.	30	34	36

3. What are the molecular formulas for magnesium hypochlorite, magnesium chlorite, and magnesium chlorate. *Choose the row in which all answers are correct.*

	magnesium hypochlorite	magnesium chlorite	magnesium chlorate
a.	$MgCl_2$	$Mg(ClO_2)_2$	$Mg(ClO_3)_2$
b.	$Mg(ClO)_2$	$Mg(ClO_2)_2$	$Mg(ClO_3)_2$
c.	$Mg(ClO)_2$	$MgClO_2$	$MgClO_3$
d.	$MgClO$	$MgClO_2$	$MgClO_3$
e.	Mg_2ClO	Mg_2ClO_2	$Mg(ClO_3)_2$
f.	$Mg_2(ClO_2)_2$	$Mg_2(ClO_3)_2$	$Mg(ClO_4)_2$
g.	$Mg(ClO)_3$	$Mg(ClO_2)_3$	$Mg(ClO_4)_3$
h.	$Mg(ClO)_4$	$Mg(ClO_2)_3$	$Mg(ClO_3)_2$

4. How many moles of oxygen atoms are in 7.5 moles of iron(II) permanganate?

    a. 7.5 mol   c. 15 mol   e. 45 mol   g. 75 mol
    b. 8 mol   d. 30 mol   f. 60 mol   h. 90 mol

5. A compound is 25.34% calcium, 30.37% carbon, 3.82% hydrogen, and 40.46% oxygen by mass. What is the empirical formula of this compound?

    a. $CaCHO$ c. CaC_2HO_2 e. CaC_2H_2O g. $CaC_4H_2O_3$
    b. $CaCHO_2$ d. $CaC_2H_3O_2$ f. CaC_2HO h. $CaC_4H_6O_4$

6. Sorbitol, a commonly used artificial sweetener, has a molecular formula $C_6H_{14}O_6$. What is the molar mass of sorbitol?

    a. 26 g mol^{-1} c. 74 g mol^{-1} e. 156 g mol^{-1} g. 207 g mol^{-1}
    b. 29 g mol^{-1} d. 133 g mol^{-1} f. 182 g mol^{-1} h. 242 g mol^{-1}

7. α–Linolenic acid $C_{18}H_{30}O_2$ (molar mass 278.42 g mol^{-1}) is an omega-3 fatty acid. What is the percent by mass of carbon in α–linolenic acid?

    a. 10.86%   c. 26.71%   e. 48.93%   g. 77.64%
    b. 11.49%   d. 36.00%   f. 57.70%   h. 89.12%

8. Balance the following equation using whole number coefficients:

    $$\_\ Fe_2O_3\ +\ \_\ H_2SO_4\ \rightarrow\ \_\ Fe_2(SO_4)_3\ +\ \_\ H_2O$$

    The sum for all of the coefficients for the reactants and products is

    a. 1   c. 4   e. 6   g. 8   i. 10
    b. 3   d. 5   f. 7   h. 9   j. 11

9. Propane C_3H_8 reacts with oxygen to produce carbon dioxide and water according to this balanced equation:

    $$C_3H_8\ +\ 5\,O_2\ \rightarrow\ 3\,CO_2\ +\ 4\,H_2O$$

    How many moles of carbon dioxide are produced from the reaction of 2 moles propane and 3 moles oxygen?

    a. 1.8 mol   c. 4.5 mol   e. 8.2 mol   g. 13.8 mol
    b. 3.0 mol   d. 6.0 mol   f. 9.5 mol   h. 15 mol

10. According to their location in the Periodic Table, how many of the following elements are transition metals?

    Pt   Ca   Fe   P   Li
    Na   Rn   U   K   Ag

    a. 1   c. 3   e. 5   g. 7   i. 9
    b. 2   d. 4   f. 6   h. 8   j. all are transition metals

11. Silicon tetrachloride is prepared by heating solid silicon in chlorine gas. In one experiment, 5.0 g silicon reacts with excess chlorine gas to produce 15 g $SiCl_4$. What is the percent yield of this reaction?

    a. 10%   c. 30%   e. 50%   g. 70%   i. 90%
    b. 20%   d. 40%   f. 60%   h. 80%   j. 100%

12. Identify all the spectator ions in this reaction:

    $$BaCl_2(aq)\ +\ Na_2SO_4(aq)\ \rightarrow\ BaSO_4(s)\ +\ 2\,NaCl(aq)$$

    a. Ba^{2+} only   d. SO_4^{2-} only   g. Ba^{2+} and SO_4^{2-}
    b. Cl^- only   e. Ba^{2+} and Na^+ h. SO_4^{2-} and Cl^-
    c. Na^+ only   f. Na^+ and Cl^-

13. What is the oxidation number of chlorine in the following molecules/ions?
    Choose the row in which all answers are correct.

	BCl_3	ClO^-	ClO_4^-
a.	+1	−1	+1
b.	−1	−1	−1
c.	−1	+1	+7
d.	+1	+2	+3
e.	−1	−2	−3
f.	0	−1	−1
g.	+2	+7	+7
h.	−1	−1	+7

14. Aluminum reacts with iron(III) oxide to produce aluminum oxide and molten iron:

    $$2\,Al(s) \; + \; Fe_2O_3(s) \; \rightarrow \; Al_2O_3(s) \; + \; 2\,Fe(l)$$

    Given the heats of formation listed below, how much heat is released when 1 mole of aluminum reacts?

    $\Delta H_f^\circ\,(Fe_2O_3(s)) = -822.2$ kJ mol^{-1}
    $\Delta H_f^\circ\,(Al_2O_3(s)) = -1669.8$ kJ mol^{-1}
    $\Delta H_f^\circ\,(Fe(l)) \quad = +12.40$ kJ mol^{-1}

a.	217.5 kJ	c.	479.2 kJ	e.	701.5 kJ	g.	1234 kJ
b.	411.4 kJ	d.	597.3 kJ	f.	822.8 kJ	h.	1646 kJ

15. How much heat is needed to heat to boiling and completely vaporize 32 g ethanol C_2H_5OH at 25 °C?

    Boiling point of ethanol = 78.4 °C
    Specific heat of liquid ethanol = 2.460 J g^{-1} K^{-1}
    Latent heat of vaporization of ethanol = 838 J g^{-1}

a.	4.2 kJ	c.	23 kJ	e.	31 kJ	g.	4.6×10^2 kJ
b.	7.9 kJ	d.	27 kJ	f.	72 kJ	h.	1.4×10^3 kJ

16. 20 g water at 80 °C is added to 100 g ice and 35 g water at 0 °C. What mass of liquid water is present at the end?

    Specific heat of water = 4.184 J g^{-1} K^{-1}
    Latent heat of fusion of ice = 333 J g^{-1}
    Latent heat of vaporization of water = 2260 J g^{-1}

a.	20 g	c.	40 g	e.	60 g	g.	90 g
b.	35 g	d.	55 g	f.	75 g	h.	155 g

17. How many of the following substances have standard heats of formation ΔH_f° equal to zero?

Ar *(g)*	N *(g)*	O_3 *(g)*	Cl_2 *(g)*
Mg *(g)*	H_2O *(l)*	Na *(s)*	Hg *(s)*

a.	0 (none)	c.	2	e.	4	g.	6	i.	8
b.	1	d.	3	f.	5	h.	7		

18. Green light has a wavelength of approximately 510 nm. What is the energy of one photon of green light?

    a. 3.9×10^{-28} J   c. 4.0×10^{-19} J   e. 7.8×10^{-11} J   g. 2.4×10^5 J
    b. 2.7×10^{-12} J   d. 5.6×10^{-17} J   f. 6.2×10^{-7} J   h. 5.9×10^{14} J

19. What type of electromagnetic radiation has more energy than visible light but less energy than x-rays?

    a. γ-ray (gamma-ray)   c. radiowave   e. ultraviolet light
    b. infrared light   d. microwave

20. $1s^2 2s^2 2p^6 3s^2 3p^6 4s^2 3d^{10} 4p^2$ is the electron configuration for which element in its ground state?

    a. Ca   c. Ti   e. As   g. Kr
    b. Ge   d. Ga   f. Sn   h. Si

21. Which of the following values is not possible for the value of the orientation atomic quantum number m_l when n = 4 and l = 3?

    a. –4   c. –2   e. 0   g. +2
    b. –3   d. –1   f. +1   h. +3

22. How many unpaired electrons are in one cobalt (Co) atom in the ground state?

    a. 0   c. 2   e. 4   g. 6   i. 8
    b. 1   d. 3   f. 5   h. 7   j. 9

23. What is the electron pair arrangement and molecular shape for SF_2?

	electron pair arrangement	*molecular shape*
a.	linear	linear
b.	tetrahedral	bent
c.	tetrahedral	linear
d.	tetrahedral	trigonal pyramid
e.	trigonal bipyramid	linear
f.	trigonal bipyramid	see-saw
g.	octahedral	bent
h.	octahedral	T-shaped

24. How many of the following molecule(s) is/are polar?

    H_2 HBr $BFCl_2$ BrF_3
    CO XeF_4 PH_3 NO_3^-

    a. 0 (none)   c. 2   e. 4   g. 6   i. all are polar
    b. 1   d. 3   f. 5   h. 7

25. What is the average bond order for the bond in a N_2 molecule?

    a. 1.0   c. 1.5   e. 2.0
    b. 1.33   d. 1.67   f. 3.0

26. A sample of gas fills a 4.0 L container at 25 °C with a pressure of 3.0 atm. Holding the temperature constant, the volume of the container is reduced to 3.0 L. What is the pressure at the new volume?

    a. 1 atm   c. 3 atm   e. 5 atm   g. 7 atm
    b. 2 atm   d. 4 atm   f. 6 atm   h. 8 atm

27. 2 moles neon, 3 moles argon and 5 moles xenon are contained in a glass bulb at a total pressure of 30 atm. Without changing the volume or temperature, helium was added to the glass bulb until the total pressure was 32 atm. What is the partial pressure of argon and helium in the container after the helium was added?

	P_{Ar}	P_{He}			P_{Ar}	P_{He}
a.	6 atm	3 atm		e.	9.6 atm	4 atm
b.	6.4 atm	6 atm		f.	15 atm	2 atm
c.	16 atm	9 atm		g.	9 atm	5 atm
d.	9 atm	15 atm		h.	9 atm	2 atm

28. Which one of the following compounds would you expect to have the *lowest* boiling point?

    a. C_2H_6 c. water   e. $CsCl(s)$ g. C (graphite)
    b. HF   d. NH_3 f. quartz (SiO_2) h. methanol (CH_3OH)

29. The boiling point of nitrogen is –196 °C. What are the signs of ΔH, ΔS, and ΔG for the vaporization of nitrogen at –150 °C?

	ΔH	ΔS	ΔG			ΔH	ΔS	ΔG
a.	–	+	+		e.	+	+	+
b.	–	+	–		f.	+	+	–
c.	–	–	+		g.	+	–	+
d.	–	–	–		h.	+	–	–

30. In what volume of water would 21.2 g of potassium phosphate be dissolved to make a 0.40 M solution?

    a. 100 mL   c. 280 mL   e. 345 mL   g. 555 mL
    b. 250 mL   d. 305 mL   f. 395 mL   h. 615 mL

31. A 30% by mass aqueous solution of hydrogen peroxide H_2O_2 has a density of 1.11 g mL^{-1}. What is the *molality (m)* of this solution?

    a. 0.079 m c. 0.431 m e. 9.79 m g. 27.0 m
    b. 0.185 m d. 0.815 m f. 12.6 m h. 90.1 m

32. An ideal solution of two compounds A (solvent) and B (non-volatile solute) contains 3 moles A and 2 moles B. At a particular temperature, the vapor pressure of pure A is 425 torr. What is the total vapor pressure above the solution?

    a. 26 torr   c. 425 torr   e. 255 torr   g. 87 torr
    b. 385 torr   d. 170 torr   f. 606 torr   h. 542 torr

33.   How many moles of ethanol C_2H_5OH are needed to lower the freezing point of 50 g water by 5 °C? (K_b H_2O = 0.5 kg K mol^{-1})

      a. 0.1 mol   c. 0.3 mol   e. 0.5 mol   g. 0.7 mol
      b. 0.2 mol   d. 0.4 mol   f. 0.6 mol   h. 0.8 mol

34.   The amide ion NH_2^- is a stronger base than the hydroxide ion OH^-. The hydroxide ion is a stronger base than ammonia NH_3. Place NH_3, H_2O and NH_4^+ in order of increasing acid strength.

      a. $NH_3 < H_2O < NH_4^+$ d. $H_2O < NH_4^+ < NH_3$
      b. $NH_3 < NH_4^+ < H_2O$ e. $NH_4^+ < NH_3 < H_2O$
      c. $H_2O < NH_3 < NH_4^+$ f. $NH_4^+ < H_2O < NH_3$

35.   In the following aqueous equilibrium, label the components according to the Brønsted-Lowry theory of acids and bases:

      $$CN^- \quad + \quad H_2O \quad \rightleftharpoons \quad HCN \quad + OH^-$$

a.	acid	acid	base	base
b.	acid	base	base	acid
c.	base	acid	acid	base
d.	acid	base	acid	base
e.	base	acid	base	base
f.	base	base	acid	acid

36.   Which solute, when dissolved in water, would produce a basic solution?

      a. NaCl   c. KNO_3 e. CH_3CO_2H g. $HClO_4$
      b. LiF   d. NH_4Cl f. KBr   h. NH_4ClO_3

37.   Consider the following disturbances on the equilibrium system shown. According to LeChatelier's principle, in which direction, if any, will the system shift to restore equilibrium in each case?

      $$3\ O_2\ (g) \quad \rightleftharpoons \quad 2\ O_3\ (g) \qquad \Delta H = +284\ kJ\ mol^{-1}$$

	decrease volume	*add O_2*	*decrease temperature*	*add catalyst*
a.	right	right	left	no change
b.	right	left	left	left
c.	left	no change	right	right
d.	no change	right	left	right
e.	right	right	no change	no change
f.	left	left	right	no change

38.   Consider the change in entropy (ΔS), change in enthalpy (ΔH) and activation energy (E_A) for a reaction. Which of these quantities, if any, would be affected by the addition of a catalyst?

      a. ΔS only   c. E_A only   e. ΔS and E_A g. ΔS, ΔH, and E_A
      b. ΔH only   d. ΔS and ΔH f. ΔH and E_A h. none are affected

39.   What is the pOH of a 0.30 M solution of hydroiodic acid?

      a. 0.21   c. 1.3   e. 8.7   g. 11.6
      b. 0.52   d. 5.6   f. 10.6   h. 13.5

40. Hydrogen iodide gas decomposes to form hydrogen gas and iodine gas according to the following balanced equation:

$$2 \, HI(g) \; \rightleftharpoons \; I_2(g) \; + \; H_2(g) \qquad K = 1.62 \times 10^{-3}$$

If 10 moles of hydrogen iodide are injected into a 2.0 L flask, what would be the concentration of iodine gas at equilibrium?

a. 0.186 M   c. 1.99 M   e. 3.03 M   g. 5.47 M
b. 0.785 M   d. 2.79 M   f. 4.63 M   h. 6.23 M

FINAL EXAMINATION

CHEMISTRY 141 Fall 2006

Wednesday December 13th 2006

1. A metal ion has 50 protons, 69 neutrons, and 48 electrons. What is the atomic number of the element, the mass number of this particular isotope, and the charge on this ion? (Choose the answer where *all* responses are correct.)

	atomic number	*mass number*	*charge*
a.	48	50	+2
b.	48	69	−2
c.	48	117	+2
d.	48	119	−2
e.	50	69	+2
f.	50	117	−2
g.	50	119	+2
h.	69	117	−2
i.	69	119	+2

2. Which one of the following polyatomic ions has the incorrect formula?

   a. nitrite NO_2^- c. sulfite SO_3^{2-} e chlorite ClO_2^- g. carbonate CO_3^{2-}

   b. nitrate NO_3^- d. sulfate SO_4^{2-} f. chlorate ClO_3^- h. bicarbonate HCO_3^{2-}

3. The following is a list of symbols for common derived SI units. Which is the derived unit for energy?

   a. N   b. W   c. Pa   d. $m\,s^{-2}$ e. $kg\,m\,s^{-2}$ f. J

4. Which of the following compounds has the greatest percent by mass of hydrogen?

   a. CH_4 c. C_2H_6 e. H_2S g. PH_3

   b. H_2O d. H_2SO_4 f. NH_3 h. N_2H_4

5. Which one of the following substances is an ionic compound?

   a. diamond   c. potassium bromide   e. water

   b. sulfur dioxide   d. hydrogen chloride   f. phosphorus trichloride

6. How many moles of carbon atoms are in 7 moles of trinitrotoluene (TNT) molecules, $C_6H_2(NO_2)_3CH_3$?

   a. 7 mol   c. 21 mol   e. 35 mol   g. 49 mol   i. 98 mol

   b. 14 mol   d. 28 mol   f. 42 mol   h. 84 mol   j. 126 mol

7. Which of the following compounds contains an alkaline earth metal?

   a. SiO_2 d. $NaNH_2$ g. COCl

   b. $FeCl_2$ e. $MgSO_4$ h. $SnCl_2$

   c. K_2NiCl_4 f. $CuCO_3$ i. K_2CO_3

8. Which one of the following elements commonly exists as a diatomic molecule?

   a. lithium   c. sulfur   e. hydrogen   g. mercury   i. xenon
   b. carbon   d. helium   f. argon   h. silicon   j. phosphorus

9. How many grams of methane (CH_4) contain the same number of molecules as 128 grams of sulfur dioxide (SO_2)?

   a. 2 g   c. 8 g   e. 32 g   g. 128 g   i. 512 g
   b. 4 g   d. 16 g   f. 64 g   h. 256 g   j. 1024 g

10. Which one of the following formulas is incorrect?

    a. KI   d. $NaCH_3CO_2$ g. CaCl
    b. $Al_2(SO_4)_3$ e. BeO   h. $LiNO_3$
    c. $MgCO_3$ f. $NaClO_4$ i. $SrSO_4$

11. What is the mass, in grams, of 8.0 moles of ammonia?

    a. 17 g   c. 51 g   e. 85 g   g. 119 g   i. 153 g
    b. 34 g   d. 68 g   f. 102 g   h. 136 g   j. 170 g

12. A 100 mL graduated cylinder contains 34.0 mL water and weighs (cylinder and water) 100 g. When a metal block is immersed in the water in the cylinder, the level of the water in the cylinder rises to 66.0 mL and the total mass (cylinder, water, and metal) becomes 173 g. What is the density of the metal?

    a. 2.28 g mL^{-1} d. 2.55 g mL^{-1} g. 3.23 g mL^{-1}
    b. 4.15 g mL^{-1} e. 0.11 g mL^{-1} h. 0.71 g mL^{-1}
    c. 3.73 g mL^{-1} f. 2.70 g mL^{-1} i. 0.34 g mL^{-1}

13. A compound containing sulfur, hydrogen, and nitrogen is burned in air and produces sulfur dioxide, water, and nitrogen dioxide. The mole ratio of the products of the reaction were 3.0 mol SO_2, 4.0 mol H_2O, and 2.0 mol NO_2. What is the empirical formula of the compound?

    a. HNS   c. $H_2N_2S_3$ e. $H_4N_2S_3$ g. $H_4N_3S_3$ i. $H_8N_3S_3$
    b. H_2NS d. $H_2N_4S_3$ f. $H_4N_4S_3$ h. $H_8N_2S_3$ j. $H_8N_2S_2O_{14}$

14. Which molecular formula is paired with an incorrect name?

    a. $HClO_3$ chloric acid   f. CCl_4 carbon tetrachloride
    b. FeF_2 iron(II) fluoride   g. NH_3 ammonia
    c. Na_3PO_4 sodium phosphate   h. H_2SO_4 sulfurous acid
    d. HBr   hydrobromic acid   i. $Al_2(SO_4)_3$ aluminum sulfate
    e. CH_3CO_2H acetic acid   j. HNO_3 nitric acid

15. Benzene (C_6H_6) burns in air to produce carbon dioxide and water. If 4.0 moles of benzene is burned in an excess amount of air, how many moles of water are produced?

    a. 1.0 mol   c. 3.0 mol   e. 6.0 mol   g. 12 mol   i. 18 mol
    b. 2.0 mol   d. 4.0 mol   f. 8.0 mol   h. 15 mol   j. 24 mol

16. The reduction of nitric oxide by ammonia is represented by the following equation:

$$\_NH_3 \ + \ \_NO \ \rightarrow \ \_N_2 \ + \ \_H_2O$$

Balance this equation using whole number coefficients. What is the sum of all four coefficients in the balanced equation?

a.	10	c.	13	e.	17	g.	19	i.	21
b.	12	d.	15	f.	18	h.	20	j.	23

17. What are the changes in the oxidation numbers of nitrogen in both NH_3 and NO in the equation listed in the previous question?

	from NH_3 *to* N_2	*from* NO *to* N_2
a.	−1	+1
b.	−2	+2
c.	−3	+1
d.	−3	+2
e.	−5	+2
f.	+2	−1
g.	+3	−2
h.	+3	−3
i.	+5	−2
j.	+5	−4

18. Which aqueous solution contains the greatest concentration of hydronium ions (H_3O^+) ions?

a.	$1.0 \ M \ H_2CO_3$	d.	$1.0 \ M \ HNO_3$	g.	$4.0 \ M \ HCN$
b.	$3.0 \ M \ HF$	e.	$1.0 \ M \ HBr$	h.	$3.0 \ M \ HCl$
c.	$2.0 \ M \ H_3PO_4$	f.	$5.0 \ M \ CH_3CO_2H$	i.	$2.0 \ M \ HClO_3$

19. How many moles of potassium nitrate must be dissolved to make 200 mL of a 2.0 M solution?

a.	0.10 mol	c.	0.30 mol	e.	0.50 mol	g.	0.75 mol	i.	1.0 mol
b.	0.20 mol	d.	0.40 mol	f.	0.60 mol	h.	0.80 mol	j.	2.0 mol

20. Aqueous ammonia and hydrochloric acid react to produce ammonium chloride:

$$NH_3(aq) \ + \ HCl(aq) \ \rightarrow \ NH_4Cl(aq)$$

Identify the spectator ion(s) in this reaction.

a.	NH_4^+	c.	H^+	e.	NH_4^+ and Cl^-	g.	NH_4^+ and OH^-
b.	Cl^-	d.	OH^-	f.	NH_4^+ and H^+	h.	NH_4^+, Cl^-, H^+ and OH^-

21. Pressure is exerted on a system so that 90 J of work is done on the system. As a result, the system warms up and liberates 35 J of heat to the surroundings. What is the change in the internal energy of the system?

a.	+35 J	c.	+55 J	e.	+90 J	g.	+125 J
b.	−35 J	d.	−55 J	f.	−90 J	h.	−125 J

22. Some substances, by definition, have a standard enthalpy of formation ΔH_f° equal to zero. Which one of the following is such a substance?

    a. $CO_2(g)$ c. $N_2(g)$ e. $H_2O(l)$ g. $I_2(g)$

    b. $Cl_2(l)$ d. $NaCl(s)$ f. $Xe(s)$ h. $C_6H_6(l)$

23. The enthalpy change when 1.0 mol of propane C_3H_8 burns in air is -2220 kJ mol^{-1} (the reaction is exothermic). How much heat is released when 1.0 kg of propane is burned?

    a. 5,000 kJ c. 20,000 kJ e. 50,000 kJ

    b. 10,000 kJ d. 25,000 kJ f. 100,000 kJ

24. A 35 g block of metal at 80°C is added to a mixture of 100 g of water and 15 g of ice in an insulated container. All the ice melted and the temperature in the container rose to 10°C. What is the specific heat of the metal?

    The specific heat of water = 4.184 J g^{-1} K^{-1}
    The latent heat of fusion ΔH_{fus} of water = 333 J g^{-1}

    a. 1.2 J g^{-1} K^{-1} d. 2.0 J g^{-1} K^{-1} g. 3.0 J g^{-1} K^{-1}

    b. 1.5 J g^{-1} K^{-1} e. 2.5 J g^{-1} K^{-1} h. 3.5 J g^{-1} K^{-1}

    c. 1.9 J g^{-1} K^{-1} f. 2.8 J g^{-1} K^{-1} i. 4.0 J g^{-1} K^{-1}

25. Use the following information to calculate the standard enthalpy of formation ΔH_f° for methane gas CH_4.

    $$CH_4(g) + 2\,O_2(g) \rightarrow CO_2(g) + 2\,H_2O(l) \quad \Delta H^\circ = -890.3 \text{ kJ}$$
    $$C(s) + O_2(g) \rightarrow CO_2(g) \quad \Delta H^\circ = -393.5 \text{ kJ}$$
    $$H_2(g) + \tfrac{1}{2}\,O_2(g) \rightarrow H_2O(l) \quad \Delta H^\circ = -285.8 \text{ kJ}$$

    a. -1569.6 kJ d. -413.6 kJ g. $+211.0$ kJ

    b. $+815.5$ kJ e. -571.6 kJ h. -74.8 kJ

    c. $+318.7$ kJ f. $+1068.4$ kJ

26. When the bonds that are broken in a chemical reaction are stronger than the bonds that are made in the reaction, then the reaction is...

    a. endothermic b. exothermic

27. What is the energy, in Joules, of a photon with wavelength of 500nm?

    a. 2.4×10^{-17} J c. 6.0×10^{14} J e. 4.0×10^{-19} J g. 7.5×10^{-34} J

    b. 3.9×10^{-28} J d. 2.5×10^{18} J f. 5.0×10^{-19} J h. 1.1×10^{-48} J

28. What are the values of n, l, and m_l for the last electron placed in a potassium atom as the ground state of the potassium atom is built up?

	n	l	m_l			n	l	m_l
a.	3	0	0		e.	2	1	-1
b.	3	1	$+1$		f.	4	1	$+1$
c.	3	2	0		g.	4	0	0
d.	2	0	0		h.	4	2	0

29.   How many unpaired electrons are there in a phosphorus atom in its ground state?

    a. 0   b. 1   c. 2   d. 3   e. 4   f. 5

30.   Start with the number of orbitals in any set of d orbitals,
      ...add the number of protons in the nucleus of a boron atom,
      ...add the number of electrons in the valence shell of a nitrogen atom,
      ...add the number of the period in which rubidium and strontium lie,
      What's the result?

    a. 16   c. 18   e. 20   g. 22   i. 24
    b. 17   d. 19   f. 21   h. 23   j. 25

31.   The electron affinity of an element depends on its:

        A. size
        B. nuclear charge
        C. electron configuration

    a. A only   c. C only   e. A and C   g. A, B, and C
    b. B only   d. A and B   f. B and C   h. none of the above

32.   The central atom in a molecule has two nonbonding pairs of electrons and two bonding pairs of electrons in its valence shell. What is the arrangement of these pairs of electrons around the central atom?

    a. linear   d. square planar   g. square pyramidal
    b. trigonal planar   e. trigonal pyramidal   h. octahedral
    c. tetrahedral   f. trigonal bipyramidal

33.   What is the shape of the molecule HArF?

    a. trigonal bipyramid   d. linear   g. T-shaped
    b. bent   e. tetrahedral   h. see-saw
    c. trigonal planar   f. trigonal pyramid i. octahedral

34.   A possible Lewis structure for the fulminate ion CNO^- is illustrated below. What are the formal charges on the elements in this structure?

       C   N   O

    a. 0   0   0
    b. −1   +1   0
    c. −2   0   +1
    d. 0   0   −1
    e. −1   +1   −1
    f. −2   +1   0
    g. 0   +1   +1
    h. −2   +1   −1
    i. −2   −1   0
    j. −1   −1   +1

$$[\ddot{\text{C}}\!=\!\text{N}\!=\!\ddot{\text{O}}\,]^-$$

35.   How many lone pairs of electrons are there in the valence shell of the central atom in the ion BrF_4^-?

    a. 0   b. 1   c. 2   d. 3   e. 4   f. 5

36. What is the hybridization of the atomic orbitals on the selenium atom in the molecule $SeCl_4$?

    a. sp   b. sp^2 c. sp^3 d. sp^2d e. sp^3d f. sp^3d^2

37. A 6.0 L vessel contains 2.0 mole H_2, 4.0 moles N_2, and 4.0 moles Ne at a pressure of 30 atm. An additional 2.0 moles of neon is then added to the vessel with no change in the volume or temperature. What is the partial pressure of neon at the end?

    a. 2.0 atm   c. 6.0 atm   e. 10 atm   g. 16 atm   i. 20 atm
    b. 4.0 atm   d. 8.0 atm   f. 12 atm   h. 18 atm   j. 24 atm

38. Suppose that a 3.0 liter vessel contains nitrogen gas at 2.0 atm pressure. Suppose that a second vessel, 3.0 liters in volume, contains hydrogen gas at 6.0 atm pressure. Now suppose that a pipe of negligible volume connects the two vessels and the two gases mix and react to form as much ammonia as possible. Assume that the temperature remains constant. What is the pressure in the apparatus at the end of the reaction?

$$N_2(g) \; + \; 3\,H_2(g) \; \rightarrow \; 2\,NH_3(g)$$

    a. ½ atm   c. 2 atm   e. 4 atm   g. 6 atm
    b. 1 atm   d. 3 atm   f. 5 atm   h. 8 atm

39. The cubic unit cell of a compound is illustrated below. The small black circles represent atom A; the large gray circles represent atom B; and the small pale circle at the center represents atom C. What is the stoichiometry of the compound?

    a. ABC   f. A_2B_3C
    b. A_2BC g. A_3B_2C
    c. A_3BC h. A_3B_3C
    d. AB_2C i. A_3B_6C
    e. AB_3C j. $A_6B_{12}C$

40. Which statement is *not* an expression of the second law of thermodynamics?

    a. All systems are driven toward equilibrium
    b. The entropy of the universe increases for any spontaneous process
    c. A system in equilibrium that is disturbed will adjust to regain equilibrium
    d. In any spontaneous process the free energy of the system will decrease
    e. The energy of the universe is conserved
    f. The entropy of an isolated system must increase for a spontaneous change in the system

41. A solution is made by adding 1.2 kg ethylene glycol $HOCH_2CH_2OH$ (molar mass 62.1 g mol^{-1}) to 4.0 kg water. What is the *molality* of the solution?

    a. 0.08 m c. 4.8 m e. 9.6 m g. 23 m
    b. 0.21 m d. 5.2 m f. 17 m h. 30 m

42. An ideal solution is prepared by mixing 4.0 moles A with 1.0 mole B. At the temperature of the liquid, the vapor pressure of pure A is 300 torr and the vapor pressure of pure B is 65.0 torr. What is the vapor pressure of B above the solution at this temperature?

    a. 13 torr   c. 52 torr   e. 253 torr   g. 65 torr
    b. 365 torr   d. 240 torr   f. 112 torr   h. 60 torr

43. The equilibrium constant K for the following reaction is 49.78.

$$H_2(g) + I_2(g) \rightleftharpoons 2\,HI(g)$$

Determine if the reaction is at equilibrium when $[H_2] = 0.350\ M$, $[I_2] = 0.450\ M$, and $[HI] = 2.80 M$. What is the relationship between the equilibrium constant K and the reaction quotient Q under these conditions and in which direction will the reaction shift (if necessary) to re-establish the equilibrium?

a. $Q < K$ shift left
b. $Q < K$ no shift
c. $Q < K$ shift right
d. $Q > K$ shift left
e. $Q > K$ no shift
f. $Q > K$ shift right
g. $Q = K$ shift left
h. $Q = K$ no shift
i. $Q = K$ shift right

44. Which one of the following will *not* disturb a system in equilibrium?

a. change in concentration
b. change in temperature
c. change in volume or pressure
d. addition of a catalyst

45. In the following aqueous equilibrium, label the components according to the Brønsted-Lowry theory of acids and bases:

$$ClO_4^- + H_2O \rightleftharpoons HClO_4 + OH^-$$

a. base   acid   base   acid
b. base   acid   acid   base
c. base   base   acid   acid
d. acid   acid   base   base
e. acid   base   acid   base
f. acid   base   base   acid

46. On which side of the equilibrium described in the previous question does the system predominantly lie?

a. the left side   b. the right side

47. What is the conjugate acid of HPO_4^{2-}?

a. PO_4^{3-} b. HPO_4^{2-} c. $H_2PO_4^-$ d. H_3PO_4

48. How many strong acids are there in the following list?

H_2SO_4	H_3PO_4	HNO_3	HF	HCl
HI	H_2CO_3	HCN	$HClO_4$	CH_3CO_2H

a. 0   c. 2   e. 4   g. 6
b. 1   d. 3   f. 5   h. 7

49. What is the pH of an $0.020\ M\,HClO_3$ solution?

a. 14.0   c. 9.2   e. 5.4   g. 1.7
b. 12.3   d. 7.0   f. 3.2   h. 0.4

50. Which salt hydrolyzes in aqueous solution to produce an acidic solution?

a. Na_3PO_4 c. KF e. $NaNO_3$ g. $NaCN$ i. KBr
b. NH_4I d. $CaCO_3$ f. $NaHCO_3$ h. $Mg(ClO_4)_2$ j. CH_3CO_2Na

FINAL EXAMINATION

CHEMISTRY 141 Spring 2007

Thursday May 3rd 2007

1. What is the formula for magnesium perchlorate?

    a. $MgClO_2$ c. $MgCrO_4$ e. $Mg(ClO_3)_2$ g. $MgCO_3$
    b. $Mg(HCO_3)_2$ d. $Mg(ClO_4)_2$ f. $MgCr_2O_7$ h. Mg_2ClO

2. Which one of the following compounds contains an alkaline earth metal?

    a. Na_3PO_4 c. KCN e. $CaSO_4$ g. CO_2
    b. $Pb(CO_3)_2$ d. FeS f. $(NH_4)_2CrO_4$ h. $AgSO_4$

3. What is the mass of 6.0 moles of N_2O?

    a. 30 g   c. 46 g   e. 168 g   g. 264 g
    b. 44 g   d. 132 g   f. 192 g   h. 276 g

4. How many oxygen atoms are in 3.0 moles of SO_2?

    a. 6.022×10^{23} atoms   d. 2.409×10^{24} atoms   g. 4.215×10^{24} atoms
    b. 1.204×10^{24} atoms   e. 3.011×10^{24} atoms   h. 4.818×10^{24} atoms
    c. 1.807×10^{24} atoms   f. 3.613×10^{24} atoms

5. One compound found in chocolate is called dimethylpyrazine ($C_6H_8N_2$). What is the percent by mass of nitrogen in dimethylpyrazine?

    a. 7.47%   c. 25.91%   e. 46.17%   g. 66.60%
    b. 12.95%   d. 28.02%   f. 52.96%   h. 85.34%

6. Balance the following reaction using whole number coefficients:

    _____ $Na_2S_2O_3$ + _____ I_2 $\rightarrow$ _____ NaI + _____ $Na_2S_4O_6$

    What is the sum of all of the coefficients?

    a. 2   c. 4   e. 6   g. 9
    b. 3   d. 5   f. 8   h. 11

7. A block of iron has a width of 5.0 cm, a length of 7.0 cm, and a height of 3.0 cm. The density of iron is 7.86 g cm^{-3}. What is the mass of the iron block?

    a. 14 g   c. 55 g   e. 117 g   g. 694 g
    b. 24 g   d. 105 g   f. 275 g   h. 825 g

8. What is the molar mass of potassium nitrite?

    a. 85 g mol^{-1} c. 77 g mol^{-1} e. 57 g mol^{-1} g. 93 g mol^{-1}
    b. 69 g mol^{-1} d. 117 g mol^{-1} f. 101 g mol^{-1} h. 65 g mol^{-1}

9. How many moles of oxygen are consumed in the complete combustion of 3.0 moles of propane C_3H_8? *(Hint: Write the balanced equation.)*

    a. 1 mole   c. 5 moles   e. 9 moles   g. 15 moles
    b. 3 moles   d. 7 moles   f. 12 moles   h. 21 moles

10. Phosphorus reacts with chlorine to produce phosphorus trichloride according to the reaction shown below. If 124 g P_4 react completely with 500 g Cl_2, how much PCl_3 will be produced?

    $$P_4(s) \; + \; 6\,Cl_2(g) \; \rightarrow \; 4\,PCl_3(l)$$

    a. 83 g   c. 641 g   e. 333 g   g. 414 g
    b. 160 g   d. 549 g   f. 94 g   h. 137 g

11. How many protons, neutrons, and electrons are in one calcium ion?

	protons	*neutrons*	*electrons*
a.	18	20	20
b.	18	40	20
c.	40	20	18
d.	40	20	19
e.	20	20	19
f.	20	20	18
g.	20	20	22
h.	20	20	20

12. An organic compound containing carbon, nitrogen, and hydrogen was burned in oxygen to produce 0.458 g CO_2, 0.374 g H_2O, and 0.146 g N_2. What is the empirical formula of the compound?

    a. CHN c. CH_4N e. CH_4N_2 g. $C_2H_2N_3$
    b. CH_2N d. C_2HN f. CH_2N_2 h. $C_2H_4N_2$

13. 1.5 mol $TiCl_4(aq)$ reacts with excess oxygen to produce 0.85 mol $TiO_2(s)$. What is the percent yield of this reaction?

    $$TiCl_4(aq) \; + \; O_2(g) \; \rightarrow \; TiO_2(s) \; + \; 2\,Cl_2(g)$$

    a. 23%   c. 42%   e. 61%   g. 83%
    b. 36%   d. 57%   f. 79%   h. 95%

14. A new element X was discovered to have two isotopes, ^{89}X (15.40% abundance, 88.989 amu) and ^{90}X (84.60% abundance, 89.855 amu). What is the atomic mass of element X?

    a. 89.00 amu   c. 89.26 amu   e. 89.50 amu   g. 89.72 amu
    b. 89.14 amu   d. 89.43 amu   f. 89.68 amu   h. 90.00 amu

15. Aqueous magnesium nitrate reacts with aqueous sodium hydroxide to produce aqueous sodium nitrate and solid magnesium hydroxide. What are the spectator ions for this reaction?

    a. Na^+ e. Na^+ and NO_3^- i. Na^+, OH^-, and NO_3^-
    b. Mg^{2+} f. Na^+ and OH^- j. Mg^{2+}, Na^+, NO_3^-, and OH^-
    c. NO_3^- g. Mg^{2+} and NO_3^-
    d. OH^- h. Mg^{2+} and OH^-

16. What is the oxidation number for iodine in each of these ions?

    I_3^- IO_4^- IO^-

    a. 0   +1   −1
    b. 0   +7   −1
    c. −1/3   +7   −1
    d. −1/3   +7   +1
    e. −1   +1   −1
    f. −1   +7   −1
    g. +1   +7   −1
    h. +1   +7   −2

17. How many mL of a 2.5 M H_2SO_4 aqueous solution must be added to water to make 0.75 L of a 0.04 M H_2SO_4 aqueous solution?

    a. 0.01 mL   c. 133 mL   e. 83 mL   g. 120 mL
    b. 40 mL   d. 12 mL   f. 7.5 mL   h. 67 mL

    Use the following information to answer questions 18 and 19:

    Specific heat of water = 4.184 J g^{-1} K^{-1}
    Latent heat of fusion of ice = 333 J g^{-1}
    Latent heat of vaporization of water = 2260 J g^{-1}

18. How much heat is needed to heat to boiling and completely vaporize 14.0 g of liquid water initially at 0°C?

    a. 10.5 kJ   c. 5.6 kJ   e. 21 kJ   g. 525 kJ
    b. 1.2 kJ   d. 37.5 kJ   f. 4.7 kJ   h. 107 kJ

19. 10.0 g of ice at 0°C was added to 30.0 g of water at 15°C. How much of the ice melts?

    a. 0 g   c. 1.2 g   e. 4.4 g   g. 7.4 g
    b. 0.8 g   d. 3.9 g   f. 5.7 g   h. 10 g

20. Which one of the following substances has a ΔH_f° <u>not</u> equal to zero?

    a. Ar*(g)*   c. Na*(s)*   e. Hg*(l)*   g. C*(s)*
    b. Pb*(l)*   d. H_2*(g)*   f. Al*(s)*   h. O_2*(g)*

21. What is the ΔH_{rxn} in kJ for the following reaction?

    $2 C_6H_6(l) + 15 O_2(g) \rightarrow 12 CO_2(g) + 6 H_2O(l)$ ΔH_{rxn} = ???

    ΔH_f° $C_6H_6(l)$ = +49 kJ mol^{-1}
    ΔH_f° $CO_2(g)$ = −393.5 kJ mol^{-1}
    ΔH_f° $H_2O(l)$ = −285.8 kJ mol^{-1}

    a. −6535 kJ   c. −728 kJ   e. −5889 kJ   g. −58.7 kJ
    b. +6535 kJ   d. +728 kJ   f. +5889 kJ   h. +58.7 kJ

22. Calculate the change in enthalpy for this reaction:

$$4\,Al(s) + 3\,O_2(g) \rightarrow 2\,Al_2O_3(s) \qquad \Delta H^\circ_{rxn} = ???$$

given this information:

$\Delta H^\circ_f\ MnO_2(s) = -520\ kJ\ mol^{-1}$
$4\,Al(s) + 3\,MnO_2(s) \rightarrow 3\,Mn(s) + 2\,Al_2O_3(s)\ \ \Delta H^\circ = -1792\ kJ$

a. +232 kJ mol^{-1} c. +2312 kJ mol^{-1} e. +3352 kJ mol^{-1} g. +5376 kJ mol^{-1}
b. −232 kJ mol^{-1} d. −2312 kJ mol^{-1} f. −3352 kJ mol^{-1} h. −5376 kJ mol^{-1}

23. According to the following equation, how much heat is produced when 1.5 moles of butane C_4H_{10} are burned in excess oxygen?

$$2\,C_4H_{10}(l) + 13\,O_2(g) \rightarrow 8\,CO_2(g) + 10\,H_2O(l)\ \ \Delta H^\circ = -5754\ kJ$$

a. 5754 kJ   c. 7672 kJ   e. 8631 kJ   g. 11508 kJ
b. 4315 kJ   d. 2877 kJ   f. 3836 kJ   h. 20139 kJ

24. Radiation has a frequency of 93.7 MHz. What is the wavelength of these radiowaves?

a. 3.2 m   c. 10.9 m   e. 37.9 m   g. 60.4 m
b. 4.5 m   d. 20.2 m   f. 56.1 m   h. 79.5 m

25. Which occupied valence orbital is highest in energy for each of the following atoms?

    B Cs Ga   B Cs Ga

a. 2p 4s 4p   e. 3p 5s 3p
b. 2p 5s 4p   f. 3p 6s 4p
c. 2p 6s 4p   g. 2s 4s 5s
d. 3p 4s 2p   h. 2s 6s 6s

26. Which element has the ground state electron configuration: $1s^22s^22p^63s^23p^64s^23d^7$?

a. Pd   c. Zn   e. Rh   g. Fe
b. Ca   d. Mn   f. Ni   h. Co

27. Which one of the following statements is <u>false</u>?

a. Radiowaves have less energy than microwaves.
b. The wavelength of red light is longer than the wavelength of blue light.
c. X-rays have more energy than ultraviolet light.
d. The frequency of orange light is greater than the frequency of green light.
e. The energy of one photon of light is equal to the frequency of that light times Planck's constant.

28. What is the name of the electron arrangement from which the molecular shape shown below was derived?

a. linear   c. trigonal planar   e. trigonal bipyramidal
b. tetrahedral   d. trigonal pyramidal   f. octahedral

29. Which one of the following molecules / ions has a central atom that does not obey the octet rule?

    a. CH_4 c. NH_3 e. CO_3^{2-} g. SBr_2
    b. $BeCl_2$ d. H_2S f. SF_3^+ h. HCN

30. What is the molecular shape of XeF_4?

    a. tetrahedral   c. see-saw   e. trigonal pyramidal   g. octahedral
    b. trigonal bipyramidal   d. trigonal planar   f. T-shaped   h. square planar

31. What is the hybridization of the valence orbitals on carbon in the molecule $COCl_2$?

    a. sp b. sp^2 c. sp^3 d. sp^3d e. sp^3d^2

32. Suppose there are two vessels connected by a tap that is closed. The first vessel is 2.0 L in volume and contains helium gas as a pressure of 6.0 atm. The second vessel is empty (contains no gas). When the tap is opened the pressure of the He gas drops to 2.0 atm. What is the volume of the second vessel?

    a. 2.0 L   c. 4.0 L   e. 8.0 L   g. 16.0 L
    b. 3.0 L   d. 6.0 L   f. 10.0 L   h. 18.0 L

33. A 4.0 L vessel contains 2.0 moles of hydrogen gas, 3.0 moles argon gas, and 6.0 moles nitrogen gas at a pressure of 15.0 atm. Keeping the temperature constant, an additional 1.5 moles of hydrogen are added. What is the partial pressure of the hydrogen gas at the end assuming that the gases behave ideally?

    a. 2.7 atm   c. 8.2 atm   e. 11.6 atm   g. 15 atm
    b. 4.8 atm   d. 10.4 atm   f. 12.3 atm   h. 17 atm

34. Methane (CH_4) gas effuses through a small hole as a rate of 3.0 moles per minute. An unknown gas under the same conditions effuses through the same hole at a rate of 1.4 moles per minute. What is the molar mass of the unknown gas?

    a. 3.48 g mol^{-1} c. 70.9 g mol^{-1} e. 28.0 g mol^{-1} g. 20.2 g mol^{-1}
    b. 73.5 g mol^{-1} d. 49.4 g mol^{-1} f. 34.3 g mol^{-1} h. 55.0 g mol^{-1}

35. A unit cell of an unknown compound contains element X in a face centered cubic arrangement. How many atoms of X are in one unit cell of this compound?

    a. 1   c. 3   e. 5   g. 7   i. 12
    b. 2   d. 4   f. 6   h. 8   j. 14

36. Arrange these substances in order of decreasing melting or boiling point: CH_4, CH_3Cl, C (diamond), and H_2O.

    a. C (diamond) H_2O CH_3Cl CH_4
    b. C (diamond) CH_3Cl H_2O CH_4
    c. CH_4 H_2O CH_3Cl C (diamond)
    d. C (diamond) H_2O CH_4 CH_3Cl
    e. CH_4 CH_3Cl C (diamond) H_2O
    f. CH_3Cl CH_4 C (diamond) H_2O

37. When solid potassium hydroxide dissolves in water, the solution gets very hot. What are the signs for ΔG, ΔH, and ΔS for this process?

	ΔG	ΔH	ΔS		ΔG	ΔH	ΔS
a.	+	+	+	e.	+	−	+
b.	+	+	−	f.	+	−	−
c.	−	+	+	g.	−	−	+
d.	−	+	−	h.	−	−	−

38. A solution is made from two volatile liquids, hexane and pentane. The mole fraction of hexane is 0.45. The vapor pressure of pure hexane is 88.7 torr at room temperature and the vapor pressure of pure pentane is 44.5 torr at room temperature. What is the total vapor pressure above this solution at room temperature?

a. 44.2 torr   c. 68.8 torr   e. 133.2 torr   g. 585 torr
b. 64.4 torr   d. 72.1 torr   f. 476 torr   h. 760 torr

39. What is the *molality* (*m*) of an 18% by mass aqueous solution of methanol CH_3OH?

a. 0.15 *m*   c. 3.65 *m*   e. 8.04 *m*   g. 142 *m*
b. 2.56 *m*   d. 6.85 *m*   f. 9.87 *m*   h. 220 *m*

40. Which one of the following aqueous solutions has the <u>highest</u> freezing point?

a. 0.35 *m* Na_2SO_4 d. 0.45 *m* KOH
b. 0.50 *m* NH_3 e. 0.30 *m* NH_4NO_3
c. 0.25 *m* K_2CrO_4 f. 0.60 *m* CH_3CO_2H

41. Which one of the following statements is <u>false</u>?

a. At equilibrium, the rate of the forward reaction is equal to the rate of the reverse reaction.
b. A catalyst lowers the activation energy of a reaction.
c. At equilibrium, the concentrations of the reactants are equal to zero.
d. The rate of a reaction is proportional to the concentrations of the reactants.
e. The change in enthalpy for a chemical reaction is a thermodynamic quantity.

42. Consider the following equilibrium:

$$H^+(aq) + CaCO_3(s) \rightleftharpoons Ca^{2+}(aq) + HCO_3^-(aq)$$

In which direction will the equilibrium shift if the following changes are made? *(Choose the row where all responses are correct.)*

	add $H^+(aq)$	add $CaCO_3(s)$	add $Ca^{2+}(aq)$	add a catalyst
a.	left	left	right	right
b.	left	right	left	right
c.	no change	left	no change	right
d.	no change	right	no change	left
e.	left	no change	right	no change
f.	right	no change	left	no change
g.	left	no change	left	no change
h.	right	no change	right	no change

43. What is the net ionic equation describing the equilibrium that is established when lithium hypochlorite is dissolved in water?

   a. $Li^+ + OH^- \rightleftharpoons LiOH$

   b. $ClO^- + H_2O \rightleftharpoons HClO + OH^-$

   c. $ClO^- + H_3O^+ \rightleftharpoons HClO + H_2O$

   d. $2 H_2O \rightleftharpoons H_3O^+ + OH^-$

   e. $ClO^- + H^+ \rightleftharpoons HClO$

   f. $LiClO \rightleftharpoons Li^+ + ClO^-$

   g. $Li^+ + OH^- + ClO^- + H_3O^+ \rightleftharpoons LiOH + HClO + H_2O$

   h. $LiClO + H_2O \rightleftharpoons LiOH + HClO$

44. Complete the following equilibrium and label the missing molecule / ion as an acid or a base.

   $$C_6H_5CO_2^-(aq) + H_2O(l) \rightleftharpoons \underline{\hspace{1cm}} + OH^-(aq)$$

   a. $C_6H_5CO_2H$, acid   d. H_3O^+, base   g. $C_6H_5CO_2^-$, acid
   b. $C_6H_5CO_2H$, base   e. CO_3^{2-}, acid   h. $C_6H_5CO_2^-$, base
   c. H_3O^+, acid   f. CO_3^{2-}, base

45. Which one of the following ions is amphiprotic?

   a. SO_3^{2-} c. HSO_4^- e. NO_3^- g. ClO_2^-
   b. SO_4^{2-} d. NO_2^- f. ClO^- h. ClO_3^-

46. Consider the following equilibrium:

   $$CO_2(aq) + H_2O(l) \rightleftharpoons H^+(aq) + HCO_3^-(aq)$$

   At equilibrium, the concentration of CO_2 is 1.8 M, the concentration of H^+ is 0.6 M, and the concentration of HCO_3^- is 0.6 M. What is the equilibrium constant K for this reaction?

   a. 0.13   c. 0.51   e. 3.7   g. 9.7
   b. 0.20   d. 1.8   f. 5.7   h. 11.2

47. What is the pH of a 0.3 M solution of magnesium hydroxide?

   a. 1.6   c. 7.0   e. 11.7   g. 13.8
   b. 3.8   d. 10.9   f. 12.2   h. 14.0

48. Consider the following equilibrium:

   $$CaC_2O_4(s) \rightleftharpoons Ca^{2+}(aq) + C_2O_4^{2-}(aq)$$

   At equilibrium, the concentrations of the calcium ion and the oxalate ion are both 2.0 M. If the concentration of the calcium ion is increased to 3.0 M, what will be the concentration of the oxalate ion after the equilibrium is reestablished?

   a. 0.75 M   c. 1.6 M   e. 2.3 M   g. 3.0 M
   b. 1.0 M   d. 2.0 M   f. 2.6 M   h. 0.40 M

49. How many of the following electrolytes will be levelled to H_3O^+ in aqueous solution?

        HBr HNO_3 H_3PO_4

        HF H_2SO_4 $HClO_4$

    a. none   c. 2   e. 4   g. all of them

    b. 1   d. 3   f. 5

50. Which of the following statements is/are <u>true</u>?

    I.   A neutral solution is one in which $[H_3O^+] = [OH^-]$.

    II. The pH of pure water at 37 °C is 6.7; therefore water at 37°C is acidic.

    III. An aqueous solution of $LiCO_3$ is basic.

    a. none are true   c. II only   e. I and II   g. II and III

    b. I only   d. III only   f. I and III   h. all are true

FINAL EXAMINATION

CHEMISTRY 141 Fall 2007

Tuesday December 11th 2007

1. What is the chemical symbol for the element silver?

   a. S   c. Ag   e. Au   g. Si
   b. Na   d. Sb   f. Pb   h. W

2. Which pair (name / formula) in the following list do not match?

   a. sulfite SO_3^{2-} f. carbonate CO_3^{2-}
   b. cyanide CN^- g. nitrate NO_3^-
   c. chlorite ClO_3^- h. chromate CrO_4^{2-}
   d. sulfate SO_4^{2-} i. acetate $CH_3CO_2^-$
   e. permanganate MnO_4^- j. phosphate PO_4^{3-}

3. Examples of an alkaline earth metal, a lanthanide, a transition metal, and a halogen, are, in that order: *Choose the row where all the descriptions fit.*

	alkaline earth metal	lanthanide	transition metal	halogen
a.	Na	Pm	Sn	Ne
b.	Mg	Pa	Fe	F
c.	Ca	Ce	Cu	Cl
d.	K	Eu	Zr	Br
e.	Ba	La	Pb	I
f.	Be	Hg	Cr	N

4. How many moles of oxygen atoms are in 3 moles of aluminum sulfate?

   a. 3 c. 6 e. 9 g. 16 i. 24
   b. 4 d. 8 f. 12 h. 18 j. 36

5. Which one of the following substances is classified as a binary molecular compound?

   a. KBr   c. H_2CO e. $MgCl_2$ g. K_3PO_4 i. HNO_3
   b. H_2 d. C_2H_5OH f. I_2 h. $XeOF_4$ j. H_2O

6. 2.50 moles of an element have a mass of 488 grams. What is the element?

   a. Rb c. Ti e. W g. Po i. Cd
   b. Cs d. Os f. Hg h. Ge j. Pt

7. What is the volume in m^3 of a box that has the dimensions 1.0 ft by 3.5 ft by 0.5 ft?

   a. $0.05 \ m^3$ c. $0.53 \ m^3$ e. $1.4 \ m^3$ g. $3.9 \ m^3$
   b. $0.14 \ m^3$ d. $0.96 \ m^3$ f. $1.7 \ m^3$ h. $4.9 \times 10^4 \ m^3$

8.   What is the mass of 6.00 moles of methane molecules (CH_4)?

      a. 16 g   c. 48 g   e. 72 g   g. 144 g
      b. 32 g   d. 64 g   f. 96 g   h. 192 g

9.   What is the molar mass of potassium dichromate?

      a. 91.1 g mol^{-1} c. 138.2 g mol^{-1} e. 177.6 g mol^{-1} g. 277.9 g mol^{-1}
      b. 105.1 g mol^{-1} d. 144.2 g mol^{-1} f. 255.1 g mol^{-1} h. 294.2 g mol^{-1}

10.   4.0 moles of propane C_3H_8 reacts with 6.0 moles of oxygen to produce carbon dioxide and water. What is the maximum amount of carbon dioxide that can be produced?

      a. 0 mole   c. 2.8 moles   e. 3.6 moles   g. 6.0 moles   i. 12.0 moles
      b. 1.2 moles   d. 3.0 moles   f. 4.8 moles   h. 10.0 moles   j. 15.0 moles

11.   0.347 g red phosphorus P_4 reacts with 2.68 g liquid bromine Br_2 to produce a phosphorus bromide. What is the empirical formula of the phosphorus bromide produced in this reaction?

      a. PBr_2 c. PBr_6 e. P_3Br_4 g. P_5Br
      b. PBr_3 d. P_3Br_2 f. P_4Br_2 h. P_5Br_2

12.   Which sample contains the greatest mass of oxygen?

      a. 3.0 moles of water H_2O e. 9.0 moles of sodium nitrate $NaNO_3$
      b. 4.0 moles of methanol CH_3OH f. 10.0 moles of hydrogen peroxide H_2O_2
      c. 5.0 moles of ozone O_3 g. 12.0 moles of sulfur dioxide SO_2
      d. 6.0 moles of sulfuric acid H_2SO_4

13.   Balance the following equation:

      $$\_ HSbCl_4 \ + \ \_ H_2S \ \rightarrow \ \_ Sb_2S_3 \ + \ \_ HCl$$

      What is the sum of *all* the coefficients in the balanced equation?

      a. 6   c. 11   e. 13   g. 17   i. 21
      b. 8   d. 12   f. 14   h. 19   j. 28

14.   Identify the spectator ions in the reaction of sodium bicarbonate with nitric acid to produce sodium nitrate, carbon dioxide, and water.

      a. Na^+ c. HCO_3^- e. Na^+ and NO_3^-
      b. NO_3^- d. H^+ f. Na^+, H^+, and NO_3^-

15.   What is the oxidation number of chlorine in $KClO_3$?

      a. −1   c. +1   e. +3   g. +6
      b. −2   d. +2   f. +5   h. −6

16.   The internal energy of an ideal system increases by 75 J as it does 120 J of work. How much heat was absorbed or released by the system?

      a. q = −45 J   c. q = −75 J   e. q = −120 J   g. q = −195 J
      b. q = +45 J   d. q = +75 J   f. q = +120 J   h. q = +195 J

17. How much heat is required to melt a 15.0 g block of ice initially at 0°C and warm the resulting water to 25°C?

    Specific heat of water   = 4.184 J g^{-1} K^{-1}
    Latent heat of fusion for water   = 333 J g^{-1}

a.	1569 J	c.	2090 J	e.	4995 J	g.	6564 J
b.	2064 J	d.	3321 J	f.	5374 J	h.	7992 J

18. According to the following balanced equation, how much energy is released when 100 g Fe reacts with excess oxygen?

    $$3\ Fe(s)\ +\ 2\ O_2(g)\ \rightarrow\ Fe_3O_4(s) \qquad \Delta H = -1118.4\ kJ$$

a.	667.5 kJ	c.	1118 kJ	e.	208.2 kJ	g.	1249 kJ
b.	2002 kJ	d.	3728 kJ	f.	334.9 kJ	h.	2476 kJ

19. Which statement is correct?

    a. molarity × moles = volume
    b. molarity × volume = number of moles
    c. mass × number of moles = molar mass
    d. volume × molarity = mass
    e. mass × molar mass = number of moles
    f. mass × volume = density

20. 160 g of sodium hydroxide NaOH was dissolved in water to make 400 mL of a concentrated solution. Sufficient water was then carefully added to dilute the solution to a volume of 1.0 L. What is the concentration of the diluted solution?

a.	1.0 M	c.	2.0 M	e.	3.0 M	g.	6.0 M
b.	1.5 M	d.	2.67 M	f.	4.0 M	h.	10.0 M

21. In old-fashioned darkrooms a "safe-light" was a light (in the visible region) that could be turned on while you were developing "slow" black and white film. Consider Planck's equation and determine the most likely color of this safe light.

    a. blue
    b. violet
    c. yellow
    d. green
    e. indigo
    f. red

22. Which of the following statements is not applicable in regard to Heisenberg's Uncertainty Principle?

    a. Electrons can behave both as particles and as waves.
    b. Light with a short enough wavelength to probe inside an atom will disrupt that atom.
    c. One cannot design an experiment that will produce precise values for both position and momentum simultaneously.
    d. Red light has a longer wavelength than blue light.
    e. Measurements on microscopic systems perturb the systems, resulting in a fundamental limit to the precision of a measurement.
    f. If you design an experiment to measure the wave nature of an electron, nature will cooperate and give you wave-like results.

23. Which element has the highest electronegativity?

a.	aluminum	c.	silicon	e.	phosphorus	g.	sulfur	i.	chlorine
b.	gallium	d.	germanium	f.	arsenic	h.	selenium	j.	bromine

24.   Which statement is true?

a.   According to the *aufbau* principle, the 3d orbitals are filled before the 4s orbital.
b.   The quantum number n indicates the shape of the orbital.
c.   If $m_l = 0$, the orbital must be a p orbital.
d.   The three p orbitals in a set have three different orientations.
e.   In the ground state electron configuration of iron, all electrons are paired (i.e. there are no unpaired electrons).
f.   If n=2, the only allowed value of l is 2.

25.   An ion of zirconium has an electron configuration [Kr]. What is the charge on this ion?

a. 4–   c. 2–   e. 1+   g. 3+
b. 3–   d. 1–   f. 2+   h. 4+

26.   What is the electron arrangement around the central atom of the polyatomic ion ICl_4^-?

a. tetrahedral   d. bent   g. trigonal bipyramidal
b. square planar   e. see-saw   h. square pyramidal
c. octahedral   f. T-shaped   i. trigonal pyramidal

27.   Which of the following molecules is/are polar?

1. PCl_3 2. NF_3 3. CH_4 4. BrF_3

a. 1 only   e. 1 and 3   i. 1, 2 and 4
b. 2 only   f. 1 and 4   j. 1, 3 and 4
c. 3 only   g. 3 and 4
d. 1 and 2   h. 1, 2 and 3

28.   How many of the hydrogen atoms in one molecule of glycine (shown on the right) are capable of participating in a hydrogen bond?

a. 0   c. 2   e. 4
b. 1   d. 3   f. 5

29.   What hybridization of atomic orbitals on the nitrogen atom in glycine (shown above) is necessary to accommodate the arrangement of electron pairs on the nitrogen atom?

a. sp   b. sp^2 c. sp^3 d. sp^3d e. sp^3d^2

30.   Two vessels, equal in volume, contain respectively hydrogen gas and chlorine gas at equal pressures and temperatures. A valve connecting the two vessels is opened; the gases mix, react, and form hydrogen chloride gas:

$$H_2(g) \ + \ Cl_2(g) \ \rightarrow \ 2\,HCl(g)$$

Assuming no change in temperature, does the total pressure inside the combined vessels...

a. decrease
b. increase
c. or stay the same?

31. A 3.0 liter vessel contains 4.0 moles of nitrogen gas and 2.0 moles of argon gas at a total pressure of 15.0 atm. 4.0 moles of helium gas are added to the mixture without changing the temperature or the volume. What is the partial pressure of nitrogen in the new mixture?

    a. 1.0 atm   c. 4.0 atm   e. 6.0 atm   g. 15.0 atm
    b. 2.5 atm   d. 5.0 atm   f. 10.0 atm   h. 25.0 atm

32. A U-tube mercury manometer is open to the atmosphere (1 atm) on the right arm and is connected to a glass vessel containing a gas on the left arm as shown. The pressure of the gas in the glass vessel is 2.25 atm. What is the difference in the levels of the mercury in the two tubes?

    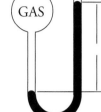

    a. 19 cm   c. 76 cm   e. 114 cm   g. 171 cm
    b. 57 cm   d. 95 cm   f. 152 cm   h. 247 cm

33. Which statement is *incorrect*?

    a. Ideal gases don't really exist.
    b. The larger a molecule is, the slower it moves.
    c. Intermolecular attraction is the most significant reason why gases deviate from ideal behavior.
    d. The vapor pressure of a liquid increases as the temperature increases.
    e. The concentration of a solute can exceed its solubility.
    f. The solid state is the most ordered state.
    g. At the same temperature, smaller molecules have a greater kinetic energy.

34. In the unit cell of an unknown compound of three elements A, B, and C shown on the right below, the grey spheres are A, the black spheres are B, and the white spheres are C.
    How many atoms of each element belong to this unit cell?

	A	B	C
a.	1	1	1
b.	1	2	1
c.	1	1	2
d.	1	2	2
e.	2	1	1
f.	2	2	1
g.	2	1	2
h.	2	2	2
i.	9	4	2

    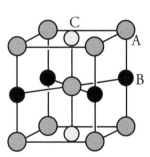

35. The heat of vaporization of liquid water is almost exactly twice the heat of vaporization of liquid ammonia. Why is this?

    a. An N–H hydrogen bond is half the strength of an O–H hydrogen bond
    b. Water is more polar than ammonia
    c. Water is normally a liquid, whereas the normal state of ammonia is as a gas
    d. To separate water molecules, twice as many hydrogen bonds need to be broken
    e. The solid-liquid line on the phase diagram for water slopes to the left instead of the right

36.   Which of the following statements is true for a system undergoing a spontaneous endothermic change?

      a.   The entropy of the system increases.
      b.   The sign for ΔH is negative.
      c.   The entropy change of the universe must be negative.
      d.   The change in the Gibbs free energy of the system is positive.
      e.   The system is at equilibrium.

37.   During which of the following processes does the entropy increase?

      1.   Water freezes to form ice.
      2.   Ethanol and water are mixed to make a solution.
      3.   A gas is cooled down.
      4.   Gasoline (C_8H_{18}) is burned to produce carbon dioxide and water.

      a.   only 1   c.   only 3   e.   2 and 3   g.   2 and 4   i.   none
      b.   only 2   d.   only 4   f.   1 and 4   h.   2, 3, and 4   j.   all

38.   Which one of the following aqueous salt solutions has the *highest* boiling point?

      a.   0.50 *m* copper(II) nitrate $Cu(NO_3)_2$
      b.   0.70 *m* sodium nitrate $NaNO_3$
      c.   0.60 *m* potassium sulfate K_2SO_4
      d.   0.80 *m* sodium acetate $NaCH_3CO_2$
      e.   0.60 *m* potassium iodate KIO_3
      f.   0.80 *m* sodium chloride $NaCl$

39.   A solution is made by adding 0.6 mole of solute to 1.6 moles of solvent. What is the mole fraction of the solute in this solution?

      a.   0.942   c.   0.600   e.   0.375   g.   0.273
      b.   0.727   d.   0.462   f.   0.321   h.   0.140

40.   An ideal solution is made from two volatile liquids, hexane and pentane. The mole fraction of hexane is 0.25. The vapor pressure of pure hexane is 88.7 torr at room temperature and the vapor pressure of pure pentane is 44.5 torr at room temperature. What is the total vapor pressure above this solution at room temperature?

      a.   22.2 torr   c.   44.5 torr   e.   62.7 torr   g.   88.7 torr
      b.   33.4 torr   d.   55.6 torr   f.   77.7 torr   h.   760 torr

41.   Which of the following changes will usually increase the rate of a reaction?

      i.   Adding a catayst
      ii.   Increasing the temperature
      iii. Increasing the concentration of the reactants

      a.   i only   c.   iii only   e.   i and iii   g.   none of them
      b.   ii only   d.   i and ii   f.   ii and iii   h.   all of them i, ii, and iii

42. The equilibrium constant K at a particular temperature for the following reaction is 25.00.

$$NO_2(g) + CO(g) \rightleftharpoons NO(g) + CO_2(g)$$

Initially, 2.0 moles each of NO_2 and CO are injected into an 1.0 liter flask. Calculate the concentration (in moles/liter) of the $CO_2(g)$ at equilibrium at this temperature.

a. 0.33   c. 0.67   e. 1.00   g. 1.50   i. 1.75
b. 0.50   d. 0.75   f. 1.33   h. 1.67   j. 2.00

43. What is the pH of a 0.0010M solution of potassium hydroxide?

a. 1.0   c. 5.0   e. 7.0   g. 11.0
b. 3.0   d. 6.0   f. 9.0   h. 13.0

44. Calculate the equilibrium constant K for the following equilibrium if the equilibrium concentration of dinitrogen tetroxide is 0.1375M and the equilibrium concentration of nitrogen dioxide is 0.525M.

$$N_2O_4(g) \rightleftharpoons 2\,NO_2(g)$$

a. 0.0722   c. 2.00   e. 11.9   g. 16.4
b. 0.500   d. 3.82   f. 14.6   h. 27.8

45. Which statement is false?

a. A solution with a pH = 7 must be neutral.
b. The ionization of strong acids in aqueous solution is essentially complete.
c. The strongest acid that can exist in water is the hydronium ion.
d. All strong acids are levelled to H_3O^+ in aqueous solution.
e. Hydrolysis will occur only if the acid or base formed is weak.
f. A lower pH means that the hydronium ion concentration is greater.
g. A strong acid is any acid stronger than the hydronium ion H_3O^+.

46. Which one of the following electrolytes is a strong acid?

a. $HClO$ c. $HClO_2$ e. HNO_2 g. HI i. HF
b. H_2SO_3 d. HCN f. H_2CO_3 h. H_3PO_4 j. CH_3CO_2H

47. The hydrogen phosphate ion HPO_4^{2-} is amphiprotic; it has both a conjugate acid and a conjugate base. In which answer are both correctly identified?

	conjugate acid	*conjugate base*
a.	H_3PO_4	PO_4^{3-}
b.	PO_4^{3-}	H_3PO_4
c.	PO_4^{3-}	$H_2PO_4^-$
d.	$H_2PO_4^-$	PO_4^{3-}
e.	$H_2PO_4^-$	H_3PO_4
f.	H_3PO_4	$H_2PO_4^-$

48. The net ionic equation representing the equilibrium established when potassium amide is added to water is shown. Label the species present as either acid or base according to Brønsted-Lowry theory.

$$NH_2^- \quad + \quad H_2O \quad \rightleftharpoons \quad NH_3 \quad + \quad OH^-$$

a.	acid	base	acid	base
b.	acid	acid	base	base
c.	acid	base	base	acid
d.	base	acid	base	acid
e.	base	acid	acid	base
f.	base	base	acid	acid

49. In which direction will the following gas-phase equilibrium shift if the indicated changes are made? The reaction is exothermic in the forward direction. *Choose the row in which all answers are correct.*

$$2\,N_2O(g) \quad + \quad 3\,O_2(g) \quad \rightleftharpoons \quad 4\,NO_2(g)$$

	increase pressure	add O_2	remove NO_2	increase temperature
a.	shift left	shift left	shift left	shift left
b.	shift left	shift right	shift right	shift right
c.	shift left	shift right	shift right	shift left
d.	shift right	shift right	shift right	shift left
e.	shift right	shift right	shift left	shift left
f.	shift right	shift left	shift right	shift right

50. Which one of the following electrolytes is weakly basic in aqueous solution?

a.	$HClO_4$	c.	KCl	e.	KNO_3	g.	LiI	i.	NaCN
b.	H_2SO_3	d.	NH_4Br	f.	$CaBr_2$	h.	H_3PO_4	j.	NH_4ClO_4

FINAL EXAMINATION

CHEMISTRY 141 Spring 2008

Monday April 28th 2008

1. If your cholesterol analysis yielded 180 mg dL^{-1}, what would this be in g L^{-1}?

    a. 180 g L^{-1} c. 18.0 g L^{-1} e. 1.8 × 10^{-2} g L^{-1} g. 0.18 g L^{-1}
    b. 1.80 g L^{-1} d. 1.8 × 10^{-4} g L^{-1} f. 1.8 × 10^{3} g L^{-1} h. 1.8 × 10^{4} g L^{-1}

2. Which one of the following would be classified as an example of an extensive physical property?

    a. mass   c. molar mass   e. temperature
    b. boiling point   d. density   f. color

3. An ion contains 23 electrons, has a net charge of +3, and its nucleus contains 30 neutrons. What is the element?

    a. V   c. Co   e. Ca   g. I
    b. As   d. Zn   f. N   h. Fe

4. Which one of the following molecules / ions is paired with an incorrect name?

    a. NO_2^- nitrite ion   e. HNO_3 nitrous acid
    b. SO_4^{2-} sulfate ion   f. MnO_4^- permanganate ion
    c. NO_2 nitrogen dioxide   g. NH_3 ammonia
    d. H_3PO_4 phosphoric acid   h. OH^- hydroxide ion

5. What is the molar mass of calcium chloride?

    a. 37.0 g mol^{-1} c. 75.5 g mol^{-1} e. 111 g mol^{-1} g. 130 g mol^{-1}
    b. 54.0 g mol^{-1} d. 99.0 g mol^{-1} f. 116 g mol^{-1} h. 134 g mol^{-1}

6. How many moles of carbon atoms are in 3.0 moles of magnesium acetate?

    a. 2   c. 4   e. 6   g. 9   i. 15
    b. 3   d. 5   f. 7   h. 12   j. 18

7. How many oxygen atoms are in 75 g potassium chlorate?

    a. 3.7 × 10^{23} c. 1.1 × 10^{24} e. 2.2 × 10^{24} g. 6.0 × 10^{25}
    b. 8.5 × 10^{23} d. 1.5 × 10^{24} f. 8.6 × 10^{24} h. 1.4 × 10^{26}

8. A compound contains 30.45% nitrogen and 69.55% oxygen. The molar mass of the compound is 92 g mol^{-1}. What is the molecular formula of the compound?

    a. NO   c. NO_2 e. N_4O_2 g. N_3O_6
    b. N_2O d. N_2O_4 f. NO_3 h. N_4O_8

9.   What is the percent mass of lithium in lithium carbonate?

     a. 10.4%   c. 18.8%   e. 34.8%   g. 65.0%
     b. 16.3%   d. 22.6%   f. 46.5%   h. 84.1%

10. Balance this equation using whole number coefficients:

     $$\underline{\quad} \, P_4O_{10} \; + \; \underline{\quad} \, H_2O \; \rightarrow \; \underline{\quad} \, H_3PO_4$$

     Add all of the coefficients in the balanced equation. The sum of all the coefficients for the reactants and products is:

     a. 3   c. 6   e. 11   g. 15
     b. 4   d. 10   f. 12   h. 18

11. During fermentation, glucose $C_6H_{12}O_6$ is converted to ethanol C_2H_5OH and carbon dioxide CO_2 according to this balanced equation:

     $$C_6H_{12}O_6 \; \rightarrow \; 2\,C_2H_5OH \; + \; 2\,CO_2$$

     How much ethanol can be produced from the fermentation of 500 g glucose?

     a. 180 g   c. 318 g   e. 539 g   g. 887 g
     b. 256 g   d. 394 g   f. 624 g   h. 1000 g

12. Propane (C_3H_8) reacts with oxygen to produce carbon dioxide and water. If 4 mol propane reacts with 10 mol oxygen, how much water is produced? *(Hint: Write the balanced equation!)*

     a. 2 mol   c. 4 mol   e. 6 mol   g. 12 mol
     b. 3 mol   d. 5 mol   f. 8 mol   h. 16 mol

13. Lithium reacts with nitrogen to make lithium nitride:

     $$6\,Li(s) \; + \; N_2(g) \; \rightarrow \; 2\,Li_3N(s)$$

     When 12.5 g lithium reacts with excess nitrogen, 5.90 g lithium nitride is produced. What is the percent yield for this reaction?

     a. 28.2%   c. 46.5%   e. 83.6%   g. 70.6%
     b. 31.9%   d. 9.40%   f. 20.9%   h. 14.7%

14. How many of the elements listed below are transition metals?

     Na   Sn   Ti   Zr
     Au   Mg   U   W

     a. 0   c. 2   e. 4   g. 6   i. 8
     b. 1   d. 3   f. 5   h. 7

15. Hydrocyanic acid reacts with sodium hydroxide to produce sodium cyanide and water. Identify all of the spectator ions in this reaction.

     a. Na^+ c. H^+ e. Na^+ and CN^- g. Na^+ and OH^-
     b. CN^- d. OH^- f. Na^+ and H^+ h. Na^+, CN^-, H^+ and OH^-

16.   What is the oxidation number of sulfur in thiosulfuric acid $H_2S_2O_3$?

   a. +1   c. +3   e. +5   g. −1
   b. +2   d. +4   f. +6   h. −2

17.   How many mL of water would you have to add to 50 mL of a 0.50 M HCl solution to make the concentration of the solution 0.20 M HCl?

   a. 5 mL   c. 15 mL   e. 50 mL   g. 100 mL
   b. 10 mL   d. 25 mL   f. 75 mL   h. 125 mL

Use this information to answer questions 18 and 19:

Specific heat of water   = 4.184 J K^{-1} g^{-1}
Specific heat of copper   = 0.385 J K^{-1} g^{-1}
Latent heat of fusion of ice = 333 J g^{-1}

18.   How much heat is needed to heat a 10 g copper block from 25°C to 55°C?

   a. 76.4 J   c. 127.2 J   e. 156.7 J   g. 205.5 J
   b. 115.5 J   d. 134.5 J   f. 184.8 J   h. 211.8 J

19.   The copper block from question 18 (after it has been heated to 55°C) is added to an insulated vessel containing 75 g ice and 50 g water. How much of the ice melts?

   a. 0.64 g   c. 11.3 g   e. 36.4 g   g. 71.8 g
   b. 7.2 g   d. 17.9 g   f. 68.6 g   h. 75.0 g

20.   Acetylene C_2H_2 reacts with oxygen to produce carbon dioxide and water:

$$2\,C_2H_2(g) + 5\,O_2(g) \rightarrow 4\,CO_2(g) + 2\,H_2O(l) \qquad \Delta H = -2599 \text{ kJ mol}^{-1}$$

How many moles of acetylene would you have to burn to produce 5000 kJ of heat?

   a. 1.92 mol   c. 3.85 mol   e. 6.04 mol   g. 8.34 mol
   b. 2.09 mol   d. 4.43 mol   f. 7.71 mol   h. 9.62 mol

21.   Calculate the enthalpy change (ΔH) in kJ for this reaction:

$$\tfrac{1}{2}\,Cl_2(g) + NaBr(s) \rightarrow NaCl(s) + \tfrac{1}{2}\,Br_2(l) \qquad\qquad \Delta H = ??? \text{ kJ}$$

given the following information:

$$CaO(s) + Cl_2(g) \rightarrow CaOCl_2(s) \qquad\qquad \Delta H = -110.9 \text{ kJ}$$
$$H_2O(l) + CaOCl_2(s) + 2\,NaBr(s) \rightarrow 2\,NaCl(s) + Ca(OH)_2(s) + Br_2(l) \;\; \Delta H = -60.2 \text{ kJ}$$
$$Ca(OH)_2(s) \rightarrow CaO(s) + H_2O(l) \qquad\qquad \Delta H = +65.1 \text{ kJ}$$

   a. +18 kJ   c. +53 kJ   e. +106 kJ   g. +116 kJ
   b. −18 kJ   d. −53 kJ   f. −106 kJ   h. −116 kJ

22.   Louis deBroglie's equation ($\lambda = h\,/\,mv$) suggests that all matter has wave-like characteristics. What is the deBroglie wavelength (in m) of a 55 g tennis ball traveling at 35 m s^{-1}? (1J = 1 kg m^2 s^{-2})

   a. 1.9×10^{-34} m   c. 4.4×10^{-38} m   e. 3.8×10^{-35} m   g. 3.4×10^{-37} m
   b. 6.3×10^{-34} m   d. 1.6×10^{-35} m   f. 3.4×10^{-34} m   h. 2.4×10^{-35} m

23.   What is the energy (in J) of a photon with a wavelength of 5.00×10^4 nm?

a. 8.94×10^{-19} J   c. 6.21×10^{-19} J   e. 6.00×10^{12} J   g. 6.89×10^{-21} J
b. 5.00×10^{-19} J   d. 3.98×10^{-21} J   f. 7.09×10^{-21} J   h. 4.21×10^{-21} J

24.   Which one of the following sets of quantum numbers does not describe an electron in a bromine atom in its ground state?

	n	l	m_l			n	l	m_l
a.	1	0	0		e.	3	2	+2
b.	2	0	0		f.	3	1	−1
c.	2	1	−1		g.	4	2	−1
d.	3	0	0		h.	4	1	+1

25.   In the ground state, strontium's (Sr) outermost electrons are in which orbital?

a.   3d   c.   4s   e.   5p   g.   4d
b.   3p   d.   4p   f.   5s   h.   4f

26.   [Kr] $5s^2 4d^{10} 5p^3$ is the ground state electron configuration for which element?

a.   Sn   c.   Sb   e.   As   g.   Bi   i.   Te
b.   Pb   d.   Pr   f.   Mo   h.   Nb   j.   Zr

27.   Which of the following atoms would you expect to have the smallest first ionization energy?

a.   Na   b.   Si   c.   K   d.   Ar   e.   Cl   f.   Al

28.   Which kind of bonding characterizes the following elements or compounds? *Choose the row in which all of the answers are correct.*

	Co	Cl_2	CO
a.	metallic	ionic	metallic
b.	metallic	nonpolar covalent	polar covalent
c.	metallic	nonpolar covalent	nonpolar covalent
d.	polar covalent	metallic	polar covalent
e.	ionic	metallic	polar covalent
f.	polar covalent	polar covalent	nonpolar covalent
g.	nonpolar covalent	ionic	metallic
h.	metallic	nonpolar covalent	ionic

29.   How many bonding pair(s) of electrons are around the central atom in SO_3?

a.   0   c.   2   e.   4   g.   6   i.   8
b.   1   d.   3   f.   5   h.   7

30.   Which of the following molecules/ions require resonance to reconcile the Lewis structure with the actual structure?

I. ClF_3 II. $CHCl_3$ III. NO_3^-

a.   I only   c.   III only   e.   I and III   g.   I, II, and III
b.   II only   d.   I and II   f.   II and III

31. What is the arrangement of electron pairs around the central atom in NF_4^+?

    a. tetrahedral   c. bent   e. square planar   g. trigonal bipyramidal
    b. trigonal planar   d. octahedral   f. see-saw   h. T-shaped

32. Water has a bent shape because of the arrangement of hybrid orbitals on the oxygen atom. What is the hybridization of the atomic orbitals on the oxygen atom in the water molecule?

    a. sp   b. sp^2 c. sp^3 d. sp^3d e. sp^3d^2

33. A sample of an ideal gas at 15°C and 1 atm pressure has a volume of 2.58 L. What volume (in L) will the same sample of gas occupy at 38°C and 2 atm pressure?

    a. 2.79 L   c. 1.40 L   e. 5.58 L   g. 2.58 L
    b. 27.9 L   d. 4.20 L   f. 3.72 L   h. 1.29 L

34. In an effusion experiment, it takes 0.10 mole of nitrogen gas 2.0 minutes to effuse through a small hole. Under the same conditions, how long would it take for 0.10 mole of hydrogen gas to effuse through the same small hole?

    a. 0.05 min   c. 0.54 min   e. 1.32 min   g. 2.01 min
    b. 0.27 min   d. 0.69 min   f. 1.86 min   h. 2.33 min

35. Identify the strongest imtermolecular force of attraction in H_2CO, CH_4, and CH_3OH.
    Choose the row where all responses are correct.

	H_2CO	CH_4	CH_3OH
a.	hydrogen bond	hydrogen bond	hydrogen bond
b.	London dispersion	dipole-dipole	London dispersion
c.	hydrogen bond	London dispersion	hydrogen bond
d.	dipole-dipole	London dispersion	dipole-dipole
e.	dipole-dipole	London dispersion	hydrogen bond
f.	dipole-dipole	dipole-dipole	dipole-dipole

36. A unit cell of a compound contains element X in a body centered cubic arrangement. How many atoms of X are in one unit cell of this compound?

    a. 1   c. 3   e. 5   g. 7   i. 9
    b. 2   d. 4   f. 6   h. 8   j. 15

37. When solid ammonium nitrate dissolves in water to make a solution, the solution gets very cold. What are the signs for ΔH, ΔS, and ΔG for this process?

	ΔH	ΔS	ΔG
a.	+	+	+
b.	+	+	−
c.	+	−	+
d.	+	−	−
e.	−	+	+
f.	−	+	−
g.	−	−	+
h.	−	−	−

38. Which one of the following statements is *false* regarding a phase diagram?

    a. The lines on a phase diagram represent two phases in equilibrium.
    b. For some substances, the solid state can exist in more than one phase.
    c. It is impossible to liquify a gas at a temperature beyond the critical point.
    d. A phase diagram can have only one triple point.
    e. The vapor pressure curve begins at the triple point and ends at the critical point.

39. What is the *molality* (*m*) of a 10% by mass aqueous solution of sodium acetate?

    a. 0.12 *m*   c. 1.77 *m*   e. 2.78 *m*   g. 4.44 *m*
    b. 1.35 *m*   d. 2.05 *m*   f. 3.36 *m*   h. 7.35 *m*

40. Which one of the following statements is true for the phase transition of water at a temperature of 0°C and a pressure of 1 atm?

    a. $\Delta H = 0$ d. The process is enthalpy driven.
    b. $\Delta S = 0$ e. The change of state is an endothermic process.
    c. $\Delta G = 0$ f. The system becomes more ordered.

41. Which one of the following aqueous solutions would you expect to have the *lowest* boiling point?

    a. 2.0 *m* NH_3 c. 1.0 *m* $Ca(OH)_2$ e. 2.2 *m* sugar   g. 1.2 *m* CH_3CO_2Na
    b. 0.6 *m* Na_3PO_4 d. 1.6 *m* HCl   f. 1.4 *m* KCl   h. 0.7 *m* Na_2CO_3

42. How many dots (electrons) are included in the Lewis dot symbol for the nitride ion?
    a. 2   c. 4   e. 6   g. 8   i. 12
    b. 3   d. 5   f. 7   h. 10   j. 14

Use this equilibrium to answer questions 43 – 45:

$$H_2(g) + I_2(g) \rightleftharpoons 2\,HI(g)$$

43. In which direction will the equilibrium shift if the following changes are made?

	add $H_2(g)$	*increase pressure*	*remove HI(g)*
a.	left	no change	left
b.	right	no change	left
c.	left	right	left
d.	right	right	right
e.	left	right	right
f.	right	no change	right
g.	no change	left	left
h.	no change	right	right

44. At equilibrium, the concentration of $H_2(g)$ is 0.0037 M, the concentration of $I_2(g)$ is 0.0037 M, and the concentration of HI(*g*) is 0.0276 M. What is the equilibrium constant K for this reaction?

    a. 0.018   c. 7.46   e. 73.2   g. 496
    b. 1.02   d. 55.6   f. 109   h. 2016

45.   The reaction quotient Q for the equilibrium shown above has a value of 65.7. Which direction will the reaction shift (if necessary) to re-establish the equilibrium?

a.   left   b.   right   c.   no shift

46.   Which of the following would increase the rate of a reaction?

   I.   increase the concentraion of the reactants
   II.   increase the temperature
   III. add a catalyst
   IV. increase the concentration of the products

a.   I only   c.   III only   e.   I and IV   g.   I and III   i.   I, III, and IV
b.   II only   d.   IV only   f.   II and III   h.   I, II, and III   j.   I, II, III, and IV

47.   What is the conjugate base of HCO_3^-?

a. H_2O c. H_3O^+ e. HCO_3^-
b. OH^- d. CO_3^{2-} f. H_2CO_3

48.   Which one of these statements is *false*?

a.   At equilibrium, the concentration of the reactants is equal to zero.
b.   When the rate of the forward reaction is equal to the rate of the reverse reaction, the system is at equilibrium.
c.   If a system at equilibrium is disturbed, the reaction will adjust itself to regain the equilibrium.
d.   Adding a catalyst will not disturb the equilibrium.
e.   At equilibrium, $\Delta G = 0$.
f.   All reactions strive to reach equilibrium.

49.   What is the pH of a 0.50M aqueous solution of HF? The K_a for hydrofluoric acid is 7.1×10^{-4}.

a.   0.30   c.   2.4   e.   5.3   g.   12.3
b.   1.7   d.   4.4   f.   11.6   h.   13.7

50.   How many of the following solutes will produce an acidic solution when dissolved in water?

   CH_3CO_2H NaCN H_3PO_4 NH_4Cl
   NH_4ClO_3 LiF   NaOH KNO_3

a.   0   c.   2   e.   4   g.   6   i.   8
b.   1   d.   3   f.   5   h.   7

FINAL EXAMINATION

CHEMISTRY 141 Fall 2008

Tuesday December 9th 2008

1. *(5 points)* Which one of the following elements exists as a diatomic gas under ordinary conditions?

   a. helium   c. sulfur   e. iodine   g. nitrogen
   b. phosphorus   d. neon   f. carbon   h. silicon

2. *(5 points)* Which one of the following elements would you classify as an alkali metal?

   a. sodium   c. sulfur   e. chlorine   g. magnesium
   b. iron   d. neon   f. lead   h. aluminum

3. Which is a correct relationship between the mass of a substance and the number of moles of that substance?

   a. mass × molar mass = number of moles   d. number of moles × mass = molar mass
   b. molar mass / mass = number of moles   e. number of moles / mass = molar mass
   c. mass / molar mass = number of moles

4. How many moles of carbon atoms are there in 3.0 moles of benzene C_6H_6?

   a. 3   c. 9   e. 18   g. 36
   b. 6   d. 12   f. 24   h. 60

5. Which one of the following samples has the greatest mass?

   a. 0.5 mol neon   e. 0.4 mol potassium hydroxide
   b. 0.4 mol calcium   f. 0.7 mol methane CH_4
   c. 0.6 mol hydrogen fluoride   g. 0.5 mol carbon monoxide
   d. 0.1 mol bromine molecules   h. 1.0 mol helium

6. Balance the following equation using whole number coefficients:

   $$\_\ P_4O_{10}\ +\ \_\ Ca(OH)_2\ \rightarrow\ \_\ Ca_3(PO_4)_2\ +\ \_\ H_2O$$

   What is the coefficient for water in the balanced equation?

   a. 1   c. 3   e. 5   g. 7   i. 9
   b. 2   d. 4   f. 6   h. 8   j. 10

7. What is the percentage by mass of copper in the mineral malachite $Cu_2CO_3(OH)_2$?

   a. 0.90%   c. 20.0%   e. 36.2%   g. 57.5%
   b. 5.43%   d. 27.4%   f. 43.9%   h. 72.1%

8. A monatomic ion of an isotope of an unknown element contains 18 electrons, 20 protons, and 20 neutrons. What is the ion?

   a. $^{38}Sr^{2+}$ c. $^{20}Ca^{2+}$ e. $^{20}Ar^{2+}$ g. $^{40}Ar^{2-}$ i. $^{38}Zr^{2-}$
   b. $^{40}Sr^{2+}$ d. $^{40}Ca^{2+}$ f. $^{38}Ar^{2+}$ h. $^{40}Zr^{2+}$ j. $^{40}Zr^{2-}$

9. The atomic mass of an unknown hypothetical element A is 33.29 g mol^{-1}. A 142.4 g sample of this unknown element combines with 97.23 g of element B to form a compound A_2B_3. What is the atomic mass (molar mass) of element B?

a. 6.500 g mol^{-1} c. 26.29 g mol^{-1} e. 52.75 g mol^{-1} g. 112.3 g mol^{-1}
b. 15.15 g mol^{-1} d. 36.91 g mol^{-1} f. 74.66 g mol^{-1} h. 167.3 g mol^{-1}

10. Nitrogen gas reacts with hydrogen gas according to the following balanced equation:

$$N_2(g) \ + \ 3\,H_2(g) \ \rightarrow \ 2\,NH_3(g)$$

If 3.0 mol nitrogen reacts with 1.5 mol hydrogen, what is the maximum amount of ammonia that can be produced?

a. 0.33 mol   c. 0.67 mol   e. 1.5 mol   g. 2.25 mol
b. 0.50 mol   d. 1.0 mol   f. 2.0 mol   h. 3.0 mol

11. Sulfonium salts crystallize from water forming crystals with a high water content often referred to as clathrates. An example is the crystal $[(C_4H_9)_3S]F.xH_2O$ where x is the number of water molecules per formula unit of the salt. The salt was analysed and found to contain 61.83% water. What is the value of x in this crystal?
Molar mass of C_4H_9 = 57.11 g mol^{-1}
Molar mass of H_2O = 18.016 g mol^{-1}

a. 6   c. 12   e. 16   g. 24   i. 30
b. 10   d. 15   f. 20   h. 27   j. 32

12. *(5 points)* What is the chloride ion concentration in a 0.20 M iron(III) chloride solution?

a. 0.10 M   c. 0.25 M   e. 0.40 M   g. 0.50 M   i. 0.70 M
b. 0.20 M   d. 0.30 M   f. 0.45 M   h. 0.60 M   j. 0.90 M

13. *(5 points)* Which one of the following acids is named *incorrectly*?

a. H_3PO_3 phosphorous acid   e. H_2SO_4 sulfuric acid
b. H_2SO_3 sulfurous acid   f. $HClO_4$ perchloric acid
c. HNO_3 nitrous acid   g. H_3PO_4 phosphoric acid
d. $HClO_3$ chloric acid   h. $HClO_2$ chlorous acid

14. Which of the following choices represents the net ionic equation for the reaction between lithium hydroxide and hydrofluoric acid in aqueous solution?

a. $Li^+ \ + \ OH^- \ + \ H^+ \ + \ F^- \ \rightarrow \ Li^+ \ + \ F^- \ + \ H_2O$
b. $LiOH \ + \ F \ \rightarrow \ Li^+ \ + \ F^- \ + \ H_2O$
c. $OH^- \ + \ H^+ \ \rightarrow \ H_2O$
d. $OH^- \ + \ HF \ \rightarrow \ F^- \ + \ H_2O$
e. $LiOH \ + \ HF \ \rightarrow \ LiF \ + \ H_2O$
f. $Li^+ \ + \ OH^- \ + \ HF \ \rightarrow \ Li^+ \ + \ F^- \ + \ H_2O$
g. $LiOH \ + \ H^+ \ + \ F^- \ \rightarrow \ Li^+ \ + \ F^- \ + \ H_2O$

15. What is the oxidation number of tungsten in WO_4^{2-}?

   a. −8   c. 0   e. +2   g. +6
   b. −2   d. +1   f. +4   h. +8

16. 50.0 g of hot water at 60°C are added to 50.0 g of ice and 50.0 g of liquid water in an insulated vessel. How much liquid water is present once the system has reached equilibrium?

   Latent heat of fusion of water = 333 Jg^{-1}
   Specific heat of water = 4.184 $J\ K^{-1}\ g^{-1}$

   a. 12.3 g   c. 50.0 g   e. 87.7 g   g. 112 g   i. 150 g
   b. 37.7 g   d. 62.3 g   f. 100 g   h. 138 g

17. A system consisting of a cylinder with a movable piston absorbs 3.00 kJ of energy as heat. As a result, the piston moves up in the cylinder and does 950 J of work against an constant external pressure of 1.0 atmosphere (1.01×10^{-5} Pa). What is the change in the internal energy ΔE of the system?

   a. +950 J   c. +3.00 kJ   e. +2.05 kJ   g. +3.95 kJ
   b. −950 J   d. −3.00 kJ   f. −2.05 kJ   h. −3.95 kJ

18. How many kJ of energy is released in the combustion of 65.0 g acetylene C_2H_2?

   $$2\ C_2H_2\ +\ 5\ O_2\ \rightarrow\ 4\ CO_2\ +\ 2\ H_2O \qquad \Delta H = -2599\ kJ\ mol^{-1}$$

   a. 1040 kJ   c. 3244 kJ   e. 6237 kJ   g. 9096 kJ
   b. 2599 kJ   d. 5198 kJ   f. 7796 kJ   h. 10400 kJ

19. Which one of the following sets of quantum numbers is not allowed?

	n	l	m_l			n	l	m_l
a.	0	0	0		e.	3	0	0
b.	1	0	0		f.	3	2	+2
c.	2	0	0		g.	4	1	0
d.	2	1	−1		h.	4	2	−2

20. *(5 points)* What is the ground state electron configuration of the sulfide ion?

   a. $1s^2\ 2s^2\ 2p^4$
   b. $1s^2\ 2s^2\ 2p^6\ 3s^2\ 3p^4$
   c. $1s^2\ 2s^2\ 2p^6\ 3s^2$
   d. $1s^2\ 2s^2\ 2p^6\ 3s^2\ 3p^2$
   e. $1s^2\ 2s^2\ 2p^6\ 3s^2\ 3p^5$
   f. $1s^2\ 2s^2\ 2p^6\ 3s^2\ 3p^6$

21. Which of the following elements would be predicted to have the lowest ionization energy?

   a. aluminum   b. silicon   c. phosphorus   d. sulfur   e. chlorine   f. argon

22. In which sequence are the colors of the visible spectrum arranged in increasing energy per photon?

a.	blue	<	indigo	<	orange	<	yellow	<	green
b.	violet	<	blue	<	yellow	<	orange	<	red
c.	indigo	<	violet	<	green	<	yellow	<	red
d.	violet	<	green	<	orange	<	blue	<	indigo
e.	red	<	yellow	<	violet	<	indigo	<	blue
f.	blue	<	violet	<	indigo	<	orange	<	red
g.	yellow	<	orange	<	blue	<	indigo	<	violet
h.	red	<	orange	<	green	<	blue	<	violet

23. What is the arrangement of bonding and non-bonding electron pairs around the central atom in the molecule BrF_5?

a. linear   c. trigonal planar   e. tetrahedral
b. trigonal bipyramidal   d. octahedral

24. Which one of the following molecules is polar?

a. CH_4 c. H_2 e. SeF_6 g. BeF_2
b. SF_4 d. BF_3 f. CCl_4 h. CO_2

25. *(5 points)* What is the hybridization of the valence atomic orbitals on the central atom in sulfur dioxide?

a. sp b. sp^2 c. sp^3 d. sp^3d e. sp^3d^2

26. What are the formal charges on the three nitrogen atoms in the structure for the N_3^- ion shown?

$$[\ \ddot{N} = N = \ddot{N}\ ]^-$$

a.	0	0	0
b.	0	−1	0
c.	+1	−1	+1
d.	−1	+1	−1
e.	−1	0	−1
f.	+1	−2	+1
g.	−2	+1	−2
h.	−1	+2	−1

27. An open-ended U-tube mercury manometer is used to measure the pressure of a gas inside a vessel. The difference in the heights of the mercury in the two sides of the manometer is 19 cm and the atmospheric pressure is 1.0 atm. What is the pressure of the gas in the vessel?

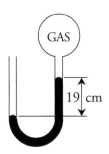

a. 0.25 atm   c. 0.75 atm   e. 1.00 atm   g. 1.50 atm
b. 0.50 atm   d. 0.975 atm   f. 1.25 atm   h. 1.75 atm

28. A 10 liter vessel contains 1.0 mole of helium gas, 1.5 moles of argon gas, and 2.5 moles of neon gas at a total pressure of 20.0 atm.

A. What is the partial pressure of argon?

An additional 3.0 moles of argon gas is added to the mixture without changing the temperature or the volume.

B. What is the partial pressure of argon in the new mixture?

Now an additional 4.0 moles of helium is added to the mixture without changing the temperature or the volume.

C. What is the partial pressure of argon now?

P_{Ar}:	A	B	C
a.	3.0 atm	3.0 atm	3.0 atm
b.	3.0 atm	6.0 atm	6.0 atm
c.	3.0 atm	18 atm	18 atm
d.	6.0 atm	3.0 atm	3.0 atm
e.	6.0 atm	6.0 atm	6.0 atm
f.	6.0 atm	18 atm	18 atm
g.	6.0 atm	6.0 atm	18 atm

29. When a salt such as ammonium nitrate dissolves in water, the solution gets very cold. The temperature drops by as much as 20°C. What are the signs for ΔG_{sys}, ΔH_{sys}, and ΔS_{sys} for this process?

	ΔG_{sys}	ΔH_{sys}	ΔS_{sys}
a.	+	+	+
b.	+	+	−
c.	+	−	+
d.	+	−	−
e.	−	+	+
f.	−	+	−
g.	−	−	+
h.	−	−	−

30. *(5 points)* How many of the following solutes would you classify as strong electrolytes in aqueous solution?

NH_4NO_3	HNO_3	KF	NH_3
H_3PO_4	KOH	HCN	$Sr(OH)_2$

a. 1   c. 3   e. 5   g. 7
b. 2   d. 4   f. 6   h. 8

31. How many grams of water must be used to dissolve 50.0 g sucrose (molecular formula $C_{12}H_{22}O_{11}$; molar mass 342 g mol^{-1}) to prepare a 1.25 *m* (molal) aqueous solution of sucrose?

a. 86 g   c. 117 g   e. 135 g   g. 183 g
b. 104 g   d. 123 g   f. 146 g   h. 207 g

32. *(5 points)* Which aqueous solution has the highest boiling point?

   a. 0.25 m K_2SO_4
   b. 0.20 m NaH_2PO_4
   c. 0.20 m $Ca(NO_3)_2$
   d. 0.30 m HNO_3
   e. 0.50 m HCN

33. Consider the following disturbances on the equilibrium system shown. In which, if any, direction will the system shift to restore the equilibrium in each case? The reaction is exothermic in the forward direction. Note that sulfur is a solid.

$$H_2(g) \ + \ 1/8 \ S_8(s) \ \rightleftharpoons \ H_2S(g)$$

	add hydrogen	*add sulfur*	*increase temperature*
a.	left	no change	right
b.	left	no change	no change
c.	right	right	right
d.	left	right	left
e.	right	no change	left
f.	left	no change	left
g.	right	no change	right
h.	right	right	left

34. What is the value of the reaction quotient, Q, for the following reaction if $[N_2]$ = 0.5 M, $[H_2]$ = 2.0 M, and $[NH_3]$ = 2.0 M?

$$N_2(g) \ + \ 3 \ H_2(g) \ \rightleftharpoons \ 2 \ NH_3(g)$$

   a. 0.5   c. 1.5   e. 2.0   g. 2.5
   b. 1.0   d. 1.75   f. 2.25   h. 3.0

35. The hydrogen oxalate ion $HC_2O_4^-$ is amphiprotic; it has both a conjugate acid and a conjugate base. In which answer are both correctly identified?

	conjugate acid	*conjugate base*
a.	$H_2C_2O_4$	$HC_2O_4^-$
b.	$HC_2O_4^-$	$C_2O_4^{2-}$
c.	$C_2O_4^{2-}$	$H_2C_2O_4$
d.	$H_2C_2O_4$	C_2O_4
e.	$H_2C_2O_4$	$C_2O_4^{2-}$
f.	$C_2O_4^{2-}$	$HC_2O_4^-$

36. Which salt will produce an acidic solution when dissolved in water?

   a. NaCl   c. KCN   e. LiF   g. $Mg(NO_3)_2$
   b. Na_2CO_3 d. NH_4NO_3 f. KNO_3 h. Na_3PO_4

37. The net ionic equation representing the equilibrium established when sodium dihydrogen phosphate is added to water is shown. Label the species present as either acid or base according to Brønsted-Lowry theory.

$$H_2PO_4^- \quad + \quad H_2O \quad \rightleftharpoons \quad H_3O^+ \quad + \quad HPO_4^{2-}$$

a.	acid	base	acid	base
b.	acid	acid	base	base
c.	acid	base	base	acid
d.	base	acid	base	acid
e.	base	acid	acid	base
f.	base	base	acid	acid

38. Which statement is *not true?*

a. A large value for K, the equilibrium constant, means that the products predominate at equilibrium.
b. A solution with a pH = 7 must be neutral regardless of the temperature.
c. The ionization of strong acids in aqueous solution is essentially complete.
d. The strongest acid that can exist in water is the hydronium ion, H_3O^+.
e. All strong acids are levelled to H_3O^+ in aqueous solution.
f. Hydrolysis will occur only if the acid or base formed in the hydrolysis is weak.
g. A lower pH means that the hydronium ion concentration is greater.
h. A strong acid is any acid stronger than the hydronium ion H_3O^+.

FINAL EXAMINATION

CHEMISTRY 141 Spring 2009

Wednesday May 6th 2009

The first 8 questions are worth 5 points each; the remaining 30 questions are worth 7 points each. The total number of points possible is 250.

1. Which one of the following elements does not exist as a diatomic molecule in nature?

   a. nitrogen   c. chlorine   e. fluorine   g. oxygen
   b. sulfur   d. hydrogen   f. bromine   h. iodine

2. What is the correct formula for the ionic compound potassium chlorate?

   a. $KClO_2$ c. $KClO_4$ e. $KClO$ g. K_2ClO_3 i. K_2CrO_4
   b. $KClO_3$ d. $K(ClO_2)_2$ f. K_2ClO_4 h. $K(ClO_4)_3$ j. K_2CO_3

3. What is the oxidation number of iodine in the compound $NaIO_3$?

   a. −1   c. −2   e. −3   g. −4   i. −5
   b. +1   d. +2   f. +3   h. +4   j. +5

4. How many unpaired electrons are in one fluorine atom in the ground state?

   a. 0   c. 2   e. 4   g. 6   i. 8
   b. 1   d. 3   f. 5   h. 7

5. How many lone pair(s) of electrons is / are around the centra

   a. 0   c. 2   e. 4   g. 6
   b. 1   d. 3   f. 5   h. 7

6. The phase diagram for a single substance is illustrated on the right. What are the signs for ΔH and ΔS moving from area C to area B (as indicated by the arrow)?

	ΔH	ΔS			ΔH	ΔS
a.	+	+		c.	−	−
b.	+	−		d.	−	+

7. What is the conjugate base of $H_2PO_3^-$?

   a. H_3PO_3 c. H_2PO_3 e. HPO_3 g. PO_3
   b. $H_3PO_3^+$ d. $H_2PO_3^-$ f. HPO_3^{2-} h. PO_3^{3-}

8. What is the pH of a 0.0316 M solution of potassium hydroxide?

   a. 1.5   c. 3.5   e. 7.5   g. 10.5   i. 12.5
   b. 2.5   d. 4.5   f. 9.5   h. 11.5   j. 13.5

9. The structural formula of vitamin C is shown to the right.
    What is the empirical formula of vitamin C?

    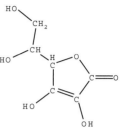

    a. CHO d. $C_3H_2O_3$ g. $C_6H_8O_6$
    b. CH_2O_3 e. $C_3H_4O_3$ h. $C_6H_4O_6$
    c. $C_2H_8O_6$ f. $C_4H_4O_6$ i. $C_6H_{10}O_3$

10. How many moles of oxygen atoms are in 2.0 moles of calcium phosphate?

    a. 4   c. 8   e. 12   g. 16   i. 20
    b. 6   d. 10   f. 14   h. 18   j. 22

11. What is the mass of 3.0 moles of sulfur hexafluoride?

    a. 51.1 g   c. 146.1 g   e. 211.4 g   g. 438.2 g
    b. 70.0 g   d. 153.2 g   f. 337.1 g   h. 634.2 g

12. A compound contains 52.15% carbon, 13.13% hydrogen, and 34.73% oxygen. What is the empirical formula for this compound?

    a. CHO c. CHO_2 e. $C_2H_6O_2$ g. $C_4H_{12}O_2$
    b. CH_5O d. C_2H_6O f. C_3H_3O h. $C_4H_6O_2$

13. Balance this equation using whole number coefficients.

    $$\_ \ Be_2C \ + \ \_ \ H_2O \ \rightarrow \ \_ \ Be(OH)_2 \ + \ \_ \ CH_4$$

    Add all of the coefficients in the balanced equation. The sum of all the coefficients for the reactants and products is:

    a. 4   c. 6   e. 8   g. 10   i. 12
    b. 5   d. 7   f. 9   h. 11   j. 14

14. 5.000 g of a sample of a hydrate of magnesium sulfate $MgSO_4 \cdot xH_2O$ was heated carefully to drive off the water. The mass was reduced to 2.442 grams. What is the value of x in the formula of the hydrate?

    a. 1   c. 3   e. 5   g. 7   i. 9
    b. 2   d. 4   f. 6   h. 8   j. 10

15. Lithium reacts with water to produce lithium hydroxide and hydrogen gas:

    $$2 \ Li(s) \ + \ 2 \ H_2O(l) \ \rightarrow \ 2 \ LiOH(aq) \ + \ H_2(g)$$

    How many grams of lithium are needed to produce 14.0 grams of hydrogen gas?

    a. 13.9 g   c. 63.2 g   e. 124.2 g   g. 178.7 g
    b. 48.6 g   d. 96.4 g   f. 148.6 g   h. 194.3 g

16. 50 mL of a 0.60 M solution of sodium chloride was diluted with water until the total volume of the solution was 300 mL. What is the molarity M of the new solution?

    a. 0.10 M   c. 0.15 M   e. 0.40 M   g. 0.51 M
    b. 0.30 M   d. 0.20 M   f. 0.36 M   h. 0.45 M

17. Ammonia reacts with oxygen to produce nitric oxide and water according to this balanced equation:

$$4\,NH_3(g)\ +\ 5\,O_2(g)\ \rightarrow\ 4\,NO(g)\ +\ 6\,H_2O(l)$$

How many moles of water can be produced from the reaction of 3.0 moles ammonia with 4.0 moles oxygen?

a. 2.0 mol   c. 4.0 mol   e. 4.8 mol   g. 6.0 mol   i. 7.5 mol
b. 3.5 mol   d. 4.5 mol   f. 5.0 mol   h. 6.8 mol   j. 10.0 mol

18. 25.0 grams of ice at 0 °C was added to 20.0 grams of warm water at 65 °C. Assuming no heat is transferred to the surroundings, how much of the ice will melt?

Specific heat of water = 4.184 J g^{-1} K^{-1}
Latent heat of fusion of ice = 333 J g^{-1}

a. 2.1 g   c. 8.7 g   e. 16.3 g   g. 21.2 g
b. 5.4 g   d. 12.4 g   f. 18.5 g   h. 25.0 g

19. Isooctane C_8H_{18} is a component in gasoline that burns in oxygen according to this balanced equation:

$$2\,C_8H_{18}\ +\ 25\,O_2\ \rightarrow\ 16\,CO_2\ +\ 18\,H_2O \qquad \Delta H = -10992\ kJ$$

How much heat (in kJ) is released when 175 g isooctane is burned?

a. 21,984 kJ   c. 10,992 kJ   e. 674 kJ   g. 8,420 kJ
b. 4,739 kJ   d. 1,053 kJ   f. 16,840 kJ   h. 96,180 kJ

20. What is the energy (in J) of one photon of light having a wavelength of 300nm?

a. 6.6×10^{-19} J   c. 3.3×10^{-5} J   e. 6.6×10^{2} J   g. 5.4×10^{14} J
b. 3.9×10^{-17} J   d. 1.0×10^{15} J   f. 3.7×10^{-36} J   h. 6.6×10^{-28} J

21. Which one of the following sets of quantum numbers is not allowed?

	n	l	m_l
a.	2	1	−1
b.	4	2	+1
c.	3	0	0
d.	1	0	0
e.	3	1	+2
f.	2	1	+1

22. Start with the number of orbitals in any one set of f orbitals

... add the number of valence electrons in a boron atom in the ground state
... add the atomic number of oxygen
... subtract the number of electrons in the 3d orbital of an iron atom in the ground state.

What is the result?

a. 2   c. 6   e. 10   g. 14   i. 18
b. 4   d. 8   f. 12   h. 16   j. 20

23. Which element, nitrogen or fluorine, has the smaller atomic radius, is more electronegative, and has the larger first ionization energy?

	Smaller Atomic Radius	More Electronegative	Larger First Ionization Energy
a.	fluorine	fluorine	fluorine
b.	fluorine	fluorine	nitrogen
c.	fluorine	nitrogen	fluorine
d.	fluorine	nitrogen	nitrogen
e.	nitrogen	fluorine	fluorine
f.	nitrogen	fluorine	nitrogen
g.	nitrogen	nitrogen	fluorine
h.	nitrogen	nitrogen	nitrogen

Use the following choices to answer questions 24 – 26:

PCl_3 CH_2Cl_2 BeF_2 ClF_5 I_3^- H_2S NO_2^-

24. How many of the compounds have a trigonal bipyramidal electron pair arrangement?

a. 0   c. 2   e. 4   g. 6
b. 1   d. 3   f. 5   h. 7

25. In how many of the compounds are the valence atomic orbitals on the central atom sp^3 hybridized?

a. 0   c. 2   e. 4   g. 6
b. 1   d. 3   f. 5   h. 7

26. How many of the compounds are not polar?

a. 0   c. 2   e. 4   g. 6
b. 1   d. 3   f. 5   h. 7

27. Which of the following processes results in a decrease in entropy ΔS?

    I. Dry ice sublimes at room temperature.
    II. Leaves are raked into a pile.
    III. Sodium chloride is dissolved in water at 25 °C.
    IV. Water condenses on a leaf in a jungle.
    V. A brand new deck of playing cards is shuffled.

a. I only   c. III only   e. V only   g. II and IV   i. I, III, and V
b. II only   d. IV only   f. I and III   h. II and V   j. all of them

28. A 0.024 mol sample of an ideal gas occupies a volume of 0.600 L at 36 °C and 1.00 atm pressure. What is the final volume occupied by the gas if the pressure decreases to 0.205 atm and the temperature decreases to 0 °C?

a. 0.11 L   c. 2.6 L   e. 7.2 L   g. 18.5 L
b. 0.14 L   d. 3.3 L   f. 10.5 L   h. 21.6 L

29. Iron crystallizes in a body-centered cubic unit cell. How many iron atoms are in one unit cell?

    a. 1   c. 3   e. 5   g. 7   i. 9
    b. 2   d. 4   f. 6   h. 8   j. 10

30. Suppose a new temperature scale (°S) was invented for which 35 °S is the freezing point of water and 150 °S is the boiling point of water. At what temperature would sulfur melt on the new scale if on the Celsius scale sulfur melts at 113 °C?

    a. 100 °S   c. 137 °S   e. 165 °S   g. 246 °S
    b. 115 °S   d. 143 °S   f. 189 °S   h. 300 °S

31. Use the bond energies given below to calculate the change in enthalpy (ΔH) for this reaction:

    $$CH_4(g) + H_2O(g) \rightarrow 3\,H_2(g) + CO(g)$$

C–H	413 kJ mol^{-1}
C–O	358 kJ mol^{-1}
C=O	732 kJ mol^{-1}
C≡O	1072 kJ mol^{-1}
O–H	463 kJ mol^{-1}
H–H	436 kJ mol^{-1}

    a. +198 kJ   c. +538 kJ   e. +1070 kJ   g. +4958 kJ
    b. −198 kJ   d. −538 kJ   f. −1070 kJ   h. −4958 kJ

32. You prepare an ideal solution consisting of pentane (pure vapor pressure = 425 torr) and hexane (pure vapor pressure = 130 torr). Calculate the mole fraction of pentane in the solution if the total vapor pressure above the solution is 350 torr.

    a. 0.15   c. 0.35   e. 0.50   g. 0.85
    b. 0.25   d. 0.45   f. 0.75   h. 0.90

33. Which one of the following statements is *true?*

    a. The activation energy is the energy released in the reaction.
    b. A catalyst provides an alternate route for a reaction with a lower activation energy.
    c. The only requirement for a successful reaction is that there is sufficient energy.
    d. A catalyst must always be in the same state as the reactants.
    e. Equilibrium is reached when the concentration of the reactants is equal to the concentration of products.
    f. The reaction rate depends only on the concentration of the reactants.

34. Initially, 5.0 moles of ammonia and 6.0 moles of oxygen gas were placed in a 1.0 L flask. The system was allowed to reach equilibrium according to the reaction shown below. After equilibrium was established, the flask was found to contain 1.5 moles of nitrogen gas. How much ammonia is in the flask at equilibrium?

    $$4\,NH_3(g) + 3\,O_2(g) \rightleftharpoons 2\,N_2(g) + 6\,H_2O(l)$$

    a. 0.75 mol   c. 2.0 mol   e. 4.25 mol
    b. 1.5 mol   d. 3.75 mol   f. 4.5 mol

35.   The process of photosynthesis can be represented by the reaction shown below. Consider the following disturbances on this equilibrium system. According to LeChatelier's principle, in which direction (if any), will the system shift to restore the equilibrium?

$$6\ CO_2(g)\ +\ 6\ H_2O(l)\ \rightleftharpoons\ C_6H_{12}O_6(s)\ +\ 6\ O_2(g)\qquad \Delta H = +2801\ kJ$$

	add a catalyst	increase temperature	increase volume	increase partial pressure of $CO_2(g)$
a.	no change	left	no change	no change
b.	left	no change	right	left
c.	no change	right	left	right
d.	right	no change	no change	no change
e.	left	right	left	no change
f.	no change	left	no change	left
g.	right	no change	left	no change
h.	no change	right	no change	right

36.   In the following aqueous equilibrium, label the species according to the Brønsted-Lowry theory of acids and bases:

$$HPO_4{}^{2-}\ +\ H_2O\ \rightleftharpoons\ H_3O^+\ +\ PO_4{}^{3-}$$

a.	acid	acid	base	base
b.	acid	base	base	acid
c.	acid	base	acid	base
d.	base	base	acid	acid
e.	base	acid	acid	base
f.	base	acid	base	acid

37.   Calculate K_b for the acetate ion $CH_3CO_2{}^-$. The K_a for acetic acid is 1.8×10^{-5}.

a. 5.6×10^{-10} c. 1.3×10^{-6} e. 5.6×10^{-18}
b. 1.8×10^{-19} d. 7.8×10^5 f. 1.8×10^9

38.   Which of the following solutes, when dissolved in water, will produce an acidic solution?

a. $NaOH$ c. K_3PO_4 e. NH_4NO_3 g. KF
b. Li_2CO_3 d. $Mg(ClO_4)_2$ f. $BaSO_4$ h. NH_3

SOLUTIONS

EXAMINATION 1

CHEMISTRY 141 FALL 2004
Solutions

1. e. number of electrons = 10
        charge = +1
        atomic number = number of protons = 10 + 1 = 11, therefore Na

2. e. nitrate is NO_3^-, nitrite is NO_2^-, and therefore hyponitrite is NO^-
        one less oxygen, same charge
        the actual hyponitrite ion exists as a dimer $N_2O_2^{2-}$

3. d. Mg^{2+} and HSO_4^-, so $Mg(HSO_4)_2$

4. g.

5. d. magnesium chloride $MgCl_2$

6. e. weighted average = $(0.35 \times 117.88) + (0.47 \times 118.80) + (0.18 \times 119.75) = 118.65$

7. h. N_2O_4, molar mass = $(2 \times 14) + (4 \times 16) = 92$ g mol^{-1}
        3 mol $\times$ 92 g mol^{-1} = 276 g

8. e. NH_2CONH_2, molar mass = $(2 \times 14) + (4 \times 1) + 12 + 16 = 60$ g mol^{-1}
        % N = $(28/60) \times 100 = 47\%$

9. d. sugar dissolving does not change the identity of the substance

10. f. magnesium phosphate is $Mg_3(PO_4)_2$

11. f. 8 C in $C_6H_5N(CH_3)_2$
        or 8 moles of C atoms in one mole of $C_6H_5N(CH_3)_2$
        $8 \times 12 = 96$ mol

12. e. 2.50 mg $\times$ (1 g/1000 mg) $\times$ (1 mol N/14 g) $\times$ (6.022×10^{23}/1 mol) = 1.08×10^{20} N

13. f. mass = density $\times$ volume = 1.58 g cm^{-3} $\times$ 4.29 cm^3 = 6.778 g
        6.778 g / 342 g mol^{-1} = 0.0198 mol sugar
        0.0198 mol sugar = 12 $\times$ 0.0198 mol C = 0.238 mol C
        0.238 mol C = 6.022×10^{23} mol^{-1} $\times$ 0.238 mol C = 1.43×10^{23} C

14. a.

	carbon	hydrogen	nitrogen	oxygen
mass:	54.8%	5.62%	7.10%	32.6
divide by molar mass:	54.8/12.01	5.62/1.008	7.10/14.01	32.6/16.00
	= 4.56	= 5.58	= 0.51	= 2.04
divide by smallest:	= 9.00	= 11.00	= 1.00	= 4.00

empirical formula is $C_9H_{11}NO_4$

15. i. $2\,CH_3NHNH_2 \; + \; 5\,O_2 \;\rightarrow\; 2\,N_2 \; + \; 2\,CO_2 \; + \; 6\,H_2O$
total = 17

16. g. $B_xH_y \; + \; oxygen \;\rightarrow\; 1\,B_2O_3 \; +2.5\,H_2O$
$\qquad\qquad\qquad\qquad$ 2 B atoms $\qquad$ 5 H atoms

therefore B_2H_5

17. d. $8.0\text{ g }O_2 \times (1\text{ mol }O_2/32\text{ g }O_2) \times (2\text{ mol }NO_2/1\text{ mol }O_2) \times (46\text{ g }NO_2/1\text{ mol }NO_2) = 23\text{ g }NO_2$

18. h. $2\,C_2H_6 \; + \; 7\,O_2 \;\rightarrow\; 4\,CO_2 \; + \; 6\,H_2O$
limiting reactant is the ethane
$3.0\text{ g mol }C_2H_6 \times (6\text{ mol }H_2O/2\text{ mol }C_2H_6) = 9.0\text{ mol }H_2O$

19. g. $2\,N_2O \; + \; 3\,O_2 \;\rightarrow\; 4\,NO_2$
$50\text{ g }N_2O = 50\text{ g}/44\text{ g mol}^{-1} = 1.136\text{ mol}$
$50\text{ g }O_2 = 50\text{ g}/32\text{ g mol}^{-1} = 1.563\text{ mol}$ — limiting reactant
[1.563/3 = 0.521 and 1.136/2 = 0.568. 0.521 is less than 0.568 so O_2 is the limiting reactant]
$1.563\text{ mol }O_2 \times (4\text{ mol }NO_2/3\text{ mol }O_2) = 2.08\text{ mol }NO_2$
$= 96\text{ g }NO_2$

20. d. $CaCO_3 \; + \; 2\,HCl \;\rightarrow\; CaCl_2 \; + \; H_2O \; + \; CO_2$
$10\text{ g }CaCO_3 = 0.10\text{ mol}$
expect 0.10 mol of $CO_2 = 4.4\text{ g }CO_2$
yield = $(3.65\text{g}/4.4\text{ g}) \times 100\% = 83\%$

EXAMINATION 1

CHEMISTRY 141 SPRING 2005
Solutions

1.   f.   mass   kilogram   kg
               length   meter   m
               time   second   s
               amount   mole   mol

2.   e.   12.0 km/s $\times$ (3600 s/1 hr) $\times$ (1 mile/1.609 km) = 2.68×10^4 mph

3.   g.   volume = 5.00^3 cm^3 = 125 cm^3
           density = 7.86 g cm^{-3}
           mass = density $\times$ volume = 7.86 g cm^{-3} $\times$ 125 cm^3 = 982.5 g
           # moles = mass / molar mass = 982.5 g / 55.84 g mol^{-1} = 17.59 mol
           Number of atoms = # moles $\times$ Avogadro's number = 17.59 mol $\times$ 6.022×10^{23} = 1.06×10^{25}

4.   c.   potassium chlorate

5.   e. $2\,C_4H_{10}$ + $13\,O_2$ $\rightarrow$ $8\,CO_2$ + $10\,H_2O$

6.   d. $6 \times C = 6 \times 12.011 = 72.066$
           $12 \times H = 12 \times 1.008 = 12.096$
           $6 \times O = 6 \times 16.000 = 96.000$
           Total = 180.16
           % C = $(72.066/180.16) \times 100\%$ = 40%

7.   e. Mg^{2+}; I^-; S^{2-}; N^{3-}; Na^+; Al^{3+}

8.   d.   individual molecules will have different masses if different isotopes are present

9.   d.   RbF

10.   b.

	chromium	silicon
mass:	73.52%	26.48%
divide by molar mass:	73.52/52.00	26.48/28.09
	= 1.414	= 0.943
divide by smallest:	= 1.50	= 1.00
multiply by 2:	= 3	= 2

           empirical formula is Cr_3Si_2

11.   g.   192 g / 16 g mol^{-1} = 12.0 mol O atoms
           it does not matter what form the oxygen is in—O, O_2, O_3—the number of atoms is the same

12.   d.   potassium dichromate is $K_2Cr_2O_7$
           there are two moles of K atoms for every mole of $K_2Cr_2O_7$

Therefore 10 moles of K in 5 moles of $K_2Cr_2O_7$
10 moles × 39.10 g mol^{-1} = 391 g

13.　c.　aluminum is the limiting reactant
0.36 mol Al × (2 mol Al_2O_3/4 mol Al) = 0.18 mol Al_2O_3

14.　g.　$2 SO_2 + O_2 \rightarrow 2 SO_3$
5 g SO_2 × (1 mol / 64 g) = 5/64 mol SO_2
5 g O_2 × (1 mol / 32 g) = 5/32 mol O_2
SO_2 is the limiting reactant:
5/64 mol SO_2 requires only 5/128 mol O_2
so 5/32 – 5/128 mol O_2 remains at end
= (15/128) mol × (32 g /1 mol) = 15/4 g O_2 = 3.75 g O_2

15.　d.　leaves decay in the winter

16.　e.　empirical mass CH_2O = 12 + 2 + 16 = 30 g mol^{-1}
molecular mass = 150 g mol^{-1}
150 / 30 = 5, so molecular formula = 5 CH_2O units, i.e. $C_5H_{10}O_5$

17.　c.　$C + 2 S \rightarrow CS_2$
C is the limiting reactant
one mole C produces one mole CS_2
9.0 moles of C produce 9.0 moles CS_2

18.　c.　Si–H compound $\rightarrow$ 2/3 SiO_2 + H_2O
or a ratio of 2 SiO_2 to 3 H_2O
therefore 2 Si and 6 H
empirical formula is SiH_3

19.　f.　61.3 g Cl_2 × (1 mol Cl_2/70.90 g Cl_2) × (1 mol PCl_5/1 mol Cl_2) × (208.2 g PCl_5/1 mol PCl_5)
= 180.0 g PCl_5
this is the theoretical yield
actual yield = 119.3 g
percent yield = 119.3/180.01 × 100% = 66%

20.　h.　mass of sulfur = 0.800 g
mass of chlorine = 4.338 – 0.800 g = 3.538 g

	sulfur	chlorine
mass:	0.800	3.538
divide by molar mass:	0.800/32.06	3.538/35.45
	= 0.02495	= 0.0998
divide by smallest:	= 1	= 4

empirical formula is SCl_4

EXAMINATION 1

CHEMISTRY 141 FALL 2005
Solutions

1. f. 95 miles/hour × (1 hr/3600 s) × (1.609 km/1 mile) × (1000 m/1 km) = 42 ms^{-1}

2. f. 5.00 gall × (3.785 L/1 gall) × (1000 mL/1 L) × (1 g/1 mL) × (1 mol/18.0 g) = 1050 mol

3. a. volume

4. c. isotopes differ in the number of neutrons in the nucleus

5. c.

6. f. five: $NaCH_3CO_2$ $Ca_3(PO_4)_2$ $NaCl$ $MgBr_2$ $Mg(NO_3)_2$

7. h. $NaSO_4$ should be Na_2SO_4

8. h. $Cu(NO_3)_2$; 6 moles O per mole of copper(II) nitrate, so 18 moles O in total

9. e. the item being counted is not specified

10. c. mass / number of moles = molar mass, so 67.0 g / 3.00 moles = 22.3 g mol^{-1}

11. f. 2 × C = 2 × 12.01 = 24.02
        1 × N = 1 × 14.01 = 14.01
        5 × H = 5 × 1.008 = 5.040
        2 × O = 2 × 16.00 = 32.00
        Total = 75.07 g mol^{-1}

12. c. 10 g × (1 mol Cl_2/70.90 g) × (6.022 × 10^{23} Cl_2 molecules/1 mol Cl_2) × (2 Cl/ 1 Cl_2)
        = 1.70 × 10^{23} atoms Cl
        or more simply: 10 g × (1 mol Cl_2/35.45 g) × (6.022 × 10^{23} Cl atoms/1 mol Cl) = 1.70 × 10^{23}
        atoms Cl

13. c. (72.975 × 0.57) + (74.729 × 0.40) + (76.899 × 0.03) = 73.794

14. d. 2 × C = 2 × 12.011 = 24.022
        6 × H = 6 × 1.008 = 6.048
        1 × O = 1 × 16.000 = 16.000
        Total = 46.07
        % O = (16.00/46.07) × 100% = 34.73%

15. d. 2 C_4H_{10} + 13 O_2 → 8 CO_2 + 10 H_2O
        26 mol of O_2 requires 4 moles of butane

16. a.

	carbon	nitrogen	hydrogen
mass:	74.04%	17.27%	8.700%
divide by molar mass:	74.04/12.01	17.27/14.01	8.700/1.008
	= 6.164	= 1.233	= 8.631
divide by smallest:	= 5	= 1	= 7

empirical formula is C_5NH_7

17. c. $B_?H_? \rightarrow B_2O_3 + 3 H_2O$

two B and six H on each side of the equation, so B_2H_6 — empirical formula BH_3

18. f. $2 NH_3(g) + 3 O_2(g) + 2 CH_4(g) \rightarrow 2 HCN(g) + 6 H_2O(g)$

19. c. ammonia: $5.0/2 = 2.5$
oxygen: $8.0/3 = 2.67$
methane: $4.0/2 = 2.0$ — limiting reactant

20. e. 4.0 mol $CH_4 \times (2$ mol $HCN/2$ mol $CH_4) = 4.0$ mol HCN

EXAMINATION 1

CHEMISTRY 141 SPRING 2006
Solutions

1. e. volume = $(0.78 \text{ cm})^3$ = 0.475 cm^3 = 0.475 mL
        density = mass / volume = 5 g / 0.475 mL = 10.5 g mL^{-1}

2. f. 2.4 miles + 112 miles + 26.2 miles
        = 140.6 miles × (1.609 km/1 mile) × (1000 m/1 km)
        = 2.26×10^5 m

3. b. dynamite explodes to form a mixture of gasses

4. e. atoms are indivisible

5. d. the atoms have different mass numbers

6. d. let x = % abundance of ^{107}Ag /100; i.e the fraction of ^{107}Ag
        107.87 = x(106.90509) + (1–x)(108.90476)
        x = 0.51746 therefore % abundance ^{107}Ag = 51.7%

7. a. alkali metals: K and Li
        alkaline earth metals: Mg and Ca
        halogens: Cl and I
        lanthanide: Pm
        transition metal: Fe
        non-metal: O
        noble gas: Ar

8. d. OH^{2-} should be OH^-
        CrO_4^{4-} should be CrO_4^{2-}
        and CO_3^- should be CO_3^{2-}

9. b. $Ca(NO_2)_2$

10. a. 10.0 g P_4 × (1 mol P_4/123.88 g P_4) × (4 mol P/1 mol P_4) = 0.323 mol P

11. c. 257 × C   = 257 × 12.01   = 3086.75
        383 × H   = 383 × 1.008   = 386.064
        65 × N   = 65 × 14.01   = 910.65
        77 × O   = 77 × 16.00   = 1232
        6 × S   = 6 × 32.07   = 192
        Total   = 5808 g mol^{-1}

12. d. use molar mass of insulin from question 11:
        (77 mol O/1 mol insulin) × (16.0 g O/1 mol O) × (1 mol insulin/5808 g insulin) × 100% = 21.2%

13. d. 4 mol $Cu(NO_3)_2$ × (187.57 g $Cu(NO_3)_2$/1 mol $Cu(NO_3)_2$) = 750.3 g $Cu(NO_3)_2$

14. b. 1 molecule PCl_5 × (1 mol/6.022 × 10²³ molecules) × (208.22 g PCl_5/1 mol PCl_5) = 3.46 × 10⁻²² g

15. h.

	carbon	nitrogen	hydrogen	oxygen
mass:	36.6%	32.0%	6.9%	24.4%
divide by molar mass:	36.6/12.01	32/14.01	6.9/1.008	24.4/16.0
	= 3.0475	= 2.2841	= 6.8452	= 1.525
divide by smallest:	= 2	= 1.5	= 4.5	= 1
multiply by 2:	= 4	= 3	= 9	= 2

    empirical formula is $C_4H_9N_3O_2$

16. c. $C_?H_?$ + O_2 → 6 CO_2 + 7 H_2O

    six C and fourteen H on each side of the equation, so C_6H_{14}, empirical formula C_3H_7

17. h. 4 $C_3H_5N_3O_9(l)$ → 12 $CO_2(g)$ + 10 $H_2O(g)$ + 6 $N_2(g)$ + $O_2(g)$

18. g.

	2 N_2O	+	3 O_2	→	4 NO_2
grams:	20		20		
divide by molar mass:	20/44.02		20/32		
moles:	= 0.4543		= 0.625		
divide by coefficient:	0.4543/2		0.625/3		
	= 0.23		= 0.208		O_2 is the limiting reactant

    0.625 mol O_2 × (4 mol NO_2/3 mol O_2) × (46.01 g NO_2/1 mol NO_2) = 38.34 g NO_2

19. d.

	Cl_2	+	3 F_2	→	2 ClF_3
	0.75 mol		4.0 mol		
divide by coefficient:	0.75/1 = 0.75		4.0/3 = 1.33		Cl_2 is the limiting reactant

    0.75 mol Cl_2 × (3 mol F_2/1 mol Cl_2) = 2.25 mol F_2 used
    4.0 mol – 2.25 mol = 1.75 mol F_2 remain

20. a. 3.03 g $C_7H_6O_3$ × (1 mol/138.12 g) = 0.02194 mol $C_7H_6O_3$ (limiting reactant)
    6.48 g $(CH_3CO)_2O$ × (1 mol/102.09 g) = 0.0635 mol $(CH_3CO)_2O$
    0.02194 mol $C_7H_6O_3$ × (1 mol $C_9H_8O_4$/1 mol $C_7H_6O_3$) × (180.154 g/1 mol) = 3.953 g $C_9H_8O_4$
    this is the theoretical yield
    % yield = (experimental/theoretical) = (3.26 g / 3.953 g) × 100% = 82.5%

EXAMINATION 1

CHEMISTRY 141 Fall 2006
Solutions

1.   e.   atomic number = 11, therefore Na
         protons = electrons, therefore no charge

2.   e.   sulfite SO_3^{2-} has a 2– charge

3.   f.   J (joule) is the derived unit for energy = force × distance = N m = $kg\ m^2\ s^{-2}$

4.   e.   greatest number of O atoms: $HClO_4$ and $HBrO_4$
         Cl has a smaller atomic mass than Br, therefore $HClO_4$

5.   f.   phosphorus pentachloride (nonmetals)

6.   e.   sum of the atomic masses = 300 g

7.   h.   2 moles N / urea × 5 moles urea = 10 moles N

8.   b.   Fe (iron) is a transition metal

9.   e.   the molecular formula is an integer multiple of the empirical formula; it may be the same but is often different

10.   e. O_2, N_2, Br_2, H_2, I_2; others are Cl_2 and F_2

11.   g.   128 g CH_4 / 16 g mol^{-1} = 8 mol CH_4

12.   i. Mg^{2+} has a 2+ charge; HSO_4^- has only a 1– charge

13.   g.   5.0 mol × 44 g mol^{-1} = 220 g

14.   b.   473 mL × (5.0 g / 100 mL) × (1.0 mol / 60 g) = 0.39 mol

15.   g.   volume of the metal block = 76.0 – 54.0 = 22.0 mL
         mass of the metal block = 194 – 123 = 71 g
         density = mass / volume = 71 g / 22.0 mL = 3.23 g mL^{-1}

16.   d.   CHN $\rightarrow$ 2 CO_2 + 1.5 H_2O + 1 NO_2
         ratio of C, H, and N on product side = C_2H_3N
         must be same on reactant side

17.   h.   number of moles of O_2 on product side: 2 CO_2 + 1.5 H_2O + 1 NO_2 = 3.75 mol O_2
         multiply by 4 to obtain 15 moles of O_2 on product side
         must multiply reactant side by 4 also, i.e. $C_8H_{12}N_4$

18.   d. $MnO_2 \; + \; 4\,HCl \; \rightarrow \; MnCl_2 \; + \; Cl_2 \; + \; 2\,H_2O$

19.   e. $Cr_2O_3 \; + \; 3\,H_2S \; \rightarrow \; Cr_2S_3 \; + \; 3\,H_2O$
          2.0 mol   2.0 mol

    H_2S is the limiting reactant
    amount of Cr_2O_3 used = 2.0 mol H_2S × (1 mol Cr_2O_3 /3 mol H_2S) = 2/3 mol Cr_2O_3
    therefore 4/3 mole Cr_2O_3 left unused

20.   e. $X \; + \; Cl_2 \; \rightarrow \; XCl_3$
         61 g   114 g

    mass of Cl_2 used = 114 − 61 = 53 g
    53 g Cl = 53 g / 35.45 g mol^{-1} = 1.5 mol of Cl in the product XCl_3

    mole ratio in product is one X to three Cl
    therefore there must be 0.50 mol of X in the product
    i.e. 61 g is 0.50 mol
    molar mass = 61 g / 0.50 mol = 122 g mol^{-1}

    element X must be antimony

EXAMINATION 1

CHEMISTRY 141 Spring 2007
Solutions

1. h. $93.7 \text{ MHz} \times (10^6 \text{ Hz} / 1 \text{ MHz}) = 9.37 \times 10^7 \text{ Hz}$

2. d. $NaHCO_3$

3. b. $11 \text{ ft} \times 13 \text{ ft} = 143 \text{ ft}^2 \times (12 \text{ in} / 1 \text{ ft})^2 \times (2.54 \text{ cm} / 1 \text{ in})^2 \times (1 \text{ m} / 100 \text{ cm})^2 = 13.3 \text{ m}^2$

4. c. density = mass / volume = $1945 \text{ g} / (9.5 \text{ cm} \times 6.5 \text{ cm} \times 7.0 \text{ cm}) = 4.5 \text{ g cm}^{-3}$

5. b. Fe (iron) is a transition metal

6. e. copper(I) chloride is a compound and can only be separated *by chemical means* into copper and chlorine

7. e. mass number = # protons + # neutrons
   atomic number = # protons;
   in a neutral atom # protons = # electrons

8. g. $3.0 \text{ mol } S_8 \times (256.5 \text{ g } S_8 / 1 \text{ mol } S_8) = 769.5 \text{ g } S_8$

9. e. SF_6 is sulfur hexafluoride

10. f. $2.0 \text{ mol } PH_3 \times (3 \text{ mol H} / 1 \text{ mol } PH_3) \times (6.022 \times 10^{23} \text{ atoms H} / 1 \text{ mol H}) = 3.61 \times 10^{24} \text{ atoms H}$

11. a. $1.0 \text{ mol } S_8 \times (8 \text{ mol S} / 1 \text{ mol } S_8) = 8 \text{ mol S}$

12. g. sum of atomic masses = $(4 \times 12.01) + (4 \times 1.008) + (2 \times 16.0) + (2 \times 14.01) = 112.1 \text{ g mol}^{-1}$

13. c. $130.8 \text{ g} / 2 \text{ mol} = 65.4 \text{ g mol}^{-1}$, therefore Zn

14. b. $3 \text{ mol Cl} \times (35.45 \text{ g Cl} / 1 \text{ mol Cl}) = 106.35 \text{ g Cl}$
    $106.35 \text{ g Cl} / 397.6 \text{ g } C_{12}H_{19}Cl_3O_8) \times 100 = 26.7\% \text{ Cl}$

15. g. $2.722 \text{ g } CO_2 \times (1 \text{ mol } CO_2 / 44 \text{ g } CO_2) \times (1 \text{ mol C} / 1 \text{ mol } CO_2) = 0.06185 \text{ mol C}$
    $0.558 \text{ g } H_2O \times (1 \text{ mol } H_2O / 18 \text{ g } H_2O) \times (2 \text{ mol H} / 1 \text{ mol } H_2O) = 0.06194 \text{ mol H}$
    $0.992 \text{ g } SO_2 \times (1 \text{ mol } SO_2 / 64 \text{ g } SO_2) \times (1 \text{ mol S} / 1 \text{ mol } SO_2) = 0.01548 \text{ mol S}$
    ratio is: $C_{0.06185}H_{0.06194}S_{0.01548}$
    divide by the smallest
    empirical formula is , C_4H_4S

16. b.

	carbon	nitrogen	hydrogen
mass:	40.0%	46.6%	13.4%
divide by molar mass:	40.0 / 12.01 = 3.3306	46.6 / 14.01 = 3.3262	13.4 / 1.008 = 13.2937
divide by smallest:	1	1	4

empirical formula is CH_4N
mass of empirical formula = 12 + 4 + 14 = 30 g mol^{-1}
therefore molecule is 2 × empirical unit
molecular formula is $C_2H_8N_2$

17. i. $CH_3CH_2OH + 3\,O_2 \rightarrow 2\,CO_2 + 3\,H_2O$
3 mol CH_3CH_2OH × (3 mol O_2 / 1 mol CH_3CH_2OH) = 9 mol O_2

18. d. $3\,PbO + 2\,NH_3 \rightarrow 3\,Pb + N_2 + 3\,H_2O$ sum = 3 + 2 + 3 + 1 + 3 = 12

19. b. determination of the limiting reactant:
124 g P_4 × (1 mol P_4 / 124 g P_4) = 1 mol P_4 / 1 = 1
323 g Cl_2 × (1 mol Cl_2 / 70.9 g Cl_2) = 4.65 mol Cl_2 / 6 = 0.76 therefore limiting reactant
4.56 mol Cl_2 × (4 mol PCl_3 / 6 mol Cl_2) × (137.32 g PCl_3 / 1 mol PCl_3) = 417 g PCl_3

20. g. there is a 1 to 1 mole ratio of CCl_4 to CCl_2F_2
therefore 1.80 mol CCl_2F_2 produced—this is the theoretical yield
% yield = (actual yield / theoretical yield) × 100 = (1.55 mol / 1.80 mol) × 100 = 86%

21. b. the actual yield cannot be larger than the theoretical yield

22. e. the atomic mass must be near 90 amu since the X–90 isotope is the most abundant by far
it must be less than 90 amu because the other isotopes have masses < 90 amu
it cannot be less than 89 amu—isotopes with masses < 89 amu have low abundances
the only logical answer is between 89 and 90 amu

if you want to calculate the answer...

atomic mass = [(0.62 / 100) × 85.925] + [(0.65 / 100) × 86.787] + [(1.86 / 100) × 87.976] + [(12.27 / 100) × 88.989] + [(84.6 / 100) × 89.855]

= 89.669 amu

EXAMINATION 1

CHEMISTRY 141 Fall 2007

Solutions

1. d. K

2. e. $3 + 4 + 5 = 12$

3. h. nitrate is NO_3^-

4. g. $1.2 \text{ in} \times 1.8 \text{ in} \times 1.0 \text{ in} \times (2.54 \text{ cm} / 1 \text{ in})^3 = 35 \text{ cm}^3$

5. a. alkali metal = sodium, halogen = chlorine, noble gas = argon, and transition metal = nickel

6. e. four: 1st, 3rd, 4th, and 6th

7. d. mass number of ^{35}Cl is 35 (18 neutrons)
        second isotope must be ^{37}Cl (with 20 neutrons)
        so that $75\% \times 35 + 25\% \times 37$ = approximately 35.5

8. e. atoms are in fact divisible into smaller particles

9. d. only three: CO, PF_5, and H_2O

10. e. the element has a molar mass (atomic mass) of 260 g /5 mol = 52 g mol^{-1}, so Cr

11. h. divide 495.5 g by 30.97 g mol^{-1} = 16 moles
        the fact that the phosphorus is present as P_4 is irrelevant

12. e. 5.0 mole $\times$ (17 g NH_3 / 1 mol) = 85 g NH_3

13. e. molar mass of Na_2CO_3 = 105.99 g mol^{-1}
        mass of sodium = 2 mole $\times$ (22.99 g mol^{-1}) = 45.98 g
        % Na = (45.98 / 105.99) $\times$ 100 = 43.38%

14. c. molar mass of NO_2 = 14.01 + 2$\times$16 = 46.01 g mol^{-1}
        divide by Avogadro's number   = 46.01 g mol^{-1}/ 6.022 $\times$ 10^{23} molecules mol^{-1}
                                        = 7.64 $\times$ 10^{-23} g molecule^{-1}

15. g.
	carbon	hydrogen	oxygen
mass:	59.96%	13.42%	26.62%
divide by molar mass:	59.96 / 12.01	13.42 / 1.008	26.62 / 16.00
	= 4.993	= 13.31	= 1.664
divide by smallest:	3.001	7.999	1.000

empirical formula is C_3H_8O

mass of empirical formula = 36 + 8 + 16 = 60 g mol^{-1}

the molar mass = 30 g / 0.50 mol = 60 g mol^{-1}

therefore the molecular formula is the same C_3H_8O

16. c.   a. 3.0 mol × 2 = 6   e. 7.0 mol × 3 = 21
          b. 4.5 mol × 4 = 18   f. 7.5 mol × 2 = 15
          c. 5.0 mol × 6 = 30   g. 9.0 mol × 1 = 9
          d. 6.0 mol × 2 = 12

17. g.   → $3 SeO_2$ + Al_2O_3
          compound must contain 3Se and 2Al, i.e. Al_2Se_3

18. i. $4 CH_3NHNH_2$ + $5 N_2O_4$ → $9 N_2$ + $12 H_2O$ + $4 CO_2$

19. i.   1.0 mol of methanol (CH_3OH) produces 2.0 mol of water (H_2O)
          2.5 mol of methanol will produce 5.0 mol of water

20. a.   7.36 g Zn = 7.36 g/ 65.39 g mol^{-1} = 0.1126 mol Zn
          6.45 g S_8 = 6.45 g/ 256.56 g mol^{-1} = 0.02514 mol S_8

          zinc is the limiting reactant—all used up

          0.1126 mol Zn × (1 mol S_8 / 8 mol Zn) = 0.01408 mol of S_8 used

          therefore 0.02514 − 0.01408 mol of S_8 left = 0.0111 mol of S_8 left
          = 2.84 g sulfur S_8 remaining at the end

21. b.   amount of sulfur used = 5.475 − 2.550 = 2.925 g
	iron	sulfur
mass:	2.550 g	2.925 g
divide by molar mass:	2.550 g / 55.85	2.925 g / 32.07
	= 0.04566	= 0.09121
divide by smaller:	1	2

empirical formula is FeS_2

22. e.   amount of water in the hydrate = 4.693 − 3.000 = 1.693 g
	$CuSO_4$	H_2O
mass:	3.000 g	1.693 g
divide by molar mass:	3.000 g / 159.6	1.693 g / 18.02
	= 0.0188	= 0.0940
divide by smaller:	1	5

empirical formula is $CuSO_4.5H_2O$

EXAMINATION 1

CHEMISTRY 141 Spring 2008
Solutions

1.   f.

2.   c. $310.15 \text{ K} - 273.15 \text{ K} = 37 \text{ °C}$

3.   d.   elements that normally exist as diatomic molecules are
          hydrogen, nitrogen, oxygen, fluorine, chlorine, bromine, and iodine.

4.   g. $4.63 \text{ km} \times (1000 \text{ m} / 1 \text{ km}) \times (100 \text{ cm} / 1 \text{ m}) = 4.63 \times 10^5 \text{ cm}$

5.   a. $200 \text{ mg} \times (1 \text{ g} / 1000 \text{ mg}) \times (1 \text{ cm}^3 / 3.52 \text{ g}) = 5.68 \times 10^{-2} \text{ cm}^3$

6.   e.   density, color, molecular mass, and temperature are intensive physical properties

7.   b.   atomic number = number of protons: ^{12}C ^{18}O ^{37}Cl ^{41}K ^{40}Ca

8.   d.   Ti, Ni, Au, and Cu are transition metals

9.   a.

10. g. ClO_4^- is perchlorate

11. d. $FeCl_3$; molar mass is the sum of atomic masses = $(1 \times 55.85) + (3 \times 35.45) = 162 \text{ g mol}^{-1}$

12. c. $0.0292 \text{ mol } C_{12}H_{22}O_{11} \times (342 \text{ g } C_{12}H_{22}O_{11} / 1 \text{ mol } C_{12}H_{22}O_{11}) = 10.0 \text{ g } C_{12}H_{22}O_{11}$

13. h. $2.0 \text{ mol } (NH_4)_2CO_3 \times (8 \text{ mol H} / 1 \text{ mol } (NH_4)_2CO_3) = 16 \text{ mol H}$

14. c. $271 \text{ g } BF_3 \times (1 \text{ mol } BF_3 / 67.81 \text{ g } BF_3) \times (3 \text{ mol F} / 1 \text{ mol } BF_3) \times (6.022 \times 10^{23} \text{ atoms F} / 1 \text{ mol F})$
          $= 7.22 \times 10^{24} \text{ atoms F}$

15. d. $0.423 \text{ g C} \times (1 \text{ mol C} / 12.01 \text{ g C}) = 0.03522 \text{ mol C}$
          $2.50 \text{ g Cl} \times (1 \text{ mol Cl} / 35.45 \text{ g Cl}) = 0.07052 \text{ mol Cl}$
          $1.34 \text{ g F} \times (1 \text{ mol F} / 19.00 \text{ g F})\quad = 0.07052 \text{ mol F}$

          divide by the smallest number; ratio is: 1 : 2 : 2
          empirical formula is CCl_2F_2

16. d. $(2 \text{ mol O} / 1 \text{ mol } C_{20}H_{24}N_2O_2) \times (16 \text{ g O} / 1 \text{ mol O}) \times (1 \text{ mol } C_{20}H_{24}N_2O_2 / 324.4 \text{ g } C_{20}H_{24}N_2O_2)$
          $\times 100 = 9.86\% \text{ O}$

17. e.

	chlorine	carbon	hydrogen
mass: divide by	71.56%	24.27%	4.07%
molar mass:	71.56 / 35.45 = 2.0186	24.27 / 12.01 = 2.0208	4.07 / 1.008 = 4.0377
divide by smallest:	1	1	2

empirical formula CNH_2 (mass of empirical unit = approximately 50 g mol^{-1})
therefore molecule is 2 × empirical unit
molecular formula is $Cl_2C_2H_4$

18. e. $\underline{1}\,(NH_4)_2Cr_2O_7 \rightarrow \underline{1}\,Cr_2O_3 + \underline{1}\,N_2 + \underline{4}\,H_2O$

19. e. $2\,KClO_3 \rightarrow 2\,KCl + 3\,O_2$

3 mol $KClO_3$ × (3 mol O_2 / 2 mol $KClO_3$) = 4.5 mol O_2

20. d.

	$2\,NH_3(g)$	+	$3\,CuO(s) \rightarrow$	$N_2(g)$	+	$3\,Cu(s)$	+	$3\,H_2O(g)$

mass: divide by	18.1 g	90.4 g
molar mass:	18.1 g/17.034 g mol^{-1} = 1.063 mol NH_3	90.4 g/79.55 g mol^{-1} = 1.1364 mol CuO
divide by coefficient:	/ 2 = 0.531	/ 3 = 0.379 —smaller, therefore limiting reactant

1.1364 mol CuO × (1 mol N_2 / 3 mol CuO) × (28.02 g N_2 / 1 mol N_2) = 10.6 g N_2

21. a. $4\,NH_3 + 7\,O_2 \rightarrow 4\,NO_2 + 6\,H_2O$

4 mol NH_3 and 7 mol O_2 are exact stoichiometric ratios of the reactants. When the reaction goes to completion (producing as much product as possible), there are zero moles of both NH_3 and O_2 remaining.

22. e. 6.40 g CH_3OH × (1 mol CH_3OH / 32.042 g CH_3OH) × (2 mol CO_2 / 2 mol CH_3OH) × (44.01 g CO_2 / 1 mol CO_2) = 8.79 g CO_2 (theoretical yield)

% yield = (actual / theoretical) × 100 = (6.21 g CO_2/ 8.79g CO_2) × 100 = 70.6%

EXAMINATION 1

CHEMISTRY 141 Fall 2008
Solutions

1. c. the base unit for mass is kg
        the base unit for volume is m^3
        density is defined as mass/volume; units $kg \ m^{-3}$

2. a. mass is extensive—depends upon how much of the matter is present

3. d. $(32.44 + 4.9 - 0.304) = 37.0$ —three significant figures with one decimal place
        the result of the division must have three significant figures as in the less precise number

4. b. iron

5. f. NH_3 is ammonia; the ammonium ion is NH_4^+ *(check question 20)*

6. h. both III (some elements exist as molecules), for example H_2, P_4, etc.,
        and VI (neutrons and protons are heavier than electrons) are true

7. d. 15 protons indicates the element P
        18 electrons compared with 15 protons indicates a charge of 3–
        16 neutrons + 15 protons = mass number of 31
        therefore $^{31}P^{3-}$

8. h. atomic mass = 10.8
        if the abundance of ^{11}B is x, then the abundance of ^{10}B is $(1 - x)$, and
        $11x + 10(1 - x) = 10.8$
        $x = 10.8 - 10 = 0.80$, which is 80%

9. c. mass / molar mass = number of moles

10. i. aluminum sulfite is $Al_2(SO_3)_3$ *(check question 18)*
        molar mass = $(2 \times 27) + 3 \times (32 + 48) = 294 \ g \ mol^{-1}$

11. h. molar mass of CO2 = $12 + 32 = 44 \ g \ mol^{-1}$
        mass of 12 moles = $12 \ mol \times 44 \ g \ mol^{-1} = 528 \ g$

12. a. magnesium chloride $MgCl_2$ $95.2 \ g \ mol^{-1} \times 0.5 \ mol$ $= 47.6 \ g$ — greatest mass
        hydrogen H_2 $2.02 \ g \ mol^{-1} \times 5.0 \ mol$ $= 10.1 \ g$
        carbon dioxide CO_2 $44.0 \ g \ mol^{-1} \times 1.0 \ mol$ $= 44.0 \ g$
        potassium K $39.1 \ g \ mol^{-1} \times 0.5 \ mol$ $= 19.6 \ g$
        methane CH_4 $16.0 \ g \ mol^{-1} \times 2.0 \ mol$ $= 32.0 \ g$
        argon Ar $40.0 \ g \ mol^{-1} \times 1.0 \ mol$ $= 40.0 \ g$
        sodium nitrate $NaNO_3$ $85.0 \ g \ mol^{-1} \times 0.25 \ mol$ $= 21.3 \ g$
        hydrogen chloride HCl $36.5 \ g \ mol^{-1} \times 1.0 \ mol$ $= 36.5 \ g$

13.　g.　$3 N_2O_4 + 8 NH_3 \rightarrow 7 N_2 + 12 H_2O$

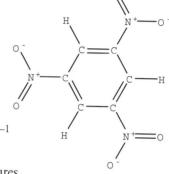

14.　h.　molecular formula $C_6H_3N_3O_6$
empirical formula is the simplest ratio C_2HNO_2

15.　b.　number of H atoms in one molecule = 10
multiply by the molar mass of H = $10 \times 1.0 = 10$ g mol⁻¹
molar mass of entire molecule = $(4 \times 12) + (10 \times 1) + 16 = 74$ g mol⁻¹
%H = $(10 / 74) \times 100 = 13.5\%$
there's no need to use atomic masses with more than 2 significant figures

16.　e.　for element X, number of moles = mass/molar mass = 27.22 g / 33.42 g mol⁻¹ = 0.8145 mol
number of moles of Y in XY_2 is twice the number of moles of X = $2 \times 0.8145 = 1.629$ mol
for element Y, molar mass = mass/number of moles = 84.10 g / 1.629 mol = 51.63 g mol⁻¹

17.　f.　unknown compound + _ $O_2 \rightarrow 1 CO_2 + 1.5 H_2O$
using whole number ratio...
unknown compound + _ $O_2 \rightarrow 2 CO_2 + 3 H_2O$
i.e. unknown compound produces C and H in the ratio 2 to 6
and therefore contains C and H in the same ratio
the only answers that fit are <u>b</u>, <u>f</u>, and <u>i</u>
<u>i</u> cannot be correct, the compound contains S
<u>f</u> has a molar mass between 60 and 70 g mol⁻¹ and is the correct answer

18.　h.　to calculate the mole ratio of H_2O to $Al_2(SO_4)_3$ we first need to know the mass % ratio
but only the % Al is provided (8.10%)

the % mass of $Al_2(SO_4)_3$　=　% mass of Al × (molar mass of $Al_2(SO_4)_3$ / 2 × molar mass of Al)
　　　　　　　　　　　　=　$8.10 \times (342.17$ g mol⁻¹ / 2 × 26.98 g mol⁻¹)
　　　　　　　　　　　　=　51.36%

therefore, % mass of water　=　100% − 51.36% = 48.64%

now convert to mole ratio:	$Al_2(SO_4)_3$	H_2O
mass:	51.36%	48.64%
divide by molar mass:	51.36 / 342.17	48.64 / 18.016
	= 0.1501	= 2.700
divide by smaller:	1	18

therefore $Al_2(SO_4)_3 \cdot 18 H_2O$

19.　g.　$4 C_3H_5N_3O_9 \rightarrow 12 CO_2 + 6 N_2 + 10 H_2O + 1 O_2$
moles of gas products = $12 + 6 + 10 + 1 = 29$ mol
according to the equation, 29 moles of gas products are produced from 4 mol $C_3H_5N_3O_9$
for one mol of nitroglycerin, the moles of gas products = 29/4 = 7.25 mol

20.　b.　O_2 is the limiting reactant

$4 NH_3 + 5 O_2 \rightarrow 4 NO + 6 H_2O$

amount of ammonia used = 2 mol O_2 × (4 mol NH_3 / 5 mol O_2) = 8/5 mol NH_3
amount of ammonia remaining at end = 3.0 mol − 8/5 mol = 7/5 mol = 1.4 mol NH_3

EXAMINATION 1

CHEMISTRY 141 Spring 2009
Solutions

1. c. 23.56 – 1.4 = 22.2 —three significant figures

2. f. velocity = $m\ s^{-1}$; acceleration = $m\ s^{-2}$; force = $kg\ m\ s^{-2}$

3. h. hydrogen, nitrogen, oxygen, fluorine, chlorine, bromine, and iodine exist as diatomic molecules
        phosphorus exists as a P_4 molecule and sulfur exists as an S_8 molecule

4. a. $CaHPO_4$

5. e. (1 mile / 11 min) × (1 min / 60 s) × (1.609 km / 1 mile) × (1000 m / 1 km) = $2.4\ ms^{-1}$

6. i. II, IV, and VI all involve changing one substance into another

7. d. let x = mass number of ^xGa
        % abundance of ^xGa = 100 – 60.1% = 39.9%
        atomic mass = 69.72 = (0.601 × 69) + (0.399 × x)
        mass number x = 71 = protons + neutrons
        therefore number of neutrons in ^xGa = 40

8. g. $C_6H_8O_6$

9. f. 3.0 mol CCl_4 × (4 mol Cl / 1 mol CCl_4) = 12 mol Cl

10. g. $Fe(CH_3CO_2)_2$; molar mass is the sum of the atomic masses
        = (1 × 55.85) + (4 × 12.01) + (6 × 1.008) + (4 × 16.00) = $173.9\ g\ mol^{-1}$

11. a. 1.0 mol KNO_3 × (1 mol N / 1 mol KNO_3) × ($6.022 × 10^{23}$ atoms N / 1 mol N)
        = $6.022 × 10^{23}$ atoms N

12. g. 2.5 mol PBr_3 × (270.67 g PBr_3 / 1 mol PBr_3) = 677 g PBr_3

13. a.

	carbon	hydrogen	oxygen
mass:	38.7%	9.70%	51.6%
divide by molar mass:	38.7 / 12.01 = 3.2223	9.70 / 1.008 = 9.6230	51.6 / 16.00 = 3.225
divide by smallest:	1	3	1

empirical formula CH_3O (mass of empirical unit = approximately $31\ g\ mol^{-1}$)

therefore molecule is 2 × empirical unit
molecular formula $C_2H_6O_2$

14. a. molar mass of $(NH_2)_2CO = 60.062$ g mol^{-1}
     mass of hydrogen = 4 mol × (1.008 g mol^{-1}) = 4.032 g
     %H = (4.032 / 60.062) × 100 = 6.71%

15. b. $2\,NaHCO_3 \rightarrow Na_2CO_3 + H_2O + CO_2$

16. f. 1 kg Ag_2O × (1000 g / 1 kg) × (1 mol Ag_2O / 231.74 g Ag_2O) × (4 mol Ag / 2 mol Ag_2O)
     = 8.63 mol Ag

17. f. $2\,X + 3\,Cl_2 \rightarrow 2\,XCl_3$

     47 g   232 g
     mass of Cl used = 232 g – 47 g = 185 g

     185 g Cl × (1 mol Cl / 35.45 g Cl) = 5.22 mol Cl

     5.22 mol Cl × (1 mol XCl_3 / 3 mol Cl) × (1 mol X / 1 mol XCl_3) = 1.74 mol X

     47 g X is 1.74 mol X so the molar mass = 47g / 1.74 mol = 27 g mol^{-1}
     element X must be aluminum

18. f. amount of water in the hydrate = 4.000 g – 2.513 g = 1.487 g

	$Ni(NO_3)_2$	H_2O
mass:	2.513 g	1.487 g
divide by molar mass:	2.513 g / 182.71	1.487 g / 18.016
	= 0.01375	= 0.08254
divide by smaller:	1	6

     empirical formula is $Ni(NO_3)_2 \cdot 6H_2O$

19. c. $4\,NH_3(g) + 5\,O_2(g) \rightarrow 4\,NO(g) + 6\,H_2O(l)$

     moles: 4.0 mol   3.0 mol
     divide by
     coefficient: 4 / 4   3 / 5
                 = 1   = 0.6   therefore O_2 is the limiting reactant

     3.0 mol O_2 × (4 mol NO / 5 mol O_2) = 2.4 mol NO

20. d. % yield = (actual yield aspirin / theoretical yield aspirin) × 100
     82.5% = (5.0 g / theoretical yield) × 100; theoretical yield = 6.06 g $C_9H_8O_4$
     6.06 g $C_9H_8O_4$ × (1 mol $C_9H_8O_4$ / 180.154 g $C_9H_8O_4$) × (1 mol $C_7H_6O_3$ / 1 mol $C_9H_8O_4$) ×
     (138.12 g $C_7H_6O_3$ / 1 mol $C_7H_6O_3$) = 4.6 g $C_7H_6O_3$

EXAMINATION 2

CHEMISTRY 141 FALL 2004
Solutions

1. e. first column: strong acids are: H_2SO_4, HCl, $HClO_3$
        second column: strong bases are: KOH, NaOH, $Mg(OH)_2$, KOH
        third column: weak acids are: all are weak acids
        fourth column: weak base is: NH_3
        fifth column: salts are: KCl, KNO_3, KCN, K_2SO_4
        e is the only row with all correct classifications

2. c. molarity = moles/liter
        moles = mass/molar mass = 10 g / 58.44 g mol^{-1} = 0.1711 mol
        volume = 500 mL = 0.500 L
        molarity = 0.1711/0.500 M = 0.34 M

3. i. the detailed ionic equation is

    $$Li^+(aq) + OH^-(aq) + H^+(aq) + Br^-(aq) \rightarrow Li^+(aq) + Br^-(aq) + H_2O(l)$$

    $Li^+(aq)$ and $Br^-(aq)$ are spectator ions

4. f. Cl +7; H is +1 and O is –2
        S –2; H is +1 with a nonmetal
        I 0; an element by itself

5. c. the oxidation numbers change, e.g. Mg from 0 to +2

6. d. heat is *not* a state function

7. b. q = +30 kJ —the system is heated and *gains* energy
        w = –25 kJ —the system does the work and *loses* energy
        ΔE = q + w = 30 – 25 = 5 kJ

8. b. heat to raise the temperature to the b.pt.:
        heat = sp ht × mass × temp change = 4.184 $JK^{-1}g^{-1}$ × 20 g × 95 K = 7950 J

        heat to vaporize the water:
        heat = latent heat of vaporization × mass = 2260 J g^{-1} × 20 g = 45200 J

        total = 7950 + 45200 = 53100 J = 53.1 kJ

9. g. heat released when the steam condenses
            = 2260 J g^{-1} × 10 g = 22600 J
        heat released when the 10 g of water cools from 100°C to 0°C
            = 4.184 $JK^{-1}g^{-1}$ × 10 g × 100 K = 4184 J
        total heat = 26784 J
        mass of ice that melts = 26784 J / 333 J g^{-1} = 80 g

10. b. Heat required to melt 100 g iron:
100 g × (1 mol/55.85 g) × (15 kJ/mol) = 26.858 kJ

Mass of acetylene required to be burned:
26.858 kJ × (2 mol C_2H_2/2600 kJ) × (26 g/1 mol) = 0.54 g

11. b. reverse & double: $2 SO_2(g) \rightarrow 2S(s) + 2O_2(g)$ ΔH° = +594 kJ

leave the same: $2S(s) + 3O_2(g) \rightarrow 2 SO_3(g)$ ΔH° = –791 kJ

add: $2 SO_2(g) + O_2(g) \rightarrow 2 SO_3(g)$ ΔH° = –197 kJ

12. g. an element in its standard state; silver metal is a solid

13. f. bonds broken: 2 H–H   2 × 436 kJ
                   1 O=O   498 kJ
   bonds formed: 4 O–H   – 4 × 467 kJ

   total: –498 kJ

14. a. radio waves < infrared < ultraviolet < gamma rays

15. e. E_{photon} = 6.626 × 10^{-34} Js × (3.0 × 10^8 m s^{-1}/10^{-6} m) = 1.988 × 10^{-19} J

for one mole of photons, Energy = 1.988 × 10^{-19} J × 6.022 × 10^{23} mol^{-1} = 1.2 × 10^5 J mol^{-1}

16. c. for 4d, n = 4 and l = 2
m_l must be a number between –2 and +2

17. e.

18. g. 2 × 3 = 6
6 – 7 = –1
–1 + 8 = 7

19. c.

20. i. Cl

EXAMINATION 2

CHEMISTRY 141 SPRING 2005
Solutions

1.   d.   first column: strong acids are: $HClO_4$, HBr, HI, $HClO_3$
             second column: strong bases are: KOH, NaOH, $Mg(OH)_2$
             third column: weak acids are: HF, HCN, HNO_2, HCO_2H
             fourth column: weak base is: NH_3
             fifth column: salts are: $MgCl_2$, $CaSO_4$, KBr, KNO_3, KCN, KH_2PO_4
             d is the only row with all correct classifications

2.   c.   molarity = 0.75 M × (10 mL/250 mL) = 0.030 M

3.   c.   the detailed ionic equation is

$$Mg(OH)_2(s) \;+\; 2\,H^+(aq) \;+\; 2\,I^-(aq) \;\rightarrow\; Mg^{2+}(aq) \;+\; 2\,I^-(aq) \;+\; 2\,H_2O(l)$$

         the iodide ion I^- is the only spectator ion

4.   e.   Cr +6
           P   0 (an element by itself)
           O +1 (F must be −1)

5.   f. H_2SO_4 is a strong acid

6.   d.   the oxidation numbers do not change

7.   a.   the reaction was exothermic—heat was released

8.   b.   q = +55 kJ —the system is heated and *gains* energy
          w = −33 kJ —the system does the work and *loses* energy
          ΔE = q + w = 55 − 33 = +22 kJ

9.   e.   mass of benzene = 86.8 mL × 0.90 g mL^{-1} = 78.1 g (one mole)

         heat to raise the temperature to the b.pt.:
         heat = sp ht × mass × temp change = 1.05 $JK^{-1}g^{-1}$ × 78.1 g × 60.1 K = 4929 J

         heat to vaporize the benzene:
         heat = latent heat of vaporization × mass = 394 J g^{-1} × 78.1 g = 30771 J

         total = 4929 + 30771 = 35,700 J = 35.7 kJ

10.   b.   heat required to vaporize the liquid nitrogen = 200 J g^{-1} × 30 g = 6000 J

         water cools to 0°C, where x = mass of water:
            heat released = 4.184 $JK^{-1}g^{-1}$ × x g × 30 K = 125.5 x J

         10.0 g of water freezes:
            heat released = 10.0 g × 333 J g^{-1} = 3330 J

total heat released = 125.5 x + 3330 J

this equals the heat required to vaporize the nitrogen
$$125.5 \text{ x} + 3330 \text{ J} = 6000 \text{ J}$$
$$125.5 \text{ x} = 2670$$
$$\text{x} = 21.3 \text{ g}$$

but 10 g of this freezes to ice, so 11.3 g remains liquid water

11. g. heat $= \Delta H_f^\circ (N_2O_4(g)) - 2 \times \Delta H_f^\circ (NO_2(g)) = +9.16$ kJ mol^{-1} $- 2 \times 33.18$ kJ mol^{-1}
$= -57.20$ kJ mol^{-1}

12. e. $2 C_2H_6 + 7 O_2 \rightarrow 4 CO_2 + 6 H_2O$

bonds broken:
2 C–C $2 \times 346 = 692$
12 C–H $12 \times 413 = 4956$
7 O=O $7 \times 498 = 3486$ ...all + energy is required

bonds formed:
8 C=O $8 \times 732 = 5856$
12 O–H $12 \times 463 = 5556$ ...all – energy is released

total = –2278 kJ
this is for 60.14 g of ethane (2 mol in the equation above)
for 50 g of ethane, the heat released will be slightly less:
$= 2278 \times (50.0/60.14) = 1894$ kJ

13. f. potassium is an element and is a solid in its standard state

14. g. multiply equation 1 by 2: $2 H_2(g) + 2 F_2(g) \rightarrow 4 HF(g)$ $\Delta H^\circ = -1074$ kJ
multiply equation 2 by 2: $2 C(s) + 4 F_2(g) \rightarrow 2 CF_4(g)$ $\Delta H^\circ = -1360$ kJ
reverse equation 3: $C_2H_4(g) \rightarrow 2 C(s) + 2 H_2(g)$ $\Delta H^\circ = -52$ kJ

add to obtain the desired equation $\Delta H^\circ = -2486$ kJ

15. f.

16. i. $2p^6 + 3p^6 + 4p^5 = 17$

17. c. the sixth electron is $1s^2\, 2s^2\, 2p^2$
$n = 2$, $l = 1$, $m_l = 0$, $m_s = +\frac{1}{2}$

18. b. $(2 - 1) \times 5 + 6 - 7 = 4$

19. g. Cl —the furthest to the upper right corner of the Periodic Table

20. a. for one molecule, the energy is $431{,}000 / 6.022 \times 10^{23}$ J $= 7.16 \times 10^{-19}$ J
frequency $= E_{photon} / h = 7.16 \times 10^{-19}$ J $/ 6.626 \times 10^{-34}$ J $= 1.08 \times 10^{15}$ s^{-1}

EXAMINATION 2

CHEMISTRY 141 FALL 2005

Solutions

1.　　d.　three are weak electrolytes: CH_3CO_2H, HF (weak acids) and NH_3 (weak base)

2.　　a.　moles = molarity × volume = 3.30 mol L^{-1} × 2.00 L = 6.60 mol
　　　　　mass = moles × molar mass = 6.60 mol × 40.0 g mol^{-1} = 264 g

3.　　g.　the equation is:

$$Li_2SO_4(aq) \; + \; Ba(NO_3)_2(aq) \; \rightarrow \; BaSO_4(s) \; + \; 2\,LiNO_3(aq)$$

　　　　　the detailed ionic equation is

$$2\,Li^+ \; + \; SO_4^{2-} \; + \; Ba^{2+} \; + \; 2\,NO_3^- \; \rightarrow \; BaSO_4(s) \; + \; 2\,Li^+ \; + \; 2\,NO_3^-$$

　　　　　the spectator ions are Li^+ and NO_3^-

4.　　a.　element reduced: N (from +5 to –3)
　　　　　element oxidized: Zn (from 0 to +2)
　　　　　moles of electrons = 1 × 8 or 2 × 4 = 8

5.　　g.　I and IV only
　　　　　H is –1 when combined with metals
　　　　　Cl, Br, I are + when combined with F or O

6.　　b.　heat = specific heat × mass × temperature change
　　　　　166.5 = specific heat $JK^{-1}g^{-1}$ × 15.0 g × 25°C
　　　　　specific heat = 0.444 $JK^{-1}g^{-1}$

7.　　e.　assuming some ice remains, the final temperature is 0°C
　　　　　heat from hot water = 4.184 $JK^{-1}g^{-1}$ × 20.0 g × 75°C = 6276 J
　　　　　this is sufficient to melt 6276 J / 333 J g^{-1} of ice = 18.85 g
　　　　　amount of ice remaining = 50.0 g – 18.85 g = 31.15 g

8.　　g.　q = –40 kJ —the system loses heat and the internal energy decreases
　　　　　w = –25 kJ —the system does the work and the internal energy decreases
　　　　　$\Delta E = q + w = -40 - 25 = -65$ kJ

9.　　g.　$C_2H_2 \; + \; 5/2\,O_2 \; \rightarrow \; 2\,CO_2 \; + \; H_2O$
　　　　　$\Delta H = [2 \times -394 - 286] - [227] = 1301$ per mole C_2H_2
　　　　　= 3903 kJ for 3.0 moles of C_2H_2

10.　　g.　Fe(s)

11.　　e.　$\lambda = 6.626 \times 10^{-34}$ Js / 0.500 kg × 30.0 ms^{-1} = 4.42 × 10^{-35} m

12.   g.   violet

13.   g. $1 + 4 + 9 + 16 + 25 = 55$

14.   g.   s d p

15.   f.   if n = 2, then l = 0 or 1 (maximum allowed value = n − 1)
            and m_l = −l through 0 to +l

16.   c.   4p

17.   e. $5 − 3 \times 2 + 5 = 9$

18.   c. $[Kr] 5s^2 4d^5$

19.   c. $(3.0 \times 10^8 \text{ ms}^{-1} / 250 \times 10^{-9} \text{ m}) \times 6.626 \times 10^{-34} \text{ Js}$
            $= 7.95 \times 10^{-19} \text{ J}$

20.   c.

EXAMINATION 2

CHEMISTRY 141 SPRING 2006

Solutions

1. e. strong electrolytes: $HClO_4$, $FeCl_3$, $Mg(OH)_2$, HBr
        weak electrolytes: NH_3, $HClO_2$, HF
        non-electrolyte: CH_3OH

2. g. H_2SO_4 is sulfuric acid, H_2SO_3 is sulfurous acid

3. d. $2\,Ag^+(aq)\;+\;CrO_4^{2-}(aq)\;\rightarrow\;Ag_2CrO_4(s)$

4. a. $+1$ (O_2F_2)
        -1 (O_2^{2-})
        -2 (ClO_3^-)

5. c. Al: 0 to +3 (oxidized)
        Pb: +2 to 0 (reduced)

6. f. $5\,L \times (0.25\ \text{mol } C_{12}H_{22}O_{11}\,/\,1\,L) \times (342\ \text{g } C_{12}H_{22}O_{11}\,/\,1\ \text{mol}) = 427.8\ \text{g } C_{12}H_{22}O_{11}$

7. d. $(10\ \text{mL}) \times (M_{conc}) = (100\ \text{mL}) \times (0.2\ \text{M})$
        $M_{conc} = 2.0\ \text{M}$

8. e. $2\,C_3H_6 + 9\,O_2 \;\rightarrow\; 6\,CO_2 + 6\,H_2O$
        bonds broken − bonds formed
        $6(C–C) + 12(C–H) + 9(O=O) − 12(C=O) − 12(H-O)$
        $6(346) + 12(413) + 9(498) − 12(803) − 12(463) = −3678\ \text{kJ}$

9. e. the aluminum is *oxidized* and the iron is *reduced*.

10. d. condense Ar: $q = 10\ \text{g} \times (6.447\ \text{kJ / mol}) \times (1000\ \text{J / 1kJ}) \times (1\ \text{mol Ar / 39.95 g Ar}) = 1613.8\ \text{J}$
        cool Ar to −189 °C: $q = 10\ \text{g} \times (1.05\ \text{Jg}^{-1}\text{K}^{-1}) \times (3\ \text{K}) = 31.5\ \text{J}$
        energy released $= 1613.8\ \text{J} + 31.5\ \text{J} = 1645\ \text{J}$

11. c. heat lost by water cooling = heat gained to melt ice
        $(15\ \text{g}) \times (4.184\ \text{Jg}^{-1}\text{K}^{-1}) \times (85\ \text{K}) =$ mass of ice melted $\times (333\ \text{Jg}^{-1})$
        mass of ice melted $= 16\ \text{g}$

12. a. $\Delta E = q + w = −20\ \text{kJ} + 30\ \text{kJ} = +10\ \text{kJ}$

13. f. elements in their standard state are $C(s)$, $P_4(s)$, $Br_2(l)$, $Cl_2(l)$, and $Hg\ (l)$

14. d. $\Delta H_{rxn} = [2(−394) + 4(−286)] − [2(−239)] = −1454\ \text{kJ}$
        $4\ \text{mol } CH_3OH \times (1454\ \text{kJ / 2 mol } CH_3OH) = 2908\ \text{kJ}$

15.   c. $E = h\nu$

$\nu = (2.84 \times 10^{-19} \text{ J}) / (6.626 \times 10^{-34} \text{ J s}) = 4.286 \times 10^{14} \text{ s}^{-1}$

$\lambda = c / \nu = (3 \times 10^8 \text{ m s}^{-1}) / (4.286 \times 10^{14} \text{ s}^{-1})$

$= 7 \times 10^{-7}$ m

$= 700$ nm which corresponds to red light

16.   e. $E_{orange} = (6.626 \times 10^{-34} \text{ J s}) \times (5 \times 10^{14} \text{ s}^{-1}) = 3.313 \times 10^{-19}$ J / photon

$E_{violet} = (6.626 \times 10^{-34} \text{ J s}) \times (7.5 \times 10^{14} \text{ s}^{-1}) = 4.970 \times 10^{-19}$ J / photon $\times$ 2 photon

$= 9.939 \times 10^{-19}$ J

9.939×10^{-19} J / 3.313×10^{-19} J = 3 photons of orange light

or

frequency of violet light is 1.5 times the frequency of orange light, therefore the photons of violet light have 1.5 times more energy than the photons of orange light
therefore three orange photons have the same energy as two violet photons

17.   b.   Se: $1s^2 2s^2 2p^6 3s^2 3p^6 4s^2 3d^{10} 4p^4$

the last electron is the 4th electron placed in the 4p orbital, n = 4, l = 1, m_l = −1, m_s = −½

18.   a. Mg^{2+}, Na^+, and F^- are an isoelectronic series:

F^- is the largest, Na^+ is in the middle and Mg^{2+} is the smallest

19.   e.   Al: $1s^2 2s^2 2p^6 3s^2 3p^1$, 7 electrons in all of the p orbitals

20.   f. l = 0 is an s orbital, l = 1 is a p orbital, l = 2 is a d orbital, l = 3 is an f orbital

EXAMINATION 2

CHEMISTRY 141 FALL 2006
Solutions

1. b. the strong acids are HNO_3 and $HClO_4$
        the HNO_3 is more concentrated

2. e. molar mass of lithium nitrate = 6.94 + 14.01 + (3 × 16) = 68.95 g mol^{-1}
        moles required = M × V = 0.10 mol L^{-1} × 50/1000 L = 0.0050 mol
        mass required = moles × molar mass = 0.0050 mol × 68.95 g mol^{-1} = 0.345 g

3. c. HNO_2 is nitrous acid

4. d. Na^+ —both NaOH and NaCN are strong electrolytes; the others are weak

5. i. V +2; K +1; U +6; Fe 2+; Cr +6

6. f. system loses 40 kJ as work done but ΔE = 25 kJ, so q = 65 kJ —so that ΔE = q + w = 65 – 40 kJ

7. d. two step process:

heat to boiling point:	heat	= specific heat × mass × temp change
		= 2.16 J g^{-1} K^{-1} × 3.9 g × (56.2 – 25) K
		= 262.8 J
vaporize:	heat	= heat of vaporization × mass
		= 525 J g^{-1} × 3.9 g
		= 2047.5 J
total:	heat	= 262.8 + 2047.5 = 2310 J = 2.31 kJ

8. e.

metal cooling:	heat	= sp ht J g^{-1} K^{-1} × 55 g × (10 – 100) K
		= – sp ht × 4950 J
ice melting:	heat	= 333 J g^{-1} × 20 g
		= 6660 J
water warming:	heat	= 4.184 J g^{-1} K^{-1} × 120 g × (10 – 0) K
		= 5021 J
sum:		– sp ht × 4950 J + 6660 J + 5021 J = zero
	sp ht	= (6660 + 5021) / 4950
		= 2.36 J g^{-1} K^{-1}

9. a. ΔH = (3 × –266.5) + (–393.7) – (–1117) – (–110.5) kJ
        = +34.3 kJ

10. d. formation of one mole of C_2H_4 from its constituent elements in their standard states

11. f. $C(s)$ + $O_2(g)$ → $CO_2(g)$ Heat released: $\Delta H = -394$ kJ

    bonds broken   *bonds formed*

    $C(s)$ $O=O$ $2\ C=O$

    +710 kJ   498 kJ

    $\Delta H = -394$ kJ = +710 kJ + 498 kJ − 2C=O

    C=O bond energy   = (710 + 498 + 394) / 2 kJ

                             = 801 kJ

12. g. γ–rays have the highest energy per photon

13. a.

14. b. $E = h\nu = 5.89 \times 10^{-26}$ J $= 6.626 \times 10^{-34}$ Js $\times \nu$

    $\nu = 5.89 \times 10^{-26}$ J $/ 6.626 \times 10^{-34}$ Js $= 88.9 \times 10^6$ s^{-1} = 88.9 MHz

15. f. m_l depends only upon l; if $l = 2$, then $m_l = +2, +1, 0, -1, -2$

16. c. Nb

17. c. two, in the 3p orbitals

18. f. number of orbitals in any set of p orbitals = 3

    number of protons in the nucleus of a carbon atom = 6

    number of d electrons in the valence shell of manganese = 5

    maximum value for l = n−1 = 5−1 = 4

    total = 18

19. g. ionization energy depends upon all three

20. c. Fe is a metallic solid

    N_2 is a molecule with a covalent bond

    CO is a molecule with a polar covalent bond

EXAMINATION 2

CHEMISTRY 141 SPRING 2007
Solutions

1. c. 3.0 moles / 5.0 L = 0.60 M

2. g. 3.0×10^8 ms^{-1} / 5.90×10^{-7} m = 5.08×10^{14} s^{-1}

3. e. ammonia NH_3 is a weak base (a weak electrolyte) and will not ionize very much in aqueous solution

4. b. the net ionic equation is: $Mg^{2+}(aq)$ + 2 $OH^-(aq)$ $\rightarrow$ $Mg(OH)_2(s)$
    the spectator ions are 2 $Na^+(aq)$ and 2 $NO_3^-(aq)$

5. c. (0.075 L $\times$ 5.0 M) / 2.0 L = 0.187 M

6. c. signs of heat and work depend on the system; system does work on surroundings (w is –) and heat transferred to the surroundings (q is +)

7. g. H is +1 (with a nonmetal); S is –2
    S is +4; O is –2
    S is +2; Cl is –1
    S is 0 (element by itself)
    K is +1; S is +6 and O is –2

8. e. element reduced: Si (from +4 to 0); change in oxidation number is –4
    element oxidized: Mg (from 0 to +2)

9. h. heat Ne to boiling: q   = (13.0 g) $\times$ (1.05 J g^{-1} K^{-1}) $\times$ (24 K)
                                    = 327.6 J

    evaporate Ne: q   = (13.0 g) $\times$ (86.3 J g^{-1})
                                    = 1121.9 J

    energy required   = 327.6 J + 1121.9 J = 1450 J

10. c. heat gained by krypton evaporating   = (10.0 g) $\times$ (107.5 J g^{-1}) = 1075 J
    heat lost by water cooling   = (5.00 g) $\times$ (4.184 J g^{-1} K^{-1}) $\times$ (25 K) = 523 J
    heat lost to form ice   = (mass of ice formed) $\times$ (333 J g^{-1})
    heat gained = heat lost: 1075 J   = 523 J + [(mass of ice formed) $\times$ (333 J g^{-1})]
    mass of ice formed   = 1.66 g

11. i. water evaporates: breaking bonds therefore endothermic
    the combustion of propane: heat released therefore exothermic
    ice forms: making bonds therefore exothermic
    2 $Na(s)$ + 2 $H_2O(l)$ $\rightarrow$ 2 $NaOH(aq)$ + $H_2(g)$ + 367.5 kJ: heat produced therefore exothermic

12. h. $\Delta H_{rxn} = [12(-242) + 4(-394)] - [5(-20) + 4(-54)] = -4164$ kJ

13. d. elements in their standard state are $N_2(g)$, K(s), and Ar(g)

14. a. equation for the molar enthalpy of formation of MnO_2 is:

$Mn(s) + O_2(g) \rightarrow MnO_2(s)$ $\qquad \Delta H_f^{\circ} = ??$

reverse equation 1 and divide by 3:

$Mn(s) + 2/3\ Al_2O_3(s) \rightarrow 4/3\ Al(s) + MnO_2(s)$ $\quad \Delta H = +597.3$ kJ

divide equation 2 by 3:

$4/3\ Al(s) + O_2(g) \rightarrow 2/3\ Al_2O_3(s)$ $\qquad \Delta H = -1117$ kJ

add to obtain the desired equation: $\qquad \Delta H_f^{\circ} = -520$ kJ

15. c. 4101 kJ $\times$ (1 mol C_2H_5OH / 1367 kJ) = 3 mol C_2H_5OH

16. d.

17. a. 2.0 GHz $= 2 \times 10^9$ Hz $= 2 \times 10^9$ s^{-1}

$E = h\nu = (6.626 \times 10^{-34}$ J s$) \times (2 \times 10^9$ s$^{-1}) = 1.33 \times 10^{-24}$ s^{-1}

18. g. E decreases as λ increases

19. f. for 5p, n = 5 and $l = 1$

m_l must be a number between -1 and $+1$

20. f. Na: $1s^2\ 2s^2\ 2p^6\ 3s^1$

Fe: $1s^2\ 2s^2\ 2p^6\ 3s^2\ 3p^6\ 4s^2\ 3d^6$

Br: $1s^2\ 2s^2\ 2p^6\ 3s^2\ 3p^6\ 4s^2\ 3d^{10}\ 4p^5$

C: $1s^2\ 2s^2\ 2p^2$

21. f. Y

22. e. Se^{2-}

EXAMINATION 2

CHEMISTRY 141 FALL 2007

Solutions

1. h. H_3PO_4 is a weak acid

2. e. molarity × volume = number of moles

3. f. 170 g KOH / 56.1 g mol^{-1} = 3.03 mol KOH in one liter
        volume (in mL) required = 1000 mL × (0.20 M / 3.03 M) = 66 mL

4. a. lithium hydroxide is a strong base—write as Li$^+$ and OH$^-$
        hydrofluoric acid is a weak acid—write as HF
        Li$^+$ is a spectator ion

5. d. $(2 \times +1) + (2 \times \underline{+6}) + (7 \times -2)$ = zero

6. f. 6 electrons are lost by the two N in the oxidation process
        6 electrons are gained by the three Pb in the reduction process

7. c. $\Delta E = q + w$
        $-180 = -40 + w$
        $w = -140$

8. h. heat to boiling: heat required = (10.0 g) × (1.05 J g^{-1} K^{-1}) × (54 K) = 567 J
        boil: heat required = (10.0 g) × (86.3 J g^{-1}) = 863 J
        total = 567 + 863 = 1430 J

9. e. melt ice: heat required = (10.0 g) × (333 J g^{-1}) = 3330 J
        warm water: heat required = (40.0 g) × (4.184 J g^{-1} K^{-1}) × (5.0 K) = 837 J
        cool aluminum: heat lost =   (15.0 g) × (0.902 J g^{-1} K^{-1}) × (ΔT)

        ΔT = (3330 + 837) / (15 × 0.902) = 308 K
        initial temperature = 308 + 5°C = 313°C

10. b. reverse equation 1 and multiply by 2: $2 Fe_3O_4$ (s) → 6 Fe (s) + 4 O$_2$ (g) ΔH = +2236.8 kJ
        multiply equation 2 by 6:   6 Fe (s) + 3 O$_2$ (g) → 6 FeO (s) ΔH = −1632.0 kJ
        add: $2 Fe_3O_4$ (s) → 6 FeO (s) + O$_2$ (g) ΔH = +604.8 kJ

11. d. according to the equation, 60.14 g (two moles) of ethane burns to produce 2856 kJ
        the mass of ethane required for 5000 kJ = 60.14 g × (5000 / 2856) = 105 g

12. i. $H_2(g)$

13.   g.   heat released by combustion is proportional to temperature increase / mass burned

for hydrogen, heat released is proportional to 14.2°C / 1.16 g = 12.24 °C g^{-1}

for methane, heat released is proportional to 7.35°C / 1.50 g = 4.90 °C g^{-1}

ratio hydrogen to methane = 12.24 /4.90 = 2.5

14.   a.   at constant pressure, $\Delta H = \Delta E + P\Delta V$

if there is an increase in volume and expansion work is done by the system, then ΔH is larger than ΔV

15.   a. $E = h\nu = hc / \lambda = (6.626 \times 10^{-34} \text{ Js}) \times (3.0 \times 10^{8} \text{ ms}^{-1}) / (1.2 \times 10^{8} \times 10^{-9} \text{ m}) = 1.7 \times 10^{-24}$ J

16.   e.   violet

17.   b.   if n = 1, then l must equal zero; i.e. the only orbital possible is an s orbital

18.   e.   Ga, Ge, As, Br; the only other possibility would be Se

19.   g.   6p

20.   d.   Ti has the configuration [Ar] $4s^2\ 3d^2$; removal of 4 electrons leads to [Ar]

21.   i.   F—the element furthest to the upper right of the Periodic Table

22.   b.   KCl is ionic

H_2O is a covalent molecule

Cu is a metal

EXAMINATION 2

CHEMISTRY 141 SPRING 2008

Solutions

1. e. HF, CH_3CO_2H, $HClO_2$ are weak acids (weak electrolytes)
        NH_3 is a weak base (weak electrolyte)
        $C_{12}H_{22}O_{11}$ is a molecule (non-electrolyte)
        NaF is a salt (strong electrolyte)

2. g. within a principal energy level there are n^2 available orbitals each holding a maximum of 2 electrons
        when n=3, there are 9 available orbitals (s, p, and d) holding a maximum of 18 electrons

3. d. the detailed ionic equation is

    $$Pb^{2+}(aq) + 2\,NO_3^-(aq) + 2\,Na^+(aq) + 2\,I^-(aq) \rightarrow 2\,Na^+(aq) + 2\,NO_3^-(aq) + PbI_2(s)$$

    $NO_3^-(aq)$ and $Na^+(aq)$ are spectator ions

4. b. H_3PO_2 H is +1, P is +1 and O is –2
        $H_4P_2O_7$ H is +1, P is +5 and O is –7
        PCl_5 Cl is –1 and P is +5
        P_4 P is 0 (an element by itself)

5. f. molar mass $C_{12}H_{22}O_{11}$ = 342.3 g mol^{-1}
        5.0 L × (0.25 mol / 1 L) × (342.3 g $C_{12}H_{22}O_{11}$ / 1 mole $C_{12}H_{22}O_{11}$) = 428 g $C_{12}H_{22}O_{11}$

6. f. (0.300 mol / L) × 0.050 L = 0.015 mol HCl in 0.300 M solution
        (0.120 mol / L) × 0.300 L = 0.036 mol HCl in 0.120 M solution
        in the new solution, the number of moles of HCl remains the same, but the volume changes;
        (0.015 mol HCl + 0.036 mol HCl) / 0.350 L = 0.146 M

7. a. evaporation (liquid to gas) is an endothermic process

8. d. heat = mass × specific heat × temp change
        180 J = 35.0 g × 0.385 J g^{-1} K^{-1} × ΔT
        ΔT = 13.4 degrees and the initial temperature of the block is 65°C - 13.4°C = 51.6°C

9. d. heat released when copper block cools = 75.0 g × 0.385 J g^{-1} K^{-1} × 100 K = 2887.5 J
        mass of ice that melts = 2887.5 J / 333 J g^{-1} = 8.7 g
        mass of liquid water present at end = 25.0 g + 8.7 g = 33.7 g

10. b. determination of the limiting reactant:
        3 mol NO / 2 = 1.5; therefore NO is the limiting reactant
        2 mol O_2 / 1 = 2
        3 mol NO × (114.1 kJ / 2 mol NO) = 171.2 kJ released

11. b. standard states of the constituent elements of NaOH are $Na(s)$, $O_2(g)$, $H_2(g)$

12. b. reverse equation 1:

$$B_2H_6(g) + 3 O_2(g) \rightarrow B_2O_3(s) + 3 H_2O(g) \qquad \Delta H = -2035 \text{ kJ}$$

reverse equation 2 and multiply by 3/2:

$$3 H_2O(g) \rightarrow 3 H_2O(l) \qquad \Delta H = -132 \text{ kJ}$$

reverse equation 3 and multiply by 3:

$$3 H_2O(l) \rightarrow 3 H_2(g) + 3/2 O_2(g) \qquad \Delta H = +858 \text{ kJ}$$

no change to equation 4:

$$2 B(s) + 3 H_2(g) \rightarrow B_2H_6(g) \qquad \Delta H = +36 \text{ kJ}$$

add to obtain the desired equation:

$$2 B(s) + 3/2 O_2(g) \rightarrow B_2O_3(s) \qquad \Delta H = -1273 \text{ kJ}$$

13. i.

14. f. 93 nm = 9.3×10^{-8} m which is ultraviolet light

15. c. $E = h\nu$; $\nu = 4.85 \times 10^{-19}$ J / 6.626×10^{-34} J s = 7.32×10^{14} s^{-1}

$c = \lambda\nu$; $\lambda = 3 \times 10^8$ ms^{-1} / 7.32×10^{14} s^{-1} = 4.10×10^{-7} m = 410 nm

16. b. $\lambda = 6.626 \times 10^{-34}$ J s / $(0.100 \text{ kg} \times 35 \text{ ms}^{-1})$ = 1.9×10^{-34} m

17. b.

18. a. the principal quantum number, n, is not allowed to equal zero

19. g. the outermost electrons are in the orbital with the highest principal quantum number

20. h.

21. d. atomic radius increases from right to left across a group

22. d. covalent bonding occurs between two highly electronegative elements (non-metals); Cl_2, CO_2, and NO

EXAMINATION 2

CHEMISTRY 141 FALL 2008

Solutions

1.   e.   molarity (mol L^{-1}) × volume (L) = number of moles (mol)

2.   d.   the formula of strontium nitrate is $Sr(NO_3)_2$
          there are 2 mol of NO_3^- ions for every mol of $Sr(NO_3)_2$
          the concentration of NO_3^- ions = 2 × 0.10 M = 0.20 M

3.   g. $HClO_3$ is chloric acid

4.   d.   the acid must be strong, i.e. HI, $HClO_4$, or HCl in the list provided
          of these, the $HClO_4$ is the most concentrated solution (2.0 M)

5.   a.   HCN is a weak electrolyte, so the detailed ionic equation is
          $Li^+(aq) + OH^-(aq) + HCN(aq) \rightarrow Li^+(aq) + CN^-(aq) + H_2O(l)$
          $Li^+(aq)$ is a spectator ion, so the net ionic equation is
          $OH^-(aq) + HCN(aq) \rightarrow CN^-(aq) + H_2O(l)$

6.   g.   Cr in $K_2Cr_2O_7$ +6
          Cr in CrO   +2
          Cr in $Cr_2(SO_4)_3 \cdot 6H_2O$ +3

7.   a.   chlorine is both oxidized (from 0 in Cl_2 to +1 in HOCl)
          and reduced (from 0 in Cl_2 to −1 in Cl^-)

8.   c.   *heat is lost by the metal as it cools to 0°C:*
          heat   = specific heat × mass × temp change
                      = 0.385 $JK^{-1}g^{-1}$ × 150 g × 86.5 K
                      = 4995 J

     this heat is used to melt ice:
          heat   = heat of fusion × mass of ice
          4995 J = 333 Jg^{-1} × mass of ice
          mass of ice = 4995/333 g = 15.0 g

9.   c. $\Delta E = q + w$
          q = +280 J (energy going *into* the system)
          w = −130 J (energy going *out of* the system)
          $\Delta E = 280 - 130 = 150$ J

10. h.   the reaction as it is written represents the combustion of one mol of acetone (= 58 g acetone)
          energy released in the combustion of 116.0 grams acetone C_3H_6O = 2 × 1790.4 kJ = 3581 kJ

          $C_3H_6O + 4O_2 \rightarrow 3H_2O + 3CO_2$ $\Delta H = -1790.4$ kJ

11. b. $4\,NH_3(g) + 3\,O_2(g) \rightarrow 2\,N_2(g) + 6\,H_2O(g)$ $\Delta H = ???$

   the idea is to manipulate the given equations so that they add up to the desired equation

   don't start with NH_3 or H_2O because they occur in both given equations

   so look at either O_2 and N_2 and match their coefficients with those in the desired equation

   that is, multiply the first equation by 3/7 and the second equation by 2/7:

   $12/7\,NH_3(g) + 3\,O_2(g) \rightarrow 12/7\,NO_2(g) + 18/7\,H_2O(g)$ $\Delta H = (-1132\text{ kJ}) \times 3/7$

   $12/7\,NO_2(g) + 16/7\,NH_3(g) \rightarrow 2\,N_2(g) + 24/7\,H_2O(g)$ $\Delta H = (-2740\text{ kJ}) \times 2/7$

   add: ————————————————————————————————

   $4\,NH_3(g) + 3\,O_2(g) \rightarrow 2\,N_2(g) + 6\,H_2O(g)$ $\Delta H = -1268\text{ kJ}$

12. b. $2\,C_4H_{10}(l) + 13\,O_2(g) \rightarrow 8\,CO_2(g) + 10\,H_2O(l)$ $\Delta H° = -5754\text{ kJ}$

   $\Delta H_{rxn} = [10(-285.8) + 8(-393.5)] - [2(\Delta H_f° \text{ of } C_4H_{10}) + 13(0)] = -5754\text{ kJ}$

   $\Delta H_f° \text{ of } C_4H_{10} = -(-5754\text{ kJ} + 6006\text{ kJ})/2 = -126\text{ kJ mol}^{-1}$

13. a. energy required to remove one electron $= 2.18 \times 10^{-18}\text{ J}$
   energy required to remove one mole of electrons $= 2.18 \times 10^{-18} \times 6.022 \times 10^{23}\text{ J} \times (1\text{ kJ}/1000\text{J})$
   $= 1313\text{ kJ}$

14. a. infrared $<$ yellow $<$ blue $<$ x-ray $<$ γ-ray

15. b. energy of a microwave photon $= h\nu = 6.626 \times 10^{-34}\text{ Js} \times 3 \times 10^8\text{ ms}^{-1}/10^{-3}\text{ m} = 2.00 \times 10^{-22}\text{ J}$
   heat required to raise the temperature of 1.0 g water by 1.0°C $= 4.184\text{ J}$
   number of photons required $= 4.184\text{ J} / 2.00 \times 10^{-22}\text{ J} = 2.10 \times 10^{22}$

16. a. it is l that equals 1 for a p orbital, not m_l

17. e. l cannot be negative and it cannot be greater than $n - 1$

18. a. same as Ar

19. f. Al^{3+} $<$ Mg^{2+} $<$ Ca^{2+} $<$ K^+ $<$ Ar $<$ Cl^- $<$ P^{3-}

20. f. argon; it has a stable configuration: $1s^2\,2s^2\,2p^6\,3s^2\,3p^6$

EXAMINATION 2

CHEMISTRY 141 SPRING 2009

Solutions

1. e. H_2SO_3 is a weak acid

2. e. N is -3; H is $+1$; C is $+3$; O is -2

3. a. zero; S^{2-} is isoelectronic with Ar and has a completely filled valence orbital set

4. f. 3d

5. e. 3.5 L $\times$ (0.45 mol NaCl / 1 L) $\times$ (58.44 g NaCl / 1 mol NaCl) = 92 g NaCl

6. a. $(M_{concentrated}) \times (V_{concentrated}) = (M_{dilute}) \times (V_{dilute})$
    volume of the dilute solution = 300 mL water + 150 mL concentrated solution = 450 mL
    (0.45 M) $\times$ (150 mL) = $(M_{dilute}) \times$ (450 mL)
    M_{dilute} = 0.15 M

7. b. N is $+3$ in HNO_2
    N is $+2$ in NO   the change in oxidation number is -1

8. a. $w = -P\Delta V = -1.0$ atm $\times$ 1.38 L $= -1.38$ L atm $\times$ (101.325 J / 1 L atm) $= -139.8$ J
    $\Delta E = q + w$
    $-180J = q - 139.8$ J
    $q = -40$ J

9. b. heat gained by CO_2 subliming $= (5.0$ g$) \times (199$ J g$^{-1}) = 995$ J
    heat lost to form ice   = (mass of ice formed) $\times$ (333 J g^{-1})
    heat gained = heat lost, so 995 J = (mass of ice formed) $\times$ (333 J g^{-1})
    mass of ice formed   = 3.0 g

10. c. 3500 kJ $\times$ (2 mol C_8H_{18} / 10992 kJ) $\times$ (114.2 g C_8H_{18} / 1 mol C_8H_{18}) = 72.7 g C_8H_{18}

11. b. reverse equation 1 and divide by 2:
    $2 CO_2(g) + 3 H_2O(l) \rightarrow C_2H_6(g) + 7/2 O_2(g)$ $\Delta H = +1560$ kJ
    multiply equation 2 by 2:
    $2 C(s) + 2 O_2(g) \rightarrow 2 CO_2(g)$ $\Delta H = -788$ kJ
    multiply equation 3 by 3/2:
    $3 H_2(g) + 3/2 O_2(g) \rightarrow 3 H_2O(l)$ $\Delta H = -858$ kJ
    add to obtain the desired equation:
    $2 C(s) + 3 H_2(g) \rightarrow C_2H_6(g)$ $\Delta H = -86$ kJ

12.   h. $-1790 = [3(-393.5) + 3(-285.8)] - [1(\Delta H_f \text{ for } C_3H_6O) + 4(0)]$
           $\Delta H_f \text{ for } C_3H_6O = -247.9 \text{ kJ mol}^{-1}$

13.   e.   Explanation of the Photoelectric Effect   Einstein
           Wave-Particle Duality   DeBroglie
           Uncertainty Principle   Heisenberg
           Quantization of Electron Energy Levels   Bohr

14.   f. $E = h\nu$; $n = E / h = 3.0 \times 10^{-19} \text{ J} / 6.626 \times 10^{-34} \text{ J s} = 4.576 \times 10^{14} \text{ s}^{-1}$
           $c = \lambda\nu$; $\lambda = c / \nu = 3.0 \times 10^8 \text{ m s}^{-1} / 4.576 \times 10^{14} \text{ s}^{-1} = 6.6 \times 10^{-7} \text{ m}$
           $6.6 \times 10^{-7} \text{ m} \times (10^9 \text{ nm} / 1 \text{ m}) = 6.6 \times 10^2 \text{ nm}$

15.   a. $89 \text{ miles hr}^{-1} \times (1 \text{ hour} / 3600 \text{ s}) \times (1.609 \text{ km} / 1 \text{ mile}) \times (1000 \text{ m} / 1 \text{ km}) = 39.78 \text{ m s}^{-1}$
           $\lambda = h / mv = 6.626 \times 10^{-34} \text{ J s} / (0.1415 \text{ kg} \times 39.78 \text{ m s}^{-1})$
           $\lambda = 1.2 \times 10^{-34} \text{ m}$

16.   a.

17.   c.

18.   i. n^2 = number of possible orbitals = 6^2 = 36 orbitals
           2 electrons in each orbital = 36 × 2 = 72

19.   h.   valence electrons in one atom of oxygen = 6
           the number of orbitals in any one set of d orbitals = 5
           number of electrons in the 3s orbital of a sodium atom in the ground state = 1
           number of electrons in the 3d orbital of a titanium atom in the ground state = 2
           6 + 5 + 1 − 2 = 10

20.   c.   more electronegative   fluorine
           larger atomic radius   nitrogen
           larger first ionization energy   fluorine

EXAMINATION 3

CHEMISTRY 141 FALL 2004
Solutions

1.   h.   I: 7 electrons and F: 5 × 7 electrons
             total 42 electrons = 5 bonding pairs and 1 nonbonding pair = 6 pairs total
             therefore octahedral

2.   a.   ammonia and chloroform are polar

3.   d. $SOCl_2$ arrangement   tetrahedral sp^3
              SO_3 trigonal planar sp^2
              SF_4 trigonal bipyramidal sp^3d

4.   f.   a little less than the tetrahedral angle of 109° due to repulsion from the lone pair

5.   b.   Xe: 8   2O: 12   2F: 14, total 34 electrons
             4 bonding pairs and 1 nonbonding pair

6.   c.   volume doubles, therefore pressure halves
             temperature decreases by (248.15/298.15), therefore pressure decreases in same ratio
             new pressure = 1 atm × (1/2) × (248.15/298.15) = 0.42 atm

7.   e.   H–C≡N
             one single bond σ
             one triple bond σ + π + π

8.   i.   pressure increases by 2.5 atm, from 5.0 atm to 7.5 atm, when the oxygen is added
            partial pressure of oxygen must be 2.5 atm
            (the other partial pressures remain the same N_2 3.5 atm and He 1.5 atm)

9.   f.   mass of H_2O_2 = 30 g in 100 g solution
            moles of H_2O_2 = 30 g / 34 g mol^{-1} = 0.88 mol
            mass of H_2O = 70 g in 100 g solution
            molality = 0.88 mol / 0.070 kg water = 12.6 *m*

10. g.   it will take longer (ethane is a larger molecule and moves more slowly)
            2.0 min × √ (30/4) = 5.5 min

11. d. $\Delta T = k \times m \times i$ i = 1 in this case
            (82.7 − 78.5) = 1.22 × *m* × 1
            4.20 = 1.22 × *m*
            m = 3.44
            moles of cinnamaldehyde = 3.44 × (175/1000) = 0.60 mol
            mass of cinnamaldehyde = 0.60 mol × 132.15 g mol^{-1} = 79.6 g

12. h.   2, 3, and 4

13. h. initial partial pressure of NO = 3.0 atm × (5.0 L/8.0 L) = 15/8 atm
    initial partial pressure of O_2 = 2.0 atm × (3.0 L/8.0 L) = 6/8 atm
    O_2 is the limiting reactant
    NO_2 formed in the reaction = 6/8 atm O_2 × (2 NO_2/1 O_2) = 12/8 atm
    NO used in the reaction = 6/8 atm O_2 × (2 NO/1 O_2) = 12/8 atm
    NO remaining unused at end = 15/8 − 12/8 atm = 3/8 atm
    Total pressure = 12/8 atm NO_2 + 3/8 atm NO = 15/8 atm

14. b. Ti: 1 center = 1
        8 corners   = 8 × 1/8 = 1
        total   = 2
        O: 2 center = 2
        4 faces   = 4 × 1/2 = 2
        total   = 4
        therefore TiO_2

15. j. all of them—all anomalous properties of water are due to the exceptionally effective intermolecular hydrogen bonding

16. j. for a spontaneous change, the entropy of the universe must increase and the free energy of the system must decrease.
    if the entropy of the system decreases, then the entropy of the surroundings must increase.
    this can only happen if the reaction is exothermic.

17. f. intermolecular attraction

18. d. $m × i$ = 0.40 × 4 = 1.60

19. f. triple point   E
        gas state   C
        normal b.pt.   G
        solid state   A
        critical point   F

20. e. freezing water is exothermic (making bonds)
    all others involve breaking bonds

EXAMINATION 3

CHEMISTRY 141 SPRING 2005
Solutions

1.   d.   two single bonds and one double bond: average = 4/3 = 1.33

2.   b.   N $2 + \frac{1}{2}(3) = 5$ formal charge 0
           C $\frac{1}{2}(8) = 4$ formal charge 0
           O $6 + \frac{1}{2}(2) = 7$ formal charge -1
           the negative formal charge is on the more electronegative element

3.   h.   I: 7 electrons and F: 3×7 electrons
           total 28 electrons = 3 bonding pairs and 2 nonbonding pairs = 5 pairs total
           therefore trigonal bipyramidal arrangement
           lone pairs are in the trigonal plane, so the shape is T–shaped

4.   g. PCl_3 and H_2O are both polar
           SF_6 is octahedral
           CCl_4 is tetrahedral
           XeF_2 is linear

5.   e.   six pairs of electrons (5 bonding and one nonbonding), therefore sp^3d^2

6.   a.   P: 5 + 2Cl: 14 + 2Br: 14, total 33 electrons, less one for the + charge, total 32
           4 bonding pairs and no nonbonding pairs

7.   e.   six σ bonds

8.   a.   25 atm × 8.0 L = (5.0 + 3.0 + 2.0) moles × 0.08206 × T
           T = 243.7 K
           T = $-29°C$

9.   g.   partial pressure of oxygen = (2/10) × 25 atm
           = 5.0 atm

10.   h.   the partial pressure remains unchanged

11.   i.   the number of moles of O_2 triples, therefore the partial pressure of O_2 triples to 15 atm

12.   f.   there are 12 moles of H_2 and 6 moles of O_2
           these combine to form 12 moles of H_2O
           the only gas remaining is the 3.0 moles of helium
           partial pressure = (3/10) × 25 atm = 7.5 atm

13.   e.   density = PM / RT = (1.0 atm × 39.95 g mol–1) / (0.08206 L atm mol^{-1} K^{-1} × 298.15 K)
           = 1.63 g L^{-1}

14.　g.　CH_4

15.　a.　Nb:　6 faces × 1/2 = 3
　　　　O:　　12 edges × 1/4 = 3
　　　　empirical formula = NbO

16.　d.　hydrogen bonding

17.　a.　hydrogen < butane < sodium chloride < diamond

18.　g.　A:　breaking bonds is endothermic　　　$\Delta H +$
　　　　B:　condensing vapor reduces disorder　$\Delta S -$
　　　　C:　equilibrium between three phases　　ΔG zero

19.　g.　assume 100 g of the solution
　　　　mass of acetic acid = 50% of 100 g = 50 g
　　　　moles of acetic acid = 50 g / 60.05 g mol-1 = 0.833 mol
　　　　mass of water = 50 g = 0.050 kg
　　　　molality = moles of solute / mass of solvent in kg = 0.833/0.050 = 16.7 m

20.　f.　require lowest ΔT
　　　　that is, lowest $m \times i$

EXAMINATION 3

CHEMISTRY 141 FALL 2005

Solutions

1.   c. PF_5 and I_3^-

2.   d.   HCN, N_2O, and I_3^-

3.   f.   HCN, $CHCl_3$, NH_3, N_2O, NO_2^-

4.   b. sp^2

5.   c.   the nitrogen has two electrons in the p_π orbital

6.   b.   one σ bond and two π bonds

7.   f. $PV = nRT$
           $50 \text{ atm} \times 4.0 \text{ L} = n \text{ mol} \times 0.08206 \text{ L atm K}^{-1} \text{ mol}^{-1} \times 298.15 \text{ K}$
           $n = 8.2 \text{ mol}$
           additional O_2 required = 6.2 mol

8.   e.   first N: 5 electrons, formal charge = 0
           second N: 4 electrons, formal charge = +1
           third N: 5 electrons, formal charge = 0
           fourth N: 5 electrons, formal charge = 0
           oxygen O: 7 electrons, formal charge = −1

9.   a.   pressure at open end = 760 torr
           pressure of gas = 760 torr − 500 mmHg = 260 torr

10.   d.   partial pressure of xenon = mole fraction × total pressure = (2.0/6.0) × 12.0 atm = 4.0 atm

11.   h.   partial pressure of xenon remains the same = 4.0 atm
           partial pressure of helium originally = (3.0/6.0) × 12.0 atm = 6.0 atm
           amount of helium is doubled, so partial pressure is doubled to 12.0 atm

12.   f.   methane is larger, it effuses more slowly (by square root (4/16))
           8 min × 2 = 16 min

13.   g.   only H_A, H_B, and H_D, hydrogen atoms attached to N

14.   h.   the vapor pressure would be lower (stronger forces of intermoleclar attraction)

15.   d.   8 corners × (1/8) = 1
           2 faces × (1/2) = 1
           4 edges × (1/4) = 1
           1 at center = 1   total 4

16. c.

17. a.

18. f. assume 100 grams of solution
mass of KOH = 15.0 grams
moles of KOH = 15.0/56.11 = 0.267 mol
mass of solvent = 85 grams = 0.085 kg
molality = 0.267/0.085 = 3.15 m

19. e. $\Delta T = K_f \times m \times i$
$-0.93 = -1.853 \times m \times 1$
$m = 0.502$
30 grams = 0.502 mol, so molar mass = 60 g mol^{-1}

20. d. $P = P_A + P_B = (X_A \times 400) + ((1 - X_A) \times 600) = 550$ torr
$400\,X_A - 600\,X_A = 550 - 600 = -50$
$200\,X_A = 50$
$X_A = 0.25$

EXAMINATION 3

CHEMISTRY 141 SPRING 2006
Solutions

1. d. BF_3

2. e. as bond order decreases, bond length increases

3. b. sp^2 (3 bonds and no lone pairs of electrons on central atom)

4. g. Cl is the central atom
       28 valence electrons, 3 bonds and 2 lone pair of electrons around Cl

5. f. single bond = 1 σ bond
       double bond = 1 σ bond + 1 π bond

6. d. H_2S; S is the central atom. 8 valence electrons, 2 bonds and 2 lone pair of electrons around S.

7. i. 1 and 6 form no bond
       2 is a σ bond
       3, 4, and 5 are π bonds

8. a. Lewis dot structure 1 has no formal charges on any of the atoms, therefore, it is the best structure.

9. e. $(P_1V_1) / T_1 = (P_2V_2) / T_2$
       (5 atm × 0.005 L) / 283 K = (1 atm × V_2) / 298 K
       V_2 = 0.0263 L × (1000 mL / 1 L) = 26 mL

10. d.

	$CH_4(g)$	+	$2 O_2(g)$	→	$CO_2(g)$	+	$2 H_2O(g)$
initial pressure:	1 × (2/3)		3 × (1/3)				
	= 2/3 atm		= 1 atm				
limiting reactant:	2/3		1/2	therefore O_2 is the limiting reactant			

   1 atm O_2 × (1 CO_2 / 2 O_2) = 0.5 atm CO_2

11. c. partial pressure of krypton must be 5.0 − 4.0 atm = 1.0 atm
       i.e one quarter that of argon
       therefore number of moles of krypton must be one quarter the number of moles of argon = 3/4 mole

    or

    $P_{Ar} = C_{Ar} \times P_T$

    4 atm = (3 mol Ar / total moles) × 5 atm = 3.75 total moles
    moles of krypton = 3.75 total − 3 mol Ar = 0.75 mol Kr

12. h. $u_{Xe} / u_{unknown}$ = square root($M_{unknown} / M_{Xe}$)
       1.6 / 2.0 = square root($M_{unknown}$ / 131.29)
       $M_{unknown}$ = 84 g mol^{-1}

13. i. methane is nonpolar therefore london dispersion force predominates
         chloromethane is polar therefore dipole-dipole force predominates
         methanol is a polar molecule that can form H-bonds
         H-bonds are the strongest intermolecular force and methanol has the highest boiling point

14. c. Sr: 1 (center) × 1   = 1
         Ti: 8 (corner) × (1/8) = 1
         O: 6 (face) × (1/2)   = 3   the empirical formula is $SrTiO_3$

15. g. 1. solid → gas ΔS +
         2. aqueous → solid ΔS −
         3. gas → liquid ΔS −
         4. diffusion ΔS +

16. b. assume 100 g solution, then 5 g CH_3CO_2H and 95 g H_2O
         5 g CH_3CO_2H × (1 mol / 60 g) = 0.0833 mol CH_3CO_2H
         95 g H_2O × (1 kg / 1000 g) = 0.095 kg H_2O
         molality = 0.0833 mol CH_3CO_2H / 0.095 kg H_2O = 0.88 *m*

17. b. $C_6H_6(l) \rightarrow C_6H_6(g)$ at 100°C
         ΔH = + (breaking bonds), ΔS = + (increasing disorder), ΔG = − (spontaneous)

18. g. $P_T = (C_A \times P_A^\circ) + (C_B \times P_B^\circ)$
         760 torr = [(1/3) × 300 torr] + [(2/3) × P_B°]
         P_B° = 990 torr (B is more volatile than A)

19. g. B and C (3 phases in equilibrium)

20. f. $\Delta T = K \times m \times i$
         $Mg(NO_3)_2$:   0.75 = K × 0.50 × 3
         K = 0.50 (for water)
         NaCl: 0.75 = 0.50 × *m* × 2
         m = 0.75

         or

         magnesium nitrate produces 1.5 times more ions than sodium chloride,
         therefore need 1.5 times more NaCl than $Mg(NO_3)_2$ = 1.5 × 0.50 = 0.75 *m*

EXAMINATION 3

CHEMISTRY 141 FALL 2006
Solutions

1.   f.   five pairs of electrons; therefore trigonal bipyramid

2.   f.   C: 4 of its own + half-share of 4 = 6; should have 4, therefore formal charge = −2
            N: 2 of its own + half-share of 6 = 5; should have 5, therefore formal charge = 0
            N: none of its own + half-share of 8 = 4; should have 5, therefore formal charge = +1

3.   b.   one lone pair and three bonding pairs: 26 divided by 8 = 3 with a remainder 2 (1 pair)

4.   d. SO_2: choice of position for the double bond

5.   b.   I: 7 and 4F: 28 plus 1 for the charge = 36: 36 divided by 8 = 4 with a remainder 4 (2 pairs)

6.   j.   all are polar

7.   g.

8.   f.   4 bonding pairs and 2 nonbonding pairs = 6 pairs total (octahedral arrangement)
            need six hybrid orbitals, so sp^3d^2

9.   i.   original partial pressure of N_2 = 40 atm × (4.0 moles N_2 / 10 moles total) = 16 atm
            partial pressure after adding 2.0 more moles of N_2
                                        = original partial pressure × (6.0 moles N_2 / 4.0 moles N_2)
                                        = 24 atm

10.   i.

	$2\,N_2O(g)$	+	$3\,O_2(g)$	→	$4\,NO_2(g)$
initial pressure:	2.0 × (2/5)		3 × (3/5)		
	= 4/5 atm		= 9/5 atm		

       $N_2O(g)$ is the limiting reactant

amount at end:	all used	(4/5) × (3/2)	
		= 6/5 atm used	
		so 9/5 − 6/5 atm left	(4/5) × (4/2)
		= 3/5 atm left unused	= 8/5 atm formed

       total pressure = 3/5 atm + 8/5 atm = 11/5 atm

11.   d.   boiling point of water on Kelvin scale = 373.15 K
            boiling point of water on Rankine scale = 373.15 × (9/5) = 671.7°R

12.   d.   methane CH_4 is a larger molecule (16 g mol^{-1}) and moves more slowly than He (4 g mol^{-1})
            difference in speeds is proportional to the square root of their molar masses, i.e. sq rt(4) = 2
            methane takes twice as long, 480 s

13. e. bcc
         number of Cu atoms = 2 on faces and 4 on edges = $(2 \times 1/2) + (4 \times 1/4) = 2$
         number of Ag atoms = 1 at center and 8 on corners = $(1 \times 1) + (8 \times 1/8) = 2$
         stoichiometry is CuAg

14. b.

15. d.

16. h.

17. b. ΔG must be negative for a spontaneous process

18. f. 0.80 mol of water $= 0.80 \text{ mol} \times 18.016 \text{ g mol}^{-1}$
                             $= 14.4 \text{ g}$
                             $= 0.0144 \text{ kg}$

         molality = 0.30 mol propanol / 0.0144 kg water = 20.8 m
         the densities are irrelevant

19. a. the solution with the smallest concentration of particles ($m \times i = 0.4 \times 2 = 0.8$)

20. a. total vapor pressure = $(2/8) \times 60.5 \text{ torr} + (6/8) \times 126.0 \text{ torr} = 109.6 \text{ torr}$

EXAMINATION 3

CHEMISTRY 141 SPRING 2007
Solutions

1. f. the square planar molecular shape is derived from the octahedral electron pair arrangement

2. f. pascal is a unit of pressure

3. d. BO_3^{3-}, boron has an incomplete octet

4. f. 3 bonding pair of electrons and one lone pair of electrons on S, therefore a tetrahedral arrangement and a trigonal pyramidal shape

5. c. NO_2^-, one single bond and one double bond: average = 3/2 = 1.5
        IO_4^-, four single bonds: average = 4/4 = 1.0
        NO_3^-, two single bonds and one double bond: average = 4/3 = 1.33

6. g. Be is an exception to the octet rule and will not form double bonds to complete the octet.

7. h. oxygen: 4 groups of electrons (2 bonding and 2 nonbonding), therefore sp^3
        carbon: 3 groups of electrons (3 bonding), therefore, sp^2
        nitrogen: 4 groups of electrons (3 bonding and 1 nonbonding), therefore sp^3

8. c. one single bond (one σ bond) and one triple bond (one σ bond and two π bonds)

9. d. 1 and 4 are σ bonds
        3 and 6 are π bonds
        2 and 5 form no bond

10. d. $P_1V_1 = P_2V_2$
        (5.0 atm × 3.0 L) = (1.5 atm × V_2)
        V_2 = 10.0 L   (this is the volume of both vessels)
        10.0 L – 3.0 L = 7.0 L (the volume of the second vessel)

11. e. PV = nRT
        P × 4.0 L = 8 moles × 0.08206 L atm $K^{-1}mol^{-1}$ × 298 K
        P = 48.9 atm (this is the total pressure in the container)
        $P_{N2} = \chi_{N2} \times P_T$ = (5/8) × 48.9 atm = 30.6 atm

        or, just considering the nitrogen gas in the mixture...

        PV = nRT
        P × 4.0 L = 5 moles N_2 × 0.08206 L atm $K^{-1}mol^{-1}$ × 298 K
        P_{N2} = 30.6 atm (this is the partial pressure of nitrogen in the container)

12. c. $H_2O(g)$ + $OCl_2(g)$ → $2\ HClO(g)$

        initial pressure: $3 \times (4/6)$ $1 \times (2/6)$

                            $= 2$ atm $= 1/3$ atm

      OCl_2 is limiting reactant:

                $1/3$ atm OCl_2 × $(2\ HClO\ /\ 1\ OCl_2)$ = $2/3$ atm $HClO$

13. f. $u_A\ /\ u_B$ = square root $(M_B\ /\ M_A)$

      $1.05\ ms^{-1}\ /\ 0.25\ ms^{-1}$ = square root $(M_B\ /\ 4\ g\ mol^{-1})$

      $M_B = 70.56\ g\ mol^{-1}$ therefore Cl_2

14. d. face centered cubic has one atom on every corner and one atom on every face

      corner: $8 \times (1/8) = 1$ atom

      face: $6 \times (1/2) = 3$ atoms

15. a. London dispersion (small molar mass) < London dispersion (larger molar mass)

      < hydrogen bonding < ionic

16. e.

17. h. a solute dissolves in a solvent to make a solution $\Delta S +$

      solid → gas $\Delta S +$

      liquid → solid $\Delta S -$

      a container of gas is heated $\Delta S +$

18. a. $\Delta G = -$ for a spontaneous reaction

      $\Delta S = -$ (4 moles of gas forming 2 moles of gas)

      therefore ΔH must be $-$

      it is the ΔH that causes ΔG to be negative, therefore enthalpy driven

19. b.

20. h. $P_T = (\chi_{toluene} \times P^\circ_{toluene}) + (\chi_{benzene} \times P^\circ_{benzene})$

      at the boiling point, the total pressure is 1 atm (atmospheric pressure).

      1 atm $= (0.70 \times 0.70) + (0.30 \times P^\circ_{benzene})$

      $P^\circ_{benzene} = 1.7$ atm

21. a. Assume 100 g solution, then 15 g $C_2H_6O_2$ and 85 g H_2O

      15 g $C_2H_6O_2$ × (1 mole $C_2H_6O_2$ / 62 g $C_2H_6O_2$) = 0.242 mol $C_2H_6O_2$

      molality = moles $C_2H_6O_2$ / kg H_2O = 0.242 mol $C_2H_6O_2$ / 0.085 kg H_2O = 2.85 *m*

22. e. require largest ΔT, that is, largest *m* × *i*

EXAMINATION 3

CHEMISTRY 141 FALL 2007

Solutions

1. e. SF_4:   valence electrons = 6 + (4×7) = 34   4 bonding pairs and 1 lone pair
       HOCl: valence electrons = 1 + 6 + 7 = 14   −2 for H = 12   2 bonding pairs and 2 lone pairs
       PO_4^{3-}: valence electrons = 5 + (4×6) + 3 = 32   4 bonding pairs and 0 lone pairs

2. e. ClF_4^+: valence electrons = 7 + (4×7) −1 = 34   4 bonding pairs and 1 lone pair
       arrangement is trigonal bipyramid
       shape of the polyatomic ion is see-saw

3. f. the Lewis structure requires two double bonds: N=N=N$^-$
       the average bond order is 2.0

4. d. IF_3:   valence electrons = 7 + (3×7) = 28   3 bonding pairs and 2 lone pairs
       arrangement is trigonal bipyramid
       required hybridization for 5 electron pairs is sp^3d

5. d. to reconcile possible Lewis structures with the actual electronic structure

6. c. two; the arrangement would have to be octahedral with two lone pairs

7. j. SF_6 is nonpolar (a symmetrical octahedral molecule)

8. g. C has 5 electrons; should have 4, so formal charge = −1
       N has 4 electrons; should have 5, so formal charge = +1 $[:C\equiv N-\ddot{\underset{..}{S}}:]^-$
       S has 7 electrons; should have 6, so formal charge = −1

9. d. 3; any H atom attached to O or N

10. f. 13

11. g. pressure is greater than 1 atm by 57 cm Hg = 570 mm Hg
                                                   = 570 torr
                                                   = 0.75 atm
       pressure = 1 + 0.75 atm = 1.75 atm

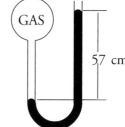

12. b. consider just one gas, for example He:
       PV = nRT so P = 3.0 moles × 0.08206 L atm K^{-1} mole^{-1} × 298.15 K / 5.0 L
                       = 14.7 atm

13. g. initial partial pressure of argon = (3/10) × 20.0 atm = 6.0 atm
       the amount of Ar is tripled, so its partial pressure must triple to 18.0 atm

14. g. both reactants are used up

P_{total} at end = partial pressure of NO_2 = 12/7 atm

15. d. hydrogen bonding

16. a. X: 4 inside = 4

    Y: 8 corners × 1/8 = 1

        4 edges × 1/4 = 1

        2 faces × 1/2 = 1

        1 inside = 1   total 4 Y   empirical formula = XY

17. c. $\Delta G = \Delta H - T\Delta S$ defines ΔG

the second law states that for a spontaneous process ΔG must be negative

18. a. $\Delta T = k \times m \times i$ —for highest b.pt., looking for the highest $m \times i$

0.60 m × 3 = 1.8

19. g. mass of solution = density × volume = 1230 g

mass of solute = 368 g

therefore mass of solvent = 862 g = 0.862 kg

moles of solute = 368 g / 98.09 g mol^{-1} = 3.75 mol

molality = moles of solute / mass of solvent in kg = 3.75 / 0.862 = 4.35 m

20. g. all three

21a. d.

21b. i. intermolecular attraction

22a. d.

22b. i. molality = moles of solute / mass of solvent in kg

EXAMINATION 3

CHEMISTRY 141 SPRING 2008
Solutions

1.   c.   one resonance structure of ozone has one double bond and one single bond

2.   a. CO_3^{2-} and SO_3

3.   c.   one single bond and one double bond: average = 3/2 = 1.5

4.   g.   Cl: 7 electrons and F: $5 \times 7 = 35$ electrons
          total 42 electrons = 5 bonding pairs and 1 nonbonding pair = 6 pairs total
          the electron arrangement is octahedral and the shape is square pyramidal

5.   b.   boron has three σ bonds in BF_3, therefore sp^2
          boron has 4 σ bonds in F_3B-NH_3, therefore sp^3

6.   a.

7.   g.   a triple bond is one σ bond and two π bonds

8.   d.   the partial pressure of helium does not change upon the addition of oxygen.
          the partial pressure of oxygen is 2.5 atm – 0.5 atm = 2.0 atm.

9.   e.

		$3 H_2(g)$	+	$N_2(g)$	$\rightarrow$	$2 NH_3(g)$
initial pressure:		$1 \times (3/5)$		$2 \times (2/5)$		
		= 3/5 atm		= 4/5 atm		
test for limiting reactant:		1/5		4/5		
		$H_2(g)$ is the limiting reactant				
final pressure:				$(3/5) \times (1/3)$		$(3/5) \times (2/3)$
				= 1/5 atm used		
				so 4/5 – 1/5		
		0 atm		= 3/5 atm unused		= 2/5 atm formed

     the total pressure is the sum of the partial pressures: 0 atm + 3/5 atm + 2/5 atm = 1 atm

10.   c. u_{Cl2} / u_{Ne} = square root (M_{Ne} / M_{Cl2})
          0.25 mol min^{-1} / (1 mol / x min) = square root (20.18 g mol^{-1} / 70.9 g mol^{-1})
          x = 2.1 min

11.   b. H_2S (although H_2O is smaller, it is able to hydrogen bond)

12.   d.   HF, H_2O and NH_2NH_2

13.   i.

14. a.   liquid $\rightarrow$ gas ΔS = +
          solid $\rightarrow$ liquid ΔS = +
          a solute dissolves in a solvent to make a solution ΔS = +

15. f. ΔH = + (solid $\rightarrow$ gas is breaking bonds)
          ΔS = + (gas is more disordered than solid)
          ΔG = – for spontaneous reaction

16. a.   diamond and graphite are the two solid phases of carbon

17. c.   assume 100 grams of solution
          mass of solute = 30 grams
          moles of solute = 30 grams × (1 mole / 90 grams) = 0.333 moles solute
          liters of solution = 100 g solution × (1 mL / 1.19 g) × (1 L / 1000 mL) = 0.084 L solution
          Molarity = moles of solute / liters of solution = 0.333 mol / 0.084 L = 4.0 M

18. f.   70 g solvent × (1 kg / 1000 g) = 0.07 kg solvent
          molality = moles of solute / kg of solvent = 0.333 mol / 0.07 kg = 4.76 *m*

19. a.   at 100°C and 1 atm pressure, water is at equilibrium therefore ΔG = 0

20. i.   lowest freezing point requires the largest ΔT, that is, largest $m \times i$

21a. d.

21b. h. S^{2-} has 8 valence electrons

22a. b.

22b. i.   P = nRT / V
          P = (2.0 mol) × (0.08206 L atm K^{-1} mol^{-1}) × (298.15 K) / 4.5 L = 10.9 atm

EXAMINATION 3

CHEMISTRY 141 FALL 2008
Solutions

1. d. P: 5 valence electrons
        O: 6 valence electrons
        Cl: 7 valence electrons × 3
        total = 32 electrons; divide by 8 = 4, no remainder, no lone pairs, so 4 pairs total

2. b. S: 6 valence electrons
        F: 7 valence electrons × 4
        total = 34 electrons; divide by 8 = 4, remainder 2, one lone pair, so 5 pairs total
        arrangement is trigonal bipyramidal

3. h. $PV = nRT$
        V is directly proportional to n and T

4. c. hydrogen bonding

5. h. SF_2, BrF_3, and SCl_4 have asymmetrical shapes and are polar

6. d. 3 π bonding pairs

7. c. formal charges are:

0 0 −1	−1 0 0	+1 0 −2
$[\ddot{O} = C = \ddot{N}]^-$	$[:\ddot{O} - C \equiv N:]^-$	$[:O \equiv C - \ddot{N}:]^-$
1	2	3
not so bad	best	worst

8. g. XeF_2: 5 electron pairs sp^3d
        XeF_4: 6 electron pairs sp^3d^2
        XeO_4: 4 electron pairs sp^3

9. d. 5 atm = 5 × (760 torr/atm) = 3800 torr
        38 cm Hg = 380 torr
        pressure is less in B, so pressure = 3800 − 380 torr = 3420 torr

10. g. $u_{O2} / u_{H2} = \sqrt{(M_{H2} / M_{O2})} = \sqrt{(2/32)} = \sqrt{(1/16)} = 1/4$

        hydrogen effuses four times faster than oxygen — it's a smaller molecule and moves 4 times faster

        i.e. oxygen takes four times longer to effuse, 4 minutes compared to 1 minute for H_2

11. d. high melting point
        the stronger the intermolecular attraction, the more energy is needed to break the molecules apart

12.   e.   initial partial pressure of helium = $\chi_{He} \times P = (2/10) \times 15$ atm = 3.0 atm
       the partial pressure of He does not change upon the addition of argon
       add 4.0 moles additional He -- number of moles of He has tripled
       therefore the partial pressure triples—to 9.0 atm

13.   a.   A atoms: 2 faces × (1/2) = 1   B atoms: 1 center = 1
                            4 edges × (1/4) = 1   8 corners × (1/8) = 1
                            total = 2   total = 2
       empirical formula is AB

14.   e.   endothermic: ΔH = +
       spontaneous: ΔG = −
       therefore: ΔS must be positive, or ΔG cannot be −.

15.   b.   the vapor pressure curve for a liquid starts at the triple point and ends at the critical point

16.   f.   assume 100 grams of solution
       mass of solute = 20 grams
       moles of solute = 20 grams × (1 mole / 58.44 grams) = 0.342 moles solute
       liters of solution = 100 g solution × (1 mL / 1.148 g) × (1 L / 1000 mL) = 0.0871 L solution
       molarity = moles of solute / liters of solution = 0.342 mol / 0.0871 L = 3.93 M
       molality = moles of solute / kg of solvent = 0.342 / (80 g × (1 kg / 1000 g)) = 4.28 *m*

17.   d.   moles of sucrose = 50.0 g / 342.3 g mol–1) = 0.146 mol
       moles of water = 100 g / 18.02 g mol–1 = 5.55 mol
       mole fraction of water = 5.55 / (5.55 + 0.146) = 0.974
       vapor pressure of solution = χ_{H2O} × vapor pressure of pure water = 0.974 × 71.9 torr = 70.0 torr

18.   b.   highest freezing point requires the smallest ΔT, that is, smallest *m* × *i*
       lowest freezing point requires the largest ΔT, that is, largest *m* × *i*

       0.15 m Na_2SO_4 *m* × *i*   = 0.15 × 3 = 0.45
       0.10 m NaBr   *m* × *i*   = 0.10 × 2 = 0.20
       0.10 m $Mg(NO_3)_2$ *m* × *i*   = 0.10 × 3 = 0.30
       0.30 m HCl   *m* × *i*   = 0.30 × 2 = 0.60

19.   c.   a catalyst changes the route of the reaction, i.e. the mechanism by which the reactants are converted into products

20.   j.   in the liquid...

       mole fraction of ethanol = 5/9
       mole fraction of butanol = 4/9
       vapor pressure due to ethanol = (5/9) × 59 torr = 32.78 torr
       vapor pressure due to butanol = (4/9) × 12.5 torr = 5.56 torr
       total vp = 32.78 + 5.56 = 38.34 torr

       therefore, in the vapor...

       mole fraction of ethanol = 32.78 / 38.34 = 0.85
       mole fraction of butanol = 5.56 / 38.34 = 0.15

EXAMINATION 3

CHEMISTRY 141 SPRING 2009

Solutions

1.   d.   Xe: 8 valence electrons
          F: $2 \times 7 = 14$ valence electrons
          total = 22 electrons = 2 bonding pairs and 3 lone pairs around the central atom

2.   h.   a single bond is one σ bond; a double bond is one σ and one π bond; a triple bond is one σ and two
          π bonds—the total number of π bonds = $1 + 2 + 2 + 2 + 2 = 9$

3.   f.   critical point   D
          liquid state   B
          normal m.pt.   H

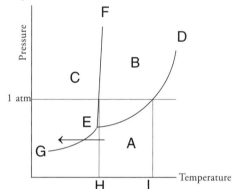

4.   c.   area A (vapor phase) $\rightarrow$ area C (solid phase)
          deposition
          $\Delta H = -$ (making bonds)
          $\Delta S = -$ (solid is less disordered than gas)

5.   b. SO_3^{2-}
          S has 6 valence electrons, O has 6 valence electrons, and 2 electrons from the 2− charge
          total 26 electrons = 3 bonding pairs and 1 nonbonding pair = 4 pairs total
          the electron arrangement is tetrahedral and the shape is trigonal pyramidal

6.   f. I_3^-
          I has 7 valence electrons and the 1− charge adds one electron
          total 22 electrons = 2 bonding pairs and 3 nonbonding pairs = 5 pairs total
          required hybridization for 5 electron pairs around the central atom is sp^3d

7.   c.   one single bond and one double bond: average = $3/2 = 1.5$

8.   c. NH_3 and BrF_5 are polar

9.   a. $CO(g)$ + $Cl_2(g)$ $\rightarrow$ $COCl_2(g)$
          bonds broken   *bonds formed*
          C≡O   Cl–Cl   2 C–Cl   and   C=O
          +1072 kJ   +242 kJ   2(−339 kJ) −732 kJ
          $\Delta H = 1072$ kJ + 242 kJ − 678 kJ − 732 kJ
          $\Delta H = -96$ kJ

10.   d. p_x and p_x are perpendicular to the internuclear axis (the y-axis)

11. c. $d = (P \times M) / (R \times T)$

   $7.71 \text{ g L}^{-1} = (2.88 \text{ atm} \times M) / (0.08206 \text{ L atm K}^{-1} \text{ mol}^{-1} \times 309.15 \text{ K})$

   $M = 67.9 \text{ g mol}^{-1}$, therefore the compound must be ClO_2

12. a.

	$2 C_2H_2(g)$ +	$5 O_2(g)$	→	$4 CO_2(g)$ +	$2 H_2O(g)$
initial pressures:	$2 \times (1/4)$	$1 \times (3/4)$		0 atm	0 atm
	= 0.5 atm	= 0.75 atm			
limiting reactant:	0.25	0.15			

   O_2 is the limiting reactant

   final pressures: $0.75 \times (2/5)$ zero $0.75 \times (4/5)$ $0.75 \times (2/5)$
   = 0.3 atm used
   so 0.5 atm − 0.3 atm
   = 0.2 atm unused   = 0.6 atm   = 0.3 atm

   the total pressure is the sum of the partial pressures:
   = 0.2 atm + 0 atm + 0.6 atm + 0.3 atm = 1.1 atm

13. e. let x = the normal human boiling point on the °A scale
   set up a proportion to compare the °A scale to the °F scale
   $(170 - x) / (170 - 20) = (212 - 98.6) / (212 - 32) = 0.63$
   $(170 - x) = 94.5$
   $x = 75.5 °A$

14. e. $u_{He} / u_{PH3} = \sqrt{(M_{PH3} / M_{He})}$
   $(0.1 \text{ mol} / 2 \text{ min}) / (0.1 \text{ mol} / x \text{ min}) = \sqrt{(33.994 \text{ g mol}^{-1} / 4.003 \text{ g mol}^{-1})}$
   $x = 5.8 \text{ min}$

15. b. London dispersion (small molar mass) < London dispersion (larger molar mass)
   < hydrogen bonding < ionic

16. i. any H atom attached to N or O

17. d. corners: $8 \times (1/8) = 1$
   face: $6 \times (1/2) = 3$ total gold atoms in one unit cell = 1 + 3 = 4

18. h. $\Delta G = -$ (spontaneous reaction)
   $\Delta H = -$ (making bonds between gas and water)
   $\Delta S = -$ (aqueous solution is less disordered than a gas)

19. b. 250 mL H_2O × (1 g / 1 mL) × (1 kg / 1000 g) × (0.35 mol NaCl / 1 kg H_2O)
   × (58.44 g NaCl / 1 mol) = 5.11 g NaCl

20. a. $\Delta T = k \times m \times i$ for the highest boiling point, look for highest $m \times i$
   $0.60 \, m \times 4 = 2.4$

FINAL EXAMINATION

CHEMISTRY 141 FALL 2004

Solutions

1. g. the charge is –3 and the number of electrons = 36
        the number of protons therefore = 36 – 3 = 33, therefore arsenic

2. d. $Ca(HCO_3)_2$

3. c. binary compounds contain two elements, not two atoms

4. e. lithium chloride LiCl

5. h. magnesium phosphate is $Mg_3(PO_4)_2$; molar mass = 282.9 g mol^{-1}
        mass of 3.00 moles = 788.6 g

6. c. moles of sugar = 39 g / 342 g mol^{-1} = 0.114 mol
        moles of H = 0.114 × 22 = 2.51 mol
        number of atoms of H = 2.51 × 6.022 × 10^{23} = 1.51 × 10^{24}

7. g.

	Gd	O	
ratio by mass	86.76%	13.24%	
ratio by moles	86.76/157.25	13.24/16.0	
	= 0.552	= 0.828	
divide by smaller	= 1	= 1.5	
multiply by 2	= 2	= 3	so Gd_2O_3

8. d. $2\,NH_3 + 5\,F_2 \rightarrow N_2F_4 + 6HF$

    2 mol F_2 × (2 NH_3/5 F_2) = 4/5 mol NH_3 = 0.80 mol

9. f. $2\,C_6H_6 + 15\,O_2 \rightarrow 12\,CO_2 + 6H_2O$

10. f. N_2O is the limiting reactant
        5.0 moles of N_2O require 5.0 mol N_2O × (3 O_2/2 N_2O) = 7.5 mol O_2
        therefore 0.50 mol remains unused

11. e. molar mass of $CoCl_2$ = 129.8 g mol^{-1}
        number of moles of $CoCl_2$ = 238.7 g/129.8 g mol^{-1} = 1.84 mol
        molarity = 1.84 mol/1.25 L = 1.47 *M*

12. c. oxidation number = +4; magnesium oxidized; reducing agent is Mg

13. c. only K$^+$; HCN is a weak acid and predominantly not ionized

14. a. Na +1 always, O almost always –2; therefore P +5

15. b. 800 J gained; 450 J lost; 350 J net gain

16. i.   heat released when steam condenses = 20 g × 2260 J g^{-1} = 45,200 J
          heat released when the water at 100°C cools to 0°C = 20 g × 4.184 J K^{-1} g^{-1} × 100 K = 8368 J
          total heat released = 45,200 J + 8368 J = 53,568 J
          mass of ice melted = 53,568 J / 333 J g^{-1} = 161 g
          mass of ice remaining = 200 g – 161 g = 39 g
          mass of water = 50 g (orig) + 20 g (from steam condensing) + 161 g (from ice melting) = 231 g

17. c.   leave eqn 1 same: $NO(g) + O_3(g) \rightarrow NO_2(g) + O_2(g)$ ΔH° = –199 kJ

          reverse eqn 2: $1.5\ O_2(g) \rightarrow O_3(g)$ ΔH° = +142 kJ

          reverse and halve eqn 3: $2\ O(g) \rightarrow O_2(g)$ ΔH° = –247 kJ

          add: $NO(g) + O(g) \rightarrow NO_2(g)$ ΔH° = –304 kJ

18. g. Cl_2 *(gas)*

19. e.   3d electron — a calcium atom does not have a 3d electron in its ground state

20. a.   Se

21. g.   3 × 2 + 2 – 2 + 8 = 14

22. b.   K

23. e. $:\!\ddot{N}\!::\!C\!::\!\ddot{N}\!:$ $^{2-}$

24. e.   36 electrons = 4 bonding pairs and 2 nonbonding pairs = 6 pairs total
          octahedral arrangement and square planar molecular shape

25. a.   sp

26. e.   slightly less than 120°

27. e.   partial pressure of first sample of N_2 gas = 5.0 atm
          partial pressure of O_2 gas = 2.5 atm
          partial pressure of second sample of N_2 gas = 7.5 atm
          total partial pressure of N_2 gas = 5.0 atm + 7.5 atm = 12.5 atm

28. g.   only 2 and 4

29. i. $2\ N_2O\ (g)$ + $3\ O_2\ (g)$ $\rightarrow$ $4\ NO_2\ (g)$
          2.0 atm × (4/10)   3.0 atm × (6/10)
            = 4/5 atm   = 9/5 atm   formed = 4/5 atm N_2O×(4NO_2/2N_2O)
          limiting reactant   used = 4/5 atm N_2O×(3O_2/2N_2O)   = 8/5 atm NO_2
                                    = 6/5 atm
                                  left unused = 9/5 – 6/5 = 3/5 atm
          total pressure at end = 3/5 + 8/5 = 11/5 atm

30. a. Pb: 8 corners × 1/8 = 1
        2 faces × 1/2 = 1
        total = 2
    O: 4 faces × 1/2 = 2
    therefore an empirical formula PbO

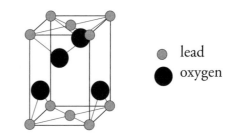

○ lead
● oxygen

31. e. spontaneous ΔG_{sys} = –
    endothermic ΔH_{sys} = +
    for ΔG_{sys} to be negative, ΔS_{sys} must be +

32. c. at the boiling point the vapor pressure must equal the atmospheric pressure

33. e. 3.50 g / 74.55 g mol^{-1} = 0.0470 mol
    0.0470 mol / 0.100 kg = 0.470 m
    $\Delta T = k \times m \times i$
        = 1.86 K m^{-1} × 0.470 m × 2
        = 1.75 K
    freezing point = –1.75°C

34. b.
	$H_2(g)$	+	$CO_2(g)$	$\rightleftharpoons$	$H_2O(g)$	+	$CO(g)$
I	0.25		0.25		0		0
C	– x		– x		+ x		+x
E	0.25 – x		0.25 – x		x		x

    $K_a = x^2 / (0.25–x)^2 = 16$
    take the square root of both sides:
    x / (0.25–x) = 4
    x = 1 – 4x
    x = 0.20
    concentration of CO_2 at equilibrium = 0.25 – 0.20 = 0.05 M

35. h. strong acids have weak conjugate bases

36. a.

37. e.
$H_2PO_4^-$	+	H_2O	$\rightleftharpoons$	HPO_4^{2-}	+	H_3O^+
acid		base		base		acid

38. b. $F^- + H_2O \rightleftharpoons HF + OH^-$

39. c. NH_4ClO_3—a salt of a strong acid and a weak base
    the ammonium ion hydrolyzes to produce H_3O^+ ions in solution.

40. c. pH = $-\log_{10}[H^+]$; $[H^+] = 10^{-4.20} = 6.31 \times 10^{-5}$ M

FINAL EXAMINATION

CHEMISTRY 141 SPRING 2005

Solutions

1. c. volume m^3
        pressure Pa
        density = mass/volume kg m^{-3}
        area m^2

2. g. mass = density × volume = 7.86 g cm^{-3} × 125 cm^3 = 983 g

3. f. ammonium perchlorate

4. g. 1 $CH_3C_6H_5$ + 9 O_2 → 7 CO_2 + 4 H_2O

5. e. 12×12.011 = 144.13
        22×1.008 = 22.18
        11×16.00 = 176.00
        _____
        342.31   176.00 / 342.31 = 0.51 51%

6. f.

	Fe	Cr	O
ratio by mass	25.0%	46.5%	28.5%
ratio by moles	25.0/55.85	46.5/52.0	28.5/16.00
	= 0.448	= 0.894	= 1.78
divide by smaller	= 1	= 2	= 4

so $FeCr_2O_4$

7. b.

8. f. 248 g / 31 g mol^{-1} = 8.0 mol

9. b. Cl_2 is the limiting reactant
        moles of Al_2Cl_6 = 0.60 mol Cl_2 × (1 mol Al_2Cl_6 / 3 mol Cl_2) = 0.20 mol Al_2Cl_6

10. d. C_2H_2 + 2 H_2 → C_2H_6

        52 g acetylene = 52 g / 26 g mol–1 = 2 mol
        10 g hydrogen = 10 g / 2 g mol–1 = 5 mol — only 4 mol required so 1 mol remains unused

11. b. empirical mass C_4H_3N = (4 × 12) + (3 × 1) + 14 = 65 g
        therefore molecular formula = 2 × C_4H_3N = $C_8H_6N_2$

12. f. MgC + excess H_2O → $Mg(OH)_2$ + C3H4

        ratio: 2 moles   1 mole
                  2 Mg   and   3 C

13. d. $3.0\ M \times (25.0/150) = 0.50\ M$

14. b. strong acids are H_2SO_4, $HClO_3$, HNO_3, HI
         bases are NH_3, KOH, NaOH
         weak acids are HF, HCN, HNO_2, HCO_2H
         salts are $MgCl_2$, $CaSO_4$, KBr, KNO_3, KCN, $CaCl_2$

15. e. +2 in $Na_2S_2O_3$; 0 in S_8; +2 in $H_4S_4O_6$; +4 in SO_2

16. f. oxygen gas

17. h. $\Delta E = q + w = 75\ kJ + 25\ kJ = +100\ kJ$

18. g. heat released by hot water = $4.184\ J\ K^{-1}\ g^{-1} \times 35\ g \times 91\ K = 13{,}326\ J$
         amount of ice that melts = $13{,}326\ J\ /\ 333\ J\ g^{-1} = 40\ g$
         total amount of water at end = 35 g (from hot water) + 35 g (original) + 40 g (from ice) = 110 g

19. c. $P_4(s)$

20. a. reverse the reaction and divide by 2

21. g. bonds broken: 2 C–H $2 \times 415\ kJ$ bonds made: 2 C–Cl $2 \times 330\ kJ$
                          2 H–Cl $2 \times 430\ kJ$ 4 O–H $4 \times 460\ kJ$
                          1 O=O   495
                                   _____   _____
                                   +2185 kJ   –2500 kJ

         net result = –315 kJ

22. c.

23. f. $4 - 1 \times 2 + 3 - 1 = 8$

24. b. K

25. d. number of electrons = $7 + (2 \times 7) + 1 = 22$
         2 bonding pairs and three nonbonding pairs

26. h. 5 pairs of electrons: trigonal bipyramidal arrangement and see-saw shape

27. f. 6 pairs of electrons: octahedral arrangement; d^2sp^3

28. b. mole fraction of oxygen = 2.0 atm / 10 atm = 0.20

29. c. partial pressure remains the same = 3.0 atm

30. i. total pressure = 10.0 atm (H_2) + 3.0 atm (He) = 13 atm

31.   d.   molar mass of acetic acid = 60 g mol^{-1}
            in 100 g of solution, there are 60 g of acetic acid = 1 mole
            molar mass of water = 18 g mol^{-1}
            in 100 g of solution there are 40 g of water = 40 g / 18 g mol^{-1} = 2.22 mole
            total moles = 3.22
            mole fraction of acetic acid = 1/3.22 = 0.31

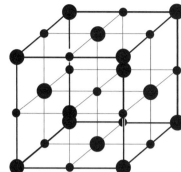

32.   a.   VC   V: one on each corner = 8 × 1/8 = 1
                              and one on each face = 6 × 1/2 = 3
                              total = 4
                  C: one at center = 1
                              one on each edge = 12 × 1/4 = 3
                              total = 4

33.   g. m × i = 2.2 × 2 = 4.4 (highest)

34.   h.   A: melting
            B: condensation
            C: triple point

35.   a.

36.   i.   K = [products] / [reactants] = $[NO][CO_2] / [NO_2][CO] = (x)^2 / (2-x)^2 = 9$
            take the square root:
            x / (2−x) = 3
            x = 3/2

37.   a. HCO_3^- + H_2O ⇌ H_2CO_3 + OH^-
               base   acid   acid   base

37.   f.   increase pressure   right
            decrease temperature   right
            add more Ti*(s)*   no change
            remove Cl_2*(g)*   left

39.   e. PO_4^{3-} + H_2O ⇌ HPO_4^{2-} + OH^-

40.   g.   pOH = $- \log_{10}[OH^-]$ = 2.30
            pH = 14 − pOH = 11.70

FINAL EXAMINATION

CHEMISTRY 141 FALL 2005

Solutions

1. d. 120 miles/hour × (1 hr/3600 s) × (1.609 km/1 mile) × (1000 m/1 km) = 53.6 ms^{-1}

2. d.

3. g. KCN, CaI_2, $AlPO_4$, Li_2CO_3, $NaBr$, $CsNO_3$

4. c.

5. h. sodium sulfate is Na_2SO_4

6. d. Na_3PO_4 four O atoms per mole × 2 moles = 8 moles O atoms

7. e.
$$
\begin{array}{rcl}
9 \times 12.011 & = & 108.099 \\
8 \times 1.008 & = & 8.064 \\
4 \times 16.00 & = & \underline{64.000} \\
& & 180.163
\end{array}
$$
    108.099 / 180.163 = 0.60   or 60%

8. h. 440 g / 5.50 moles = 80 g mol^{-1}

9. g. 1 $C_8H_{18}O_3$(l) + 11 O_2(g)   →   9 H_2O(g) +   8 CO_2(g)

10. a. oxygen is the limiting reactant
        amount of CO_2 produced = 4 moles O_2 × (8 mol CO_2 / 11 mol O_2) = 2.9 mol CO_2

11. a. Mg^{2+} is smaller than Ca^{2+}
        Ca^{2+} is smaller than Ca

12. e. HF —weak acid

13. d. NaHCO3: molar mass = 84.01 g mol^{-1}
        22 g = 22/84.01 moles = 0.262 moles
        molality = 0.262 mol / 0.078 kg = 3.36 *m*

14. i. 40 + 25 J = 65 J

15. a. K$^+$ only

16. e. heat = [2.1 J g^{-1} K^{-1} × 15 g × 20 K] + [333 J g^{-1} × 15 g] = 5625 J = 5.625 kJ

17. e. eqn 1 stays the same: NO(g) + O(g)   → NO_2(g)   ΔH° = −304 kJ
        eqn 2 stays the same: O_3(g)   →   1.5 O_2(g)   ΔH° = −142 kJ
        divide eqn 3 by 2:   0.5 O_2(g)   →   O(g)   ΔH° = +247 kJ
        _____
                                    NO(g) + O_3(g)   → NO_2(g) + O_2(g)   ΔH° = −119 kJ

18. b. hydrogen is reduced; tin is oxidized; number of moles of electrons = 2

19. g. 97.5 MHz × (10^6 Hz / 1 MHz) × 6.626 × 10^{-34} Js = 6.46 × 10^{-26} J

20. g. E = hν = hc/λ
    if λ is 1.5 times larger, the E is 2/3, so need 150 photons of red light

21. e. maximum *l* is n−1

22. f. $2p^6$ and $3p^4$, total 10

23. b. Zr

24. f. CH_3OH, N_2H_4, HF, H_2O, CH_3CO_2H

25. d. trigonal bipyramidal arrangement; see-saw shape

26. b. sp^2

27. e. must be the charge on the ion, −1

28. d. I_3^- three lone pairs on the central I

29. a. 38 cm Hg = 0.5 atm
    1.0 atm − 0.5 atm = 0.5 atm

30. f. 15 atm × (3 mol/10 mol) = 4.5 atm

31. d. partial pressures of N_2 and He remain the same (3.0 atm and 4.5 atm)
    the partial pressure of H_2 doubles to 15 atm

32. d. H_2 effuses faster—it's a smaller molecule
    1 mol × $\sqrt{(40/2)}$ = 4.5 mol

33. c. face-centered cubic

34. g. largest *m* × *i*

35. h. A, B, and D

36. a.

37. e. CO_3^{2-} + H_2O ⇌ HCO_3^- + OH^-

38. a. too much reactant, Q will be less than K

39. a.

40. b. pH = $-\log_{10}$[H+] = $-\log_{10}$(0.04) = 1.4

FINAL EXAMINATION

CHEMISTRY 141 Spring 2006
Solutions

1. d. density = mass / volume = 50 g / 4.76 mL = 10.5 g mL^{-1}
       volume of cube = $(2.2 \text{ cm})^3$ = 10.6 cm^3 = 10.6 mL
       mass of cube = 10.6 mL × (10.5 g / 1 mL) = 112 g

2. h. nickel has 28 protons, ^{58}Ni = 30 neutrons, ^{62}Ni = 34 neutrons, ^{64}Ni = 36 neutrons

3. b. magnesium hypochlorite $Mg(ClO)_2$
       magnesium chlorite $Mg(ClO_2)_2$
       magnesium chlorate $Mg(ClO_3)_2$

4. f. 7.5 mol $Fe(MnO_4)_2$ × (8 mol O / 1 mol $Fe(MnO_4)_2$) = 60 mol O atoms

5. h.

	Ca	C	H	O
mass of Ca = 25.34%				
mass of C = 30.37% ratio by mass	25.34	30.37	3.82	40.46
mass of H = 3.82% ratio by moles	25.34/40.08	30.37/12.01	3.82/1.008	40.46/16.00
mass of O = 40.46%	= 0.6322	= 2.529	= 3.789	= 2.529
divide by smallest	= 1	= 4	= 6	= 4

    $CaC_4H_6O_4$

6. f. molar mass of sorbitol = (6 × 12.01) + (14 × 1.008) + (6 × 16.0) = 182 g mol^{-1}

7. g. (18 mol C/1 mol α-linolenic acid) × (1 mol/278.42 g α-linolenic acid) × (12.01 g C/1 mol) × 100%
       = 77.64% C

8. g. 1 Fe_2O_3 + 3 H_2SO_4 → 1 $Fe_2(SO_4)_3$ + 3 H_2O

9. a.
       C_3H_8 + 5 O_2 → 3 CO_2 + 4 H_2O
       2 mol   3 mol
       divide by coefficient   2/1 = 2   3/5 = 0.6 O_2 is the limiting reactant

       3 mol O_2 × (3 mol CO_2 / 5 mol O_2) = 1.8 mol CO_2

10. c. Pt, Fe, and Ag are transition metals

11. e. 5.0 g Si × (1 mol Si / 28.09 g Si) × (1 mol $SiCl_4$ / 1 mol Si) × (169.89 g $SiCl_4$ / 1 mol $SiCl_4$)
       = 30 g $SiCl_4$
       % yield = (actual yield / theoretical yield) × 100 = (15 g / 30 g) × 100 = 50%

12. f. Na^+ and Cl^-

13. c. −1 in BCl_3; +1 in ClO^-; and +7 in ClO_4^-

14. b. ΔH_{rxn} = [−1669.8 + (2 × 12.40)] − [−822.2] = −822.8 kJ
       1 mol Al × (822.8 kJ / 2 mol Al) = 411.4 kJ

15. e. heat to boiling point: $q = 32 \text{ g} \times 2.460 \text{ J g}^{-1} \text{ K}^{-1} \times 53.4 \text{ K} = 4203.65 \text{J}$
         vaporize: $q = 32 \text{ g} \times 838 \text{ J g}^{-1} = 26816 \text{ J}$
         total heat $= 4203.65 \text{ J} + 26816 \text{ J} = 31019 \text{ J} = 31 \text{ kJ}$

16. f. heat lost (hot water cooling) = heat gained (ice melting)
         $20 \text{ g} \times 4.184 \text{ J g}^{-1} \text{ K}^{-1} \times 80 \text{ K} = m \times 333 \text{ J g}^{-1}$
         m = 20 g ice melted
         mass of liquid water = 20 g (ice melted) + 20 g (hot water) + 35 g (cold water) = 75 g water

17. d. $Ar(g)$, $Na(s)$, and $Cl_2(g)$

18. c. $\lambda = 510 \text{ nm} = 510 \times 10^{-9} \text{ m}$
         $\nu = c/\lambda = 3.0 \times 10^8 \text{ m s}^{-1} / 510 \times 10^{-9} \text{ m} = 5.88 \times 10^{14} \text{ s}^{-1}$
         $E = h\nu = 6.626 \times 10^{-34} \text{ Js} \times 5.88 \times 10^{14} \text{ s}^{-1} = 4.0 \times 10^{-19} \text{ J}$

19. e. in order of increasing energy: radiowave < microwave < infrared < visible < ultraviolet < γ–ray

20. b. germanium

21. a. m_l cannot be less than $-l$ or larger than $+l$

22. d. Co: $[Ar] 4s^2 3d^7$

23. b. tetrahedral arrangement of electron pairs; bent (V) shape

24. f. CO, HBr, $BFCl_2$, PH_3, and BrF_3

25. f. triple bond

26. d. $P_1V_1 = P_2V_2$
         $P_2 = (3 \text{ atm} \times 4 \text{ L}) / 3L = 4 \text{ atm}$

27. h $P_{Ar} = C_{Ar} \times P_T = (3/10) \times 30 \text{ atm} = 9 \text{ atm}$
         (The partial pressure of Ar will not change with the addition of He.)
         $P_{He} = 2 \text{ atm}$

28. a. C_2H_6 is a nonpolar small molecule

29. f. $\Delta H = +$ (breaking bonds), $\Delta S = +$ (creating disorder), $\Delta G = -$ (spontaneous)

30. b. 21.2 g K_3PO_4 × (1 mol / 212.27 g K_3PO_4) × (1 L / 0.4 mol) × (1000 mL / 1 L) = 250 mL

31. f. assume 100 g solution, then 30 g H_2O_2 × (1 mol / 34.016 g H_2O_2) = 0.882 mol H_2O_2
         70 g H_2O × (1 kg / 1000 g) = 0.070 kg H_2O
         molality = mol H_2O_2 / kg H_2O = 0.882 mol H_2O_2 / 0.070 kg H_2O = 12.6 *m*

32. e. The vapor pressure for a non-volatile solute equals zero.
         $P_T = C_A \times P_A° = (3/5) \times 425 \text{ torr} = 255 \text{ torr}$

33.   e. $\Delta T = K \times m \times i$
            $m = \Delta T / (K \times i) = 5 / (0.5 \times 1) = 10$ mol ethanol / kg H_2O
            50 g $H_2O \times$ (1 kg / 1000 g) $\times$ (10 mol ethanol / kg H_2O) = 0.5 mol ethanol

34.   a. $NH_3 < H_2O < NH_4^+$

35.   c.   CN$^-$ + H_2O $\rightleftharpoons$ HCN   +   OH$^-$
            base   acid   acid   base

36.   b.   LiF, salts of weak acids hydrolyze to make a basic solution

            F$^-$ + H_2O $\rightleftharpoons$ HF   +OH$^-$

37.   a.   decrease volume   right
            add O_2 right
            decrease temperature   left
            add catalyst   no change

38.   c.   entropy and enthalpy are state functions
            the changes in entropy and the change in enthalpy are independent of the route taken between the reactants and products

39.   h. $[H_3O^+] = 0.30$ M
            pH $= -\log_{10} [H_3O^+] = -\log_{10} (0.30) = 0.523$
            pH + pOH = 14
            pOH = 14 – 0.523 = 13.5

40.   a.   2 HI(g) $\rightleftharpoons$ $I_2(g)$ + $H_2(g)$ $K = 1.62 \times 10^{-3}$

            [Initial]   5   0   0
            [Change]   –2x   +x   +x
            [Equilibrium]   5–2x   x   x

            $K = [H_2][I_2] / [HI]^2 = 1.62 \times 10^{-3} = x^2 / (5-2x)^2$
            x = 0.186 M

FINAL EXAMINATION
CHEMISTRY 141 Fall 2006
Solutions

1. g. atomic number = number of protons = 50
   mass number = number of protons + neutrons = 50 + 69 = 119
   charge = difference between the number of protons and electrons = 50 – 48 = +2

2. h. the bicarbonate ion (hydrogen carbonate) has a charge of 1– not 2–

3. f. J is the derived unit for energy, heat, and work

4. a. 4/16 or 25%

5. c. potassium bromide

6. g. 7 moles TNT × (7 moles C / 1 mole TNT) = 49 moles C

7. e. Mg is an alkaline earth metal (Group 2)

8. e. H_2 is a diatomic molecule

9. e. if the numbers of molecules (or moles) in the two samples are the same, then the masses must be in the same ratio as their molar masses:
   mass of CH_4 = mass of SO_2 × (16 g mol^{-1} / 64 g mol^{-1}) = 128 g × 1/4 = 32 g

10. g. should be $CaCl_2$

11. h. 8.0 moles NH_3 × 17 g mol^{-1} = 136 g

12. a. mass of metal block = 173 – 100 g = 73 g
    volume of metal block = 66.0 – 34.0 mL = 32 mL
    density = mass / volume = 73 g / 32 mL = 2.28 g mL^{-1}

13. h. on the product side: 3.0 mol S, 8.0 mol H, and 2.0 mol N
    must be the same on the reactant side: $H_8N_2S_3$

14. h. H_2SO_4 is sulfuric acid

15. g. C_6H_6 + 15/2 O_2 → 6 CO_2 + 3 H_2O
    moles of water = 4 moles C_6H_6 × (3 mol H_2O / 1 mol C_6H_6) = 12 moles H_2O

16. i. 4 NH_3 + 6 NO → 5 N_2 + 6 H_2O sum = 4 + 6 + 5 + 6 = 21

17. g. NH_3 → N_2 change +3
    NO → N_2 change –2

18. h.   strong acids are HNO_3, HBr, HCl, and $HClO_3$
          the HCl is the most concentrated

19. d.   number of moles = molarity × volume = 2.0 mol L^{-1} × 200/1000 L = 0.40 mol

20. b. NH_3 is a weak electrolyte; HCl and NH_4Cl are strong; Cl^- is the only spectator ion

21. c.   w = +90 J —system gains energy
          q = –35 J —system loses energy
          ΔE = q + w = –35 + 90 = +55 J

22. c.   an element in its standard state

23. e.   1.0 mol propane = 44 g propane
          heat released for 1.0 kg (= 1000 g) = 2220 kJ × (1000 g / 44 g) = 50,000 kJ

24. i.   metal cooling: heat   = sp ht J g^{-1} K^{-1} × 35 g × (10 – 80) K
                                     = – sp ht × 2450 J

          ice melting: heat   = 333 J g^{-1} × 15 g
                                     = 4995 J

          water warming: heat   = 4.184 J g^{-1} K^{-1} × 115 g × (10 – 0) K
                                     = 4812 J

          sum: – sp ht × 2450 J + 4995 J + 4812 J = zero
                               sp ht   = (4995 + 4812) / 2450
                                       = 4.00 J g^{-1} K^{-1}

25. h.   equation for the formation of CH_4 gas:
          $C(s)$ + $2H_2(g)$ → $CH_4(g)$ ΔH = ?
          equation 2 as is:
          $C(s)$ + $O_2(g)$ → $CO_2(g)$ ΔH = –393.5 kJ
          equation 3 × two:
          $2H_2(g)$ + $O_2(g)$ → $2H_2O(l)$ ΔH = –571.6 kJ
          reverse equation 1:
          $CO_2(g)$ + $2H_2O(l)$ → $CH_4(g)$ + $2O_2(g)$ ΔH = +890.3 kJ
          add these three equations to obtain desired equation above
                                      ΔH = 890.3 – 393.5 – 571.6 kJ = –74.8 kJ

26. a.   endothermic

27. e.   E = hν = hc / λ = 6.626 × 10^{-34} Js × 3.0 × 10^8 m s^{-1} / 500 × 10^{-9} m = 4.0 × 10^{-19} J

28. g.   the $4s^1$ electron

29. d.   3

30. e.   5 + 5 + 5 + 5 = 20

31. g. all three

32. c. four pairs of electrons, therefore tetrahedral

33. d. 1 + 8 + 7 = 16, one bonding pair to H, another to F, leaving three nonbonding pairs on the Ar
         5 pairs total, therefore trigonal bipyramidal arrangement and a linear shape

34. f. C: 4 of its own + half-share of 4 = 6; should have 4, therefore formal charge = –2
         N: none of its own + half-share of 8 = 4; should have 5, therefore formal charge = +1
         O: 4 of its own + half-share of 4 = 6; should have 6, therefore formal charge = 0

35. c. Br: 7 and 4F: 28 plus 1 for the charge = 36: 36 divided by 8 = 4 with a remainder 4 (2 pairs)

36. e. $SeCl_4$: trigonal bipyrmidal arrangement; 5 pairs of electrons around the Se
         require 5 hybrid orbitals, so sp^3d

37. h. original partial pressure of Ne = 30 atm × (4.0 moles Ne / 10 moles total) = 12 atm
         partial pressure after adding 2.0 more moles of Ne
                                  = original partial pressure × (6.0 moles Ne / 4.0 moles Ne)
                                  = 18 atm

38. c.
	$N_2(g)$	+	$3 H_2(g)$	$\rightarrow$	$2 NH_3(g)$
initial pressure:	2.0 × (3/6)		6.0 × (3/6)		
	= 1.0 atm		= 3.0 atm		

     correct mole ratio—no limiting reactant

amount at end:	all used	all used	1.0 atm N_2 × (2/1)
			= 2.0 atm

39. h. A: 6 on faces × 1/2 = 3
         B: 12 on edges × 1/4 = 3
         C: 1 at center = 1
         stoichiometry = A_3B_3C

40. e. this is the first law

41. c. moles of solute = 1200 g / 62.1 g mol–1 = 19.3 mol ethylene glycol
         mass of solvent = 4.0 kg water
         molality = moles solute / mass solvent = 19.3 / 4.0 *m* = 4.83 *m*

42. a. Raoult's law: vapor pressure of B, $P_B = \chi_B P_B^\circ = (1/5) \times 65.0$ torr = 13 torr

43. h. Q = K = 49.78, therefore the system is at equilibrium and will not shift

44. d. addition of a catalyst enables the sytem to reach equilibrium faster, but the equilibrium reached is the
         same as without a catalyst

45. b.

46. a. salts do not hydrolyse to form a strong electrolyte—$HClO_4$ is a strong electrolyte (acid)

47. c. conjugate acid of HPO_4^{2-} is $H_2PO_4^-$ (add one H+)

48. f. 5 H_2SO_4 HI HNO_3 $HClO_4$ HCl

49. g. $HClO_3$ is a strong acid; 0.02 moles of $HClO_3$ will produce 0.02 moles of H^+ in solution

    $pH = -\log_{10}[H^+] = -\log_{10}[0.02] = 1.7$

50. b. NH_4^+ will hydrolyse to produce NH_3 (a weak electrolyte) releasing H^+ making the solution acidic

FINAL EXAMINATION

CHEMISTRY 141 Spring 2007

Solutions

1. d. $Mg(ClO_4)_2$

2. e. calcium is an alkaline earth metal

3. g. 6.0 mol N_2O × (44.02 g N_2O / 1 mole N_2O) = 264 g N_2O

4. f. 3.0 mol SO_2 × (2 mol O / 1 mol SO_2) × (6.022×10^{23} atoms / 1 mol O) = 3.613×10^{24} atoms

5. c. (2 mol N / 1 mol $C_6H_8N_2$) × (14.01 g N / 1 mol N) × (1 mol $C_6H_8N_2$ / 108.144 g $C_6H_8N_2$) × 100
    = 25.91% N

6. e. $2\ Na_2S_2O_3\ +\ I_2\ \rightarrow\ 2\ NaI\ +\ Na_2S_4O_6$ sum = 2 + 1 + 2 + 1 = 6

7. h. volume = 5.0 cm × 7.0 cm × 3.0 cm = 105 cm^3
    mass = density × volume = (7.86 g / 1 cm^3) × 105 cm^3 = 825 g

8. a. KNO_2 molar mass = 39.10 + 14.01 + (2 × 16.00) = 85.11 g mol^{-1}

9. g. $C_3H_8\ +\ 5\ O_2\ \rightarrow\ 3\ CO_2\ +\ 4\ H_2O$
    3 mol C_3H_8 × (5 mol O_2 / 1 mol C_3H_8) = 15 mol O_2

10. d.
	P_4	+	$6\ Cl_2$	$\rightarrow$	$4\ PCl_3$
mass:	124 g		500 g		
divide by molar mass:	124/124		500/70.9		
	= 1		= 7		
limiting reactant:	1/1 = 1		7/6 = 1.17		

    therefore P_4 is the limiting reactant
    1 mol P_4 × (4 mol PCl_3 / 1 mol P_4) × (137.32 g PCl_3 / 1 mol PCl_3) = 549 g PCl_3

11. f. Ca^{2+}: 20 protons, 20 neutrons, 18 electrons

12. c. 0.458 g CO_2 × (1 mol CO_2 / 44 g CO_2) × (1 mol C / 1 mol CO_2) = 0.0104 mol C
    0.374 g H_2O × (1 mol H_2O / 18 g H_2O) × (2 mol H / 1 mol H_2O) = 0.0415 mol H
    0.146 g N_2 × (1 mol N_2 / 28 g N_2) × (2 mol N / 1 mol N_2) = 0.0104 mol N
    $C_{0.0104}H_{0.0415}N_{0.0104}$
    divide by the smallest: CH_4N

13. d. % yield = actual yield / theoretical yield × 100
    theoretical yield = 1.5 mol $TiCl_4$ × (1 mol TiO_2 / 1 mol $TiCl_4$) = 1.5 mol TiO_2
    % yield = (0.85 mol / 1.5 mol) × 100 = 57%

14. g. atomic mass = (0.154 × 88.989) + (0.846 × 89.855) = 89.72 amu

15.   e. $Mg(NO_3)_2(aq) + 2\,NaOH(aq) \rightarrow 2\,NaNO_3(aq) + Mg(OH)_2(s)$ (overall reaction)
           $Mg^{2+}(aq) + 2\,NO_3^-(aq) + 2\,Na^+(aq) + 2\,OH^-(aq) \rightarrow 2\,Na^+(aq) + 2\,NO_3^-(aq) + Mg(OH)_2(s)$
                                                                   (detailed ionic reaction)

           spectator ions: Na^+ and NO_3^-

16.   d. I_3^-:   iodine is $-1/3$
           IO_4^-:   oxygen is -2, iodine is $+7$
           IO^-:   oxygen is -2, iodine is $+1$

17.   d. $M_1V_1 = M_2V_2$ $(2.5\ M)(V_1) = (0.04\ M)(0.75\ L)$
           $V_1 = 0.012\ L = 12\ mL$

18.   d.   heat water to boiling point = $14\ g \times 4.184\ J\ g^{-1}\ K^{-1} \times 100\ K = 5857.6\ J$
           heat to vaporize water = $14\ g \times 2260\ J\ g^{-1} = 31640\ J$
           total heat = $5857.6\ J + 31640\ J = 37497.6\ J = 37.5\ kJ$

19.   f.   heat released from hot water = $30\ g \times 4.184\ J\ g^{-1}\ K^{-1} \times 15\ K = 1882.8\ J$
           amount of ice that melts = $1882.8\ J / 333\ J\ g^{-1} = 5.65\ g$

20.   b.   the standard state of lead is solid $Pb(s)$

21.   a. $\Delta H_{rxn} = [12(-393.5) + 6(-285.8)] - [2(49)] = -6534.8\ kJ$

22.   f. $3\,Mn(s) + 3\,O_2(g) \rightarrow 3\,MnO_2(s)$ $\Delta H°_f = 3 \times -520\ kJ$ (multiply by 3)
           $4\,Al(s) + 3\,MnO_2(s) \rightarrow 3\,Mn(s) + 2\,Al_2O_3(s)$ $\Delta H = -1792\ kJ$ (no change)
           add:
           $4\,Al(s) + 3\,O_2(g) \rightarrow 2\,Al_2O_3(s)$ $\Delta H_{rxn} = (3 \times -520) + (-1792) = -3352\ kJ$

23.   b. $1.5\ mol\ C_4H_{10} \times (5754\ kJ / 2\ mol\ C_4H_{10}) = 4315\ kJ$

24.   a. $93.7\ MHz \times (10^6\ Hz / 1\ MHz) = 9.37 \times 10^7\ Hz$
           $\lambda = c / \nu = 3 \times 10^8\ m\ s^{-1} / 9.37 \times 10^7\ s^{-1} = 3.2\ m$

25.   c.   B: $1s^2 2s^2 \underline{2p^3}$
           Cs: $1s^2 2s^2 2p^6 3s^2 3p^6 4s^2 3d^{10} 4p^6 5s^2 4d^{10} 5p^6 \underline{6s^1}$
           Ga: $1s^2 2s^2 2p^6 3s^2 3p^6 4s^2 3d^{10} \underline{4p^1}$

26.   h.   Co

27.   d.   increasing frequency: R O Y G B I V

28.   f.   square planar is derived from the octahedral electron arrangement

29.   b.   Be is an exception to the octet rule and will not form double bonds.

30.   h.   36 valence electrons / 8 = 4 bonds and 4 lone electrons (2 lone pair of electrons)
           electron arrangement = octahedral, molecular shape = square planar

31.   b.   24 valence electrons / 8 = 3 bonds and 0 lone electrons
           electron arrangement = trigonal planar, hybridization = sp^2

32.   c. $P_1V_1 = P_2V_2$
           $(6.0 \text{ atm} \times 2.0 \text{ L}) = (2.0 \text{ atm} \times V_2)$
           $V_2 = 6.0$ L   (volume of both vessels)
           6.0 L $- 2.0$ L $= 4.0$ L (volume of the second vessel)

33.   b.   total pressure after adding additional hydrogen: $P_1/n_1 = P_2/n_2$
           15 atm / 11 mol = P_2 / 12.5 mol
           $P_2 = 17$ atm
           $P_{hydrogen} = \chi_{hydrogen} \times P_{total} = (3.5 / 12.5) \times 17 \text{ atm} = 4.8 \text{ atm}$

34.   b.   Graham's law: the unknown gas effuses more slowly – it is larger.
           $(3 / 1.4) = $ square root $(x / 16)$
           $x = 73.5$ g mol $^{-1}$

35.   d.   face centered cubic has one atom on every corner and one atom on every face
           corners = $8 \times (1/8) = 1$ atom
           face= $6 \times (1/2) = 3$ atoms

36.   a.   covalent network > hydrogen bond > dipole-dipole > London dispersion

37.   g. $\Delta G = -$ (spontaneous reaction)
           $\Delta H = -$ (exothermic reaction)
           $\Delta S = +$ (increase in disorder)

38.   b. $P_T = (\chi_{hexane} \times P^o_{hexane}) + (\chi_{pentane} \times P^o_{pentane})$
           $P_T = (0.45 \times 88.7 \text{ torr}) + (0.55 \times 44.5 \text{ torr}) = 64.4 \text{ torr}$

39.   d.   *molality* = moles CH_3OH / kg H_2O
           assume 100 g solution, then 18 g CH_3OH and 82 g H_2O
           18 g $CH_3OH \times (1 \text{ mol} / 32 \text{ g}) = 0.5618$ mol CH_3OH
           molality = 0.5618 mol CH_3OH / 0.082 kg H_2O = 6.85 *m*

40.   b.   0.35 *m* Na_2SO_4 *m* × *i* = 0.35 × 3 = 1.05
           0.50 *m* NH_3 *m* × *i* = 0.50 × 1 = 0.50 — smallest ΔT, highest freezing point
           0.25 *m* K_2CrO_4 *m* × *i* = 0.25 × 3 = 0.75
           0.45 *m* KOH   *m* × *i* = 0.45 × 2 = 0.90
           0.30 *m* NH_4NO_3 *m* × *i* = 0.30 × 2 = 0.60
           0.60 *m* CH_3CO_2H *m* × *i* = 0.60 × 1 = 0.60

41.   c.

42.   f. $H^+(aq)$ + $CaCO_3(s)$ $\rightleftharpoons$ $Ca^{2+}(aq)$ + $HCO_3^-(aq)$
           add $H^+(aq)$ *add $CaCO_3(s)$*   *add $Ca^{2+}(aq)$*   *add a catalyst*
           right   no change   left   no change

43.   b. Li^+ will not hydrolyze (Li^+ is a spectator ion)
           ClO^- will hydrolyze to make a basic solution: $ClO^- + H_2O \rightleftharpoons HClO + OH^-$

44.   a. $C_6H_5CO_2H$, acid

45.   c. HSO_4^-

46.   b. K = [products] / [reactants] = $(0.6 \times 0.6) / 1.8 = 0.2$

47.   g.   for every $Mg(OH)_2$, there are two OH^-, therefore $[OH^-] = 2\,[Mg(OH)_2]$
           $pOH = -\log_{10}[OH^-] = -\log_{10}(2 \times 0.3) = 0.2$
           $pH = 14 - pOH = 14 - 0.2 = 13.8$

48.   c.

	$CaC_2O_4(s)$	$\rightleftharpoons$	$Ca^{2+}(aq)$	+	$C_2O_4^{2-}(aq)$	
initial equilibrium:			2.0 M		2.0 M	$K = 2.0 \times 2.0 = 4.0$
initial:			3.0 M		2.0 M	
change:			$-x$		$-x$	
equilibrium:			$3 - x$		$2 - x$	$4.0 = (3-x)(2-x)$
						$x = 0.4385$ M

  $[C_2O_4^{2-}] = 2 - 0.4385 = 1.56$ M

49.   e.   strong acids are levelled to H_3O^+ in aqueous solution
           the strong acids are HBr, HNO_3, H_2SO_4, and $HClO_4$

50.   f.   I and III are true; II is false

FINAL EXAMINATION

CHEMISTRY 141 Fall 2007

Solutions

1. c. Ag is the symbol for silver

2. c. the chlorite ion is ClO_2^- not ClO_3^-

3. c. Ca (alkaline earth) Ce (lanthanide)   Cu (transition metal)   Br (halogen)

4. j. 3.0 mol of $Al_2(SO_4)_3$ contains 36 mol of O atoms (i.e. $3 \times 4 \times 3 = 36$)

5. j. H_2O is a molecule containing just two elements

6. j. 488 g / 2.50 mol = 195 g mol^{-1}, therefore Pt

7. a. 1.0 ft × 3.5 ft × 0.5 ft = 1.75 ft^3
       1.75 ft^3 × (12 in/1 ft)^3 × (2.54 cm/1 in)^3 × (1 m/100 cm)^3 = 0.0496 m^3

8. f. 6.00 mol × 16.0 g mol^{-1} = 96 g CH_4

9. h. $(2 \times 39.1) + (2 \times 52.0) + (7 \times 16.0) = 294$ g mol^{-1}

10. e. limiting reactant is oxygen: C_3H_8 + $5 O_2$ → $3 CO_2$ + $4 H_2O$
       amount of CO_2 produced = 6.0 mol O_2 × (3 CO_2 / 5 O_2) = 3.6 mol CO_2

11. b.
		P_4	+	Br_2	→	?
mass:		0.347 g		2.68 g		
divide by molar mass:		0.347/30.97		2.68/79.90		
		= 0.0112		= 0.0335		
divide by smaller:		1		3		therefore formula is PBr_3

12. e. $9 \times 3 = 27$ moles

13. f. $2 HSbCl_4$ + $3 H_2S$ → $1 Sb_2S_3$ + $8 HCl$ total = 2 + 3 + 1 + 8 = 14

14. e. Na^+ + HCO_3^- + H_3O^+ + NO_3^- → Na^+ + NO_3^- + CO_2 + $2 H_2O$
       spectator ions are Na^+ and NO_3^-

15. f. +5

16. h. $\Delta E = +75$ J
       w = −120
       therefore q = +195 J

17.   g.   heat to melt ice = 333 J g^{-1} × 15.0 g = 4995 J
             heat to warm water = 4.184 J g^{-1} K^{-1} × 15.0 g × 25 K = 1569 J
             total = 6564 J

18.   a.   3 moles of Fe (3 × 55.85 g) produces 1118.4 kJ
             100 g would produce 1118.4 kJ × (100 /(3 × 55.85 g) = 667.5 kJ

19.   b.

20.   f.   160 g NaOH = 4.0 mol
             the diluted solution contains 4.0 mol NaOH in 1.0 L

21.   f.   low energy end of the visible spectrum

22.   d.   this statement has nothing to do with Heisenberg's Uncertainty Principle

23.   i.   chlorine

24.   d.

25.   h.   four electrons have been removed

26.   c.   ICl$_4^-$:   number of valence electrons = 7 + (4 × 7) + 1 = 36
                          divide by 8: 4 bonding pairs + 2 nonbonding pairs = 6 total; therefore octahedral

27.   i.   CH$_4$ is nonpolar

28.   d.   any H attached to N, O, or F

29.   c.   three single bonds and one lone pair; therefore tetrahedral and sp^3

30.   c.   equal moles of gases on both sides of the equation

31.   f.   partial pressure of nitrogen will not change = (4/6) × 15.0 atm = 10.0 atm

32.   d.   the difference in the heights of mercury corresponds to the difference in pressures = 1.25 atm
             difference = 1.25 atm × 76 cm = 95 cm

33.   g.   all gases have the same average kinetic energy at the same temperature

34.   e.   A: 8 corners + 1 at center = 2
             B: 4 edges = 1
             C: 2 faces = 1

35.   d.

36.   a.   if the change is endothermic (ΔH = +), then ΔS must be + for ΔG to be − (spontaneous)

37. g.

38. c. highest ΔT, or highest $m \times i$
         for 0.60 m K_2SO_4, $m \times i = 0.60 \times 3 = 1.80$

39. g. moles of solute = 0.60 moles
         total moles of solute and solvent = 0.60 + 1.60 = 2.20 moles
         mole fraction of solute = 0.60 / 2.20 = 0.27

40. d. total vp = $\chi_{hexane}P^\circ_{hexane} + \chi_{pentane}P^\circ_{pentane}$ = (0.25 × 88.7) + (0.75 × 44.5) = 55.6 torr

41. h.

42. h.
         $$NO_2 \quad + \quad CO \quad \rightleftharpoons \quad NO \quad + \quad CO_2$$
         initial: 2.0 M   2.0 M

         equilibrium: 2.0 – x   2.0 – x   x   x

         $K = 25.0 = [NO][CO_2] / [NO_2][CO] = x^2 / (2.0 - x)^2$
         take square root of both sides:
         $x / (2.0 - x) = 5$
         $x = 1.67$

43. g. KOH is a strong base
         $[OH^-] = 0.0010 = 10^{-3}$ M
         pOH = 3
         pH = 14 – 3 = 11

44. c. $K = [NO_2]^2 / [N_2O_4] = (0.525)^2 / (0.1375) = 2.00$

45. a. a neutral solution has a pH of 7 only at 25°C

46. g. HI is one of the seven strong acids

47. d. the conjugate acid has one more H^+; the conjugate base has one less H^+

48. e. the acid is always the H^+ ion donor; the base accepts the H^+

49. d.

50. i. NaCN salt of a strong base (NaOH) and a weak acid (HCN)
         the CN^- ion will hydrolyze to form HCN (the weak acid from which the salt is made) and OH^-
         it is the OH^- ion that makes the solution basic

FINAL EXAMINATION

CHEMISTRY 141 Spring 2008
Solutions

1.   b. $180 \text{ mg dL}^{-1} \times (1 \text{ g} / 1000 \text{ mg}) \times (10 \text{ dL} / 1 \text{ L}) = 1.8 \text{ g L}^{-1}$

2.   a.   mass

3.   h.   23 electrons and a charge of +3 means there must be 26 protons, therefore Fe

4.   e. HNO_3 is nitric acid

5.   e. $CaCl_2$; $(1 \times 40.08) + (2 \times 35.45) = 111 \text{ g mol}^{-1}$

6.   h. $3 \text{ mol Mg(CH}_3\text{CO}_2)_2 \times (4 \text{ mol C} / 1 \text{ mol Mg(CH}_3\text{CO}_2)_2 = 12 \text{ mol C}$

7.   c. $75 \text{ g KClO}_3 \times (1 \text{ mol KClO}_3 / 122.55 \text{ g KClO}_3) \times (3 \text{ mol O} / 1 \text{ mol KClO}_3) \times$
   $(6.022 \times 10^{23} \text{ O atoms} / 1 \text{ mole O}) = 1.1 \times 10^{24} \text{ O atoms}$

8.   d.

	nitrogen	oxygen
mass:	30.45%	69.55%
divide by molar mass:	30.45 / 14.01 = 2.17	69.55 / 16.0 = 4.34
divide by the smaller:	1	2

   empirical formula is NO_2
   mass of empirical formula = 46 g mol^{-1}; therefore molecule is $2 \times$ the empirical unit
   molecular formula is N_2O_4

9.   c. $(2 \text{ mol Li} / 1 \text{ mol Li}_2\text{CO}_3) \times (6.941 \text{ g Li} / 1 \text{ mol Li}) \times (1 \text{ mol Li}_2\text{CO}_3 / 73.89 \text{ g Li}_2\text{CO}_3) \times 100$
   $= 18.8\%$

10.   e. $\underline{1} \text{ P}_4\text{O}_{10} + \underline{6} \text{ H}_2\text{O} \rightarrow \underline{4} \text{ H}_3\text{PO}_4$

11.   b. $500 \text{ g C}_6\text{H}_{12}\text{O}_6 \times (1 \text{ mol C}_6\text{H}_{12}\text{O}_6 / 180.16 \text{ g C}_6\text{H}_{12}\text{O}_6) \times (1 \text{ mol C}_2\text{H}_5\text{OH} / 1 \text{ mol C}_6\text{H}_{12}\text{O}_6)$
   $\times (46 \text{ g C}_2\text{H}_5\text{OH} / 1 \text{ mol C}_2\text{H}_5\text{OH}) = 256 \text{ g C}_2\text{H}_5\text{OH}$

12.   f. $\qquad\qquad C_3H_8 + 5 O_2 \rightarrow 3 CO_2 + 4 H_2O$
   $\qquad\qquad\qquad\; 4 \text{ mol} \quad 10 \text{ mol}$

   limiting reactant: 4/1 = 4   10/5 = 2
   therefore O_2 is the limiting reactant: $10 \text{ mol O}_2 \times (4 \text{ mol H}_2\text{O} / 5 \text{ mol O}_2)$
   $\qquad\qquad\qquad\qquad\qquad\qquad\qquad\qquad\qquad\qquad = 8 \text{ mol H}_2\text{O}$

13.   a. $12.5 \text{ g Li} \times (1 \text{ mol Li} / 6.941 \text{ g Li}) \times (2 \text{ mol Li}_3\text{N} / 6 \text{ mol Li}) \times (34.88 \text{ g Li}_3\text{N} / 1 \text{ mol Li}_3\text{N})$
   $= 20.9 \text{ g Li}_3\text{N}$ (theoretical yield)
   % yield = (actual yield / theoretical yield) $\times 100 = (5.90 \text{ g} / 20.9 \text{ g}) \times 100 = 28.2\%$

14.   e.   Au, Ti, Zr, W

15.　a.　the detailed ionic equation is:

$$HCN(aq) + Na^+(aq) + OH^-(aq) \rightarrow Na^+(aq) + CN^-(aq) + H_2O(l)$$

the sodium ion Na^+ is the only spectator ion

16.　b.　H is +1; S is +2; O is −2

17.　f.　$(0.5\ M) \times (50\ mL) = (0.2\ M) \times (V_{dilute})$
$V_{dilute} = 125\ mL - 50\ mL$ (from concentrated solution) = 75 mL water

18.　b.　heat = mass × specific heat × ΔT = (10 g) × (0.385 J K^{-1} g^{-1}) × (30 K) = 115.5 J

19.　a.　heat lost by copper block cooling = heat gained to melt ice
(10 g) × (0.385 J K^{-1} g^{-1}) × (55 K) = mass of ice melted × (333 J g^{-1})
mass of ice melted = 0.64 g

20.　c.　5000 kJ × (2 mol C_2H_2 / 2599 kJ) = 3.85 mol C_2H_2

21.　d.　multiply equations 1, 2, and 3 by ½:

½ CaO(s) + ½ Cl$_2$(g) → ½ CaOCl$_2$(s)　　　　　　　　　　　　　　　ΔH = −55.45 kJ
½ H$_2$O(l) + ½ CaOCl$_2$(s) + NaBr(s) → NaCl(s) + ½ Ca(OH)$_2$(s) + ½ Br$_2$(l)　ΔH = −30.1 kJ
½ Ca(OH)$_2$(s) → ½ CaO(s) + ½ H$_2$O(l)　　　　　　　　　　　　　　ΔH = +32.55 kJ

add to obtain the desired equation:　　　　　　　　　　　　　　　　　ΔH = −53.0 kJ

22.　f.　λ = 6.626 × 10^{-34} J s / (0.055 kg × 35 m s^{-1}) = 3.44 × 10^{-34} m

23.　d.　ν = c / l = (3 × 10^8 m s^{-1}) / (5 × 10^{-5} m) = 6 × 10^{12} s^{-1}
E = h × ν = (6.626 × 10^{-34} J s) × (6 × 10^{12} s^{-1}) = 3.98 × 10^{-21} J

24.　g.　in the ground state bromine does not have electrons in the 4d orbital

25.　f.　5s

26.　c.　Sb

27.　c.　K

28.　b.　Co is metallic, Cl$_2$ is nonpolar covalent, CO is polar covalent

29.　e.　SO_3 has a trigonal planar electron arrangement and shape; one double bond is required to complete the octet of S; resonance is required

30.　c.　NO_3^-

31.　a.　32 total valence electrons; 4 bonds and no lone pairs of electrons, therefore tetrahedral

32.　c.　electron arrangement is tetrahedral; hybridization is sp^3

33. c. $(P_1 \times V_1) / T_1 = (P_2 \times V_2) / T_2$
$(1 \text{ atm} \times 2.58 \text{ L}) / 288 \text{ K} = (2 \text{ atm} \times V_2) / 311 \text{ K}$ $V_2 = 1.40 \text{ L}$

34. c. $u_{nitrogen} / u_{hydrogen} = \sqrt{(M_{hydrogen} / M_{nitrogen})}$
$(0.1 \text{ mol} / 2 \text{ min}) / (0.1 \text{ mol} / x \text{ min}) = \sqrt{(2.016 \text{ g mol}^{-1} / 28.02 \text{ g mol}^{-1})}$
$0.05 \text{ mol min}^{-1} / (0.1 \text{ mol} / x \text{ min}) = 0.26823$ $x = 0.54 \text{ min}$

35. e. H_2CO is polar (dipole-dipole); CH_4 is nonpolar (London dispersion); CH_3OH can hydrogen bond

36. b. body centered cubic has one X on each corner $(8 \times 1/8) = 1$ and one X in the center $= 1$

37. b. ΔG is – (spontaneous reaction); ΔH is + (heat absorbed); ΔS is + (solution is more disordered)

38. d.

39. b. molality = number of moles of solute / mass of solvent in kg
assume 100 g solution, then there are 10 g $NaCH_3CO_2$ and 90 g H_2O
10 g $NaCH_3CO_2 \times (1 \text{ mol } NaCH_3CO_2 / 82 \text{ g } NaCH_3CO_2) = 0.1219 \text{ mol } NaCH_3CO_2$
molality = 0.1219 mol / 0.09 kg = 1.34 *m*

40. c. water is at equilibrium, therefore $\Delta G = 0$

41. a. require the smallest ΔT, that is, smallest $m \times i$

42. g. N^{3-} has 8 valence electrons

43. f. $H_2(g) + I_2(g) \rightleftharpoons 2 HI(g)$ *add $H_2(g)$*   *increase pressure*   *remove HI(g)*
                                                         move right   no change   move right

44. d. $K = [HI]^2 / ([H_2] \times [I_2]) = (0.0276)^2 / (0.0037 \times 0.0037) = 55.6$

45. a. $Q > K$, therefore shift left to restore equilibrium

46. h.

47. d. CO_3^{2-}; the conjugate base has one less H^+ than the acid

48. a.

49. b.   HF   + $H_2O \rightleftharpoons F^-$ + H_3O^+ $K_a = 7.1 \times 10^{-4}$
         initial: 0.5   0   0
         change: –x   +x   +x
         equilibrium: 0.5 – x   x   x
         0.5 – x is approximately equal to 0.5, so $7.1 \times 10^{-4} = x^2 / 0.5$
         $x = 0.0188 = [H_3O^+]$ pH = $-\log[H_3O^+] = -\log(0.0188) = 1.72$

50. e. CH_3CO_2H, NH_4ClO_3, H_3PO_4, NH_4Cl

FINAL EXAMINATION
CHEMISTRY 141 Fall 2008
Solutions

1. g. nitrogen N_2

2. a. sodium Na

3. c. mass / molar mass = number of moles

4. e. 3.0 mol $C_6H_6 \times (6$ mol C $/ 1$ mol $C_6H_6) = 18$ mol C

5. e.

Ne	0.5×20 g mol^{-1}	$= 10$ g
Ca	0.4×40 g mol^{-1}	$= 16$ g
HF	0.6×20 g mol^{-1}	$= 12$ g
Br_2	0.1×160 g mol^{-1}	$= 16$ g
KOH	0.4×56 g mol^{-1}	$= 22$ g —greatest mass
CH_4	0.7×16 g mol^{-1}	$= 11$ g
CO	0.5×28 g mol^{-1}	$= 14$ g
He	1.0×4 g mol^{-1}	$= 4$ g

6. f. $P_4O_{10} + 6\,Ca(OH)_2 \rightarrow 2\,Ca_3(PO_4)_2 + 6\,H_2O$

7. g. 2 Cu $\qquad\qquad 127$ g
    $Cu_2CO_3(OH)_2 \qquad 221$ g
    %Cu $= (127/221) \times 100 = 57.5\%$

8. d. 20 protons indicates Ca
    18 electrons compared with 20 protons indicates a 2+ charge
    20 protons + 20 neutrons indicates a mass number $= 40$
    therefore $^{40}Ca^{2+}$

9. b. number of moles of A $= 142.4 / 33.29 = 4.278$ mol
    therefore, number of moles of B in $A_2B_3 = 4.278 \times (3/2) = 6.416$ mol
    molar mass of B = mass / number of moles $= 97.23 / 6.416 = 15.15$ g mol^{-1}

10. d. limiting reactant is H_2
    mol of ammonia produced $= 1.5$ mol $H_2 \times (2$ mol $NH_3 / 3$ mol $H_2) = 1.0$ mol NH_3

11. f.

	$[(C_4H_9)_3S]F$	H_2O
mass:	38.17%	61.83%
divide by molar mass:	38.17 / 222.40	61.83 / 18.015
	= 0.1716	= 3.432
divide by the smaller:	1	20

formula is $[(C_4H_9)_3S]F.20H_2O$

12. h.   0.20 M $FeCl_3$ × (3 mol Cl^- / 1 mol $FeCl_3$) = 0.60 M Cl^-

13. c. HNO_3 is nitric acid

14. d. OH^- + HF → F^- + H_2O
          the Li^+ ion is a spectator ion

15. g.   +6

16. h.   the hot water cools from 60°C to 0°C
          heat released = specific heat × mass × temp change = 4.184 $JK^{-1}g^{-1}$ × 50 g × 60 K = 12552 J
          this heat melts some of the ice:
          mass of ice that melts = 12552 J / 333 Jg^{-1} = 37.7 g
          water present at equilibrium = 50 g orig present + 50 g hot water + 37.7 g from ice = 138 g

17. e.   q = +3000 J
          w = −950 J
          ΔE = 3000 − 950 = 2050 J = 2.05 kJ

18. c.   according to the equation, 2 mol C_2H_2 (52.08 g) releases 2599 kJ energy
          energy released by 65.0 g = 2599 × (65.0 / 52.08) = 3244 J

19. a.   n cannot equal 0

20. f. $1s^2\ 2s^2\ 2p^6\ 3s^2\ 3p^6$

21. a.   aluminum

22. h.   ROY G BIV

23. d.   octahedral—5 bonding pairs and one nonbonding pair

24. b. SF_4—see-saw shape

25. b. sp^2

26. d. $$\left[\ \ddot{\text{N}}=\text{N}=\ddot{\text{N}}\ \right]^-$$
          −1   +1   −1

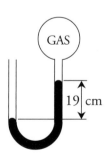

27. c.   19 cm Hg = 190 mm Hg = 0.25 atm
          pressure inside vessel = 1.0 atm − 0.25 atm = 0.75 atm

28. f.   A   initial partial pressure = mole fraction × total pressure = (1.5 / 5.0) × 20 atm = 6.0 atm
          B   increase number of moles of Ar by (4.5 / 1.5), partial pressure increases by a factor of 3 to 18 atm
          C   addition of another gas has no effect on the partial pressure of Ar (V and T constant)

29. e.   ΔG − (spontaneous), ΔH + (endothermic), ΔS + (increase in entropy)
          note that ΔS must be positive or ΔG could not be negative

30. e. salts: NH_4NO_3 and KF
    strong acids: HNO_3
    strong bases: KOH and $Sr(OH)_2$
    total: 5 strong electrolytes

31. c. 50 g sucrose = (50 g / 342 g mol^{-1}) = 0.146 mol
    (0.146 mol / mass of solvent in kg) = 1.25 m
    mass of solvent in kg = 0.146 / 1.25 = 0.117 kg = 117 g

32. a. 0.25 m K_2SO_4 $m \times i$ = 0.25 × 3 = 0.75
    0.20 m NaH_2PO_4 $m \times i$ = 0.20 × 2 = 0.40
    0.20 m $Ca(NO_3)_2$ $m \times i$ = 0.20 × 3 = 0.60
    0.30 m HNO_3 $m \times i$ = 0.30 × 2 = 0.60
    0.50 m HCN $m \times i$ = 0.50 × 1 = 0.50

33. e. $H_2(g)$ + 1/8 $S_8(s)$ ⇌ $H_2S(g)$
    add hydrogen   *add sulfur*   *increase temperature*
    right   no change   left

34. b. $N_2(g)$ + 3 $H_2(g)$ ⇌ 2 $NH_3(g)$
    K = $[NH_3]^2$ / $[N_2][H_2]^3$ = 2^2 / 0.5 × 2^3 = 1.0

35. e. *conjugate acid* $HC_2O_4^-$ *conjugate base*
    $H_2C_2O_4$ $C_2O_4^{2-}$

36. d. NH_4NO_3 salt of a weak base and a strong acid
    the ammonium ion hydrolyses to produce hydronium ions

37. a. $H_2PO_4^-$ + H_2O ⇌ H_3O^+ + HPO_4^{2-}
    acid   base   acid   base

38. b. the pH of a neutral solution depends upon the temperature
    the value of K_w increases if the temperature increases

FINAL EXAMINATION
CHEMISTRY 141 Spring 2009
Solutions

1. b. sulfur exists as an S_8 molecule

2. b. $KClO_3$

3. j. Na is +1; O is −2; I must be +5

4. b. F: $1s^2 \, 2s^2 \, 2p^6 \, 3s^2 \, 3p^5$

5. b. number of electrons = $6 + (4 \times 7) = 34$
        4 bonding pairs and 1 lone pair

6. a. area C (solid) to area B (liquid)
        ΔH = + (breaking bonds) and ΔS = + (increase in disorder)

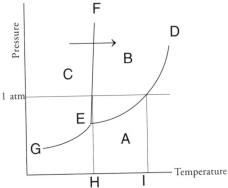

7. f. $HPO_3{}^{2-}$; the conjugate base has one less H^+ than the acid

8. i. KOH is a strong base and will completely dissociate; $[KOH] = [OH^-] = 0.0316$ M
        $pOH = -\log[OH^-] = -\log(0.0316) = 1.5$
        $pH = 14 - pOH = 14 - 1.5 = 12.5$

9. e. $C_3H_4O_3$; the empirical formula is the simplest ratio of atoms

10. g. 2.0 mol $Ca_3(PO_4)_2 \times$ (8 mol O / 1 mol $Ca_3(PO_4)_2$) = 16 mol O

11. g. 3.0 mol $SF_6 \times$ (146.07 g / 1 mol) = 438.2 g

12. d. 52.15 g C × (1 mol / 12.01 g) = 4.342 mol C
        13.13 g H × (1 mol / 1.008 g) = 13.026 mol H
        34.73 g O × (1 mol / 16 g)   = 2.171 mol O
        divide by the smallest number; ratio is: 2 : 6 : 1
        empirical formula is C_2H_6O

13. e. 1 Be_2C + 4 H_2O → 2 $Be(OH)_2$ + 1 CH_4

14. g. amount of water in the hydrate = 5.000 g − 2.442 g = 2.558 g

	$MgSO_4$	H_2O
mass:	2.442 g	2.558 g
divide by molar mass:	2.442 / 120.4	2.558 / 18.02
	= 0.02029	= 0.14195
divide by smaller:	1	7

empirical formula is $MgSO_4 \cdot 7H_2O$

15. d. 14.0 g H_2 × (1 mol H_2 / 2.016 g H_2) × (2 mol Li / 1 mol H_2) × (6.941 g Li / 1 mol Li)
= 96.4 g Li

16. a. (0.60 M) × (50 mL) = (M_{dilute}) × (300 mL)

M_{dilute} = 0.10 M

17. d.
$$4 NH_3(g) + 5 O_2(g) \rightarrow 4 NO(g) + 6 H_2O(l)$$
amount: 3.0 moles   4.0 moles
divide by
coefficient: / 4   / 5
= 0.75   = 0.80   (NH_3 is the limiting reagent)
3.0 mol NH_3 × (6 mol H_2O / 4 mol NH_3) = 4.5 mol H_2O

18. e. heat lost by water cooling = heat gained to melt ice
(20.0 g) × (4.184 J g^{-1} K^{-1}) × (65 K) = mass of ice melted × (333 J g^{-1})
mass of ice melted = 16.3 g

19. g. 175 g C_8H_{18} × (1 mol / 114.2 g) × (10992 kJ / 2 mol C_8H_{18}) = 8420 kJ

20. a. 300 nm × (1 m / 10^9 nm) = 3 × 10^{-7} m
ν = c × λ = (3 × 10^8 m s^{-1}) × (3 × 10^{-7} m) = 1 × 10^{15} s^{-1}
E = h × ν = (6.626 × 10^{-34} J s) × (1 × 10^{15} s^{-1}) = 6.6 × 10^{-19} J

21. e. if l = 1, m_l = −1, 0, +1

22. f. 7 + 3 = 10
10 + 8 = 18
18 − 6 = 12

23. a. fluorine has the smaller atomic radius, is more electronegative, and has the larger first ionization energy

24. b. I_3^-

25. d. PCl_3, CH_2Cl_2, H_2S

26. c. BeF_2, I_3^-

27. g.

28. c. (P_1V_1) / T_1 = (P_2V_2) / T_2
(1 atm × 0.6 L) / 309 K = (0.205 atm × V_2) / 273 K
V_2 = 2.6 L

29. b. body-centered cubic: corners = 8 × (1/8) = 1
center = 1 × 1   = 1
total atoms   = 2

30. e. let x = the melting point of sulfur on the °S scale

set up a proportion to compare the °S scale to the °C scale

$(150 - x) / (150 - 35) = (113 - 100) / (100 - 0)$

$x = 165\ °S$

31. a. $CH_4(g)\quad +\quad H_2O(g)\quad \rightarrow\quad 3\ H_2(g)\quad +\quad CO(g)$

bonds broken   *bonds formed*

4 C–H   2 O–H   3 H–H   and   C≡O

4(+413) kJ 2(+463) kJ   3(–436 kJ) –1072 kJ

$\Delta H = 1652\ kJ\ +\ 926\ kJ\ -\ 1308\ kJ\ -\ 1072\ kJ$

$\Delta H = +198\ kJ$

32. f. $P_T = (\chi_{pentane} \times P°_{pentane}) + (\chi_{hexane} \times P°_{hexane})$

350 torr $= (\chi_{pentane} \times 425\ torr) + [(1 - \chi_{pentane}) \times 130\ torr]$

$\chi_{pentane} = 0.75$

33. b.

34. c. $4\ NH_3(g)\quad +\quad 3\ O_2(g)\quad \rightleftharpoons\quad 2\ N_2(g)\ +\ 6\ H_2O(l)$

Initial: 5 M   6 M   0   0

Change: –4x   –3x   +2x   +6x

Equilibrium: 5 – 4x   6 – 3x   2x   6x

= 1.5   therefore, x = 0.75

$[NH_3] = 5 - (4 \times 0.75) = 2.0$

35. h. $6\ CO_2(g)\ +\ 6\ H_2O(l)\quad \rightleftharpoons\quad C_6H_{12}O_6(s)\ +\ 6\ O_2(g)$ $\Delta H = +2801\ kJ$ (endothermic)

	increase	*increase*	*increase partial*
add a catalyst	*temperature*	*volume*	*pressure of $CO_2(g)$*
no change	right	no change	right

36. c.

37. a. $K_a \times K_b = K_w$

$(1.8 \times 10^{-5}) \times K_b = (1 \times 10^{-14})$

$K_b = 5.6 \times 10^{-10}$

38. e. NH_4^+ will hydrolyze to produce the weak base NH_3 and H_3O^+, therefore acidic